Canada in the Atlantic Economy

VOLUME 2

The Impact of Trade Liberalization: 1

comprising three studies
of the "Canada in the Atlantic Economy" series

Research Director: H. Edward English

Published for the
Private Planning Association
of Canada by
University of Toronto Press

To William B. Lambert

These studies of "Canada in the Atlantic Economy" are dedicated with respect and gratitude to the late William B. Lambert, Chairman of the Board of the Private Planning Association of Canada from 1965 to 1967, who played a vital role in the development and supervision of the Atlantic Economic Studies Program, on which the publications are based.

His interest went far beyond his formal responsibility; he held a deep conviction concerning the importance of international cooperation among the North Atlantic nations. His untimely death came when the first draft studies had entered the early stages of publication.

Editorial Note

The studies in this series are issued individually as paperbacks, but they are also being published in groups, each dealing with one aspect of Canada in the Atlantic economy. Such "group" volumes will bear a distinctive title and be casebound; pagination will follow that of the paperbacks. This book, the second of the "group" volumes, incorporates the fourth, fifth, and sixth studies of the series.

H. E. E.

Contents

Canada in the Atlantic Economy

CANADA IN THE ATLANTIC ECONOMY

Published:

1. David W. Slater, *World Trade and Economic Growth: Trends and Prospects with Applications to Canada*
2. H. Edward English, *Transatlantic Economic Community: Canadian Perspectives*
3. Harry G. Johnson, Paul Wonnacott, Hirofumi Shibata, *Harmonization of National Economic Policies under Free Trade*
4. Gerald I. Trant, David L. MacFarlane and Lewis A. Fischer, *Trade Liberalization and Canadian Agriculture*
5. W. E. Haviland, N. S. Takacsy, E. M. Cape, *Trade Liberalization and the Canadian Pulp and Paper Industry*
6. David E. Bond and Ronald J. Wonnacott, *Trade Liberalization and the Canadian Furniture Industry*

Forthcoming:

7. Jacques J. Singer, *Trade Liberalization and the Canadian Steel Industry*
8. John Munro, *Trade Liberalization and Transportation in International Trade*
9. John F. Earl, *Trade Liberalization and the Atlantic Provinces Economy*
10. G. David Quirin, *Trade Liberalization and the Mineral Industries*
11. R. A. Shearer, G. R. Munro, and J. H. Young, *Trade Liberalization and the British Columbia Economy*
12. Richard E. Caves and Grant L. Reuber, *Canadian Economic Policy and the Impact of International Capital Flows*
13. Jacques J. Singer and Eric C. Sievwright, *Trade Liberalization and the Canadian Primary Textiles Industry*
14. Hirofumi Shibata, *Harmonization of Fiscal Policy under Freer Trade*
15. R. A. Matthews, *Easing the Adjustment to Freer Trade: A Program of Transitional Policies for Canada*
16. Eric Hehner, *Non-Tariff Barriers Affecting Canada's Trade*
17. David W. Slater, Bruce W. Wilkinson, and H. Edward English, *Canada in a Wider Economic Community*

Other studies to be published later in the series will deal with policies for the transitional period and problems of harmonizing customs practices, transport policies, etc. There will also be a summary study in which the implications of the more specialized studies will be drawn together in an assessment of the over-all impact of trade liberalization on the Canadian economy.

Trade Liberalization and Canadian Agriculture

Gerald I. Trant
David L. MacFarlane and Lewis A. Fischer

Published for the
Private Planning Association of Canada by University of Toronto Press

To William B. Lambert

These studies of "Canada in the Atlantic Economy" are dedicated with respect and gratitude to the late William B. Lambert, Chairman of the Board of the Private Planning Association of Canada from 1965 to 1967, who played a vital role in the development and supervision of the Atlantic Economic Studies Program, on which the publications are based.

His interest went far beyond his formal responsibility; he held a deep conviction concerning the importance of international cooperation among the North Atlantic nations. His untimely death came when the first draft studies had entered the early stages of publication.

© University of Toronto Press 1968 / Printed in Canada / SBN 8020 3209 5

Foreword

There have been two outstanding developments in international trade policy during the past twenty years—the multilateral dismantling of trade barriers under the General Agreement on Tariffs and Trade, which has been the agency for several rounds of successful tariff negotiations since its inception in 1947, and the establishment of the European Economic Community and the European Free Trade Association in the late 1950s. In a period of reconstruction and then sustained growth, these policies have helped the participating nations of the Atlantic area to experience the benefits of international specialization and expanding trade. The wealth generated by trade and domestic prosperity has also made possible external aid programs to assist economic growth in the developing countries.

Whatever the trade and economic development problems of the future, it is widely acknowledged that the industrially advanced countries of the North Atlantic region must play an important role. It is also generally conceded that the ability of these countries to maintain their own economic growth and prosperity and to contribute to that of the less advanced nations will be greatly enhanced if they can reduce or remove the remaining trade barriers among themselves. Cooperation among Atlantic countries is now fostered by the GATT and by the Organisation for Economic Co-operation and Development. But the success of these and other approaches depends on the assessment by each country of the importance of international trade liberalization and policy coordination for its domestic economy and other national interests. This is particularly true for countries such as Canada which are heavily dependent upon export markets.

The Atlantic Economic Studies Program of the Private Planning Association of Canada was initiated to study the implications for Canada of trade liberalization and closer economic integration among the nations bordering the North Atlantic. It is planned to issue at least twelve paperbound volumes, incorporating over twenty studies by leading Canadian and foreign economists. Despite the technical nature of much of the subject matter, the studies have been written in language designed to appeal to the non-professional reader.

The directors and staff of the Private Planning Association wish to acknowledge the financial support which made this project possible—a grant from the Ford Foundation and the contributions of members of the Association. They are also appreciative of the help that has been provided by very many individuals in the preparation and review of all the studies—in discussions and correspondence with authors, at the Association's November, 1966, conference on "Canada and the Atlantic Economy," and on other occasions.

H. E. ENGLISH
Director of Research
Atlantic Economic Studies Program

Contents

The Impact of Trade Liberalization on Canadian Agriculture

Gerald I. Trant

I. Introduction

When relative costs differ among nations, the law of comparative advantage implies that real incomes may be increased by trade. The present paper examines, first, Canada's comparative advantage in agricultural production in an aggregate sense and, subsequently, the ability of Canadian farmers to compete with those of other nations in the production of particular agricultural products. The estimates of Canada's economic competitiveness for individual products are essentially estimates of absolute advantage, although, when considered together, they may serve as a basis for determining comparative advantage.

This study is essentially limited to an analysis of the competitive factors in agriculture itself. For the purpose, it has seemed advisable to make certain assumptions about variables of economic significance, of which the more important are

1. that international exchange rates, particularly between Canada and the United States, remain stable;
2. that there will be no major changes in production techniques in agriculture (a change of the magnitude of the conversion from horse power to tractor power, for example);
3. that intranational institutional arrangements will remain relatively unchanged;
4. that there will be no major changes in consumer preferences for agricultural products.

The ability to make distinctions, with greater or less precision, as to whether Canada will maintain an absolute advantage or disadvantage in the production of a particular product, depended not only on the assumptions made above, but also on fundamental economic interrelationships and adequacy of data. Data availability and completeness ranged from excellent in the case of wheat and coarse grains to very poor for greenhouse production. However, the most serious gap in data was encountered for Communist countries, many of which are producers of temperate agricultural products. Therefore, inferences drawn from the study should be modified by these restraints.

Canadian agriculture has depended heavily on exports as a source of cash income. Table I indicates the importance of agricultural exports to farm cash income. Large exports have typically been associated with high farm cash income, and low levels of exports have tended to dampen farm cash income. For individual commodities, such as wheat and flax, export sales have been even more important than for agriculture in general. Although the value of Canadian agricultural exports has exceeded the value of imports for many years, there is no guarantee that this situation will continue indefinitely. In fact, Table I suggests that the export surplus narrowed in a disturbing manner in several years.

TABLE I

CANADIAN FARM CASH INCOME AND
AGRICULTURAL EXPORTS AND IMPORTS
(million Canadian dollars)

Year	Farm cash income	Exports of agricultural products	Imports of agricultural products
1950	2,158	818	604
1951	2,793	1,020	711
1952	2,864	1,220	564
1953	2,788	1,147	541
1954	2,378	853	594
1955	2,384	801	639
1956	2,647	1,013	690
1957	2,575	909	709
1958	2,855	1,034	683
1959	2,811	970	739
1960	2,854	909	747
1961	2,988	1,193	813
1962	3,186	1,157	857
1963	3,199	1,359	1,004
1964	3,464	1,702	1,047

Sources: Canada Department of Agriculture, *Canada: Prices, Policy and Trade, 1963–64*; and Dominion Bureau of Statistics, *Farm Cash Income*, various issues.

There can be little doubt that U.S. agriculture and agricultural trade have been dominant influences on Canadian agriculture. This can be inferred from Table II, which shows Canada's agricultural trade with the world in general and with the United States in particular. In products other than

TABLE II

CANADIAN EXPORTS AND IMPORTS OF AGRICULTURAL PRODUCTS
(million Canadian dollars)

Calendar year	Exports to		Imports from	
	All countries	United States	All countries	United States
1950	818	302	604	274
1951	1,020	383	711	340
1952	1,220	303	564	280
1953	1,147	298	541	263
1954	853	235	594	301
1955	801	183	639	316
1956	1,013	206	690	362
1957	909	239	709	373
1958	1,034	289	683	362
1959	970	217	739	389
1960	909	193	747	427
1961	1,193	225	813	467
1962	1,157	224	857	479
1963	1,359	223	1,004	514
1964	1,702	332	1,047	550

Source: Canada Department of Agriculture, *Canada: Prices, Policy and Trade, 1963–64.*

grains, Canada has exported to the United States a much larger share than Table II suggests. Little Canadian grain has gone to the United States, although grain exports have frequently accounted for nearly half of the value of Canada's total agricultural exports. Aside from trading with each other, Canada and the United States have been directly competing in world markets for many farm products (as will become evident in subsequent sections dealing with individual products). This is to be expected, since they share, to a large extent, similar agricultural resources and production techniques.

Given that the United States is Canada's strongest competitor in world agricultural trade over a wide range of products, a comparison of the two countries' respective agricultural productivity may serve as a useful tool to indicate their comparative advantages. Different measures have been used from time to time to estimate productivity in agriculture, of which some appear to be more useful than others.[1] To express comparative advantage,

[1]See, for example, G. A. MacEachern and D. L. MacFarlane, "The Relative Position of Canadian Agriculture in World Trade," *Conference on International Trade and Canadian Agriculture*, Economic Council of Canada and the Agricultural Economics Research Council of Canada, Ottawa, Queen's Printer, 1966, pp. 95–104.

a measure of productivity must reflect value of output in relation to costs. In other words, the ideal measure of productivity would be the ratio of value of output to value of input for the industry in question. Superficially, many measures of productivity appear to meet this criterion, but on closer inspection they fall short of it. For example, measures of labour productivity, such as gross domestic product per man-hour or per active person employed in agriculture, are ratios of total value of output to a single factor of production—i.e., labour. Since land, machinery, livestock, and other productive resources are also required in agricultural production, they ought to be part of the denominator in the ratio of value of output to value of input if a meaningful measure of productivity is to result. No measure of labour productivity alone will, therefore, be adequate. It can be argued that other measures of productivity which embody a ratio of total value of agricultural output to the quantity or value of a single resource are similarly inaccurate. On these grounds, one must also reject such measures of productivity as value of output per animal, or value of output per acre, etc.

Another way of measuring productivity is simply to use total values of output and then to compare changes in output among different nations over a given period of time.[2] This method has defects of its own. It implies that the values of inputs used in production either do not change at all over time or else change at the same rate for all nations during the time period considered.

While no measure of productivity is free from flaws, one type which appears to avoid some of the inaccuracies discussed above is the ratio of an index of *total value of agricultural output* to an index of *total value of inputs used in agriculture*. Recently, indices of this type have been calculated for Canadian and U.S. agriculture for the period 1935 to 1964. They indicate that, over the whole thirty-year period, there has been an average annual increase in Canadian agricultural productivity of 2.2 percent, while U.S. agricultural productivity has increased at an average annual rate of 1.6 percent.[3] Since 1946, Canadian agricultural productivity has averaged an increase of 2.6 percent a year, and U.S. agricultural productivity has averaged a yearly increase of 1.4 percent. This result stands in marked contrast to productivity estimates obtained by using ratios of total output to a single factor of production.[4]

Increases in Canadian agricultural productivity have resulted from the interaction of two forces—an increase in output and a *decrease* in the

[2]*Ibid.*, p. 101.
[3]I. F. Furniss, "Productivity Trends in Canadian Agriculture, 1935 to 1964," *Canadian Farm Economics*, vol. 1, no. 1, pp. 18–22.
[4]MacEachern and MacFarlane, "The Relative Position of Canadian Agriculture in World Trade," pp. 97, 98, 101.

inputs used to produce that output.[5] Agricultural productivity in the United States has also been subject to changes in output and inputs. However, in the U.S. economy the forces have tended to work against each other: increases in output have been produced by increases in the amounts of resources used.[6] This result is consistent with the view that, in the United States, agricultural production has increased chiefly in response to relatively high price supports; at the same time U.S. agriculture has been encouraged to increase excessively its factors of input. On the other hand, Canadian agriculture, with a similar technology at its disposal, has had to adjust to the forces of a relatively free market, with the result that surplus resources have tended to be squeezed out of Canadian agriculture.

In any event, it is critically important to observe that, although Canada's comparative advantage in agriculture has improved relative to that of the United States, similar gains in productivity might very well be possible for U.S. agriculture under a somewhat freer market situation.

It may be reasonably inferred from the above that Canadian agriculture has a head start over U.S. agriculture along the road to improved productivity. However, with a common pool of technology and free movement of many productive resources between Canada and the United States, there is little reason for believing that Canada's current lead would be maintained under free trade. A more accurate understanding of Canadian competitive strength in agricultural production can be gained by the more detailed examination of individual products that follows.

The commodity studies presented in this and succeeding sections examine agricultural commodities of economic importance to Canada, with a view to discovering how Canadian prices and quantities would be affected if barriers to international trade were lowered. Furthermore, attention has been directed towards changes of a permanent, rather than to those of a temporary, nature.

Many agricultural commodities employ common factors of production, and a good deal of primary agricultural output is used to produce secondary products. Consequently, this paper considers both direct and indirect effects of changes in prices and quantities and examines relative changes of prices and quantities within agriculture.

As an aid to analysis and exposition, it seemed useful, first, to select one commodity whose position under free trade could be established with a considerable degree of certainty and then, where appropriate, to determine the relative position of other related commodities. Wheat was selected as the benchmark commodity because of its great importance to Canadian

[5]Furniss, "Productivity Trends," p. 18.
[6]*Ibid.*, p. 21.

agriculture as well as because of the fact that international and domestic statistics were more readily available for this commodity than for most other Canadian agricultural products.

II. Grain

Wheat

This section demonstrates that Canada has a considerable absolute advantage in wheat production over most of the world's wheat producers and exporters and that, with the freeing of world production and international movement of this commodity, Canada could expect to export as much wheat as at present, or more, and at prices relatively higher than those that have been in effect in recent years. The outline of the case for Canada's strong competitive position in wheat is straightforward; in effect, the paper argues that Canada has the potential to produce large quantities of wheat of superior quality at equal cost to, or at lower cost than, comparable wheat from other regions.

Since the early 1920s, Canada has been a major exporter of wheat and wheat flour in an expanding world trade in this grain. From the twenties until the Second World War, Canada was the world's leading wheat exporter. Since then, the United States has taken over first place, with Canada as a very strong second, leading Australia and Argentina by a wide margin. Since the early 1950s, France has also emerged as an important wheat exporter of about the same size as Argentina (Table III).

Although Canada has been delivering a declining percentage of world wheat exports, total Canadian wheat exports have been maintained, and even increased, in recent years. While Table III indicates that Canada has maintained a relatively strong position in world wheat trade, it also suggests that this country has been losing ground to the United States in wheat exports. The data of Table III, however, give only a partial view of Canada's competitiveness in wheat deliveries vis-à-vis the United States. A considerable portion of U.S. wheat exports in recent years has been of a non-commercial nature, involving a large degree of subsidy in price or terms of sale. These non-commercial exports have obscured the true competitive relationship between Canada and the United States in wheat production. A more accurate view of Canada's competitive position may be secured by comparing Canadian wheat exports with commercial U.S. wheat exports in recent years. It has been noted by J. M. Stam that, during the periods 1951–54, 1955–60, and 1961–63, commercial U.S. exports averaged 100 million bushels per year less than average yearly Canadian

TABLE III

WHEAT AND WHEAT FLOUR: WORLD EXPORTS, PRINCIPAL COUNTRIES

Year (beginning July)	Argentina Quantity (million bushels)	Argentina % of world total	Australia Quantity (million bushels)	Australia % of world total	Canada Quantity (million bushels)	Canada % of world total	France Quantity (million bushels)	France % of world total	United States* Quantity (million bushels)	United States* % of world total	World total (million bushels)
1920–29†	154	18.4	89	10.5	267	31.8			222	26.4	840
1930–39†	130	18.3	114	16.1	201	28.3			75	10.6	710
1945–49†	76	8.7	83	9.4	252	28.7			415	47.3	878
1952	29	3.0	99	10.0	392	39.7			317	32.1	987
1954	132	13.6	93	9.6	253	26.1	88	9.1	274	28.2	971
1956	98	7.4	126	9.5	282	21.2	14	1.1	549	41.3	1,328
1958	103	7.8	75	5.7	300	22.7	38	2.9	443	33.5	1,321
1960	70	4.4	183	11.6	343	21.8	57	3.6	662	42.0	1,576
1961	86	5.0	230	13.3	365	21.0	68	3.9	718	41.4	1,734
1962	55	3.5	200	12.7	320	20.3	109	6.9	615	38.9	1,580
1963	102	5.0	287	14.2	554	27.4	98	4.8	849	41.9	2,025
1964‡	156	8.5	238	12.9	435	23.6	169	9.2	718	39.0	1,840

Sources: 1920 to 1962 (excluding France): U.S. Department of Agriculture, *The Wheat Situation*, April 1963. France, 1954 to 1962: U.S. Department of Agriculture, *Agricultural Statistics*, 1963. 1963 and 1964: United Nations, Food and Agricultural Association, *World Grain Trade Statistics, 1964/65* (data converted from metric tons, wheat equivalent, at the rate of 36.744 bushels per metric ton).
*U.S. export statistics include 32 million bushels of wheat for 1963/64 and 35 million bushels for 1964/65 reported as shipped to Canada but actually representing only transit trade through Canadian ports and accordingly not included in Canadian import statistics.
†Averages
‡Preliminary.

exports.[1] In the same article, the author observed that Public Law 480 appeared to have more strongly affected U.S. commercial exports than Canadian exports, in the sense that the former declined more rapidly than the latter to countries where they were both in direct competition with PL480 exports. In point of fact, there is good reason to believe that Canada has shown a *long-term ability* to export large amounts of commercial wheat in competition with the United States.

Although Canada is sufficiently competitive vis-à-vis the United States in terms of quantity of wheat exports, its strongest advantage exists in the quality of its wheat. There are many reasons for believing that Canadian wheat has superior bread-baking qualities to that produced by any other major exporter. L. A. Fischer reports a ranking for wheat exports to the Common Market countries that places Manitoba grades 1 to 4 above all other grades and varieties, including Northern spring and Hard Red winter wheat from the United States, and Plata wheat from Argentina.[2] Other evidence indicates that, on the basis of protein and sedimentation, Canada's top four grades are better than top wheat grades from the United States and markedly superior to wheat from Belgium, France, Italy, the Netherlands, and West Germany.[3] Furthermore, Canada produces very large amounts of the top grades of wheat; for example, numbers 1, 2, and 3 Northern together accounted for more than three-quarters of the Canadian wheat crop during the five-year period 1959 to 1963.[4] A large number of countries import small quantities of Canadian hard wheat for blending with other wheat to produce a flour that is suitable for bread-baking (Table IV and Appendix Tables I and II).

Possibly the most compelling evidence of the high quality of Canadian wheat comes from the large purchases of Canadian wheat by countries that are net exporters of wheat. France has regularly purchased some Canadian wheat during the 1960s, despite the fact that it has been a net exporter of this grain for many years. Even the United States has made small but continuous purchases of Canadian wheat, other than seed, for domestic use (Appendix Tables I and II).

Sustained exports and a high-quality product are only part of the essential picture required for evaluating Canada's competitive position in wheat production. Although there might well have been reason for Canadian wheat to receive a price premium that would have been reflected back

[1]J. M. Stam, "The Effects of Public Law 480 on Canadian Wheat Exports," *Journal of Farm Economics,* vol. 46, no. 4.
[2]L. A. Fischer, *Future of Canadian Wheat Exports to the Common Market Countries,* mimeograph, Macdonald College, McGill University, 1964, p. 69.
[3]*Ibid.,* Table 31, p. 72.
[4]Canadian Wheat Board, *Annual Report,* various issues.

TABLE IV

PERCENTAGE DISTRIBUTION OF EXPORTS OF WHEAT AND WHEAT FLOUR
(WHEAT EQUIVALENT)

Exporting country	1959/60*	1960/61	1961/62	1962/63	1963/64
to Western Europe					
Argentina	41.1	38.5	59.7	47.7	17.8
Australia	25.9	30.9	28.6	16.4	14.7
Canada	59.2	53.6	46.9	46.4	29.8
France	41.8	46.6	47.7	22.2	50.4
United States	15.3	24.5	24.9	15.4	13.9
to Eastern Europe					
Argentina	—	—	0.4	—	7.9
Australia	—	0.6	—	0.5	0.5
Canada	1.8	4.9	7.6	5.6	13.8
France	—	1.9	—	19.3	19.8
United States	5.3	6.2	2.4	3.2	7.8
to USSR					
Argentina	—	—	—	—	4.0
Australia	—	—	—	—	21.5
Canada	—	2.2	—	—	30.8
France	—	—	—	—	5.6
United States	—	—	—	—	7.5
to North and Central America					
Argentina	—	—	—	—	—
Australia	—	—	—	0.1	0.3
Canada	5.8	5.1	4.1	4.6	4.8
France	5.2	4.0	5.7	2.0	2.8
United States	4.1	1.9	1.7	2.0	1.9
to South America					
Argentina	56.0	56.6	33.4	44.3	34.7
Australia	—	—	—	0.4	—
Canada	3.0	2.2	1.5	2.7	1.6
France	3.6	1.0	1.6	1.2	0.4
United States	12.7	9.9	13.1	13.2	9.6
to Near East Asia					
Argentina	1.4	2.4	—	—	—
Australia	15.1	9.6	4.6	5.4	6.2
Canada	1.7	1.5	0.7	0.9	0.5
France	3.0	1.7	1.7	1.4	0.6
United States	7.2	9.4	11.5	7.1	4.6
to Far East Asia					
Argentina	—	—	3.7	5.4	35.6
Australia	43.9	49.7	57.1	69.1	50.9
Canada	24.0	28.8	37.0	35.7	17.5
France	2.1	3.7	14.6	33.1	10.1
United States	44.0	36.3	28.3	43.4	41.2
to Africa					
Argentina	—	0.5	1.7	2.6	—
Australia	6.6	4.8	6.0	3.8	2.6
Canada	4.4	1.6	2.1	4.0	0.8
France	42.6	34.7	27.6	20.3	9.6
United States	10.2	10.3	15.7	15.6	13.2

TABLE IV (continued)

Exporting country	1959/60*	1960/61	1961/62	1962/63	1963/64
to Oceania					
Argentina	—	—	—	—	—
Australia	8.0	4.4	3.6	4.3	3.3
Canada	—	0.1	0.1	0.1	0.1
France	0.9	0.4	0.9	0.5	0.7
United States	—	—	—	—	—

Source: International Wheat Council, *World Wheat Statistics,* various issues.

Note: Total exports of wheat and wheat flour for each country per crop year = 100 percent.

*July–June years.

to producers in terms of higher prices, such has not been the case. Basic producer prices have been lower for Canadian farmers than for virtually any other nation's wheat producers. Table V, in conjunction with Table III, strongly supports the contention that Canadian wheat producers have the ability to compete with the rest of the world's wheat producers. Total Canadian wheat exports have been increasing throughout the world, while basic producer prices in Canada have remained below those of other nations.

Instead of using basic producer prices to compare competitiveness among wheat-producing nations, some authors have calculated the cost advantage enjoyed by Canadian producers using producer prices for a given time in the past. Recent estimates of this type suggest that, during the 1964/65 crop season, Canada had a cost advantage of 31 cents a bushel over the United States, 22 cents a bushel over Argentina, and about 7 cents a bushel over Australia.[5] Such estimates for a single point in time, however, tend to reflect short-term supply and demand forces as well as more persistent ones and hence may be most useful as additional evidence of absolute advantage.

Canadian wheat production has varied considerably from year to year as a result of changes in weather conditions and changes in wheat acreages. Table VI shows that variations in average yield have been more important than changes in seeded acreage as factors in the year-to-year fluctuation. There has been a remarkable stability in the seeded acreage of wheat during the period under study; in no year did it exceed thirty million acres,

[5]MacEachern and MacFarlane, "The Relative Position of Canadian Agriculture in World Trade," pp. 34, 35.

TABLE V

BASIC PRODUCER PRICES IN SELECTED COUNTRIES
(U.S. dollars* per bushel)

Country	1960/61	1961/62	1962/63	1963/64	1964/65
Europe:					
Belgium†	2.56	2.56	2.61	2.65	2.65
France†	2.20	2.24	2.33	2.36	2.39
Germany, Federal					
Republic†	2.82–2.95	2.82–2.95	3.01	3.01	3.01
Ireland	2.27	2.25	2.25	2.25	2.25
Italy†	2.83	2.83	2.72	2.67	2.68
Netherlands†	2.33	2.31	2.31	2.53	2.69
Sweden	2.47	2.37	2.67	2.79	2.89
Switzerland	4.23	4.23	4.36	4.36	4.36
United Kingdom	2.02	2.02	2.02	1.99	1.99
North and Central America:					
Canada	1.30	1.38‡	1.38	1.38	1.38
Mexico	1.99	1.99	1.99	1.99	1.99
United States	1.78	1.79	2.00	1.82	1.30§
South America:					
Argentina	1.25	1.41	1.28	1.45	1.42
Chile	1.99	2.01	1.36	2.29	—
Asia:					
India	1.99	‖	1.99	2.14	2.14
Japan	2.84	3.01	3.18	3.26	3.41
Turkey	1.66	1.90	2.21	2.21	2.21
Africa:					
South Africa	2.19	2.21	2.15	2.21	2.30
Tunisia	2.72	2.72	2.72	2.72	2.18
United Arab Republic					
(Egypt)	2.11	2.11	2.11	2.11	—
Oceania:					
Australia	1.70	1.76	1.77	1.61	1.63
New Zealand	1.88	1.88	1.88	1.88	1.88

Source: International Wheat Council, *World Wheat Statistics*, various issues. These prices and definitions are used as a basis for government guarantees to producers and are not necessarily comparable between countries.

*Converted at IMF par values except for Argentina, Chile, and Tunisia, where the IMF exchange rate for the first month of each country's crop year was used. 1964/65 prices for Argentina and Tunisia are based on their devalued currencies.

†Intervention prices for August, 1962 (applying to 1962/63 crop year), July, 1963 (for 1963/64), and July, 1964 (for 1964/65), respectively, for Belgium and the Netherlands, for the surplus areas in France and Italy and for the deficit area in Germany. Prices increase on a seasonal scale to take account of storage costs and interest charges and refer to soft wheat of national quality standards in 1963/64 (except those of Germany) and of EEC standard quality.

‡On March 1, 1962, the price was raised by 10 cents to $1.50 per bushel, retrospective to the beginning of the Canadian marketing year.

§Does not include producer subsidy of nearly 40 cents (U.S.).

‖In 1961 the Indian government did not fix guaranteed floor prices.

TABLE VI

CANADIAN WHEAT PRODUCTION, EXPORTS, DOMESTIC USE, AND STOCKS

Crop year	Production			Exports (million bushels)	Apparent domestic use (million bushels)	Year-end stocks (million bushels)
	Seeded acreage (million acres)	Total production (million bushels)	Average yield (bushels per seeded acre)			
1940/41	29	540	18.8	231	130	480
1941/42	22	315	14.3	226	145	424
1942/43	22	556	25.8	215	170	595
1943/44	17	282	16.9	344	177	357
1944/45	23	415	18.3	343	171	258
1945/46	23	316	13.6	343	158	74
1946/47	24	412	16.9	239	160	86
1947/48	24	339	14.0	195	153	78
1948/49	24	381	16.1	232	125	102
1949/50	27	366	13.4	225	131	112
1950/51	27	466	17.1	241	148	189
1951/52	25	554	21.9	356	170	217
1952/53	26	702	26.8	386	150	383
1953/54	26	634	24.0	255	144	619
1954/55	26	332	13.0	252	162	537
1955/56	23	519	22.9	312	164	580
1956/57	23	573	25.2	264	155	734
1957/58	22	393	18.2	320	159	649
1958/59	22	398	18.0	295	168	588
1959/60	24	445	18.2	277	148	600
1960/61	25	518	21.1	353	147	608
1961/62	25	283	11.2	358	142	391
1962/63	27	566	21.1	331	138	487
1963/64	28	723	26.2	595	157	459
1964/65	30	600	30.2	399	146	515

Source: DBS, *Handbook of Agricultural Statistics, 1908–63*, and supplementary data from Farm Crops section.

and in only one year was it less than twenty million acres. Typically, seeded acreage varied less than 10 percent from one year to the next.

Since 1939, Canadian wheat producers have faced two major crises during which it became increasingly difficult for them to market their wheat; one of these occurred in the first years of the Second World War, the other during the early 1950s. The response of wheat producers to these two, somewhat similar, situations gives a useful insight into producers' reactions to the limited production alternatives available to them. Two large crops at the beginning of the war, without compensating increases in exports, raised wheat stocks to record levels. The government reacted by offering an acreage bonus for land taken out of wheat production. This bonus amounted to $4.00 per acre for land taken out of wheat and put into summer fallow, and $2.00 for land taken out of wheat and put into coarse grains or grass.[6] Faced with little prospect of delivering their wheat, producers reduced sowings of this crop by nearly six million acres. This cutback was stimulated by a twofold incentive: government compensation for reduced wheat acreage and the prospect of substitute income from coarse-grain crops. Stocks of wheat continued to build up as a result of a large crop in the 1942/43 crop year. The government became more concerned and made it abundantly clear that little would be gained from wheat production in the 1943/44 crop season. Canadian wheat acreage reached a record low in that year. This was compensated for, to some degree, by an increase in coarse-grain and flaxseed acreage. With renewed prospects of higher exports and increased farm deliveries to the Wheat Board, seeded acreage of wheat rose by six million acres in the next year. From 1944/45 until the end of the 1940s, surplus wheat production did not constitute a problem for Canadian wheat producers.

However, a second wheat-marketing crisis soon developed. A series of heavy crops between 1950 and 1954 raised wheat stocks to unprecedented levels. Above-normal crops continued until, by the end of the 1956/57 crop year, Canada was holding nearly three-quarters of a billion bushels of wheat. Since then, expanded exports (notably to the Communist countries) have reduced wheat stocks; but record levels of production have counteracted, and wheat stocks have remained disturbingly large. Producer response during the 1950s and 1960s has been particularly interesting. From 1953 to 1957, seeded acreage was reduced by an average of less than 5 percent per year; from 1957 to 1964, it increased steadily to a record level of nearly thirty million acres. It seems that, as marketing became difficult, wheat acreage was reduced only gradually, despite the large build-up of stocks which hampered deliveries from farms to the Wheat Board. This was in marked distinction to the response in the early 1940s, when wheat acreage had been cut back drastically and rapidly. The essential difference between the situation in the 1940s and that of the 1950s was that in the 1940s producers had received a bonus for choosing the next-best alternative to wheat production and, accordingly, had increased their coarse-grain acreage and summer fallow (Table VII). In the 1950s, the switch to coarse-grain production was much less pronounced

[6]G. E. Britnell and V. C. Fowke, *Canadian Agriculture in War and Peace, 1935–1950*, Stanford, Calif., Stanford University Press, 1962, p. 206.

TABLE VII

SEEDED ACREAGE AND SUMMER FALLOW, PRAIRIE PROVINCES
(million acres)

| Year | Seeded acreage | | | Summer fallow | Total† |
	Wheat	Coarse grains*	Flaxseed		
1940/41	28	13	–	17	58
1941/42	21	14	1	23	59
1942/43	21	17	2	20	59
1943/44	16	19	3	21	59
1944/45	22	18	1	20	60
1945/46	22	17	1	21	61
1946/47	24	15	1	20	60
1947/48	23	16	2	20	61
1948/49	23	16	2	21	61
1949/50	27	14	–	22	63
1950/51	26	15	1	22	63
1951/52	24	17	1	22	64
1952/53	25	17	1	21	65
1953/54	26	16	1	23	66
1954/55	25	16	1	26	66
1955/56	22	19	2	25	66
1956/57	22	15	3	24	65
1957/58	21	15	3	25	65
1958/59	21	15	3	26	66
1959/60	24	14	2	27	66
1960/61	24	13	2	27	65
1961/62	25	10	2	28	68
1962/63	26	13	1	27	68
1963/64	27	13	2	27	69
1964/65	29	11	2	26	69
1965/66	28	13	2	27	69

Source: DBS, *Handbook of Agricultural Statistics, 1908–63*, and supplementary data from Farm Crops section.
*Oats, barley, and rye.
†May not always be exact addition of component columns due to rounding.

than it had been in the 1940s, although there was a marked movement into flaxseed. This reluctance to change crops without a compensatory incentive suggests that wheat producers have few worthwhile production alternatives.

The reactions by producers to crises in Canadian wheat marketings suggest that Canada's low cost of wheat production results from a lack of good production alternatives. Canadian hard spring wheat is produced on prairie land that has very little rainfall; consequently, the alternatives to wheat production have been restricted to coarse grains, oilseeds, and ranching. Although coarse-grain production uses the same productive resources as does wheat production, an increase in the demand for coarse grains requires an increase of the grain-consuming livestock population. This is a difficult objective to achieve in the short run. Other things being equal, a large increase in grain-consuming livestock, such as hogs, will depress hog prices and subsequently drive down prices for coarse grains. Moreover, when wheat stocks are high, there appears to be a tendency to use low grades of wheat for livestock feed. This is suggested in Table VI, which shows high levels for "apparent domestic use" where year-end stocks are high. In other words, a build-up of wheat stocks depresses feed-grain prices to a considerable extent because feed wheat is a good substitute for other feed grains. Table VIII shows that gross returns per acre from wheat have consistently exceeded gross returns per acre from alternative crops. Assuming similar production costs, it can be concluded that it has generally been more profitable for the Prairie provinces to grow wheat than to grow alternative crops.

TABLE VIII

GROSS RETURNS, PRAIRIE PROVINCES, FIVE-YEAR AVERAGES
(Canadian dollars per acre)

Period	Wheat	Oats	Barley	Rye	Flaxseed
1950–54	29.41	24.15	28.50	18.62	27.96
1955–59	26.21	20.12	20.71	13.02	24.03
1960–64	36.81	29.68	34.12	20.15	31.70

Source: DBS, *Handbook of Agricultural Statistics, 1908–63*, and supplementary data from Farm Crops section.

In view of these considerations it can be inferred that the opportunity costs of wheat production in western Canada are low. A reduction in wheat prices would divert production to alternative, resource-competitive crops whose prices would drop as stocks increased. This, in turn, would reduce the prices of resources used in wheat and feed-grain production, provided wheat prices were to remain low for a considerable period of time. Farmers would probably continue to produce wheat as long as they expected to cover direct cash costs of operation, including their own wages. Their last economic alternative would be to use the land for range purposes. However, this would require a substantial increase of cattle to utilize the range.

Such an increase would be biologically impossible to achieve in the short run.

It must reasonably be expected that most regions growing high-quality wheat would face similar adjustments if wheat prices were to decline. Since Canada's strongest competitor for wheat, in terms of quality, is the United States, direct comparison between Canadian and U.S. spring-wheat production is relevant. Table IX shows that, until 1960, Canadian yields slightly

TABLE IX

AVERAGE YIELDS, SPRING WHEAT
(bushels per seeded acre)

Period	Canada	United States
1930–39	12.5	8.1
1940–49	16.5	15.1
1950–59	20.2	15.7
1960	20.9	20.2
1961	10.6	13.0
1962	20.9	26.3
1963	26.0	20.3
1964	20.0	21.2*
1965	23.8	23.5*

Sources: Canadian data: Dominion Bureau of Statistics, *Handbook of Agricultural Statistics, 1908–63* and the *Wheat Review*, various issues.
U.S. data: U.S. Department of Agriculture, *Wheat Situation,* various issues up to February, 1966.
*Adjusted to seeded acreage basis by reducing bushels per harvested acre by two bushels per acre.

exceeded those in the United States. Since then, the two countries appear to have had nearly identical yields.[7] The situations facing producers in the two countries have been significantly different. Canadian farmers have been faced with a lower wheat price than have U.S. producers and, on these grounds, have had less incentive to seek high yields per acre. Furthermore, their U.S. counterparts receive price supports on an acreage basis contingent upon acreage limitations. Under the Temporary Wheat Reserves Act, Canadian wheat producers also receive small subsidies, principally in the

[7]With relatively free trade in productive factors such as machinery, fertilizers, and chemicals between Canada and the United States, and land being the main fixed resource in wheat production, yield per acre is a better indication of productive efficiency than it would be for agriculture as a whole, as discussed in the first section of the study.

form of assistance of storage costs on excess reserves. Canadian railroads have made less obvious subsidies to Canadian grain producers in the form of statutory grain rates, which appear to be below variable costs.[8] Taken together, Canadian subsidies appear to be in the order of 10 cents per bushel, while U.S. direct subsidies on wheat exports are nearly three times as great. There seems little reason for doubt that, under relatively free trade, Canada would be able to produce spring wheat at a cost at least as low as that in the United States.

Given that spring wheat yields only about one-third of total U.S., but nearly all of Canadian, wheat production, Canada may be expected, under conditions of free trade, to expand its exports of wheat to most countries, relative to U.S. exports, by selling a product generally accepted as being of superior quality at an equal or lower price.

Communist bloc countries have purchased substantial amounts of Canadian wheat in recent years, thus relieving what would otherwise have been a heavy surplus position. A rising standard of living in Communist bloc countries can be expected to increase their demand for wheat to replace inferior bread grains in the diet. While one can offer only conjecture on this subject, it appears probable that Communist countries will attempt to become self-sufficient producers, and even perhaps net exporters, of wheat. However, since available evidence suggests that only a small region in the Ukraine produces a product whose quality is comparable to that of Canadian wheat, it seems doubtful that Communist bloc exports would pose a serious threat to Canadian wheat exports in anything approaching a free market situation.

Barley

Canada has exported barley (for feed, seed, and malting) and malt in widely varying quantities for many years. During the 1930s Canadian barley exports averaged fourteen million bushels per year. This level was drastically reduced during the first years of the Second World War but nearly doubled in the later war years. Between 1940 and 1959 Canada exported as little as three million bushels, and as much as 122 million bushels, in individual years. The late 1940s and the 1950s witnessed a drastic increase in Canada's barley exports (Table X). In the 1960s exports remained at high levels but declined substantially below those of the previous decade. Canada's relative position as an exporter of barley has shifted a great deal, as the above-mentioned changes suggest. During a

---

[8]J. L. McDougal, "The Relative Level of Crow's Nest Grain Rates in 1899 and in 1965," *Canadian Journal of Economics and Political Science*, XXXII (February 1966).

TABLE X

CANADIAN EXPORTS OF BARLEY
(million bushels)

Period	Amount
1930–39 average	14.0
1940/41	4.6
1941/42	3.0
1942/43	34.9
1943/44	37.2
1944/45	40.0
1945/46	5.1
1946/47	7.7
1947/48	4.3
1948/49	24.6
1949/50	20.8
1950/51	27.4
1951/52	73.5
1952/53	122.1
1953/54	93.7
1954/55	80.9
1955/56	68.7
1956/57	81.5
1957/58	80.3
1958/59	70.5
1959/60	63.8
1960/61	47.2
1961/62	42.9
1962/63	15.4
1963/64	46.9
1964/65	.37.0

Sources: DBS, *Handbook of Agricultural Statistics, 1908–63* and *Grain Trade of Canada, 1963–64*; Canadian Wheat Board, *Annual Report, 1964–65*.

recent five-year period, Canada ranked second twice, third twice, and fifth once, among principal exporting countries. Other major barley exporters have been the United States, France, Australia, and Argentina; in some years, Denmark, the Netherlands, the United Kingdom, and Sweden have also been large exporters of barley.[9]

[9]United Nations, Food and Agricultural Organization, "Barley Exports From Specified Exporting Countries," *World Grain Trade Statistics, 1964/65* and previous issues.

During the last half of the 1940s, Canadian barley was exported primarily to the United States and to Europe; large shipments to the United States continued throughout the 1950s. While the United States has imported a good deal of Canadian barley in the 1960s, the amounts have been much lower than they were during the previous decade. During the 1950s, continental Europe's purchases of Canadian barley declined somewhat, but there was a compensatory increase in the United Kingdom's imports. At the same time, Canada developed a considerable export trade in barley to the Far East. Since the beginning of the 1960s, Canada has virtually left the continental European market, although exports to the United Kingdom have remained important. Exports of barley to the Far East have increased substantially, amounting to more than 40 percent of total Canadian barley exports during the first part of the 1960s.[10]

Canada's strong competitive position as a barley producer is implied by its sustained ability to export large quantities of barley to the United States despite a tariff barrier and regardless of the fact that *the United States has been the world's main exporter of barley* for many years. However, it would be overly optimistic to assume that free trade would immediately produce a large increase in U.S. purchases of Canadian barley. A major component of U.S. imports appears to have been malting-quality barley, the demand for which may be expected to increase only slowly. The dominant feature of Canada's advantage in barley production lies perhaps not on the demand side but on the production side.

A considerable change has taken place in the geographical pattern of barley production during the last thirty-five years. During the 1930s the Prairies produced about 72 percent of Canadian barley; by 1965, 94 percent was produced in the Prairies.[11] It is interesting to observe that, under conditions of relatively free movement of resources, barley production shifted from the east to the west, despite the fact that per-acre yields of barley were higher in the east than in the west. For example, from 1957 to 1963 eastern barley yields were more than ten bushels per acre greater than yields in the Prairie provinces.[12] While it is true that freight subsidies paid on feed grain transported from west to east increased western barley prices relative to eastern prices, a similar development in oat prices did not have nearly the same effect on regional specialization in oat production.

Barley competes for the same resources as does wheat, but its gross returns are less than those from wheat (Table VIII). In western Canada

[10]Canadian Wheat Board, *Annual Report, 1964–65.*
[11]Dominion Bureau of Statistics, *Handbook of Agricultural Statistics, 1908–63*, and *Grain Trade of Canada, 1964–65*; Canadian Wheat Board, *Annual Report, 1964–65.*
[12]DBS, *Handbook of Agricultural Statistics, 1908–63.*

it is grown in conjunction with wheat for two main reasons: one, to provide on-farm feed supplies, and the other, to provide an alternative source of cash income in case deliveries to the Wheat Board are suspended. The greatest force affecting acreage and production of barley has been the market outlook for wheat. When wheat acreages declined, as during the early 1940s and throughout most of the 1950s, barley acreages increased to replace the wheat. Increased wheat acreages in the 1960s have resulted in a decrease in the acreage of barley. This is shown clearly in Table VII.

To sum up: under conditions of free trade, greater export opportunities and higher returns from wheat sales would induce Canadian wheat farmers to expand production, or at least to maintain production at high levels. If wheat acreage expands, barley acreage contracts because the two crops are resource-competitive. In other words, free trade would tend to increase the income of Canadian grain growers through expanded wheat sales. However, this would increase the opportunity cost of barley production and, in consequence, lead to a relative decline in Canada's competitive position as a barley producer.

Oats

World trade in oats has been small relative to trade in other grains. The United States, Australia, and Argentina have been the leading exporters of oats in recent years. Canada, like a number of other countries, has been an important but erratic exporter of oats. During the past twenty years, Canada has sent nearly 90 percent of its oat exports to Europe and the United States and has imported virtually no oats since 1935. World trade in oats has been as variable as that in barley, with countries entering the world market as large exporters for a year, then dropping back to their previous positions.[13]

The Prairie provinces have been the centre of Canadian oat production virtually since the west was opened up for agriculture. However, between 30 and 50 percent continues to be grown in the eastern provinces.[14] Almost all the Canadian oat crop—which has always been very large, running a close second to wheat in most years and occasionally exceeding it—is used domestically for feed. Less than 10 percent is exported in a typical year.

In the Prairie provinces oats have been grown as a secondary crop whose production has been dominated by wheat. Increased acreages of wheat have meant decreased acreages of oats, as Table VII indicates. In the eastern provinces, with their cooler, more humid growing seasons, oats have retained a strong position as a feed grain.

[13]FAO, *World Grain Trade Statistics, 1964/65* and previous issues.
[14]DBS, *Handbook of Agricultural Statistics, 1908–63*.

Canada's competitive position in world oat production appears to be relatively strong, as suggested by Table XI. Despite a sometimes adverse price level and a small but important tariff,[15] Canada has continued to export oats to the United States, itself the world's leading exporter of oats.

TABLE XI

CANADIAN EXPORTS OF OATS

Period	Exports to	
	All countries (million bushels)	United States (percentage of total exports)
1945/46	43.9	35
1946/47	29.8	4
1947/48	10.2	22
1948/49	23.2	85
1949/50	20.5	89
1950/51	35.4	88
1951/52	70.6	84
1952/53	65.4	92
1953/54	70.7	94
1954/55	22.2	68
1955/56	4.1	52
1956/57	18.7	96
1957/58	26.2	83
1958/59	7.5	20
1959/60	6.1	20
1960/61	2.7	42
1961/62	3.4	36
1962/63	21.7	12
1963/64	18.2	9
1964/65	15.2	17

Sources: D.B.S., *Handbook of Agricultural Statistics, 1908–63*; and Canadian Wheat Board, *Annual Report, 1964–65*.

Under free trade, Canada could be expected to maintain its oat production in the face of foreign competition. However, Canada's improved competitive position in wheat production as a result of free trade would reduce somewhat the volume of Canadian oat exports, as western oat acreage would decline due to increased wheat production. On the other hand, in eastern Canada, where oats is mainly used as livestock feed on the farm where it is produced, oat acreage would probably remain unchanged, as it has for nearly twenty years.[16]

[15]The U.S. tariff on oats has been 4 cents a bushel.
[16]DBS, *Handbook of Agricultural Statistics, 1908–63*.

Grain corn

Corn is one of the few types of grains which Canada produces but does not export in large quantities. For the last twenty-five years Canadian exports of grain corn have been negligible; since 1915 Canada has imported a large proportion of its grain-corn requirements (Table XII). Nearly all these imports have come from the United States. In recent years, grain-corn imports into Canada from the United States have had to climb an 8-cents-per-bushel tariff wall; but despite the tariff, substantial amounts have moved across the border, particularly during the 1960s. On the surface, this suggests that the United States has an advantage over Canada in corn production. While this may well be so, a number of factors complicate the situation.

TABLE XII

CANADIAN PRODUCTION AND IMPORTS OF GRAIN CORN

Period	Seeded acreage (thousand acres)	Total production (million bushels)	Imports	
			(million bushels)	(% of total production)
1915–19*	235	11.9	8.8	73.9
1919–29*	239	10.2	12.1	118.6
1930–39*	158	6.3	10.0	158.7
1940–49*	261	11.0	5.7	51.8
1950–59*	442	25.3	8.5	33.6
1960/61	455	26.1	21.4	82.0
1961/62	400	29.2	29.6	101.4
1962/63	421	32.0	31.2	97.5
1963/64	500	32.8	23.0	70.1
1964/65	—	53.0	20.8	39.2

Sources: DBS, *Handbook of Agricultural Statistics, 1908–63* and *Trade of Canada, Imports by Countries,* 1963 and 1964. Supplementary data received through direct communications with Dominion Bureau of Statistics.
*1915–59 annual averages.

For many years, U.S. corn producers have received price supports by participating in the loan program of the Commodity Credit Corporation. The popularity of this program among farmers suggests that it has provided a good deal of actual price support. Further complications arise from the acreage-diversion requirements of the U.S. price-support programs. These stipulations demand that corn producers who wish to be eligible for corn price support divert part of their corn acreage to other crops designated to be of a soil-conserving nature. Such institutional arrangements make comparisons of corn-production costs between Canada and the United States poor indicators of absolute cost differences.

However, Table XIII indicates that for the past ten years, despite the price supports in the United States, U.S. corn prices have been below

TABLE XIII

CANADIAN AND U.S. GRAIN-CORN YIELDS AND PRICES
(prices in domestic currencies)

Crop year	Canada		United States	
	Average yield (bushels per seeded acre)	Average farm price (dollars per bushel)	Average yield (bushels per harvested acre)	Seasonal average price* (dollars per bushel)
1955	62.2	1.06	42.0	1.35
1956	54.6	1.20	47.4	1.29
1957	57.8	1.18	48.3	1.11
1958	60.3	1.21	52.8	1.12
1959	63.7	1.16	53.1	1.04
1960	57.3	1.23	54.5	1.00
1961	73.0	1.12	62.0	1.08
1962	76.0	1.20	64.1	1.08†
1963	65.5	1.37	67.6	1.09†
1964	80.2	1.25	62.1	1.15†

Sources: Canadian data: DBS, *Handbook of Agricultural Statistics,
1908–63* and supplementary data from Farm Crops section. U.S. data:
U.S. Department of Agriculture, *Agricultural Statistics*, various issues,
and *Supplement to 1964 Grain and Feed Statistics.*
*Obtained by weighting state prices by quantity sold.
†Preliminary.

Canadian corn prices by an amount roughly equal to the Canadian tariff and exchange. It could be expected, therefore, that under free trade Canadian grain-corn prices would decline to a level comparable to that in the United States. In addition, there is reason to believe that U.S. corn is differentiated from Canadian corn on a quality basis, in much the same way that Canadian hard wheat and cheddar cheese are distinctive products with specific markets. From 1952 to 1956, inclusive, Canadian grain-corn prices were below those in the United States; yet substantial imports of grain corn (three and a half to five million bushels) entered Canada each year.[17] This observation suggests that purchasers were willing to pay a premium for U.S. grain corn. Discussion with persons in Canadian corn-processing industries (such as breakfast-food manufacturers and distillers) reveals that U.S. corn is available in a wider range of grades and types and hence is more suitable than Canadian corn for manufacturing purposes.

However, in the agricultural economy of southern Ontario, corn has occupied a rather special place in recent years; and despite large U.S. imports, Canadian corn production has increased. New varieties and improved production techniques have raised acreage yields to levels which compare very well with those of other crops in the southwestern part of Ontario. A recent Ontario study revealed that corn tended to be more profitable per acre than other grain crops such as rye, fall wheat, barley, oats, and soybeans.[18] Since (with the exception of soybeans) these crops are substitutes for one another, a reduction in corn prices would result in an absolute reduction in other grain prices; but in relation to each other, prices would remain comparatively unchanged. Thus, under free trade, corn production may be expected to increase slightly or to remain at present levels, simply because it would offer the best returns among available crops to many farmers.

Canada's absolute advantage in grain production

Three distinct but related factors have worked together to give Canada an absolute advantage in its major grain crops—wheat, oats, and barley. First, there has been a low real cost of production of these grains, chiefly because the Prairie provinces have had virtually no short-term production alternatives. The next best alternative to cropping—cattle raising—offers substantially lower returns per acre, especially since the existing cattle population cannot be significantly increased in the short run. Other factors that have kept costs of grain production down have been the substitution of machinery for labour and the increasing size of farm units.

The second factor that has helped to ensure Canada an absolute advantage in grain production has been the high quality of Canadian grains. Good seed and cultivation practices (while not exclusive to Canada) and the favourable factor endowment of land and climate together produce grains that are of nearly unique quality. It is this special natural advantage

---

[17]*Ibid.*
[18]This conclusion is suggested by M. J. Dorling in a mimeographed release, "Grain Corn Acreages and Production in Ontario in Recent Years," University of Guelph, 1961; see also Department of Agricultural Economics, "Production Opportunities on Ontario Tobacco Farms," University of Guelph, April 1965.

that enables Canada to produce a distinctly differentiated product for export.

The third factor to secure Canada an absolute advantage in grain production has been the application of strict grading standards. This system has been so successful that it now serves as the basis for grading grains in international trade. The rigid enforcement of this practice has permitted the sale of Canadian grains by predetermined grades—an advantage enjoyed by few other countries.

III. Tobacco

Canada produces a nominal amount of burley and cigar tobaccos, but flue-cured tobacco has accounted for nearly 90 percent of Canadian tobacco output for the past twenty years. Ontario grows more than 95 percent of Canada's total output of flue-cured tobacco, which is largely used for cigarette production (Appendix Tables V and VI). As a world producer of flue-cured tobacco, Canada has taken third or fourth place after the United States, Rhodesia, and sometimes Japan (Table XIV).

TABLE XIV

ESTIMATED PRODUCTION OF FLUE-CURED TOBACCO
(million pounds, farm weight)

	1961	1962	1963
United States	1,257.8	1,408.4	1,329.1
Rhodesia	236.8	234.4	198.6
Japan	173.7	190.9	190.8
Canada	195.4	187.6	187.7
India	154.6	163.5	147.5
Brazil	128.8	93.3	121.7
Rest of world	822.1	943.0	1,036.6
World total	2,969.2	3,221.1	3,212.0

Source: U.S. Department of Agriculture, *Annual Report on Tobacco Statistics,* 1961, 1962, 1963.

The United Kingdom has long been the world's largest importer of tobacco, and the United States has been its chief supplier, accounting for nearly 45 percent of British imports. Rhodesia, Zambia, and Malawi together have accounted for 30 percent, while Canada and India each have had about 10 percent of the U.K. market. Unlike Rhodesia, which produces primarily for export, Canada consumes about 80 percent of its tobacco domestically and exports the residual 20 percent. Canadian imports have amounted to about 1 percent of production in recent years.[1]

Almost every country taxes tobacco at some stage between production and consumption, and quotas and other controls abound in the industry. Canadian tobacco production has been heavily protected from international competition by a tariff of 20 and 30 cents per pound on stemmed and unstemmed tobacco, with the result that Canadian imports have been very small indeed. Canada's chief competitors in tobacco production have been the United States and Rhodesia. The United States has been able to sell its tobacco at a higher price than Canada for many years. Canada, at least recently, has managed to sell at a slightly higher price than Rhodesia (see Table XV).

TABLE XV

TOBACCO PRICES IN CANADA, RHODESIA, AND
THE UNITED STATES
(U.S. dollars per kilogram)

Year	Canada	Rhodesia	United States
1950	0.89	0.97	1.14
1951	0.96	0.89	1.13
1952	0.92	1.10	1.09
1953	0.97	1.02	1.14
1954	0.95	0.99	1.12
1955	0.95	1.04	1.17
1956	1.02	0.85	1.18
1957	1.08	1.01	1.23
1958	1.04	0.94	1.32
1959	1.22	0.89	1.28
1960	1.18	0.88	1.34
1961	1.04	0.87	1.41

Source:Department of Agricultural Economics, *Production Opportunities on Ontario Tobacco Farms*, University of Guelph, April 1965.

Both Canada and the United States have had stringent controls on tobacco production for many years, such as acreage allotments or legal rights granted to farmers to produce a given acreage of tobacco. The allotment system has produced considerable variations in the sizes of tobacco farms between the United States and Canada. The average acreage

[1]Rachel Berthiaume, *Exports, Imports, and Domestic Disappearance of Agricultural Products as a Percentage of Production, 1935–1962*, Canada Department of Agriculture, February 1965.

allotment of Ontario farms has been about thirty-four acres.[2] However, the effective size of acreage per grower in Ontario is a good deal larger because many growers own more than one farm; in some instances, husband and wife own a separate farm each.[3] In the United States, the typical flue-cured-tobacco allotment has been three acres, while in Rhodesia, where no production control exists, the typical grower owns sixty-five acres for the production of flue-cured tobacco.

If world trade in flue-cured tobacco were to be freed and production controls eliminated, Canadian producers could be expected to enlarge their plantings in order to reduce unit costs. The same type of adjustment, although it might take a little longer, could be expected to take place in the United States. The over-all result would be a reduction in world tobacco prices and, in turn, a reduction of Ontario tobacco-land prices.

Even if substantial price reductions were to result, Ontario growers would probably maintain, or even increase slightly, production of flue-cured tobacco as long as prices remained above 35 cents. This estimate is based on a study which investigated alternative opportunities to flue-cured-tobacco production in Ontario.[4] The study found that grain corn and potatoes appeared to be the next-best alternatives to tobacco production. Since, as the previous section on corn indicated, grain-corn prices would be expected to decline under free trade, the opportunity costs of tobacco production in Ontario would also be reduced under free trade. However, since free trade would eliminate much of the protection which Commonwealth countries now enjoy, the United States could expect to gain more from free trade than would Canada and Rhodesia. The net effect would probably leave Canadian tobacco producers slightly worse off, with little or no expectation of increasing production of tobacco except in Ontario, where resources and skills have been developed.

IV. Sugar

Canada is largely a net sugar importer in world trade; more than 80 percent of its sugar is imported, usually in the form of raw sugar, which is domestically further refined. There are no quantity restrictions on sugar

[2]G. Klosler, "Opportunity Costs of Resources Used in Tobacco Production in Norfolk County," unpublished Master's thesis, Ontario Agricultural College, University of Guelph.
[3]F. A. Stinson, *Report of Ontario Flue-cured Tobacco Industry Inquiry Committee*, February 1964.
[4]Department of Agricultural Economics, *Production Opportunities on Ontario Tobacco Farms*, University of Guelph, April 1965.

imports. Commonwealth tariff preference rates, which apply to Canadian sugar imports, have been most pronounced in the case of sugar for further refining. At between 24 and 36 cents per hundredweight, they have been one-fifth to one-quarter of the full rate. Canada has typically imported more than three-quarters of its sugar needs from Commonwealth countries, in particular from Australia, Jamaica, and Guyana.[1]

Canadian sugar production has been confined to beet sugar. Table XVI compares acreages, yields, and prices in Canada and the United States for

TABLE XVI

CANADIAN AND U.S. SUGARBEET PRODUCTION AND PRICES
(prices in domestic currencies)

	Canada			United States		
Crop year*	Harvested acreage (thousand acres)	Average yield (tons/har- vested acre)	Average farm price (dollars per ton)	Harvested acreage (thousand acres)	Average yield (tons/har- vested acre)	Average price† (dollars per ton)
1954	90	11.10	12.06	876	16.1	10.80
1955	82	11.98	13.42	740	16.5	11.20
1956	79	11.33	17.33	785	16.6	11.90
1957	84	12.58	13.24	878	17.7	11.20
1958	98	13.55	14.47	891	17.0	11.70
1959	90	13.70	12.78	905	18.8	11.20
1960	86	12.76	14.36	957	17.2	11.60
1961	85	13.02	13.13	1,077	16.4	11.20
1962‡	85	13.06		1,104	16.5	13.50
1963	95	13.83				

Sources: Canadian data: DBS, *Handbook of Agricultural Statistics, 1908–63*.
U.S. data: U.S. Department of Agriculture, *Agricultural Statistics*, various issues.
*Years for United States relate to years of harvest but, for California, include some acreage harvested in the beginning of the following year.
†Prices do not include government payments under Sugar Act.
‡Preliminary figures for United States.

the decade 1954–64. In recent years, Canadian sugarbeet production has been concentrated in the provinces of Alberta and Manitoba, but Ontario and Quebec still produce significant quantities.

Sugarbeet production has been supported by the Canadian Agricultural Stabilization Board for a number of years by means of variable deficiency payments to producers, which effectively insulate Canadian producers from

[1]International Sugar Council, *The World Sugar Economy Structure and Policies*, vol. 1. London, Haymarket House, 1963.

world changes in sugar prices.[2] Although Canadian sugarbeet production has grown considerably in recent years, removal of price supports could reduce Canadian beet-sugar production drastically. Since, as noted in "Trade in Agricultural Products,"[3] the guaranteed price to sugarbeet producers was 100 percent higher than the international price, it may be presumed that other nations producing sugarbeets would encounter similar price, and consequent production, declines.

V. Oilseeds

For many years Canada has had an active trade in oilseeds and oilseed products; both exports and imports have shown a long-term upward trend (Table XVII). Until recently exports exceeded imports slightly, but this relationship was reversed in 1963 and 1964. Flaxseed, rapeseed, and soybeans, in that order, have been the main crops in Canada's oilseed trade.

TABLE XVII

CANADIAN EXPORTS AND IMPORTS OF
OILSEEDS AND OILSEED PRODUCTS
(million Canadian dollars)

Year	Exports	Imports
1959	78	71
1960	86	70
1961	89	89
1962	99	90
1963	94	97
1964	96	115

Source: Canada Department of Agriculture, *Canada's Trade in Agricultural Products with the United Kingdom, the United States and All Countries*, various issues.

Flaxseed

For many years, Canada has been one of the world's principal exporters of flaxseed (Table XVIII), which has therefore become rather important in western Canada, where most of the Canadian crop is grown. Since 1955, more than 50 percent of Canada's production has been exported every year, and in some years the proportion has been as high as 80 percent.

[2]*Ibid.*
[3]General Agreement on Tariffs and Trade, "Trade in Agricultural Products," *Reports of Committee II on Country Consultation*, Geneva, 1962.

TABLE XVIII

EXPORTS OF FLAXSEED
(metric tons)

Exporting regions*	1959	1960	1961	1962	1963
Europe:					
Belgium, Luxembourg	9,598	15,076	20,250	18,512	25,443
Hungary			1,436		207
Netherlands	8,700	12,007	11,949	8,922	13,997
North and Central America:					
Canada	319,095	368,521	351,917	292,486	293,065
United States	214,670	105,401	115,000	100,141	86,575
South America:					
Argentina		63,038	98,955	6,638	20,692
Brazil			4,491	6,957	24,511
Uruguay			5,474	27,327	1,639
Asia:					
Iraq	8,369	4,860	4,964	6,883	1,836
Nepal	4,380	3,889	5,361	3,503	
Turkey	19,985	7,814	584		
Africa:					
Ethiopia	10,378	18,825	16,434	25,908	
Morocco	2,564	10,169	2,179	2,326	1,831
Tunisia	65	1,027	1,427	745	574

*Countries whose exports exceeded one thousand metric tons in any one year.
Source: FAO, *Trade Yearbook*, 1960 and 1964.

As in the case of many temperate crops, Canada's chief competitors in flaxseed have been the United States and Argentina. Cost differences between the United States and Canada have been difficult to establish with accuracy because flaxseed has been under price support in the United States, while it has faced a 10-cent tariff per bushel in Canada. Table XIX suggests that, while Canadian prices, until 1959 at least, remained typically below those in the United States, yields and total production of Canadian flaxseed have been sustained. However, as with feed grains, costs of flax-seed production in Canada are probably predominantly determined by opportunity costs, particularly opportunity costs for the production of wheat. Table VII indicates that high wheat acreages tend to drive down flaxseed acreage and production, while low wheat acreages appear to have the reverse effect. Since, as Table VIII implies, wheat tends to produce a larger gross income per acre than flaxseed, increased incentives to grow wheat would raise opportunity costs of flaxseed production. Consequently, it seems reasonable to conclude that Canada's share of flaxseed in world export markets would decline under free trade conditions. In any event, the main products of flaxseed—linseed oil and linseed-oil meal—are being replaced by artificial drying oils and soybean meal, respectively. It can be expected, therefore, that the importance of flaxseed will decline in world markets with or without free trade,[1] unless new processing outlets are found to stimulate world demand.

Rapeseed

During the 1950s, there began a phenomenal increase in Canadian rapeseed production (Table XX), most of which has been exported to the Far East and Europe. Canada also produces some rape oil crushed from rapeseed, which is a close substitute for soybean oil as a human food. But Canada's rape-oil production is small relative to its output of soybean oil. Rapeseed meal, which can be used successfully as a feed for cattle and poultry, appears to be less satisfactory for feeding swine. Its use as a high-protein feed supplement is unpopular because of toxic side effects. Aside from the toxicity problem, rapeseed meal produces less energy and contains less protein than soybean meal.

Improved varieties, at some future stage, could make rapeseed meal more competitive vis-à-vis soybean meal. Until such time, it is unlikely that rapeseed meal will replace soybean meal as a feed supplement.

Canada imposes no tariff on rape oil in either its denatured or undenatured form. However, there is a Canadian tariff of 5 to 7½ percent on rapeseed, and of 15 to 20 percent on rapeseed meal. As suggested above, it is unlikely that rapeseed meal would enter Canada even without a tariff; hence it can be concluded that the Canadian rapeseed industry is operating under conditions approaching those of free trade. Consequently, given the steady rise of Canadian rapeseed production and given its leading position in world exports of rapeseed since 1957, Canada appears to have an absolute advantage in the production of this oilseed.

Soybeans

Soybean production in Canada has been confined almost entirely to southwestern Ontario. Before the Second World War, Canadian soybean acreage and production were of little significance, but since then they have increased remarkably (Table XXI). Domestic consumption, however, has outgrown production, with the result that Canada has been a net importer of soybeans since 1940. Interestingly enough, Canada also exports important amounts

[1]A. Burnett, *Fats and Oils: A Review of Recent World Trends in Production,* University of Guelph, February 1963.

TABLE XIX

FLAXSEED PRODUCTION AND PRICES
(prices—domestic currencies)

Crop year	Canada				United States			
	Seeded acreage (thousand acres)	Total production (thousand bushels)	Average yield (bushels per seeded acre)	Average farm price (dollars per bushel)	Seeded acreage (thousand acres)	Total production (thousand bushels)	Average yield (bushels per seeded acre)	Season average price* (dollars per bushel)
1940	382	3,049	8.0	1.07	3,364	30,924	9.2	1.42
1941	1,043	6,780	6.5	1.26	3,462	32,133	9.3	1.79
1942	1,536	15,470	10.1	1.99	4,698	40,976	8.7	2.36
1943	2,984	18,432	6.2	2.15	6,182	50,009	8.1	2.83
1944	1,217	8,882	7.3	2.52	2,887	21,665	7.5	2.91
1945	873	6,225	7.1	2.50	3,953	34,557	8.7	2.89
1946	886	6,774	7.6	2.99	2,641	22,588	8.6	4.03
1947	1,791	13,822	7.7	5.24	4,264	40,618	9.5	6.15
1948	1,958	18,449	9.4	3.81	5,121	54,803	10.7	5.71
1949	312	2,242	7.2	3.31	5,348	42,976	8.0	3.63

1950	584	4,959	8.5	3.47	4,274	40,236	9.4	3.34
1951	1,159	9,478	8.2	3.90	4,116	34,696	8.4	3.72
1952	1,110	11,660	10.5	3.16	3,445	30,184	8.8	3.73
1953	956	9,748	10.2	2.44	4,759	37,656	7.9	3.64
1954	1,178	10,998	9.3	2.54	5,947	41,274	6.9	3.05
1955	1,836	18,990	10.3	2.77	5,148	40,415	7.9	2.90
1956	3,041	34,991	11.5	2.56	5,786	47,037	8.1	2.99
1957	3,486	19,205	5.5	2.53	5,481	25,113	4.9	2.94
1958	2,551	22,342	8.8	2.62	3,862	37,409	9.7	2.69
1959	2,052	17,191	8.4	3.06	3,268	21,237	6.5	3.00
1960	2,513	22,571	9.0	2.75	3,437	30,402	8.8	2.65
1961	2,086	14,478	6.9	3.32‡	2,975	22,178	7.5	3.26
1962†	1,445	16,042	11.1	3.35‡	3,087	31,952	10.4	2.84
1963	1,685	21,176	12.6	3.20‡				
1964	1,978	20,313	10.3	3.20				
1965§	2,239	27,954	12.5					

Sources: Canadian data: DBS, *Handbook of Agricultural Statistics 1908–63* and supplementary data from Farm Crops section. U.S. data: U.S. Department of Agriculture, *Agricultural Statistics*, various issues.

*Obtained by weighting state prices by quantity sold.
†Preliminary for United States.
‡Average of western daily price quotations.
§Preliminary for Canada.

TABLE XX

CANADIAN RAPESEED PRODUCTION AND PRICES

Crop year	Seeded acreage (thousand acres)	Estimated production (million pounds)	Average yield (pounds per seeded acre)	Average farm price (cents per pound)
1950	4	.1	300	3.8
1951	7	6.0	925	3.5
1952	19	13.9	751	3.4
1953	30	24.6	832	3.6
1954	40	28.9	722	3.3
1955	138	77.9	565	3.5
1956	352	299.8	852	3.5
1957	618	433.1	701	3.2
1958	626	388.1	620	2.5
1959	214	178.0	834	4.0
1960	763	556.0	729	3.3
1961	710	561.0	790	3.6
1962	371	293.0	789	
1963	484	443.0	916	
1964	691	661.5	835	
1965	1,435	1,140.0	795	

Source: DBS, *Handbook of Agricultural Statistics, 1908–1963* and supplementary data from Farm Crops section.

of soybeans and soybean meal and oil to the United Kingdom. This trade is mainly a result of the favourable tariff arrangements which Britain grants Canada as a member of the Commonwealth. Table XXII shows the relationship of Canada's exports and imports to production.

Soybean production has at times received price support from the federal government, but realized prices have, in fact, been above support levels for the past five years. At the same time, soybeans, soybean meal, and soybean oil for manufacturing have all entered Canada free of duty. For all intents and purposes, therefore, the Canadian soybean industry—on the import side—has been operating under conditions closely approximating those of free trade. Table XXI indicates that acreage and production of soybeans in Canada have been well maintained during the past five years, which implies that, under conditions of free trade, Canadian soybean producers could well compete with the larger U.S. soybean industry. At the same time, however, it would be unduly optimistic to suggest any large or rapid increase in Canada's soybean acreage because suitable land in south-western Ontario is confined to four or five counties. The principal loss to

TABLE XXI

CANADIAN SOYBEAN PRODUCTION AND PRICES
(prices—domestic currencies)

Crop year	Canada				United States			
	Seeded acreage (thousand acres)	Total production (thousand bushels)	Average yield (bushels per seeded acre)	Average farm price (dollars per bushel)	Harvested acreage (thousand acres)	Total production (thousand bushels)	Average yield (bushels per harvested acre)	Season average price* (dollars per bushel)
1940	11	844	18.3	1.90	4,807	78,045	16.2	.90
1945	46	3,323	23.4	2.55	10,740	193,167	18.0	2.08
1950	142	5,993	26.4	2.09	13,807	299,249	21.7	2.47
1955	227	5,001	22.1	2.03	18,620	373,682	20.1	2.22
1960	257	6,631	31.3	2.25	23,655	555,307	23.5	2.13
1961	212	6,608	29.9	2.48	27,008	679,566	25.2	2.28
1962†	221	5,002	21.9	2.80	27,857	675,197	24.2	2.34
1963	228	6,976	30.2	2.87				
1964	231	8,030	30.3					
1965‡	265							

Sources: Canadian data: DBS, *Handbook of Agricultural Statistics, 1908–63* and supplementary data from Farm Crops section.
U.S. data: U.S. Department of Agriculture, *Agricultural Statistics,* various issues.
*Obtained by weighting state prices by quantity sold.
†Preliminary for United States.
‡Preliminary for Canada.

TABLE XXII

CANADIAN EXPORTS AND IMPORTS OF
SOYBEANS AND SOYBEAN PRODUCTS
(percentage of production)

Year	Exports	Imports
1960	28	245
1961	55	201
1962	37	223

Source: Canada Department of Agriculture, *Exports, Imports, and Domestic Disappearance of Agricultural Products as a Percentage of Production, Canada, 1935–62*, Feb. 1965.

Canada from free trade would occur in exports to the United Kingdom, which are at present greatly enhanced by the Commonwealth preference.

VI. Fruit, Vegetables, and Miscellaneous Products

Fruit

For reasons mainly of climate, Canada has been, and probably will continue to be, a net importer of fruits of all kinds. While this observation needs no explanation in the case of tropical fruits, it may require discussion where temperate-climate fruits are concerned. For more than three decades, Canadian imports of temperate-climate fruit (excluding apples) have closely approximated total Canadian production.[1] With the possible exception of blueberries, which Canada has exported in substantial quantities in recent years, Canadian exports of fruit have been small, amounting to less than 10 percent of total domestic fruit output. At present, apple production is close to balancing consumption, but with improved varieties and controlled-atmosphere storage, Canada could probably increase its exports.

Fresh fruit entering Canada in direct competition with domestic field production faces a differential tariff, which provides increased protection during the Canadian growing season and reduced support during the remainder of the year. Commonwealth countries are exempt from this tariff; but they do not, in any case, ship significant quantities of fresh temperate-climate fruit to Canada. Removal of this tariff could therefore be expected to lower Canadian in-season prices for many fresh fruits and, indeed, to lead to difficult conditions for farmers if regional "dumping"

[1]Berthiaume, *Exports, Imports, and Domestic Disappearance of Agricultural Products.*

were to be practised following "bumper" crops. The over-all volume of imports could not be expected to increase significantly, but it might rise by a small margin. Total Canadian fruit production would probably decline slightly under free trade, except for blueberries and, perhaps, apples.

Vegetables

Canada has imported vegetables, mostly from the United States, at about four times the level of its exports.[2] This statistic does not include potatoes, in which Canada has had a small export surplus.

Canada's vegetable production has been protected by a differential but moderate tariff. Under free trade many domestic vegetable producers would face conditions similar to those foreseen for fruit producers: increased competition from abroad, pressure on domestic prices, and "dumping" practices in response to heavy crops in the United States.

One of the little known features of Canadian agriculture is the greenhouse industry, which has shown a very rapid growth in recent years. Canadian greenhouse area increased from 3.2 million square feet in 1951 to 23.7 million square feet in 1963.[3] The industry has grown most rapidly in the production of vegetables, especially tomatoes, cucumbers, and lettuce in that order. About two-thirds of Canada's greenhouse industry is located in southwestern Ontario (mostly in Essex county). No protection other than that given to field-grown crops has been extended to the greenhouse-vegetable industry, but it has flourished. Today, it supplies a substantial share of cucumber and, to a lesser extent, tomato output during peak production months.[4]

Competition for Canadian greenhouse growers does not come so much from their rivals in the northern United States, but rather from field producers in Texas, California, and Mexico. However, provided high-quality production is maintained, there seems every likelihood that Canada's greenhouse industry could survive under free trade.

Miscellaneous products

For specific agricultural commodities, such as maple products, turnips, and clover seed, Canada has, in fact, achieved an export surplus which is large relative to the size of trade involved. These products would be expected to gain from free trade, but large absolute increases in exports (particularly in maple products) would be unlikely.

[2]Canada Department of Agriculture, *Canada's Trade in Agricultural Products with the United Kingdom, the United States and All Countries.*
[3]DBS, *Greenhouse Industry,* 1963 and previous issues.
[4]W. G. Phillips, "The Greenhouse Vegetable Industry," unpublished Ph.D. thesis, University of Windsor, 1961.

VII. Beef

Canada's international trade in cattle has included four distinct groups, each of which warrants separate consideration.

Beef cattle

For many years, Canada's chief export market for live beef cattle has been the United States (Table XXIII). Considerable numbers of cattle used to be shipped to the United Kingdom, but since 1939 shipments, if any, have been negligible. Canadian beef-cattle exports have mostly been feeders—calves or animals more nearly ready for fattening. However, from time to time substantial numbers of slaughter animals have been exported as well. At the same time, Canada has consistently imported a small number of live beef animals, mostly from the United States and almost exclusively for slaughter. Occasionally these imports have become large, as they did in 1959 and 1964, chiefly as a result of temporary shortages of Canadian slaughter cattle. Virtually no feeder cattle appear to have entered Canada. The usual pattern of Canadian trade in live beef cattle thus emerges as a series of flows across the Canadian-U.S. border in both directions, but predominantly from Canada to the United States, consisting primarily of movements of feeder cattle from north to south and of slaughter cattle from south to north. The two-directional flow is simply a matter of local supply imbalances, which are settled internationally rather than intra-nationally.[1]

Two main factors have tended to isolate Canadian-U.S. cattle trade from competition by other countries. First, livestock disease-prevention measures enforced jointly by Canada and the United States prohibit imports of live cattle and uncooked meat from countries whose herds are infected with foot-and-mouth disease. These regulations virtually eliminate commercial movements of cattle from Latin American and many European countries to North America. Second, imports of live cattle from disease-free areas such as Australia and New Zealand are inhibited by barriers of high-cost, long-distance transportation.

Both factors leave Canada with an absolute advantage in supplying feeder cattle to the U.S. market. Free trade alone would not greatly benefit any potential exporters of cattle, such as Paraguay and Argentina, unless accompanied either by substantial easing of U.S.-Canadian disease-prevention regulations or by effective measures towards eradication of livestock diseases in those countries. If the latter goal were to be achieved, free trade

[1]This has been, at least in part, due to the relatively low tariff—1½ to 2½ cents per pound liveweight.

might well lead to increased cattle exports to the United States and might divert some U.S. imports away from Canadian suppliers. Even in that event, however, really significant changes in the present pattern would be unlikely because transportation costs would continue to pose a problem for most exporting countries.

In any case, it seems unlikely that livestock disease-prevention measures will change or that potential exporter nations will solve their disease-control problems; hence Canada may expect to continue substantial exports of beef cattle to the United States. Despite tariff protection of 1½ cents or 2½ cents per pound liveweight in recent years, and higher rates previously, the United States has been a substantial net importer of Canadian beef cattle (Table XXIII). Canada's high level of net exports has been accompanied by an increase in the beef-cattle population (Table XXVII) and in the per capita consumption of beef in Canada. The only substantial reductions in exports of Canadian beef cattle to the United States in recent years have been associated with special circumstances, such as the Canadian wartime embargo on beef-cattle exports (1942–48), the outbreak of foot-and-mouth disease in Canada (1952) and the resultant U.S. embargo (1952–53), and the Canadian cattle inventory build-up during 1956.

With only a relatively minor tariff on beef animals it can be argued that the existing trading pattern between Canada and the United States is quite similar to that which would develop under Canadian-U.S. free trade. Removal of the tariff between Canada and the United States would tend to shift farming operations to wheat production, increase opportunity costs for range land and feeding grains, and decrease profitability of feeding operations. An increasing number of Canadian feeder cattle would be sent to the U.S. corn belt to be fattened before being shipped back to Canada.[2] If these animals were to be slaughtered and processed before being returned to Canada, this could cause an important short-term dislocation of resources used in the Canadian economy.

Fresh (chilled) or frozen beef

Canada's trade in fresh beef, as in beef cattle, has been largely confined to the U.S. market for reasons of cattle-disease prevention. Under special

---

[2]With present fairly high feed-conversion ratios in cattle, and in the absence of feed freight assistance, it is cheaper as a general rule to ship cattle than feed. If feed freight assistance were to continue in Canada, there is reason for believing that feed and cattle would continue to be shipped directly from western to eastern Canada. This has been discussed by A. Wood in the *Canadian Journal of Agricultural Economics*, Vol. XIII. Somewhat similar results have been presented by T. C. Kerr in "An Economic Analysis of the Feed Freight Assistance Policy," a mimeographed publication of the Agricultural Economics Research Council of Canada, Ottawa.

TABLE XXIII

CANADIAN EXPORTS* AND IMPORTS OF CATTLE AND BEEF

Year	Purebred dairy to all countries	Exports of cattle†			Imports of cattle§	Exports of beef‡ to			Imports of beef‖
		All countries	United Kingdom	United States		All countries	United Kingdom	United States	
		(thousand animals)				(million pounds)			
1940	23.0	233.8	—	229.5	.2	3.9	—	.5	10.8
1941	29.8	254.1	—	250.6	.1	7.9	—	.9	8.8
1942	34.5	215.8	—	212.4	.1	16.0	—	4.3	5.6
1943	57.3	62.7	—	58.6	.1	13.5	.4	—	6.0
1944	53.8	59.1	—	53.3	.3	107.4	98.1	—	5.7
1945	71.4	79.5	‡‡	70.7	.2	194.8	184.4	.1	.7
1946	97.0	104.6	‡‡	96.4	.5	138.2	123.8	.1	—
1947	76.5	83.2	‡‡	74.5	.5	51.0	32.8	.1	3.0
1948	132.7	457.4	—	420.5	.7	133.8	35.4	84.0	.6
1949	69.0	420.7	—	417.6	.8	106.9	—	99.5	10.1

1950	70.7	458.8	—	456.7	.8	90.7	—	87.7	11.9
1951	57.0	239.1	—	237.6	1.2	96.9	—	94.9	33.7
1952	8.0	15.4	—	14.1	3.7	68.1	63.8	2.2	22.6
1953	42.2	69.5	—	67.3	2.8	28.8	6.6	18.7	24.4
1954	33.3	89.2	—	86.8	3.5	22.6	8.2	11.3	32.4
1955	41.8	67.6	—	63.4	6.4	12.8	—	9.7	34.7
1956	48.4	56.5	—	49.4	9.4	18.6	—	16.2	39.7
1957	40.8	387.5	‡	384.1	6.3	55.3	—	53.0	54.0
1958	46.7	670.5	—	667.0	4.5	63.9	—	61.3	58.0
1959	37.1	342.7	—	340.4	33.4	30.0	—	27.2	66.3
1960	37.6	272.9	‡	269.0	9.1	25.9	—	22.7	49.5
1961	44.3	503.1	‡	495.3	3.8	37.5	—	34.0	53.1
1962	39.7	492.2	‡	484.9	3.6	27.7	—	24.2	55.6
1963	34.6	278.6	‡	272.1	3.5	25.6	.3	21.3	63.8
1964	38.1	222.2	‡	214.4	36.9	42.8	.1	34.9	47.8

Source: This table was derived from a G. E. Britnell and V. C. Fowke, *Canadian Agriculture in War and Peace*, Stanford University Press, Stanford, Calif., 1962; and DBS, *Farm Livestock and Animal Products*, various issues.
*Includes exports to Newfoundland until federation with Canada on March 31, 1949.
†Includes calves, although in practice cattle accounted for all exports to the United Kingdom and most exports to the United States and other countries.
‡Includes fresh (chilled) or frozen, pickled in barrels, etc.
§Includes purebred dairy and beef cattle. Imports other than purebred were negligible until 1952.
‖Includes fresh (chilled) or frozen, canned, salted or pickled in barrels, edible offal of beef, etc.
#Less than 400 head.

circumstances, Canada has shipped substantial quantities of beef to the United Kingdom. Such shipments were made as a wartime arrangement and during the 1952 outbreak in Canada of foot-and-mouth disease, which diverted exports to the United Kingdom because the United States imposed severe regulations. Typically, Canadian beef has not been shipped to the United Kingdom because it has not been price-competitive with beef from Argentina, Australia, and other suppliers (Table XXIV). Fresh or frozen beef imports have amounted to between a quarter and a third of total Canadian beef imports since the late 1950s. At the same time, nearly nine-tenths of Canadian beef exports have been fresh beef, nearly all of which has gone to the United States.

TABLE XXIV

FRESH (CHILLED) OR FROZEN BEEF EXPORT PRICES
(U.S. dollars per metric ton)

Year	United States	Canada	Australia	New Zealand	Mexico	Argentina	Uruguay
1959	1,392.8	930.3	537.0	688.0	457.3	420.8	435.2
1960	1,335.5	869.2	649.7	620.4	514.3	445.0	412.9
1961	1,340.7	754.4	659.8	640.4	607.8	412.5	392.0
1962	1,510.6	835.8	644.9	612.2	756.5	351.9	360.9
1963	1,570.9	858.0	670.1	635.2	794.5	381.9	331.7

Source: FAO, *1964 Trade Year Book*, 1964.

Under free trade, Canada could be expected to continue to export some fresh beef to the United States. However, no clear-cut evidence is available to suggest that Canada has an absolute advantage in fresh beef relative to the United States.

South American countries, such as Argentina and Uruguay, enjoy a large cost advantage in fresh-beef production over Canadian and U.S. producers (Table XXIV). Eradication of foot-and-mouth disease by these countries could result in considerable exports of their beef to the United States and Canada, with a considerable initial dampening effect on Canadian beef prices. In view of the magnitude of the Canadian-U.S. market and a fairly high income elasticity for beef, long-term adjustments under the above assumptions would probably not depress relative beef prices much below the present levels, provided that per capita incomes in the United States and Canada continue to rise.

Canada exports virtually no frozen beef and imports only small quantities of it, chiefly from Australia and New Zealand. Available evidence suggests that these imports are primarily used for processing into meat products in Canada. Processed beef products are discussed in more detail below.

Processed beef and beef products

More than two-thirds of Canada's beef imports consist of pickled or canned beef. Australia, Argentina, Paraguay, Brazil, and Uruguay have been the most important exporters of canned beef to Canada in the last decade. Australian canned beef has been permitted to enter Canada duty-free. Although these products are classed as beef, they do not appear to be close substitutes for fresh beef and are more directly comparable to cow beef, which is used in the Canadian meat-processing industry. Since free trade in beef products already exists between Canada and Australia, there seems little reason for believing that Canada's import-export pattern for processed beef would change substantially under free trade with all nations.

Purebred dairy cattle

Exports of purebred dairy cattle have been the most stable component of Canada's beef and cattle trade over the last decade (Table XXIII). Most of these exports have gone to U.S. milk producers. Since there are no tariffs between Canada and the United States on purebred dairy cattle, this traditional pattern of trade suggests that Canada has an absolute advantage in purebred dairy-cattle production relative to the United States.

VIII. Pork

The international pattern of Canada's trade in pork and hogs during the past twenty-five years has been similar to that in beef. During the 1940s, as a result of wartime contracts and heavy supplies of feed grains, Canada produced and exported to the United Kingdom considerable amounts of pork (Table XXV). In the early 1950s, the pattern of exports changed abruptly, with a reduction in total exports of pork, accompanied by a switch to the United States as the main importer. Since then, Canada's trade in pork and hogs, like that in beef, has consisted largely of a two-way flow across the U.S.-Canadian border.

Canada has consistently exported, but not imported any, live hogs. Canadian imports of pork products have increased substantially since 1960, to the extent that, in 1963, Canada was a net importer of this commodity (Table XXV). The pattern of pork exports and imports between Canada and the United States has differed from that of beef. Canadian pork exports to the United States have been specialty products, which, in the 1960s, have sold in quantities of about fifty million pounds a year, virtually independent of the prices charged.[1] Imports into Canada, on the other

[1]These products have included back bacon and hams. The back bacon has been so well accepted in many parts of the United States that the term "Canadian bacon" is used to refer to back bacon of domestic U.S. origin in many of the northern States.

TABLE XXV

CANADIAN EXPORTS* AND IMPORTS OF HOGS AND PORK PRODUCTS

	Export of hogs† to			Exports of pork products					
				All products to		Bacon and hams to‖		Pork meat** to all countries	
Year	All countries	United States	Imports of hogs§	All countries	United States††	All countries	United Kingdom#			Imports of pork products‡
	(thousand animals)					(million pounds)				
1940	7.2	.3	—	353.0	—	345.6	344.1	7.4		37.2
1941	37.2	33.9	—	482.0	—	464.6	460.8	17.4		5.2
1942	6.0	.2	—	537.4	—	528.1	525.0	9.3		.9
1943	9.3	.5	—	587.5	—	563.0	560.3	24.5		2.3
1944	9.7	.2	—	717.8	—	695.8	692.3	22.0		.7
1945	9.2	.8	—	462.0	—	449.8	446.1	12.2		—
1946	7.6	1.5	—	300.8	—	289.3	286.0	11.5		.7
1947	11.2	3.1	—	251.2	—	235.8	232.0	15.4		5.9
1948	7.4	2.2	—	229.5	—	204.7	200.1	24.8		1.6
1949	2.3	1.4	—	77.9	—	67.1	65.6	10.8		5.5
1950	1.6	1.2	—	85.1	6.6	78.5	72.3	6.6		5.7
1951	4.3	3.9	—	33.0	22.2	6.1	1.9††	26.9		22.5
1952	.7	.4	—	32.1	22.5	3.5	—	28.6		4.7
1953	21.1	20.8	—	78.1	66.6	7.0	—	71.1		.5
1954	26.5	24.9	—	76.1	66.9	8.9	—	67.2		1.5

Year									
1955	8.9	8.3	—	80.1	69.6	10.9	—	69.2	.2
1956	1.7	.7	—	67.9	56.6	8.8	—	59.1	.2
1957	1.9	.5	—	43.5	74.6	5.2	—	38.3	1.5
1958	8.1	7.5	—	69.4	60.2	6.2	—	63.2	1.7
1959	4.5	3.9	—	76.1	56.1	6.3	—	69.8	1.4
1960	6.8	5.6	—	73.1	47.3	6.6	—	66.5	17.7
1961	27.6	2.4	—	58.4	44.3	6.3	—	52.1	42.0
1962	4.6	2.7	—	52.3	46.3	6.8	—	45.5	35.7
1963	3.6	3.2	—	52.4	46.6	8.2	—	44.2	89.8
1964	4.2	3.7	—	59.5	51.2	8.2	—	51.3	53.9

Sources: Britnell and Fowke, *Canadian Agriculture in War and Peace*, pp. 458–9; DBS, *Trade of Canada: Exports and Imports*, 1940–59, and *Farm Livestock and Animal Products*, various issues.

*Includes exports to Newfoundland until federation with Canada on March 31, 1949.

†Includes swine for improvement of stock and for slaughter.

‡Includes bacon and hams, shoulders and sides; pork—fresh (chilled) or frozen, dry-salted, barreled in brine; canned hams; and pork content of sausage, beginning 1950.

§Includes only swine for improvement of stock, not classified separately after 1943. Imports (by weight) of hogs for slaughter averaged 120 thousand lbs. a year from 1900 to 1904, inclusive; 5.3 million lbs. in 1905; 6.6 million lbs. in 1906; less than 10 thousand lbs. a year from 1907 to 1930; and were negligible from 1931 to 1960.

‖Includes bacon and hams, shoulders and sides, cured or smoked.

#Includes exports to Northern Ireland and Eire prior to 1926.

**Includes pork—fresh (chilled) or frozen, dry-salted; bologna, beginning 1946; canned hams and uncanned cooked hams, beginning 1951.

††Exports to United Kingdom became insignificant after expiration of wartime contracts.

hand, appear to have risen during the same period, partially as a result of pork prices in Canada exceeding those in the United States. Another important reason for the expansion of U.S. exports into Canada since 1960 has been the removal of the Canadian embargo on uncooked pork products of U.S. origin, which had been in effect because of the presence of the disease vesicular entheme in the United States. Fresh-pork imports, which had not exceeded 10 percent of total pork imports during the period 1956–60, rose to a level of 80 percent between 1960 and 1964.

Relative to other countries, particularly the United States, Canada does not appear to enjoy any sustained advantage in pork production. On the contrary, available price evidence implies that Canada is a high-cost pork producer relative to many other important pork-producing nations (Table XXVI).

Under free trade, Canada could hope to maintain, or perhaps to increase slightly, its exports of high-quality specialty pork products to the United States. On the other hand, free trade might result in higher feed-grain costs for Canada because factors would shift into wheat production. Consequently, Canada's hog production costs would rise above, or at best remain at, present levels, and imports of pork (probably from the United States) might well increase.

IX. Sheep and Lambs

Livestock and farm outputs of sheep and lambs, unlike those of cattle and hogs, have steadily declined over the last thirty years (Table XXVII). Exports have also been diminishing and, since 1950, have amounted to less than 10 percent of production. Imports have risen from 12 to over 100 percent of production during the same period. Most of Canada's trade in sheep and lambs, as in other livestock, has been with the United States. Most imports of mutton and lamb, however, have come from Australia and New Zealand. Frozen lamb and mutton have been more readily accepted by consumers than frozen beef, leading to one of the essential differences in the marketability of these products.

There has been relatively free access for lamb and lamb products to the Canadian market—a tariff of half a cent per pound on lamb and mutton, and a zero tariff on wool in the grease. Free trade would be expected to increase slightly Canada's imports of lamb and mutton and to accelerate moderately the downward trend in the Canadian sheep industry. The latter development, in turn, would lead to increased wool imports to meet domestic requirements, even without a rise in domestic demand.

TABLE XXVI

FRESH (CHILLED) OR FROZEN SWINE MEAT EXPORT PRICES
(U.S. dollars per metric ton)

Year	Belgium-Luxembourg	Denmark	Netherlands	Sweden	Yugoslavia	Canada	United States	Argentina
1959	729.0	661.4	652.5	503.3	560.2	748.3	338.7	450.0
1960	566.2	579.8	660.8	478.4	572.4	690.1	538.4	497.3
1961	754.1	639.7	728.5	516.6	594.5	868.9	642.5	512.5
1962	642.1	644.8	669.4	515.0	676.8	833.5	633.6	595.1
1963	909.7	754.9	794.6	659.3	772.3	838.3	609.5	709.7

Source: FAO, *Trade Yearbook*, 1964.

TABLE XXVII

LIVESTOCK AND FARM OUTPUT* OF CATTLE, HOGS, AND SHEEP AND LAMBS IN CANADA
(thousand animals)

Year†	Cattle		Hogs		Sheep and lambs	
	Livestock	Farm output	Livestock	Farm output	Livestock	Farm output
1930	7,686	970	3,735	3,976	3,438	1,440
1935	8,973	1,388	3,651	4,720	3,224	1,613
1940	8,380	1,560	6,002	7,244	2,887	1,284
1945	9,632	2,478	4,964	8,718	3,032	1,578
1950	8,343	2,107	4,372	6,794	1,579	829
1955	10,603	2,330	4,800	6,941	1,634	745
1956	11,011	2,466	4,731	6,860	1,620	757
1957	11,265	2,816	4,758	6,297	1,628	752
1958	10,990	2,908	5,931	7,474	1,630	740
1959	11,058	2,454	6,519	9,666	1,608	735
1960	11,337	2,640	5,070	7,811	1,607	716
1961	11,934	2,852	5,331	7,550	1,548	773
1962	12,075	2,751	4,973	7,653	1,433	767
1963	12,305	2,821	5,210	7,605	1,340	660
1964	12,817	3,031	5,620	8,305	1,286	643

Sources: Britnell and Fowke, *Canadian Agriculture in War and Peace*, 1962. The figures are based on data from Livestock Section, Agriculture Division, Dominion Bureau of Statistics. (Data for 1930 are not fully comparable with the revised data from that year forward.) 1956–64 data: DBS, *Farm Livestock and Animal Products*, 1964.
*"Farm output" includes commercial marketings plus estimates of farm and local slaughter.
†For livestock data, "year" as of June 1st.

X. Dairy Products

Cheese

Canada had a well-developed market for dairy products, mostly cheddar cheese, in the United Kingdom from 1900 until 1946. With the termination of wartime cheese contracts, the United Kingdom sought dairy products from non-dollar producers and drastically reduced its imports of Canadian cheese (Table XXVIII). It is significant that Canadian cheddar cheese exported to the United Kingdom commands a premium over similar cheeses produced by other nations. For example, in 1964–65 Canadian finest white cheese sold in London at a premium of between 11 and 19 cents per pound over New Zealand finest white cheese and at a considerable premium over most other cheeses of comparable types from England, Denmark, the

TABLE XXVIII

CANADIAN EXPORTS OF BUTTER, CHEESE, AND CONCENTRATED WHOLE MILK PRODUCTS AND IMPORTS OF BUTTER AND CHEESE (million pounds)

Year	Exports*							Imports	
	Butter		Cheese		Condensed milk	Evaporated milk	Milk powder†	Butter	Cheese
	United Kingdom	All countries	United Kingdom	All countries					
1940	.0	1.3	103.2	106.6	6.8	34.7	4.4	.0	1.0
1945	—	5.6	132.9	135.4	18.7	70.8	6.0	.0	.7
1950	—	1.6	59.2	63.1	3.9	33.6	9.2	.0	10.2
1955	.0	7.4	12.6	13.7	1.3	5.3	16.1	.0	12.7
1956	.0	2.1	10.9	12.2	2.6	6.3	17.3	.0	9.0
1957	—	.0	7.5	8.5	.7	4.6	16.4	.0	9.4
1958	—	.0	14.9	15.7	—	3.2	17.5	.0	11.2
1959	10.5	10.5	19.2	20.0	—	5.0	18.4	.0	13.0
1960	2.9	3.0	17.7	18.8	—	3.3	36.7	.0	13.2
1961	—	.0	18.3	19.5	—	4.7	25.8	—‡	14.7
1962	—	.0	26.1	27.3	—	6.1	20.2	—	14.6
1963	5.6	5.6	24.6	25.8	—	5.9	17.1	—	15.4
1964	36.5	113.7	30.0	31.7	—	18.1	18.4	—	15.3

Source: Britnell and Fowke, *Canadian Agriculture in War and Peace*, p. 463.
*Includes exports to Newfoundland until federation with Canada on March 31, 1949.
†Whole milk powder.
‡Less than 500 lbs.

Netherlands, and West Germany. However, it would be incorrect to infer on the basis of this premium price that Canada has an absolute advantage in cheese production. New Zealand's exports of cheese have been, in a typical year, about ten times as large, and Denmark's about eight times as large, as Canada's exports. The Netherlands has exported even more (Table XXIX). Since these nations have consistently been exporting cheese in large quantities at prices substantially below Canada's (Table XXX), they appear to have an absolute advantage over Canada in cheese production. While Canada does enjoy the advantage of exporting a specialized, differentiated product, the market for that product appears to be fairly limited. There is little reason to assume that exports of Canadian cheddar

TABLE XXIX

EXPORTS OF CHEESE AND CURD
(metric tons)

Exporting region*	1959	1960	1961	1962	1963
Europe:					
Austria	7,177	6,056	6,986	8,063	9,276
Belgium-Luxembourg	416	775	2,060	6,311	4,563
Bulgaria	6,944	8,759	10,694	10,495	3,951
Denmark	79,015	75,925	78,972	81,455	78,913
Finland	17,852	16,962	17,793	16,860	17,263
France	28,210	31,261	39,349	36,199	45,476
Germany, Fed. Rep.	8,862	12,178	11,835	18,054	18,923
Hungary	5,563	5,965	7,783	7,510	8,824
Ireland	754	754	2,370	4,397	6,904
Italy	21,397	23,454	23,181	26,671	25,651
Netherlands	105,580	109,152	107,901	109,187	117,517
Norway	9,700	10,366	9,502	9,536	13,833
Poland	4,984	6,431	3,590	1,892	1,221
Sweden	3,997	3,209	3,399	5,536	6,682
Switzerland	28,787	31,057	33,356	32,317	33,731
United Kingdom	2,472	3,112	2,979	2,868	2,716
North America:					
Canada	9,076	8,554	8,862	12,370	11,721
United States†	6,428	4,236	4,118	3,286	15,374
South America:					
Argentina	3,441	3,084	3,882	3,924	5,412
Oceania:					
Australia	14,642	19,230	18,326	22,737	26,356
New Zealand	84,790	80,686	89,011	93,774	92,015

Source: FAO, *Trade Yearbook*, 1960 and 1964.
*Countries whose exports exceeded 5,000 metric tons in any one year.
†Includes re-exports.

TABLE XXX

EXPORT AND IMPORT VALUES OF CHEESE AND CURD, SELECTED COUNTRIES
(U.S. dollars per metric ton)

Country	1959	1960	1961	1962	1963
Exports					
Denmark	603.32	610.30	613.84	613.57	665.37
France	987.10	1,026.07	929.60	947.32	862.48
Italy	1,131.33	1,253.05	1,190.59	1,137.00	1,224.40
Netherlands	619.48	567.57	601.04	598.89	595.88
Switzerland	1,110.36	1,123.06	1,303.27	1,130.71	1,173.25
Canada	834.51	783.61	706.27	672.92	715.89
United States	875.93	1,013.03	1,153.75	1,080.48	697.38
Australia	683.38	581.18	563.19	512.60	517.98
New Zealand	729.90	644.00	625.61	555.77	548.89
Imports					
Belgium-Luxembourg	713.62	694.48	724.24	739.14	776.31
France	937.15	1,001.48	1,099.51	1,012.50	1,077.43
Germany, Fed. Rep.	567.87	555.83	606.01	594.01	615.29
Italy	825.43	827.66	795.51	773.70	793.18
United Kingdom	776.11	670.42	644.79	650.95	658.43
Canada	1,062.63	1,125.46	1,113.46	1,073.42	1,081.22
United States	1,065.01	1,092.66	1,035.16	1,032.38	989.19

Source: FAO, *Trade Yearbook*, 1964.

cheese to the United Kingdom could expand by a large amount without an accompanying reduction in price. Canada's trade in cheese with the United Kingdom is already in fairly free competition with that of New Zealand and other Commonwealth countries; and under free trade, Canadian cheddar cheese exports and premium prices would be expected to remain approximately at present levels.

Canada exports significant quantities of cheddar cheese but consumes most of its production domestically. Increasing amounts of specialty cheeses have entered Canada since 1950 (Table XXVIII), most of which have faced a substantial tariff if imported from non-Commonwealth countries. There is little doubt that in the short run, zero tariffs would lead to a significant increase in Canadian imports of specialty cheeses.

Butter

Canada is not an important world exporter of butter (Table XXXI) and consumes most of its butter production domestically. As Table XXVIII suggests, Canada has had a virtual embargo on butter for many years. In the interest of domestic products, it has not imported any butter since 1953. To maintain domestic production at adequate levels, large price-

TABLE XXXI

EXPORTS OF BUTTER
(metric tons)

Exporting region*	1959	1960	1961	1962	1963
Europe:					
Austria	5,295	5,340	3,260	3,534	4,185
Belgium-Luxembourg	44	6,329	9,466	3,577	4,472
Bulgaria	2,187	2,570	1,704	1,791	761
Denmark	117,950	118,082	120,043	114,717	102,358
Finland	21,432	25,725	17,499	10,209	15,772
France	12,192	23,145	51,224	30,316	40,699
Hungary	4,964	5,723	4,008	4,663	5,481
Ireland	1,332	7,638	15,399	16,282	19,541
Netherlands	39,924	39,269	31,133	32,586	40,673
Norway	6,371	6,754	5,425	5,134	3,798
Poland	22,687	28,599	26,691	27,461	18,563
Sweden	4,211	11,833	8,572	16,954	10,608
United Kingdom†	2,481	2,717	3,252	3,129	2,033
North America:					
Canada	4,764	1,367	3	2	2,544
United States†	9,721	584	335	2,619	26,378
South America:					
Argentina	23,203	24,303	14,098	11,096	13,321
Africa:					
Kenya	2,597	2,506	2,185	3,392	2,963
South Africa	1,891	1,035	13,578	4,845	1,137
Oceania:					
Australia	79,720	79,355	63,823	80,789	81,133
New Zealand	196,073	159,569	167,686	171,139	166,726

Source: FAO, *Trade Yearbook*, 1960 and 1964.
*Countries whose exports exceeded 2000 metric tons in any one year.
†Includes re-exports.

support expenditures have been required (Table XXXII). From time to time, such price supports have resulted in surplus butter production in Canada, as in 1960, 1961, and 1962. Canada's absolute disadvantage in butter production can be most clearly inferred from the fact that New Zealand butter has been sold in large quantities in the United Kingdom at a price nearly 20 cents below the Canadian support price of 64 cents per pound. Even with price supports, Canada does not produce enough butter to be a consistent exporter. Free trade would undoubtedly increase Canada's imports of butter and force domestic prices down.

TABLE XXXII

ASSISTANCE PAID ON (SPECIFIC) COMMODITIES BY THE CANADIAN GOVERNMENT, DEPARTMENT OF AGRICULTURE
(thousand dollars)

Commodity	54/55	55/56	56/57	57/58	58/59	59/60	60/61	61/62	62/63	63/64
Hogs and pork*	6,041	5,886	5,698	5,442	7,202	38,005	35,610	8,732	12,906	14,185
Lamb					281	361	101		627	585
Fowl	118	490	55	154	423	138	†	1,423		
Eggs				1,483	3,426	4,810	2,096	38	663	10
Wool					1,541	1,219	1,253	1,236	956	727
Butter‡	1,790	5,303	4,711	2,777	342	3,409	2,442	2,482	45,239	108,957
Cheese§	719	596	641	845	1,523	923	1,122	1,549	1,950	6,162
Dry skim milk						8,108	7	100	1,052‖	1,168†
Milk for manufacturing				1,094	6,957	9,844	11,433	12,371	13,258	1,865
Whole milk powder for international relief									4,914	
Assistance to western grain producers	18,699	16,333	17,164	17,778	40,588		40,430	39,974	113#	
Other supports to grains	4,585	486	187	480	63,471	64,878	68,610	66,956	50,264	59,547
Potatoes					367	96	36	597	619	
Tomatoes					52					
Asparagus					106					
Sugarbeets						2,657	2,716	1,670	1,983	2
Soybeans						1,217	867			
Sunflower seed for crushing							44			
Apples	602		182		769					
Peaches					*	357	268			
Raspberries						31		7		
Honey								91	371	76

Source: Canada Department of Agriculture, *Supplement to Federal Agricultural Assistance Programme*, various issues.
*Includes hog premiums paid on quantity actually shipped and graded during the fiscal year.
†Less than $500.
‡Includes assistance to imported butter.
§Includes quality premiums.
‖Includes product for international relief and sale for export programs.
#Excludes $26,740 refunded from previous year's expenditure—provincial breakdown for this refund was not available.

Condensed milk and milk powder

For products such as condensed or evaporated milk and milk powder, too few data are available to reach definite conclusions about Canada's competitive position. Canada has, however, exported a small but fairly steady quantity of evaporated milk and milk powder for many years.

General trends

Canada's dairy industry has received substantial tariff protection, as well as direct financial support, for many years (Table XXXII). Despite such protection, dairy-cattle production has steadily declined in Canada (Table XXVII). Consequently, it can be inferred that Canada's dairy industry is at an absolute disadvantage in relation to other nations. It also appears to be at a comparative disadvantage relative to other lines of agricultural production in Canada. There can be little doubt that Canadian dairy farming would decline substantially under the economic pressures that would be brought upon it by free trade. The decline of the Canadian dairy industry might be somewhat mitigated by new sales outlets for fluid milk to large U.S. population centres such as Detroit or Buffalo. This possibility would depend entirely upon the way in which the United States decided to change the boundaries of the areas supplying milk to the cities in question. In any event, it is not clear whether fluid milk would tend to move from Canada to the United States or from the United States to Canada.

Any decline in the Canadian dairy industry would affect some provinces more than others. In recent years, the number of dairy cows has been increasing in the province of Quebec but declining in most others.[1] This has been attributed to the limited alternatives available to Quebec farmers, who have been faced with a short growing season more suitable for forage production than for grain crops required for the fattening of livestock. Consequently, while most Canadian dairy producers would be hurt by free trade, Quebec producers, because of their limited alternatives, would be more likely to remain in dairying than producers in other provinces.

While the decline, under free trade, of the Canadian dairy industry would be an important development in itself, it is likely that more serious contractions would occur in the secondary industries that use the output of dairy farms as raw materials. Moreover, the dairy-products industry purchases a great deal from other sectors of the Canadian economy,[2] so that a large-scale substitution of imports for domestically produced dairy products may affect the over-all pattern of the Canadian economy.

[1]DBS, *Dairy Statistics*, various issues.
[2]For a discussion of interrelationships in the economy, see T. Josling and G. I. Trant, *Interdependence among Agriculture and Other Sectors of the Canadian Economy*, Agricultural Economics Research Council of Canada, Ottawa.

XI. Poultry and Eggs

Since the Second World War, Canada's poultry industry has been directed primarily towards the domestic market. From 1950 to 1963 poultry exports reached less than 1 percent of total poultry production, while imports were around 3 percent. During the same period Canadian exports of eggs hovered at or below 3 percent, and imports around 1 percent, of production,[1] while virtually all poultry-meat and live-poultry imports into Canada came from the United States.[2] Eggs have been imported from many sources.

   There can be little question that changes in production techniques have had a decisive impact on the poultry industry in the last two and a half decades. Within a few years poultry production changed from a small-scale, supplementary, family-owned enterprise, present on nearly every North American farm, to a highly specialized and, by agricultural standards, large-scale enterprise. Before 1945 a typical Canadian chicken flock raised for meat production comprised around five hundred birds; usually only one flock was raised for marketing each year. By 1966 the capacity of a broiler-growing plant in Ontario averaged twenty thousand birds, and at least four lots of birds were produced annually. Turkey and egg production have gone through similar, though less spectacular, expansions.

   Poultry production, whether for meat or eggs, has required the following factors of production: baby chicks, feed and medication, housing and fuel, and equipment. All these factors have become so highly developed that a complete poultry plant can be established nearly anywhere. Interchange of production techniques between Canada and the United States has reached an extremely high level. In fact, it would be virtually impossible to tell merely by inspecting the plant whether one was in a Canadian or in a U.S. poultry factory. The essential point is that, although poultry production employs highly specialized techniques, these have become so well developed and widely known that they have become, in a sense, completely mobile across national boundaries.

   Canada's competitive position in poultry production vis-à-vis the United States can be compared in the following way. There have been few significant qualitative differences in the resources used for poultry production between the two countries in recent years. However, feed costs have been lower in the United States than in Canada, chiefly because of the U.S. advantage in grain-corn and soybean production. Slightly higher costs are also expected to have prevailed in Canada for poultry equipment (because of Canadian tariffs on these items) and for heating expenditures

[1]Berthiaume, *Exports, Imports, and Domestic Disappearance of Agricultural Products.*
[2]Canada Department of Agriculture, *Canada's Trade in Agricultural Products with the United Kingdom, the United States, and All Countries,* various issues.

(as a consequence of the generally less favourable Canadian climate). Labour costs in Canada have typically been less than in the United States. Furthermore, the poultry industry in the United States has been more highly integrated than in Canada, probably resulting in a slightly higher level of managerial skill.

These differences in factor costs have given U.S. poutry-meat producers a cost advantage over Canadian producers. This advantage is reinforced because feed is a major component of total poultry-meat production costs. Heating and equipment costs tend to raise Canadian production costs, but to a lesser degree. While building costs and labour costs in Canada may have been lower than those in the United States, they represent such a low cost component per bird that they cannot compensate for the higher feed costs in Canada.

Table XXXIII reflects the competitive disadvantage that Canada appears to have in broiler production relative to the United States. Under free trade, Canadian broiler producers would enjoy somewhat lower feed and equipment costs than at present but would still be expected to retain a slight absolute disadvantage relative to the United States.

Relative to poultry-meat production, egg production requires a much larger proportion of labour. The slightly lower cost of Canadian labour relative to U.S. labour can, therefore, more effectively offset the higher Canadian feed prices. This appears to be confirmed by Table XXXIV, which shows that egg prices in Canada have been maintained at lower levels than those in the United States. It may thus be concluded that Canada's egg industry could survive in a satisfactory manner under free trade.

XII. Summary and Conclusions

This survey of Canadian agriculture indicates Canada's strong competitive position vis-à-vis world agriculture. However, Canadian competitiveness appears unevenly distributed among agricultural commodities. Our conclusions have led us to recognize four categories of products, classified by degree of competitiveness:

1. Products in which Canada has a strong absolute advantage:
   wheat, oats, barley, flax, rapeseed, beef feeder cattle, and purebred dairy cattle.
2. Products in which Canada has a slight absolute advantage:
   cheddar cheese and specialty pork products.
3. Products in which Canada has no ascertainable absolute advantage:
   tobacco, grain corn, fresh beef, fresh pork, eggs, soybeans, dried milk powder, and fluid milk.

TABLE XXXIII

CANADIAN AND U.S. DOMESTIC PRICES FOR CHICKEN BROILERS

(cents per pound liveweight in domestic currency)

Year	Country	Jan.	Feb.	Mar.	Apr.	May	June	July	Aug.	Sept.	Oct.	Nov.	Dec.
1961	Canada	17.5	19.0	18.5	16.5	14.5	14.5	16.5	16.5	13.0	12.5	14.5	15.5
	United States	16.4	17.6	16.6	14.9	14.0	12.8	12.4	12.7	11.8	11.8	12.4	15.2
1962	Canada	15.5	16.5	15.5	19.0	17.0	18.0	19.5	20.5	20.5	20.0	14.5	19.0
	United States	16.3	16.7	16.1	14.7	14.3	14.2	15.0	15.5	16.3	15.0	14.1	14.5
1963	Canada	19.0	20.5	19.0	19.5	19.0	18.5	19.0	20.0	20.0	19.0	16.5	19.0
	United States	14.7	15.9	15.5	15.4	14.9	14.4	14.6	14.4	13.9	14.2	14.5	13.3
1964	Canada	18.0	18.5	18.0	16.5	16.5	18.0	20.0	18.0	17.0	17.0	16.5	17.0
	United States	14.2	14.2	14.3	13.7	13.7	14.0	14.8	14.7	14.7	14.4	14.5	13.6
1965	Canada	17.5	19.0	18.5	18.0	17.0	18.5	19.0	19.5	19.5	19.5	19.5	19.5
	United States	14.6	15.1	15.6	15.0	15.4	15.7	15.5	15.2	14.5	14.2	14.6	14.6

Sources: Canadian data: Canada Department of Agriculture, *Poultry Products Market Review*, 1961–65.
U.S. data: U.S. Department of Agriculture, *Supplement to the Poultry and Egg Situation*, revised May 1966.
Note: Canadian prices, given for the Toronto markets, are for broilers and fryers for 1961 and 1962, and for chickens under five pounds from 1963 to 1965.

TABLE XXXIV

EGG PRODUCTION IN CANADA AND CONSUMPTION AND PRICES
IN CANADA AND THE UNITED STATES

	Production	Consumption		Price	
Year	Canada (thousand dozens)	Canada (dozens eggs	United States per capita)	Canada (domestic cents	United States per dozen)
1950	293,727	19.7	30.3	34.9	36.3
1951	291,235	20.0	30.4	48.1	47.7
1952	342,527	22.2	30.2	35.1	41.6
1953	355,184	22.9	29.5	43.0	47.7
1954	385,819	23.9	29.3	33.7	36.6
1955	386,011	24.0	28.8	38.1	39.5
1956	399,758	24.0	28.8	38.1	39.3
1957	439,843	25.0	27.9	31.4	35.9
1958	441,438	24.2	27.3	32.7	38.5
1959	448,236	23.3	26.6	29.2	31.4
1960	435,606	23.0	25.5	29.8	36.0
1961	429,923	22.6	24.7	31.3	35.5
1962	434,200	22.5	24.5	29.9	33.6
1963	417,920	21.5	24.0	33.6	34.4
1964	437,906	21.5	23.6	26.2	33.8
1965	432,795	21.4	23.2	31.4	33.7

Sources: Canadian data: DBS, *Production of Poultry and Eggs*, various issues; Canada Department of Agriculture, *Poultry Products Market Review*, various issues. U.S. data: U.S. Department of Agriculture, *Selected Statistical Series for Poultry and Eggs through 1965.*

4. Products in which Canada has an absolute disadvantage:
    fruit and vegetables, sugar, poultry meat, butter, mutton, lamb, and wool.

There can be relatively few surprises in the results presented above. The important grain crops, which account for more than 50 percent of the value of Canada's agricultural exports, show a clear-cut absolute advantage, while relatively few commodities appear to be at an absolute disadvantage. All in all, Canadian agriculture seems to be sufficiently competitive to look after itself in the event of free trade.

Although most of Canadian agriculture buys little from, and sells less to, the rest of the Canadian economy, the beef and the dairy industries provide the essential raw materials for the meat-products industry and the dairy-products industry, respectively. Both these secondary industries contribute substantially to Canadian income by making large purchases from other sectors of the economy. Consequently, the total reduction in Canadian national product resulting from a decline of the Canadian dairy industry under free trade (which may be expected because of Canada's absolute disadvantage in butter production) would be greater than the estimated loss from a contraction of the butter industry alone. Similarly, while Canada appears to have an absolute advantage in feeder-cattle production, increased exports of feeder cattle for fattening and processing in the United States mean a reduction in the output of the meat-products industry. Consequently, the export gain in this case might seem to be illusory in the short run.

Appendix

TABLE A-I

EXPORT CLEARANCES OF CANADIAN WHEAT TO SMALL BUYERS*
INCLUDING COUNTRIES WHICH ARE TRADITIONALLY NET EXPORTERS OF WHEAT
CROP YEARS 1960/61–1964/65
(thousands of bushels)

Destination	1960/61	1961/62	1962/63	1963/64	1964/65
Commonwealth countries:					
Africa:					
Federation of Rhodesia and Nyasaland	109	75	8	37	48
Union of South Africa	—	504	7,883	3,038	945
Asia:					
Hong Kong	524	617	579	668	905
Malaya and Singapore†	—	—	124	453	929
Pakistan	2,099	1,856	362	355	3,199
Caribbean:					
British West Indies	—	—	11	10	12
Europe:					
Malta	1,199	1,238	1,095	1,546	980
Non-Commonwealth countries:					
Africa:					
Mozambique	437	618	562	102	35
Nigeria	—	272	667	651	603
Asia:					
Burma	356	222	—	79	171
Israel	1,592	829	1,789	1,603	529
Kuwait	—	—	—	—	350
Philippines	987	3,855	6,710	7,301	6,482
Saudi Arabia	—	556	648	783	590
Taiwan	140	172	116	411	735
U.S. Oceania	313	474	520	462	76
Europe:					
Albania	2,355	2,102	—	3,696	5,025
Austria	1,529	1,626	1,554	1,191	1,660
Bulgaria	—	—	—	7,586	5,753
Finland	439	2,456	1,682	726	343
France	9,903	1,036	6,877	4,884	5,553
Germany, Eastern	1,918	8,040	—	—	10,552
Ireland	3,413	2,318	3,470	2,235	2,224
Italy	14,933	3,878	4,915	3,875	3,915

TABLE A-I (continued)

Destination	1960/61	1961/62	1962/63	1963/64	1964/65
Norway	3,301	1,729	1,828	1,703	1,601
Sweden	19	30	169	22	67
Switzerland	7,316	8,033	2,923	8,072	3,919
USSR	7,511	—	—	212,204	8,844
Yugoslavia	—	—	3,920	3,502	—
North and Central America:					
Cuba	5	—	—	7,454	8,121
Dominican Republic	923	1,490	1,156	852	704
El Salvador	18	385	580	1,018	777
Guatemala	60	47	255	275	408
Honduras	5	—	—	—	53
Nicaragua	—	—	—	—	505
United States	2,519	1,487	1,169	1,026	—
South America:					
Colombia	—	265	—	—	367
Ecuador	1,191	1,157	1,200	1,087	1,370
Peru	1,816	—	535	731	938
Venezuela	2,658	4,736	6,677	7,904	9,122

Sources: Export clearances for all countries except U.S.: Board of Grain Commissioners for Canada, Statistics Branch, *Canadian Grain Exports*, Ottawa, Queen's Printer, various issues; U.S. data compiled from returns of Canadian elevator licensees and shippers and advice from American grain correspondents.

*Less than 10 million bushels (in latest year shown).

†From 1963/64 on, Malaysia.

TABLE A-II

CUSTOMS EXPORTS OF CANADIAN WHEAT FLOUR TO SMALL BUYERS*
CROP YEARS 1960/61–1964/65
(thousands of bushels)

Destination	1960/61	1961/62	1962/63	1963/64	1964/65
Commonwealth countries:					
Africa:					
Gambia	—	—	—	8	63
Nigeria	852	1,752	550	18	8
Federation of Rhodesia and Nyasaland	38	33	38	31	2
Asia:					
Aden	—	—	—	—	28
British Middle East	15	32	28	38	20
Europe:					
Gibraltar	31	64	36	32	3
Caribbean:					
British Honduras	18	36	37	40	43
Oceania:					
Fiji	7	6	4	6	8
South America:					
British Guiana (Guyana)	203	31	23	39	57

TABLE A-II continued

Destination	1960/61	1961/62	1962/63	1963/64	1964/65
Non-Commonwealth countries:					
Africa:					
Angola	18	—	4	6	7
Cameroon Republic	—	—	—	—	48
French Equatorial Africa	5	4	—	—	25
Guinea Republic	—	—	—	—	1
Ivory Coast	—	—	—	3	4
Liberia	19	36	65	61	85
Malawi	—	—	—	—	21
Mozambique	5	21	27	34	43
Nyasaland	—	—	—	—	11
Tanganyika†	17	33	15	11	2
Asia:					
Indonesia	206	390	153	126	17
Iran	2	2	4	4	2
Japan	1,588	1,081	516	85	47
Jordan	1	110	1	1	10
Kuwait	26	25	77	31	10
Portuguese Asia	44	16	10	21	14
Saudi Arabia	9	1	7	6	1
Syria	7	2	6	1	1
Europe:					
Denmark	2	3	11	5	3
Greece	10	7	30	16	16
Iceland	17	24	15	5	3
Italy	4	19	5	1	7
Netherlands	6	2	5	6	8
North and Central America:					
El Salvador	190	215	83	12	2
French West Indies	4	2	4	2	8
Guatemala	62	81	52	16	46
Haiti	—	—	28	110	22
Honduras	76	105	68	64	50
Nicaragua	381	463	489	277	2
Panama	324	440	419	155	80
St. Pierre and Miquelon	7	10	16	21	21
South America:					
Chile	12	8	12	6	1
Peru	5	22	41	64	75
Surinam	83	76	67	74	80
Venezuela	35	11	2	—	1
Oceania:					
French Oceania	1	1	2	1	1
U.S. Oceania	29	2	3	2	14

Source: Canadian Wheat Board, *Annual Report*, various issues.
*Less than 100,000 bushels (in latest year shown).
†From 1964/65 on, Tanzania.

TABLE A-III

BARLEY PRODUCTION AND PRICES, ANNUALLY, 1948-65

Crop year	Canada Production — Total acres seeded (000 acres)	Total yield (mil. bu.)	Average yield per seeded acre (bu.)	Average farm price* Canada ($/bu.)	Ontario ($/bu.)	United States — Total acres seeded† (mil. acres)	Production — Total yield (mil. bu.)	Average yield per seeded acre‡ (bu.)	Average price*§ ($/bu.)
1948	6.4	152.3	23.8	0.96	1.11	13.1	315.5	24.2	1.16
1949	5.9	118.0	19.9	1.31	1.25	11.1	237.1	21.3	1.06
1950	6.5	167.5	25.7	1.13	1.30	13.0	303.8	23.3	1.19
1951	7.8	245.4	31.3	1.10	1.30	10.8	257.2	23.8	1.26
1952	8.5	291.6	34.4	1.06	1.35	9.2	228.2	24.8	1.37
1953	8.9	262.1	29.4	0.86	1.07	9.6	246.7	25.7	1.17
1954	7.8	175.2	22.3	0.89	1.06	14.7	379.3	25.7	1.09
1955	9.9	251.1	25.4	0.87	1.05	16.3	403.1	24.7	0.92
1956	8.4	269.1	32.1	0.79	1.06	14.7	376.7	25.6	0.99
1957	9.4	216.0	23.0	0.76	0.98	16.4	442.8	27.0	0.887
1958	9.3	237.8	25.6	0.77	0.98	16.2	477.4	29.6	0.90
1959	7.7	215.6	27.3	0.74	0.99	16.8	422.4	25.1	0.86
1960	6.9	193.5	28.2	0.80	0.99	15.6	431.3	27.6	0.838
1961	5.5	112.6	20.4	1.05	1.05	15.8	395.7	25.1	0.981
1962	5.3	165.9	31.4		1.068	14.7	429.5	29.2	0.927
1963	6.2	220.7	35.8		1.078	11.6	405.6	35.1	
1964	5.5	166.8	30.6		1.078	1.1	403.1	37.8	
1965‖	6.0	214.6	35.5			9.5	207.7	42.8	

Sources: Canadian data: DBS, *Handbook of Agricultural Statistics, 1908–63*, and Ontario Department of Agriculture, *Agricultural Statistics for Ontario*, 1964; supplementary data received through direct communication with DBS.
U.S. data: U.S. Department of Agriculture, *Agricultural Statistics*, various issues.

*All prices in domestic currencies.
†Estimates of seeded average relate to the over-all average of barley sown for all purposes, including barley sown in the preceding fall.
‡Calculated from total acres seeded and total yield.
§Obtained by weighting state prices by quantity sold. Includes an allowance for loans redeemed at the end of the crop marketing season and for quantities bought by the government under purchase agreements when such transactions are of significant volume.
‖Preliminary for Canada.

TABLE A-IV

OAT PRODUCTION AND PRICES, ANNUALLY, 1948–65

Crop year	Canada					United States			
	Production			Average farm price		Production			Average price‡ ($/bu.)
	Total acres seeded (000 acres)	Total yield (mil. bu.)	Average yield per seeded acre (bu.)	Canada ($/bu.)	Ontario ($/bu.)	Total acres seeded* (mil. acres)	Total yield (mil. bu.)	Average yield per seeded acre† (bu.)	
1948	10.8	345.3	31.8	0.70	0.82	43.8	1,450	33.1	0.717
1949	11.0	304.6	27.7	0.79	0.84	43.1	1,220	28.3	0.655
1950	11.2	401.8	35.9	0.78	0.90	45.0	1,369	30.4	0.788
1951	11.9	493.9	41.5	0.76	0.89	41.0	1,278	31.2	0.820
1952	11.1	471.1	42.6	0.67	0.82	42.3	1,217	28.8	0.789
1953	9.9	414.0	41.9	0.63	0.72	43.2	1,153	26.7	0.742
1954	10.0	306.4	30.5	0.67	0.77	46.9	1,410	30.1	0.714
1955	11.0	399.4	36.5	0.67	0.76	47.5	1,496	31.5	0.600
1956	10.5	467.5	44.6	0.58	0.78	44.2	1,151	26.0	0.686
1957	8.8	316.9	35.9	0.61	0.70	41.8	1,290	30.8	0.605
1958	9.2	345.7	37.4	0.64	0.71	37.7	1,401	37.2	0.578
1959	9.1	344.2	37.9	0.69	0.74	35.1	1,052	30.0	0.646
1960	9.6	398.5	41.4	0.68	0.76	31.5	1,155	36.6	0.598
1961	8.5	284.0	33.2	0.75	0.81	32.5	1,011	31.1	0.641
1962§	10.6	493.6	46.6		0.80	30.2	1,032	34.2	0.617
1963	9.5	453.1	47.8		0.776				
1964	8.2	357.2	43.6		0.771				
1965‖	8.7	415.0	47.9						

Sources: Canadian data: 1962–64 Ontario prices from Ontario Department of Agriculture, *Agricultural Statistics for Ontario*, 1964; all other Canadian data from DBS, *Handbook of Agricultural Statistics, 1908–63* (also data by province, brought up to date from DBS data).

U.S. data: 1948 data from U.S. Department of Agriculture, *Agricultural Statistics* 1962; 1949–62 data from *Agricultural Statistics*, 1963.

*Estimates of seeded average relate to the total average of oats sown for all purposes, including oats sown in the preceding fall.

†Calculated from data of seeded acres and production.

‡Obtained by weighting state prices by quantity sold. Includes an allowance for loans unredeemed at the end of the crop marketing season and for quantities bought by the government under purchase agreements when such transactions are of significant volume.

§Preliminary for United States.

‖Preliminary for Canada.

TABLE A-V

TOBACCO PRODUCTION AND PRICES—ALL TYPES OF TOBACCO, ANNUALLY, 1948-64

Crop year	Canada						United States			
	Total acres harvested (000 acres)		Production (mil. lbs.)		Average farm price (¢ per lb.)		Total acres harvested (000 acres)	Production* (mil. lbs.)	Average yield per acre harvested (lbs.)	Average price per lb. received by farmer (¢)
	Canada	Ontario	Canada	Ontario	Canada	Ontario				
1948	111	98	127	113	39.7	41.01	1,554	1,980	1,274	48.2
1949	109	99	140	132	39.7	40.57	1,623	1,969	1,213	45.9
1950	102	93	120	111	42.64	43.85	1,599	2,030	1,269	51.7
1951	119	110	154	145	43.05	45.83	1,780	2,332	1,310	51.1
1952	92	84	140	131	40.74	41.20	1,772	2,256	1,273	49.9
1953	101	92	139	129	42.82	43.57	1,633	2,059	1,261	52.3
1954	132	121	185	174	42.10	42.73	1,667	2,244	1,346	51.1
1955	110	97	135	121	42.78	44.25	1,495	2,193	1,466	53.2
1956	128	116	162	152	44.50	45.52	1,363	2,176	1,596	53.7
1957	137	127	165	156	47.67	48.38	1,122	1,667	1,486	56.1
1958	134	125	197	188	45.4	45.83	1,078	1,736	1,611	59.9
1959	128	118	170	158	53.2	54.18	1,153	1,796	1,558	58.3
1960	136	124	214	200	53.56	54.58	1,142	1,944	1,703	60.9
1961	138	127	210	198	50.23	51.13	1,174	2,061	1,755	63.8
1962†	131	122	203	190	47.24	50.50	1,226	2,309	1,884	59.0
1963	114	104	201	190	45.06	45.48				
1964	85	76	154	143	54.08	54.81				

Sources: Canadian data: DBS, *Reference Papers*, 1950, *Canada Year Book*, 1949, *Leaf Tobacco Acreage, Production, and Value, Quarterly Bulletin of Agricultural Statistics.*
U.S. data: 1948 data from U.S. Department of Agriculture, *Agricultural Statistics*, 1962; 1949–62 data from *Agricultural Statistics*, 1963.
*Production figures are on a farm-sales-weight basis.
†Preliminary for United States.

TABLE A-VI

FLUE-CURED TOBACCO PRODUCTION AND PRICES, ANNUALLY, 1948–64

Crop year	Canada						United States			
	Production				Average farm price (¢ per lb.)		Production		Average yield per acre harvested (lbs.)	Average price per lb. received by farmer (¢)
	Total acres harvested ('000 acres)		Total yield (mil. lbs.)				Total acres harvested ('000 acres)	Total yield* (mil. lbs.)		
	Canada	Ontario	Canada	Ontario	Canada	Ontario				
1948	91	85	102	98	42.5	42.7				
1949	91	86	117	114	42.1	42.25	935	1,114	1,191	47.2
1950	92	87	108	104	44.49	44.72	958	1,257	1,312	54.7
1951	111	106	144	140	44.24	46.44	1,110	1,453	1,309	52.4
1952	86	81	132	127	41.73	41.61	1,111	1,365	1,229	50.3
1953	96	91	132	127	43.70	43.77	1,022	1,272	1,245	52.8
1954	123	117	173	168	43.18	43.21	1,042	1,314	1,261	52.7
1955	98	92	118	112	45.29	45.48	991	1,483	1,479	52.7
1956	118	111	149	144	46.11	46.30	875	1,422	1,625	51.5
1957	126	121	152	148	49.23	49.29	663	975	1,471	55.4
1958	123	117	181	176	46.54	46.57	639	1,081	1,691	58.2
1959	117	111	152	147	55.39	55.57	693	1,081	1,559	58.3
1960	129	124	205	199	54.55	54.65	692	1,251	1,808	60.4
1961	128	122	195	190	51.58	51.70	698	1,258	1,801	64.3
1962†	122	117	188	180	48.28	51.04	731	1,400	1,916	60.1
1963	106	99	187	180	45.92	45.81				
1964	80	73	143	137	55.61	55.63				

Sources: Canadian data: DBS, *Reference Papers*, 1950, *Canada Year Book*, 1949, *Leaf Tobacco Acreage, Production, and Value, Quarterly Bulletin of Agricultural Statistics.*
U.S. data: 1949–57 data from U.S. Department of Agriculture, *Agricultural Statistics*, 1962; 1958 from *Agricultural Statistics*, 1963.
Note: Premiums for farm-typing and grading of flue-cured tobacco have not been applicable beginning with the 1958 crop (except in Ontario).
*Production figures are on a farm-sales-weight basis.
†Preliminary for United States.

TABLE A-VII

EXPORTS OF UNMANUFACTURED TOBACCO
SELECTED YEARS
(metric tons)

Exporting region*	1948–52	1958	1963
Europe	108,000	162,000	193,000
EEC	11,000	19,600	20,000
Bulgaria	44,600	43,800	86,000
Czechoslovakia	—	1,900	3,000
Greece	28,900	62,400	62,000
Hungary	7,600	—	—
Poland	—	1,500	3,000
United Kingdom†	4,600	1,100	1,500
Yugoslavia	10,600	23,200	17,000
North and Central America	255,000	270,000	263,000
Canada	11,500	13,400	17,800
Cuba	14,400	26,000	—
Dominican Republic	16,100	11,500	—
Honduras	1,900	—	1,500
Mexico	200	300	12,500
United States‡	210,400	218,800	230,800
South America	38,000	39,000	83,600
Argentina	400	1,700	17,500
Brazil	29,600	30,400	44,300
Colombia	3,800	4,500	11,200
Paraguay	3,900	2,400	10,600
Asia	127,000	210,000	154,000
China, Taiwan	—	200	1,300
Cyprus	600	800	1,000
India	42,400	48,100	67,900
Japan	400	3,700	6,900
Philippines	6,000	14,100	24,800
Syria (UAR)‡	1,900	300	1,500
Thailand	—	5,800	3,800
Turkey	58,600	56,100	44,600
Africa	69,000	81,000	104,300
Algeria	11,200	7,800	—
Cameroon	400	1,000	1,000
Madagascar	3,100	4,300	3,700
Rhodesia, Nyasaland†	1,800	65,000	96,800
USSR	—	6,200	1,800

Source: FAO, *Trade Yearbook*, various issues.
*Countries exporting 1,000 metric tons or more in 1963.
†Including re-exports.
‡From September 28, 1961, on, Syria.

TABLE A-VIII

IMPORTS OF UNMANUFACTURED TOBACCO
SELECTED YEARS
(metric tons)

Importing region*	1948/52	1958	1963
Europe	350,000	464,000	584,700
EEC	125,600	177,000	263,600
EFTA	178,000	194,000	209,900
Czechoslovakia	—	15,500	13,000
Finland	4,500	4,800	7,000
Germany, Democratic Republic†	—	18,900	29,200
Ireland	8,100	6,100	6,400
Poland	4,800	11,800	19,300
Spain	21,100	29,300	26,900
Yugoslavia	1,200	900	10,000
North and Central America	47,000	71,000	84,900
Canada	800	1,300	1,200
El Salvador	1,200	1,500	1,400
Mexico	1,000	2,400	2,600
United States	42,600	62,900	76,100
South America	10,000	3,000	5,600
Argentina	4,700	—	—
Chile	300	300	2,100
Uruguay	3,600	1,700	2,700
Asia	46,000	56,000	41,200
Ceylon	700	600	1,200
China, Taiwan	100	500	2,200
Hong Kong	5,200	5,000	8,300
Israel	600	800	1,500
Japan	2,500	2,700	15,800
Philippines	6,600	2,400	2,300
Thailand	1,700	5,300	3,700
Vietnam, Republic of	—	1,800	2,500
Africa	37,000	40,000	32,900
Congo, Leopoldville	—	—	4,000
Morocco	4,000	2,600	4,000
Nigeria	2,500	2,400	1,700
South Africa	1,800	1,400	2,400
Tunisia	2,800	3,700	2,200
United Arab Republic	12,500	11,900	12,400
Oceania	15,000	23,000	15,500
Australia	12,200	19,400	12,400
New Zealand	2,700	3,400	2,500
USSR	—	84,300	93,400

Source: FAO, *Trade Yearbook*, various issues.

*Countries importing 1,000 metric tons or more in 1963.

†Data are estimates based on import and export data by origin or destination of countries reporting trade, or were derived from unofficial sources by the FAO.

Prospects
for Trade Liberalization In Agriculture

David L. MacFarlane and Lewis A. Fischer

I. Introduction

The problem

The agricultural industries of the North Atlantic area are characterized by a jungle of laws and regulations aimed largely at raising the level of prices and the incomes of farmers. The jungle consists of tariffs, national price supports and production-control programs, import-quota arrangements, European Common Market negotiations for a Common Agricultural Policy (CAP), export subsidies and provision of credit for surplus disposal, state trading, and international commodity agreements. These policy measures, taken at a national level or at the level of a regional trading bloc such as the EEC, have led to severe restrictions on international trade in farm products. In fact, throughout the history of postwar trade negotiations, agriculture has been given "special status," meaning that it has been practically exempt from such negotiations. In view of all these circumstances, the economist can with only limited profit employ customary analytical procedures.[1]

There are two challenges to the writers of this study. The first, related to the task of evaluating the prospects for trade liberalization in agriculture, is to cut through the maze of political factors that afflict the industry. Only

---

[1]While agricultural trade restrictions in all their varied forms have become noticeably worse during the post-1945 period, their historical roots go back a very long way. By 1800 most European countries and Britain had well-developed mechanisms for protecting their domestic farm industries. Then Britain began in 1844 a period of some ninety years of free trade, and the consequences were what the economists would expect: lower land rents and farm-labour returns. These were accompanied by extreme hardship in the farm areas. While the major countries which developed as agricultural exporters in the nineteenth century maintained and encouraged a climate of economic freedom for the agricultural sectors, this came to an end with the depression of the 1930s. From that time until the present, importing and exporting countries have appeared to vie with one another in devising measures for the protection of their agriculture. As we shall see, there are indications that, in the 1960s, this climate has been changing. There is a good prospect that serious discussion of the costs of agricultural protectionism and of the possible gains from freeing the farm industry will be possible.

in this way can we determine whether (and in what forms) freer trade in farm products might be realized. An equally difficult task is to assess the effects of such possible changes on agricultural trade patterns, on farm output, on the prices of farm products, and on the incomes of farmers.

Stated in other terms, the purpose of this study is to assess whether an accommodation can be negotiated between the apparent need for agricultural supports and the desirability of maintaining and expanding trade in farm products. In doing this, we must keep in mind that the intricate network of controls that now distinguishes agriculture arose in large part from two special characteristics of the industry. Historically, both in countries that employ widespread use of restrictive measures and in those that do not, labour returns have been much lower in agriculture than in other industries. In addition, farm prices and incomes are subject to highly erratic fluctuations, in part associated with irregular yields and output, leading to a high degree of instability in the industry.

The difficulty of breaking through the maze of controls must not be underestimated. National governments have shown a willingness to discuss their problems on an international level but have shown little interest in reform at home. Nevertheless, there are some signs that encourage us to make this analysis of the opportunities for trade liberalization. Recognition of the costs, both to the importing and to the exporting countries, of the ludicrous policies employed over the past two decades may now be leading to more rational farm and trade policies. In the past four years there has been a clear improvement in farm prices and incomes, and in the United States this has been accompanied by the freeing of one farm product after another from some of the most objectionable controls.

Scope and method

The development of an Atlantic trading community is a particularly interesting approach to the freeing of agriculture from international trade and other restrictions. For present purposes an Atlantic trading group would include Canada, the United States, the European Economic Community (EEC), the European Free Trade Association (EFTA), and possibly the Caribbean countries not already members of the Latin American Free Trade Area (LAFTA).

Although emphasis is placed on the Atlantic grouping, prospective trade with Japan, the USSR, eastern Europe, and China, and with the developing countries will greatly influence trends in the Atlantic community and must be taken into account. The other explicit assumptions underlying this study are as follows. (1) There will be no change in foreign exchange rates. (2) Since non-tariff barriers are inordinately important in agriculture, it is assumed that progress in reducing them must accompany, and be harmonized with, reductions in tariff barriers. (3) Since it is highly unrealistic in the case of agriculture to suggest, even for purposes of economic analysis, either a rapid or a total removal of barriers, it is assumed that there will be a gradual removal of both. Implicit in this assumption is the continuance by governments of some protective or stabilizing measures to aid their farm industries. In this context, a transition period of five to twenty years is suggested. (4) An overriding assumption is that the long-term objective of international trade policy is the most rapid sustainable growth of the world economy as a whole.

The study will consider, first, the postwar agricultural trade patterns (particularly in the North Atlantic community) applicable to those Canadian farm products that are important in foreign trade. It will then turn to an examination of the maze of national, regional, and international policies that influence Canada's present and prospective trading position in agriculture vis-à-vis that of important competitors. This will be followed by a consideration of the prospects for freer trade in farm products in the North Atlantic area and of the means by which this might be realized, taking account of the nature of the barriers. And finally, the implications of freer trade for Canadian farm producers will be considered.

II. The Canadian Farm Industry and Its Foreign Trade

The Canadian farm industry accounts for about 4 to 6 percent of net national product.[1] Annual gross output of the industry ranged, during the period 1950–65, from a low of $2,122 million in 1950 to a high of $3,776 million in 1965. During the same period, annual net output ranged from a low of $975 million in 1961 to a high of $1,645 million in 1965.

Canada is the world's fourth largest exporter of farm products. These exports represent about one-third of Canadian farm production. Total Canadian agricultural exports increased substantially between the early 1950s and 1963–64, when they averaged $1,530 million. In the early postwar years, farm exports accounted for between one-quarter and one-third of Canada's total merchandise exports; in recent years they have accounted for about 20 percent.

Trends in Canada's agricultural trade

Some interesting changes have taken place in the destination of Canadian farm exports. Until the early 1950s, the United States was Canada's most

[1]Moreover, by their non-farm work, members of the agricultural labour force make an additional contribution estimated at half their contribution through agriculture.

TABLE 1

CANADA, MAJOR AGRICULTURAL EXPORTS, BY COMMODITY, 1956 AND 1961–65
(thousands of dollars)

Commodity	1956	1961	1962	1963	1964	1965
Total exports	4,789,746	5,754,985	6,178,631	6,798,500	8,094,360	8,522,953
Agricultural products	959,741	1,223,584	1,187,949	1,275,040	1,624,605	1,525,920
as percentage of all products	20.0	21.3	19.2	18.7	20.1	17.9
Wheat and wheat flour	584,630	724,267	658,561	849,420	1,123,771	906,580
Barley	94,977	48,966	29,927	24,524	51,254	43,679
Other cereals—milled and unmilled	32,759	30,605	30,567	40,613	33,646	35,432
Flaxseed	43,623	46,269	41,920	38,560	48,662	51,658
Rapeseed	3,000	13,850	20,667	16,156	10,152	30,900
Oil seed—cake and meal	20,891	11,419	19,064	23,123	22,409	26,485
Other feeds of vegetable origin	8,563	10,750	12,977	19,007	22,082	21,276
Vegetables and vegetable preparations	8,851	15,810	23,998	27,341	30,943	41,889
Other crude vegetable products	11,485	13,227	13,856	12,512	13,233	14,053
Fruits and fruit preparations	11,791	13,226	17,691	22,768	21,636	20,093
Tobacco	17,674	28,025	35,182	29,541	38,365	35,363
Live animals	12,948	66,901	68,054	41,971	34,514	79,133
Meats and meat preparations	37,035	42,898	42,781	44,421	51,698	76,244
Other animal products	24,056	20,593	20,785	19,637	21,496	33,539

Source: Dominion Bureau of Statistics, *Trade of Canada, Exports,* and *Canada Yearbook,* various years.

important customer, taking almost half our total farm exports. With the institution in the 1950s of U.S. quantitative import restrictions arising from their farm programs, this market has been effectively eroded, so that in 1963–64 it accounted for only 14 percent of agricultural exports. The USSR, eastern European countries, and mainland China have become important importers of wheat and accounted for 25 percent of total farm exports in 1963–64. The EEC countries reduced their shares from over 16 percent in the period 1954–58 to 12 percent in 1963–64. On the other hand, other countries increased their shares from 14 percent in 1950–51 to 19 percent in 1963–64. Japan's remained relatively constant in the decade from 1954–64.

If wheat is excluded from agricultural exports, a somewhat different picture emerges. Prior to 1939, over 60 percent of Canada's agricultural exports (excluding wheat) found markets in Britain, and one-quarter in the United States. In recent years the situation has reversed, with only 25 percent of these products going to Britain, and nearly one-half to the United States.[2] EEC countries take about 10 percent, followed by Japan with a somewhat smaller share.

Wheat and wheat flour are by far the most important among Canadian farm exports, in terms of both the value of exports and the proportion of production sold abroad. In the 1960s, average annual exports have been 435 million bushels, valued at about $853 million. These two commodities have accounted for some 60 percent of agricultural exports since 1960. Among the other grains, only barley exports have been on a scale sufficient to warrant mention here. These have averaged 38 million bushels annually, valued at about $40 million in the crop years of the 1960s. All other cereals, processed and unprocessed, have had export values of about $35 million annually.

Other crop exports worthy of note are the oilseeds (flaxseed and rapeseed): annual exports of flaxseed have averaged about $45 million annually, and those of rapeseed about $18 million. Tobacco exports have been averaging about $30 million. There have been relatively small exports of fruits and vegetables and processed preparations from them, such as maple products, seeds, and fodder.

In the category of livestock and livestock products, exports of live animals, particularly feeder cattle, slaughter cattle, and dairy cattle, have been most important, averaging about $58 million annually in the 1960s. Other animal products (hides and skins, other meats and meat preparations) have averaged about $70 million annually. Cheese exports, largely

[2]F. S. Shefrin, *Trends in Canada's Agricultural Trade Pattern*, Ottawa, Department of Agriculture, 1966, p. 9.

to Britain under an export subsidy scheme, have averaged about 25 million pounds a year, valued at some $10 million.

In the Atlantic area, Britain has been the largest buyer of Canadian wheat, averaging over 70 million bushels a year. EEC countries have been purchasing 60 to 70 million bushels annually. Purchases by Japan have been averaging about 50 million bushels a year. Eastern European countries and the USSR have made large purchases in recent years, as has mainland China. However, the prospect is that most of these countries will again become self-sufficient in a relatively short period. South American and Caribbean countries have been purchasing 20 to 25 million bushels annually in recent years. A minuscule import quota is applicable to Canadian wheat exports to the United States.

The destination of Canadian barley exports is largely the Common Market countries, Britain, Japan, the United States, and China. Oilseed exports go mainly to Britain, the Common Market countries, and Japan. Tobacco is exported very largely to Britain under a preferential tariff arrangement.

Virtually all live animals and fresh, chilled, and frozen meats are exported to the United States. Other meats and meat products are also exported mainly to the United States, as well as to the EEC countries and Britain. Hides and skins, offal products, and tallow are shipped largely to the United States, the Common Market countries, and to Britain. As we have noted, almost all Canadian cheese exports go to Britain.

Canada has very large food imports. In 1963–64, they averaged $1,022 million, compared with agricultural exports averaging $1,530 million. A fairly large proportion (perhaps one-third) are imports of products which are produced in Canada, and this proportion has been increasing over the past ten years. Canada has sizable imports of feed grains, of temperate-climate fruits and vegetables, and of meats, as well as of poultry and dairy products. The increased imports of some of these products suggest Canadian agriculture has not made technological (and cost) progress comparable to that of the United States, from which a very large proportion of these imports come. Most of the food imports from the United States are processed, and their import into Canada reflects the existence of larger-scale and more-efficient processing plants in the United States.

Canada's position in world trade in farm products

Since a separate study in the present series is devoted to Canada's comparative-cost or comparative-advantage position, only a few summary points will be made here. In the study referred to, Professor Gerald I. Trant[3] has grouped farm products according to their competitive position. According to his grouping, products in which Canada has a strong absolute advantage are wheat, oats, barley, flax, rapeseed, beef feeder cattle, and pure-bred dairy cattle. Products in which Canada has a slight absolute advantage include cheddar cheese and specialty pork products. Products in which Canada has no ascertainable absolute advantage are tobacco, grain corn, fresh beef, fresh pork, eggs, soybeans, dried milk powder, and fluid milk. Products in which Canada has an absolute disadvantage include fruits and vegetables, sugar, poultry meat, butter, mutton, lamb, and wool.

Dr. G. A. MacEachern states about Canada that "a relatively stable absolute advantage is enjoyed by many commodities, for example, wheat, barley, flaxseed, rapeseed, milk production, grade dairy cattle, some cheeses, and other milk products, tobacco, turnips, and some fruit. For a number of other commodities, a competitive advantage exists with selected countries, but is unstable relative to the United States, varying by seasons of the year and due to regional production and transport costs, for example, feeder and slaughter cattle, hogs, a variety of meats, eggs, apples, and potatoes."[4]

There is substantial agreement between these two writers in regard to Canada's comparative advantage in farm products.

III. The Atlantic Area Farm-Policy Maze

The prospects for greater Canadian trade in farm products in the Atlantic region depend on three factors: (1) the demand for farm products in the area, (2) the degree of competitive advantage (in a purely economic context) which Canada enjoys, and (3) the adjustment of the complex of barriers that now inhibit trade. The first and third of these are examined in some detail in the following pages, with emphasis placed on Canada's position and the effects of freer trade on Canadian agriculture. The second has just been touched on here, it being the subject of a separate study in this series.

Trade liberalization possibilities cannot be explored without first examin-

[3]"The Impact of Trade Liberalization on Canadian Agriculture," in the present volume.
[4]G. A. MacEachern and David L. MacFarlane, "The Relative Position of Canadian Agriculture in World Trade," *Conference on International Trade and Canadian Agriculture*, Economic Council of Canada and the Agricultural Economics Research Council of Canada, Ottawa, Queen's Printer, 1966, p. 134.

ing the agricultural policies of the major trading countries and blocs in the Atlantic area. Of particular importance are those policy aspects that have resulted in barriers to trade in agricultural products.

One of the most significant economic phenomena of the postwar years has been the agricultural protectionist measures adopted by most countries in the world. Incomes of agricultural workers in the more developed countries have been one-third to two-thirds lower than those earned by comparable workers in the non-agricultural sectors of the various economies. Virtually all governments around the world have developed domestic programs to assist agriculture, partly as a result of political pressure from farm people, and to some extent in the hope that agricultural aids would speed the rationalization of the industry. But the success of these programs has required the increased use of barriers to agricultural imports.

The European Economic Community

The most significant developments in agricultural policy of the past decade and a half, and certainly within the context of this study, are those of the European Economic Community. Over a protracted period of discussion and negotiation, these countries maintained the policy of increasingly protecting their farmers. In fact, failure to agree on the Common Agricultural Policy (CAP) continually threatened the disintegration of the Community. Only in late 1966, after a year's boycott of negotiations by France on the issue of supranationality, was the CAP agreed upon. It became effective on July 1, 1968.

The basis of agreement is the creation of a common internal agricultural market (with a few temporary exceptions in cases of special difficulty) and of a system of import levies aimed at bringing import prices of basic commodities to the level of those established by the EEC Commission. Provisions have been made for fixed tariffs on some products and for quantitative restrictions of imports if they should threaten the farmers of any signatory country. The levies will be paid into the European Agricultural Guidance and Guarantee Fund. Member countries have been paying assessments into the Fund since 1962 and will continue to do so until the CAP is fully operative. In the first year, assessments totalled $36.2 million (U.S.) and were expected to rise to $700 million in 1966–67. It is expected that the levies will yield to the Fund more than $1,500 million in the first year of its operation.

The Fund will be used for three purposes: (1) price supports and export subsidies, (2) measures designed to improve the structure of agriculture, and (3) special payments to Germany, Italy, and Luxembourg to compensate for the reduction of grain prices in these countries. Estimates are that 65 percent of the sum will be used for the first purpose, 21 percent for the second, and 14 percent for the third.

Dr. J. A. Richter[1] writes of the CAP arrangements:

To sum up the main content of the EEC's agricultural market and price policy, we might say that the most rigid protection is planned for the basic (so-called target price) commodities. Others will be more flexibly protected. Grains, sugar, and dairy products are the basic commodities for which target prices are to be approximated systematically by variable import levies and/or subsidies.

Pork, eggs, and poultry will be protected by fixed tariffs and 'derived' variable levies. . . . Fruits and vegetables will be mainly protected by fixed tariffs and market interventions.

For products other than the basic ones . . . , minimum import or gate prices may be decreed and realized by special levies.

For oilseeds, it is not unlikely that a system of manufacturing taxes (margarine) will be imposed to regulate interproduct competition affecting highly protected animal fats.

Of greatest interest to Canada is the protection afforded wheat producers within the Community. In recent years about one-third of the gross wheat imports into the EEC were supplied by Canada. The threshold price of wheat (the price applicable to imports at the frontier which would assure that the internal target price, and thus the farm price, would be guaranteed) was set in 1964 at $3.12 (Can.). The difference between the landed price at the frontier and the threshold price is covered by a variable levy.

While the CAP provides guidelines for agricultural development in each of the member countries, each member country will continue to pursue its own internal policies with respect to agriculture, to the extent that they do not interfere with the provisions of the CAP. It is very difficult to secure complete and reliable data concerning the costs of the purely internal programs, but it has been estimated that they currently cost over $2 billion (U.S.) and will rise to $2.5 billion by 1970. Thus, through the internal domestic programs and the levies, the total cost of farm programs will probably exceed $4 billion in 1970. This should be considered in the context of a projected GNP for the Community of $280 billion (U.S.) in that year. An additional burden is created by the fact that food prices in the Community are inordinately high.

In addition to the maintenance of a wide measure of independence in agricultural policy in individual Common Market countries, these countries also have widely differing agricultural-resource endowments. Before assessing the implications for Canada of the CAP, we will examine the farm industries within the Community—first in France, which is by far the

[1]*Agricultural Protection and Trade: Proposals for an International Policy*, New York, Praeger, 1964, pp. 33–4.

largest agricultural producer (and a surplus producer interested in markets now shared by Canada), and then in the other five countries, which are important customers for our commercial agricultural exports.

France joined the EEC partly because she believed she would become the breadbasket of, and a dominant supplier of other farm products to, the Community. Forty-six percent of the Community's farm land is in France. When the French government stated that in 1963–64 there were ten million acres of uncultivated farm land, it created the myth of the gigantic potential of French agriculture. While there are significant possibilities of augmenting aggregate farm output by employing presently unused land, these possibilities are questionable, at least for the near future.

Of the 86 million acres of farm land currently in use in France, some 35 million require consolidation. The Fourth Plan foresees the consolidation of 1.7 million acres per year at a cost of $60 million per year of public funds. In other words, twenty, if not twenty-five, years would be needed to implement this project.[2]

Land devoted to the nine leading crops decreased 15 percent, from 13 million hectares to 11 million hectares, from the beginning of the 1950s to 1962–63. Nonetheless, acreage of wheat, corn, and barley increased over these years. The farm-labour force decreased at an annual rate of 3 to 4 percent, but this was accompanied by an increase in farm output averaging 4.2 percent per year. Purchased inputs, such as fertilizers and farm machinery, account for much of the production increases over the period. Table II shows striking increases of these inputs in the 1950s. Tractors have increased over the twelve-year period to more than five times their initial number.

In the early 1960s about 150,000 persons of African origin were employed in French agriculture. The majority will leave the country soon under present French policies. Their replacement suggests the substitution of more-expensive labour and/or further mechanization.

State aids to agriculture were $400 million (U.S.) in 1954, $733 million in 1959, $1,322 million in 1962, and $1,763 million in 1964–65. More than one-half of the last figure was used as an aid to the production adjustments. Income supports ranked next, followed by export subsidies. Farmers' terms of trade have improved markedly, since prices received by farmers increased by 22 percent during the period 1960 to 1964, while the prices paid by farmers rose by only 8 percent over the same period.

The choice of the commodities selected for support takes account of preferential status implied in membership in the EEC, as well as of the

[2]Ambassade de France, *France and Agriculture*, New York, Service de Presse et d'Information, p. 8. Unless otherwise indicated, data are from this publication.

TABLE II

FRANCE, SELECTED PURCHASED INPUTS IN AGRICULTURE

Input	1948-49 to 1952-53	1962-63	1962-63 inputs as percent of 1948-49 to 1952-53 inputs
Fertilizers ('000 metric tons)			
Nitrogenous	252	683	171
Phosphate	454	1,034	128
Potash	362	910	151
Tractors	148,142	804,400	443
Combined harvester-threshers	17,738	68,500	286

Source: United Nations, Food and Agriculture Organization, *Production Yearbook*, no. 18, Rome, 1964.

TABLE III

FRANCE, AIDS TO AGRICULTURE, 1964-65

Type of Aid	Amount (mil. $ U.S.)
Export subsidies	237.5
Income support	513.8
Aids to adjustment of production	890.7
Other	121.0
Total	1,763.0

Source: *Agrarpolitische Revue*, Brugg, Switzerland, April 1965, p. 306.

shifting demand resulting from improved incomes in western Europe. Another factor in French policy is the planned expansion of trade with both underdeveloped and eastern European countries.

In summary, the main objectives of current French agricultural policy are to control the grain market in West Germany and Benelux by displacing wheat imports from non-members, particularly the United States, and to expand animal production in order to benefit from the increasing demand for meat throughout the EEC. There are no limits on meat production in the current French plan.

The value of final agricultural production increased from $4.7 billion to $7.5 billion (U.S.) between 1954 and 1961. Yet French agriculture is probably still far from an optimum production level, in an economic context. In 1955 France's gross agricultural product per capita was half that of the Benelux countries and one-third that of the United States, and the value of gross agricultural output per acre of land was lower than the average for the EEC. Over 75 percent of the farms enumerated in the 1955 census were less than twenty acres in size. Thus large increases in output are possible through the difficult processes of rationalization and consolidation of holdings. They will also come about through the use of more purchased inputs and improvement in the quality of inputs. By 1963–64 France had achieved 110 percent of self-sufficiency in grains, 100 percent in meats, and produced small surpluses of dairy products.

Inquiry into the farm policies of Benelux, West Germany, and Italy is limited largely to their relevance to Canada's trade position. Netherlands agriculture shows the highest productivity rates, as well as the relatively highest per capita income of the rural population, among the EEC members. Her gross agricultural product increased between 1949 and 1961 by 60 percent. Input of farm labour decreased by 20 percent, whereas purchased inputs, including imported feed, increased by 110 percent during the same period.

Analyzing the Dutch economy, Mr. H. Saudie concludes that "agricultural practices in the Netherlands are already so near to the technological optimum that little can be expected from further reduction of that distance to that optimum. . . . As inputs rise faster than outputs, value added will tend to grow very slowly indeed."[3] The Netherlands is the only country where fertilizer input has not increased in recent years. Total funds allocated for agriculture in 1965 were $203 million (U.S.), whereas $217 million was budgeted for 1964. This decline is largely due to reductions in direct subsidies to farmers. All other items of the agricultural budget have been raised, with land development getting the largest increase.

In Belgium the predominance of fragmented farm units characterizes agriculture. The creation of the EEC has encouraged industrial expansion; hence, labour has transferred from agriculture to other sectors of the economy. The number of tractors increased from 12,000 to 60,000 from 1950 to 1963. Nitrogenous fertilizer use increased from 77,000 to 151,000 metric tons. Concurrently, yields of wheat and barley increased from 3,200 to 3,770 kilograms per hectare and from 3,000 to 3,600 kilograms, respectively. Comparable aggregate figures for meat production are 124,000 to 274,000 metric tons.

The Federal Republic of Germany is Canada's most important customer among the Common Market countries. Improved management and a great expansion in the application of purchased inputs have resulted in substantial productivity increase in agriculture (see Table IV). Monthly farm

[3]"Possible Economic Growth in the Netherlands," *Europe's Future in Figures*, Amsterdam, North Holland Publishing Co., 1962, p. 169.

TABLE IV

WEST GERMANY, SELECTED INPUT AND PRODUCTION DATA

Item	1948–52	1965
Number of tractors ('000)	164.1	1,053.2
Fertilizers used ('000 metric tons):		
Nitrogenous	365.0	746.4
Phosphate	405.5	755.7
Potash	660.3	1,125.4
Yield per hectare ('00 kilos):		
Wheat	26.2	35.1
Barley	23.9	31.1
Maize	22.4	36.4
Production ('000 metric tons):		
Meat (except poultry)	1,407	2,964
Poultry meat	42	121

Source: FAO, *Production Yearbook*, no. 18.

wages rose from the equivalent of $16.70 (U.S.) in 1950 to $71.20 in 1963, an increase of 326 percent. The number of paid farm workers was reduced from 885,000 in 1951 to 299,000 in 1963–64, as a result of migration from farms. Non-wage inputs measured in current values almost trebled over the same period.

In Italy, farming was characterized by low outputs and generally by an insufficient use of resources other than labour prior to the land reforms initiated in 1950. The major objective of these reforms was to increase productivity and adjust production patterns to market requirements. EEC policy created comparative advantages for the production of maize, fruits, and vegetables. The government "green plans" also encourage the restriction of wheat production. Generally, the plans have contributed large support for improvement measures, but the amount of these funds has not been published.

The target presented in the Saraceno report is to "create the necessary conditions in agriculture to enable agricultural productivity to match non-agriculture productivity."[4] The report estimates that 150,000 people a year are leaving farms. The number of tractors increased by 431 percent and the use of nitrogenous fertilizers by 158 percent during a recent fifteen-year period. These are modest increases. Taking the average of 1948–53 as a basis of comparison, wheat acreage has declined by about 8 percent, while total output has been practically unchanged. On the other hand, maize yields and total output have increased by 79 and 60 percent, respectively.

[4]Report to Italian Parliament on Italy's Economic Situation, 1963.

This, along with feed grain imports, has provided the basis for doubling meat production.

Community production of meats has not kept up with demand. Self-sufficiency in these products is less today than ten to fifteen years ago. The gap between supply of, and demand for, meat, hard wheat, and fruit has increased sharply. On the other hand, both expansion of quantity and improvement of quality of fruits in Italy and some regions of France have occurred. The expansion of feed grain production and the use of purchased inputs have made possible a rapid increase of livestock production with improvement in quality. But all students of EEC agriculture hold the view that feed grain requirements cannot be met by production within the Community.

Since July 1, 1967, there has been a common market for grain, having all the characteristics of a domestic market. A single levy is imposed on imports of the various cereals from third countries, while intra-Community trade in cereals is free from levies. Refunds or subsidies on intra-Community export trade have been eliminated; for exports, the amount of the subsidy has been unified.

The application of the full levies based on the level of agreed-upon common prices for barley and corn has increased the cost of imports of these grains appreciably. Taking this into account, the Ministers agreed to make an exception for Italy. The levy on barley and corn imported by sea into Italy from third countries has been reduced by $7.50 per metric ton until the end of the 1971–72 marketing year. A special provision has also been made for Durum wheat. This assures producers a price higher than would be obtained on the basis of the agreed target price of $125 per ton.

The results of the foregoing and earlier policies, expressed in terms of output per capita, are presented in Table V. Apart from the Netherlands, the output per capita increased moderately over the seven years

TABLE V

EEC COUNTRIES, INDEX NUMBERS OF TOTAL AGRICULTURAL PRODUCTION PER CAPITA
1956–57 TO 1963–64
(1952–53 to 1956–57 = 100)

Country	1956–57	1957–58	1958–59	1959–60	1960–61	1961–62	1962–63	1963–64
Belgium-Luxembourg	99	105	108	100	109	107	116	116
France	100	99	100	106	116	108	117	113
West Germany	100	101	105	101	113	100	111	114
Italy	102	99	114	112	104	112	110	112
Netherlands	95	101	109	109	109	108	109	105

Source: FAO, *Production Yearbook*, no. 18, p. 34.

from 1956–57 to 1963–64. However, the great bulk of the increase was in livestock and livestock products. Nonetheless, with the rapid increase in demand for these products, the Community was less self-sufficient in 1962–63 than in 1950–53. While incomes have risen sharply in the EEC, they do not seem to have kept pace with family expenditures on food. Thus in West Germany expenditures on food for a typical family of four rose 106 percent from 1950 to 1963, by 25 percent from 1958 to 1963, and by 15 percent from 1960 to 1963.[5] Faced with a comparable situation, France has employed food price controls widely, and they are still in effect. The fact that food accounts for about 35 percent of family living expenditures, compared with 20–23 percent in North America, indicates that western Europe still suffers from high food costs.

The CAP must be regarded as a necessary part of an over-all integration of the six western European economies. The striking industrial achievement of the Community has had an important influence on the agriculture of the area. This is most clearly shown in the change in the composition of diets as a result of higher real incomes. Higher real incomes, the increased cost of marketing services, and increased farm prices have each contributed to the increased retail cost of food. Farm prices have generally risen less than either retail food prices or the cost of living, as indicated in Table VI. To some extent this has been due to the use of a "guided" food and agricultural pricing policy, including the use of consumer subsidies, in all member countries.

TABLE VI

SELECTED COUNTRIES, PERCENTAGE INCREASES IN
SELECTED INDEXES, 1958–64

Country	Farm prices	Retail food prices	Cost of living
France	18	9	8
Germany	11	14	14
Italy	11	17	24
Netherlands	13	22	19
Belgium	14	11	11
Canada	2	8	8
United States	−9	4	7

Source: FAO, *Production Yearbook*, 1965, pp. 432–6.

The widespread use of imported labour in the EEC is well known. This has had an unfavourable influence on the rationalization of agriculture.

[5]H. Hix, "Die Entwicklung der Nahrungsausgaben nach Verbrauchergruppen," *Agrarwirtschaft*, Heft 4, 1965, p. 202.

Were it not for this policy, the increased labour requirements for non-farm industries would have been drawn from the agricultural sector—a type of shift which has been perhaps the most important factor in speeding the rationalization of Canadian agriculture.

The following quotation from Professor John O. Coppock[6] stresses the difficulties of developing a common policy for an industry beset with countless protective devices:

. . . governments have put their national difficulties onto the international bargaining table without showing perceptible interest in "reform" of policies at home. Lacking this interest in taking national action to correct at least part of the international disarray, the discussions within an international framework have no prospect of important success. In this rather futile battle the main importing countries have the best of things. Their domestic agricultural policies may be, and normally are, as economically absurd as those of the exporting countries. . . . By using this (import) control, in conjunction with any of various techniques to tax imports, the net importing countries can sustain their structure of high farm prices internally with little difficulty, if they choose to do so—and most of them have so chosen.

The Common Market has settled most of its internal differences . . . that settlement, however, was wedded to a common policy clearly aimed at greater self-sufficiency with little regard for comparative costs.

Confronted with such an obviously difficult situation for Canadian agriculture, there are, nevertheless, reasons for a restrained optimism. First, continued rapid economic growth in the EEC will lead to a moderate growth in the demand for food through income effects alone. To this must be added population growth. Professor Sol Sinclair states that ". . . the growth of the economy of the EEC, both before and after the CAP, provides an opportunity to increased trade with non-member countries if the latter are willing to make some adjustment."[7] Second, there are already rumblings of discontent about the cost of supporting the farm industry of the EEC. These may increase, particularly if the Community were to suffer a recession of any seriousness, and might result in governmental measures to reduce these costs. In West Germany, France, and Benelux, there is discontent which blames the CAP for high food prices and threatened inflation. Third, to the extent that rationalization measures succeed, the agriculture of the EEC should become more competitive in an international context and thus require less in the way of subsidies. Finally, while the EEC may become a net exporter of wheat, all such exports will be of soft

[6]*Atlantic Agricultural Unity: Is It Possible?*, New York, McGraw-Hill, 1966, pp. 17 and 57.
[7]"EEC's Trade in Agricultural Products with Non-member Countries," in *International Journal of Agrarian Affairs*, IV, 5 (1965), p. 287.

wheat. Continued demand for Canadian (and other) hard wheats by the Community is expected, but probably in a declining trend.

Under section 110 of the Treaty of Rome, the EEC is committed to maintaining and expanding international trade. A more positive stricture is included in the provisions of GATT. As contracting parties to GATT, the Six, in forming a customs union, must adopt schedules of duties and other regulations of commerce which "shall not on the whole be higher or more restrictive than the general level of duties and regulations of the commerce" applicable before the customs union was established.[8]

Our final summary statement on the CAP is to emphasize its real costs expressed in a misallocation of resources and of higher food costs. An important aspect of the former is that, with a more liberal trade policy and larger food imports, much of the large investments made in agriculture, as well as a substantial part of current operating expenses, would be available for investment in more productive enterprises. This could clearly affect the capacity of the EEC countries to be competitive in international markets for industrial products.

Policies of Britain and other European Free Trade Association (EFTA) countries

Agriculture is exempted from the EFTA arrangements. Since Britain purchases more than 90 percent of Canada's exports to the Association countries, it is particularly important to consider the farm policies of that country. In 1965 total exports to EFTA countries were $359 million, of which $323 million went to Britain.

Generally the EFTA area developed out of fear among some of the outer seven countries that they would not be able to participate, even economically, in the EEC, but more particularly from a resistance to the original political implications of joining the Community.

The EFTA countries have a total population of 97 million and account for about 10 percent of world income. The countries are highly dependent on international trade, with exports accounting for 23 percent of gross national product. These countries have had a long history of close economic relationship. While the Stockholm Convention excludes farm products from its provisions for tariff reductions, it provides for increasing agricultural trade through bilateral arrangements. This has been of considerable advantage to Denmark and Portugal. Thus, in the early years of the Convention, agricultural products accounted for some 10 percent of total trade within the area. This figure has risen more than one-third—paralleling gains in non-agricultural trade.

[8]GATT, *Basic Instruments and Selected Documents*, III, Geneva, 1958, p. 48.

In postwar Britain the position of agriculture has been guaranteed by the Agricultural Act of 1947. Its basic purpose was to increase the level of self-sufficiency in food from one-third to more than one-half. Warrant for this has been in an appeal to defence policy, general social policy, and to an effort to conserve foreign exchange. The program mechanism has been very largely through deficiency payments. These in recent years have absorbed more than 60 percent of government expenditures on agriculture, which have recently run at $700–$1,000 million per year.

This system does not apply to horticultural crops, which are supported by seasonally variable levies, nor to eggs and milk, for which domestic prices are fixed and the consumer subsidizes the farmer directly. Payments to farmers to assist in making structural improvements (drainage, irrigation, etc.) have taken another 20 percent of total expenditures on agriculture by government, while direct aids, such as fertilizer subsidies, have accounted for some 15 percent. Cost to the government is equivalent to 70 to 80 percent of the net output of the industry. This fact of high support for an inefficient industry, plus the heavy drain on the treasury, has led to misgivings about the policy; over the past several years there has been a determined effort to hold the budgetary line and even to effect cutbacks. Some guaranteed prices have been reduced, and the "standard quantities" to which they apply have been limited. But on the latter it has been difficult to hold the line. However, the cost to the Treasury in 1965 and 1966 was about $700 million, and it was expected to rise to about $780 million in 1967.

Cereals policy is of great importance to Canada. Under a 1960 agreement, minimum import prices have been agreed upon between major export countries. The internal price was $2.04 (Can.) in 1965–66 on domestically produced wheat. Support at the full level of domestic wheat is presently limited to 127 million bushels per year, the standard quantity in the program. Exporting countries compete to fill the annual import quota. Levies are applied to imports other than those from Agreement countries— the levy serves to bring the landed price of imports up to the internal level. Canada is in an advantageous position because of the demand for high-protein wheat. The policy seeks to ensure the import position of traditional foreign suppliers, but in recent years the standard quantities (on which domestic subsidies apply) have been increased to cover increases in domestic requirements.

There has been a steady increase in acreage over the past five years— the 1965 figure exceeded nine million acres. Only if imports threaten to fall significantly below the nine million tons per year imported in the three years before June, 1964, does the government assure remedial action. At the present time the only hopeful notes for Canada's wheat exports to Britain are (1) an ability to bid for a larger share of the rather rigidly limited, and probably declining, total import quota, and (2) the less encouraging prospect for freer trade in the farm products that Britain and Europe import. Canadian wheat exports to Britain have already been declining, and it is not unlikely that Britain will within a year or two request a reduction in the nine-million-ton over-all import quota. Changing technology in the baking industry detracts from the advantage held by Canadian hard red wheats—and this could become a serious problem for Canada, not only in the British market, but in all her export markets. The implications of Britain's possible entry into the EEC will be considered later.

Canadian cheddar cheese, once a major Canadian export to Britain, is now exported in modest quantities, 20 to 30 million pounds a year, but under an export subsidy. It commands a 10 to 12 percent premium over pasteurized cheddars produced in New Zealand and England. Its position in the British market will become increasingly secure as British incomes rise. Apple exports from Canada to Britain, very important in the pre-1939 period, are now faced with an eighty-thousand-ton import quota from all dollar countries. Canada has been filling an increasing proportion of the quota. If Britain should overcome her balance of payments difficulties, the prospect for apple exports would be good.

As noted earlier, Britain is making a determined effort to rationalize her agriculture. This is regarded as a necessary aspect of her traditional cheap (at retail levels) food policy. Without substantial improvement in productivity, costs to the government could mount to clearly unacceptable levels. While output per worker increased by 6 percent per year (1960–64), this was achieved by means of heavy new investments—thus injuring in some measure other industries requiring capital. Even in the face of this encouraging improvement in labour productivity, when considered against the postwar experience of major agricultural exporters, it appears that Britain has lost ground relatively over the entire postwar period.

In the other EFTA countries—in fact, for the whole area—it is clear that over-all gains could be secured from freer trade in farm products. All employ tariffs and/or quantitative restraints, though these are practically non-existent in Denmark. Efforts to support farm incomes in that country have been pursued increasingly, though not by import restraints. In the Scandinavian countries, the emphasis of farm policy is on aiding families on small farms—and is thus just as much or more a matter of social as of agricultural policy. On the whole, Sweden, Switzerland, and Denmark have followed relatively liberal policies vis-à-vis their EFTA partners on agricultural products. Austria, Norway, and Finland have tended to be more protectionist, and their imports of farm products have increased little over the years this economic area has been in existence.

Denmark and Austria have been anxious to join the EEC if the terms were right; and, in fact, Austria has begun negotiations. Norway has also made overtures in that direction. Switzerland shows no enthusiasm for joining, while the position of Finland, because of her special relationship to Russia, is most uncertain.[9] But if Britain or Britain, Austria, and Denmark should join the EEC, EFTA would cease to have much economic meaning, and the other countries might be forced into some kind of associate membership.

Policies of the United States

While barriers to international trade in agricultural products were implicitly a part of the American agricultural adjustment legislation of the early 1930s, they did not become really serious until after the Second World War. Then the Havana Charter, which became the basis for GATT, clearly established exceptional treatment for agricultural products. This document, drafted in Washington, justified the use of export subsidies and import restrictions on farm products. Thus, more than any country up to that time, the United States placed agricultural products outside the scope of GATT negotiations. The "necessity" for such interventions arose from the United States' choosing (as the EEC has done in recent years) to protect farm incomes through supporting farm prices.

In briefest terms, for more than thirty years the United States has attempted to secure the income gains which would come from restriction of output of products whose demand is inelastic. And during the whole period the success of these measures has been frustrated by the slow growth of demand, by the advance of technology, and by structural changes in the industry. Even with vigorous efforts to restrain production, it has increased year by year, while farm prices in 1964 were below 1957–59 levels. But as noted elsewhere, 1965 and 1966 have seen significant increases in farm prices—and these may be sustained or even further increased. However, recent gains are due more to American economic development and to events abroad than to the farm policies of the United States.

The current programs in the United States had their origin in the Agricultural Act of 1933, which provided acreage allotments and price supports for "basic" farm products: wheat, corn, cotton, rice, tobacco, and peanuts. This was, and is, known as the "parity" program, since its

9See S. J. Wells, "EFTA—The End of the Transition," *Lloyds Bank Review*, no. 82, Oct. 1966, pp. 18–33.

objective was to bring the prices of these products into a farm-purchasing-power-parity relationship with the period 1910–14. Special land-use and rural-welfare programs were begun soon after 1933. Surpluses continued in the 1930s, but these became a national blessing during the Second World War. They appeared again in the late 1940s, and while some disappeared in the Korean War period, they became serious by 1954. In that year the surplus disposal law (the Agricultural Trade Development and Assistance Act, PL480), was passed, and within two years 40 percent of U.S. farm exports were moving under that program.[10] Continued difficulties from surpluses and low prices led to the Soil Bank program, begun in 1956. This provided for payments equivalent to rent for fifty to sixty million acres put in a conservation reserve and not cropped. During the later Eisenhower years, reduction in price supports on wheat and feed grains was accompanied by some general relaxation of production controls, and surpluses again became a serious problem, despite sales under PL480.

The policy developments which had been under way gradually for nearly a decade were formalized and extended in the Food and Agriculture Act of 1965. The emphasis in this legislation is on extending a two-price system, with high price supports limited to that part of production required for domestic consumption. For instance, the basic loan or support level in the case of wheat is $1.25 per bushel, which makes American wheat fully competitive in world markets. Domestic consumption of wheat is subsidized to the extent of $1.32 per bushel. Thus, in reality, a large export subsidy continues under the new program. The essence of the new arrangement is to substitute aggressive American competition in foreign markets for a policy of holding large commodity stocks in the hands of the government.

Accompanying these changes in domestic agricultural programs, the Food for Freedom Act of 1966 made generally consistent changes in the American food-aid and surplus-disposal operations. Emphasis was placed on expanding international trade in farm products, implicitly on a commercial basis. Local currency sales, which over the past ten years have accounted for almost two-thirds of all PL480 exports, are to be very largely phased out by 1971, by which time almost all concessional sales will be on the basis of long-term loans.

So much for a general overview intended to present the broadest outline of the American problem and policies over the years since 1945. The background of the problem rests not only in the cruelly distressing farm situation of the depression of the 1930s, but more deeply in history, and

---

[10]The Act provides for four types of programs. Title I covers sales for foreign currencies; Title II covers famine and relief; Title III includes domestic donations; and Title IV, long-term credit sales.

in the nature of agricultural development reflecting the particular resource and market problems of the American farmer. There was rural poverty in wide areas, the fluctuations of farm prices and incomes were erratic, and the gap in the living standards between the rural and the urban populations was extreme.

The United States is the world's largest exporter of agricultural commodities. Agricultural products account for about one-quarter of total U.S. exports. Several of its crops depend heavily on the export market. However, in general, the importance of farm exports and the range of commodities involved reflect much more the failure of crop-restriction programs than the comparative advantages of the various sectors of the industry.

The major crop exports and the percentage of total production of each important export in the 1965/66 fiscal year are presented in Table VII. The United States also had substantial exports of fruits and fruit preparations ($327 million), dairy products ($174 million), oilcake and meal ($216 million), tallow ($159 million), vegetables and preparations ($170 million), hides and skins ($139 million), poultry products ($72 million), variety meats ($56 million), and lard ($23 million). Total agricultural exports of the United States in the fiscal year 1965/66 were $6,681 million. This is the highest figure on record. Over the earlier years of the decade, agricultural exports varied from $4,517 million to $6,096 million.

While the U.S. government describes exports other than those under PL480 as commercial, moderate to large-scale subsidies have continued to

TABLE VII

UNITED STATES, AGRICULTURAL EXPORTS, 1965/66 FISCAL YEAR

Crop	Exports Quantity (millions)	Value (mil. $)	Percentage of crop exported	Percentage of crop exported under PL480 and AID*
Wheat and wheat flour	859 bus.	1,403	67	67
Feed grains	25.9 met. tons	1,383	47	9
Soybeans	257 bus.	734	30	1
Cotton	3.1 bales	386	20	26
Tobacco	472 lb.	395		27
Soybean and cottonseed oil	1,390 lb.	189	18	68
Rice	30.4 bags	222	48	32

Source: United States, Department of Agriculture, *Export Fact Sheet* and *Import Fact Sheet*, 1966.
*Agency for International Development.

apply to most of the price-supported products moving into competitive world markets.[11] Table VIII shows the unit and total subsidies required to move a selected group of commodities into commercial export markets in the fiscal year 1963/64. These, of course, are over and above PL480 subsidies. It will be noted that meats and livestock products (except dairy products) and fruits and vegetables are not included in Table VIII. Thus exports of these products are truly commercial.

TABLE VIII

UNITED STATES, EXPORT SUBSIDIES, 1963/64 FISCAL YEAR

Commodity	Unit	Payment per unit ($)	Payment total (mil. $)
Wheat and flour	bushel	.56	427
Cotton	bale	42.50	219
Rice	cwt.	2.28	71
Milk, non-fat, dry	pound	.082	55
Butter	pound	.34	35
Milkfat	pound	.42	5
Cheese	pound	.16	
Tobacco	pound	.193	3
Flaxseed	pound	.06	*
Peanuts	pound	.07	4
Total			820

Source: *International Federation of Agricultural Producers News*, July 1965, p. 3.
*Less than 0.5.

American farm exports do not clearly reflect the comparative-advantage position of the industry. Nor do production trends reflect domestic needs. Crop output in the United States has been increasing, in recent years, twice as rapidly as consumption of farm products. Although the prospect of overproduction has been moderated by phenomenal export demands (largely food for the developing countries), it will probably continue to be a problem. In addition to this, the oversupply of farmers and the trend to increased productivity in U.S. agriculture will aggravate the situation.

An examination of productivity trends in American agriculture indicates

[11]U.S. government publications euphemistically describe "commercial sales" as including "in addition to unassisted commercial transactions, shipments of some commodities with governmental assistance in the form of (1) credits for relatively short periods; (2) sales of government-owned commodities at less than domestic market prices; and (3) export payments in cash and kind." United States, Department of Agriculture, *Export Fact Sheet* and *Import Fact Sheet*, 1966. These subsidies have been employed on a very large scale over the past fifteen years.

tremendous advances over the past twenty years. Total production increased from an index value of 87 in 1949 to 115 in 1965 (1957–59 = 100), while total inputs showed almost no change. The composition and the quality of inputs, however, have been changing rapidly. This reflects the relative decline in the costs of farm inputs derived from the non-farm industrial sector, as compared with the wages of labour. Over the past fifteen years, relative to the cost of farm labour, the cost of fertilizer has dropped by 70 percent, that of farm machinery by 50 percent, and that of all capital inputs by 59 percent.[12]

TABLE IX

UNITED STATES, INDEX NUMBERS OF MAJOR INPUTS, 1949–64
(1957–59 = 100)

Year	Total input	Farm labour	Farm real estate	Mechanical power and machinery	Fertilizer and lime	Feed, seed, and livestock purchases*	Miscel-laneous
1949	101	152	95	80	61	69	82
1950	101	142	97	86	68	72	85
1951	104	143	98	92	73	80	88
1952	103	136	99	96	80	81	88
1953	103	131	99	97	83	80	91
1954	102	125	100	98	88	82	91
1955	102	120	100	99	90	86	94
1956	101	113	99	99	91	91	98
1957	99	104	100	100	94	93	95
1958	99	99	100	99	97	101	100
1959	102	97	100	101	109	106	105
1960	101	92	100	100	110	109	106
1961	101	89	100	99	114	123	109
1962	101	85	100	96	124	121	113
1963	102	83	101	99	132	124	115
1964	103	81	102	101	137	123	120

Source: *Economic Report of the President*, Washington, D.C., U.S. Government Printing Office, 1965, p. 279.
*Non-farm portion of feed, seed, and livestock purchases.

Thus the total labour input in American agriculture declined by 47 percent from 1949 to 1964; power and machinery inputs increased by 26 percent; fertilizer and lime, by 125 percent; purchased feed, seed, and livestock inputs, by 78 percent; and miscellaneous inputs, by 46 percent. These data are presented in Table IX. Accompanying these changes, the

[12]*U.S. Agriculture in 1980*, Ames, Iowa State University, 1966, p. 6.

number of farms declined by an estimated 40 percent, while the size of farms roughly doubled.

The consequences of the developments described may be summarized in terms of changes in productivity. The appropriate data are presented in Table X.

TABLE X

UNITED STATES, FARM OUTPUT PER
UNIT OF INPUT, 1949–65
(1957–59 = 100)

Year	Productivity index
1949–52	86
1953–56	93
1957–60	101
1961	106
1962	107
1963	110
1964	109
1965	112

Source: U.S., Department of Agriculture, *Agricultural Statistics*, 1965, p. 458, and earlier issues of the same annual.

While the productivity gains are modest—less than 2 percent per year—they are not unimpressive, considering that farm prices were depressed under the pressure of large surpluses during most of the period. (These productivity measures are all in deflated value terms.) However, when considered on the basis of labour productivity, the gains are much more striking. Over the period from 1949 to 1965, farm output per man-hour increased by 168 percent. This large increase of labour productivity indicates unmistakably the revolutionary changes occurring in the agricultural industries.

The changes which have occurred in American agriculture must be regarded as one of the most important economic phenomena of the postwar years. This statement is made in the context that even without export subsidies the vast surplus-producing agricultural industry of the United States will press its output on every world market and will probably increasingly expose the high economic and social costs involved in agricultural protectionism in Britain, western Europe, and other countries—including Canada.

There is little doubt that the pace of economic change which has transformed American agriculture in the postwar years will not only continue but will accelerate. Education, communication, and mobility among the regional and economic sectors are becoming more effective. Agriculture, once intractable, has become knowledgeable about, and acclimated to, the process of economic growth. And competition within the industry is gathering momentum as resources move into the hands of stronger managers.[13] Capital now represents 75 percent of all inputs, and it is projected that this figure will rise to 90 percent in twenty years or less. The Iowa study projects a decline of more than 50 percent in numbers of farmers and about 40 percent in the farm labour force by 1980. It also projects that the agriculture of 1980 could still produce large surpluses over domestic requirements.

The important implications that past and projected changes in the structure of American agriculture hold for prospects in agricultural trade are considered in a later chapter.

Canadian agricultural development and policies

Reference has been made to the extent and importance of agricultural exports in the Canadian economy and also to the relatively strong comparative advantage of Canadian agriculture in several important commodities. We turn now to an examination of the structure of the industry and of how structural changes may strengthen the position of agriculture in a world trade context.

In the period 1951–61, the amount of improved acreage in farmland increased by 7 percent, from 96.9 million acres to 103.4 million. This was mainly the result of an 11 percent expansion in the Prairie provinces. During the same period there was a decrease in the Maritimes, Quebec, and Ontario of 22, 11, and 5 percent, respectively. British Columbia increased improved acreage by 14 percent. With a large decline in the numbers of farms over the decade,[14] the average size of farms, as indicated in Table XI, increased very substantially—more than one-third for Canada as a whole. This by itself would obviously greatly strengthen the position of the farm industry, beset as it has historically been by problems of small scale and inadequate capitalization.

In a broad sense the relative strength of the agriculture of the various regions of Canada is revealed by measures showing the proportion of farm units which are too small or inadequately capitalized to allow efficient production. By an arbitrary definition it may be assumed that an adequately

[13]See *ibid*.
[14]Fourteen percent for Canada, based on the 1951 definition of a farm; 25 percent for the Atlantic provinces, 19 percent for Quebec, 20 percent for Ontario, 16 percent in the Prairie provinces, and 9 percent in British Columbia.

TABLE XI

CANADA AND REGIONS, AVERAGE SIZE OF FARMS
(acres)

Region	Total land			Improved land		
	1951	1961	Percentage change 1951–61	1951	1961	Percentage change 1951–61
Atlantic	123	132	7	37	55	49
Quebec	125	140	12	66	82	24
Ontario	139	149	7	85	99	14
Prairies	498	609	22	288	384	33
British Columbia	178	194	9	44	65	48
Canada	279	336	20	156	215	38

Source: *U.S. Census of Agriculture* and S. H. Lane, "Recent and Comparative Changes in Canadian Agriculture," Canadian Agricultural Economics Society, *Workshop Report*, 1963, p. 11.

TABLE XII

CANADA AND REGIONS, PERCENTAGE OF FARMS WITH ANNUAL SALES OF
$10,000 OR MORE, AND PERCENTAGE OF AGRICULTURAL OUTPUT
FROM SUCH FARMS, 1958

Region	Percentage of farms with annual sales of $10,000 or more	Sales by these farms as percentage of sales by all farms
Maritimes	3	20
Quebec	5	22
Ontario	14	45
Prairies	9	32
British Columbia	9	48
Canada	9	34

Source: J. M. Fitzpatrick and C. V. Parker, "Distribution of Income in Canadian Agriculture," p. 5 (mimeo).

capitalized farm might have annual sales of $10,000 or more. The proportion of census farms and the percentage of total farm sales in this category in 1958 are shown in Table XII. Thus only a small proportion of Canadian farms (from 3 to 14 percent, depending on the region) are adequately capitalized by this definition, and from 20 to 48 percent of agricultural output comes from such farms. The data reveal an important feature of the Canadian farm industry—the comparatively large output produced by the largest 9 percent of the farms. With size of farms increasing rapidly since 1958, the 9 percent largest farms at the present time would probably account for well over 40 percent of total sales.

Between 1951 and 1964, the labour force employed in agriculture declined by one-third, from 939,000 to 630,000, and accounted for less than 10 percent of the total labour force in 1964.[15] The downward trend took place in all provinces. The greatest reduction in the farm labour force was in Quebec, where it amounted to some 50 percent. Next was the Maritime provinces, with a 39 percent reduction. In Ontario, the Prairie region, and British Columbia, the labour force was reduced by 33, 23, and 21 percent, respectively.

The rate of decline is highly dependent on the nearby non-agriculture employment opportunities and on the rate at which mechanization of farm production increases. More people have left agriculture in regions where alternative job opportunities were available. According to Professor Lane, "Regionally, we find that Ontario and British Columbia offered the greatest opportunities for new employment during the decade 1951–61. Although there was an absolute growth in employment in the Prairie region during this period, the rate of growth was less than the national average."[16]

Capital inputs in agriculture may be divided into two groups, capital investments and operating expenses (exclusive of labour).

Table XIII shows the changes which took place in machinery and equipment investment between 1951 and 1961. The number of tractors increased by 30 percent in Canada. In general, the increase was greater in eastern Canada than in the West. The number of trucks used for farm purposes rose 54 percent in Canada during the same period. The number of grain combines increased by 72 percent. The increase in the Prairie provinces, although smaller than in the eastern provinces, was still very significant. In Manitoba and Saskatchewan the number of grain combines increased by 55 and 51 percent, respectively, whereas in Alberta the number rose by 85 percent.

In the same period, the number of electric motors increased by 126 percent, the largest increase taking place in the Prairie provinces. In 1961, the number of electrified farms in Canada was reported at 409,882. The percentage of farms making use of electric power in 1951 and in 1961 is shown by province in Table XIV.

As in other countries, the increase in purchased inputs is one of the most significant structural changes in agriculture in the postwar period. Purchased inputs are measured for Canada by the cash operating-expense

[15]Dominion Bureau of Statistics, *The Labour Force*, April 1965.
[16]Lane, "Recent and Comparative Changes in Canadian Agriculture," pp. 10, 12.

TABLE XIII

CANADA AND REGIONS, NUMBER OF FARM MACHINES AND EQUIPMENT, 1951 AND 1961

Item	Year	Maritimes	Quebec	Ontario	Prairie provinces	British Columbia	Canada
Automobiles	1951	19,288	41,602	114,870	141,337	12,557	329,667
	1961	18,526	55,385	110,773	158,938	14,322	357,944
Trucks	1951	12,650	19,167	41,486	113,512	9,291	196,122
	1961	14,590	26,597	62,812	185,983	12,004	302,012
Tractors	1951	12,430	31,971	105,204	236,930	13,148	399,683
	1961	4,351	70,697	150,046	290,700	16,974	549,789
Combines	1951	245	420	10,031	79,117	687	90,500
	1961	1,570	3,046	22,387	127,276	1,331	155,611
Balers	1951	—	—	—	—	—	—
	1961	4,081	13,212	28,061	41,488	2,679	89,522
Forage harvesters	1951	—	—	—	—	—	—
	1961	396	1,551	8,945	4,663	1,208	16,764
Milking machines	1951	4,188	17,632	37,464	8,770	3,129	70,883
	1961	6,553	34,724	44,284	17,191	3,365	106,119

Source: DBS, *Census of Agriculture*, 1951 and 1961.

TABLE XIV

CANADA AND REGIONS, PERCENTAGE OF FARMS
USING ELECTRIC POWER, 1951 AND 1961

Area	1951	1961
Newfoundland	38	66
Nova Scotia	71	91
Prince Edward Island	22	78
New Brunswick	60	96
Quebec	67	97
Ontario	74	95
Manitoba	48	90
Saskatchewan	16	66
Alberta	25	72
British Columbia	59	87
Canada	51	85

Source: Calculated from DBS, *Census of Agriculture*, 1951 and 1961.

item in DBS farm net income statistics. They increased by 63 percent from 1951 to 1964, while cash income from farming operations increased by only 22 percent. In fact, cash operating expenses now take up 85 and 83 percent of cash farm income in Nova Scotia and New Brunswick (Table XV). This leaves only 15 and 17 percent of cash income to be set against depreciation charges, interest on owned capital, and labour and management return—obviously entirely inadequate.

TABLE XV

CANADA AND REGIONS, OPERATING COSTS AS PERCENTAGE OF
CASH FARM RECEIPTS, 1951–64

Area	1951–54	1955–58	1959–61	1962–64
Prince Edward Island	55	61	66	72
Nova Scotia	86	76	80	85
New Brunswick	69	69	75	83
Quebec	54	64	71	70
Ontario	48	60	66	66
Manitoba	42	51	50	51
Saskatchewan	39	45	43	42
Alberta	43	46	46	49
British Columbia	71	62	63	59
Canada	47	54	57	57

Source: Compiled from DBS, *Quarterly Bulletin of Agricultural Statistics*, various numbers.

One of the largest inputs included in operating costs is fertilizer. Table XVI shows the fertilizer expenditures in constant dollars (1935–39 = 100) between 1951 and 1964. Total expenditures on fertilizer between the periods 1951–54 and 1962–64 increased by 84 percent; the most significant increases took place in Alberta, Saskatchewan, and British Columbia. In Alberta the fertilizer input in real terms rose by 340 percent; in Saskatchewan, by 146 percent; and in British Columbia, by 105 percent. The lowest increases occurred in the Maritime provinces.

TABLE XVI

CANADA AND REGIONS, FERTILIZER EXPENDITURES, 1951–64

Area	1951–54	1955–58	1959–61	1962–64	Percentage increase 1951–54 to 1962–64
Prince Edward Island	1,390	1,650	1,648	1,686	21
Nova Scotia	1,023	924	967	1,100	8
New Brunswick	2,200	2,085	2,182	2,237	2
Quebec	4,426	5,054	6,872	8,136	84
Ontario	13,600	15,755	18,242	24,099	77
Manitoba	1,597	976	1,506	2,450	43
Saskatchewan	1,839	1,249	2,052	4,518	146
Alberta	1,955	2,051	4,230	8,596	340
British Columbia	1,337	1,577	2,029	2,536	105
Canada	29,075	31,111	38,955	53,544	84

Source: Computed from farm income data in DBS, *Quarterly Bulletin of Agricultural Statistics*, various numbers.

The number of milk cows changed little over the period 1951 to 1964. A slight downward trend is evident in the Maritime provinces, Manitoba, and Saskatchewan, offset by a small upward trend in Quebec and British Columbia. Cattle other than milk cows show a definite increase in Canada. From just over five million head in 1951, the number increased to over nine million head in 1964. The most significant increase took place in the Prairie provinces, where the number has more than doubled since 1951. However, upward trends are also shown in the other provinces. The number of hogs, although fluctuating cyclically, has been fairly constant since 1951. The small number of sheep in Canada has also changed very little since 1951.

In an important work on the changing input structure and productivity of Canadian agriculture,[17] I. F. Furniss provides measures respecting eight

[17]"Productivity Trends in Canadian Agriculture, 1935–64," *Canadian Farm Economics*, vol. I, no. 1 (1966).

TABLE XVII

INDEXES OF INPUTS, BY SELECTED CATEGORIES, 1939–65
(1949 = 100)

Year	Real estate*	Labour†	Capital							Total capital	Total inputs
			Machinery and equipment‡	Livestock§	Purchased feed and seed	Fertilizer and limestone	Electric power	Miscellaneous‖			
1935–39	112	137	52	102	41	34	22	61	53	106
1945	99.4	99.1	77.0	118.4	106.7	75.3	40.6	67.2	87.5	95.5
1946	103.3	110.1	82.4	114.8	125.3	80.5	53.1	87.0	97.5	104.8
1947	102.7	104.2	87.4	110.1	147.7	87.7	63.9	99.2	107.6	105.0
1948	101.3	101.8	93.2	91.4	108.0	89.5	82.3	103.5	98.1	100.5
1949	100.0	100.0	100.0	100.0	100.0	100.0	100.0	100.0	100.0	100.0
1950	98.3	94.5	114.5	101.1	93.5	102.4	128.4	98.7	105.4	98.7
1951	96.9	87.7	110.6	115.5	95.0	106.2	153.0	95.3	105.0	94.8
1952	96.6	82.7	115.0	124.9	93.4	101.4	173.6	91.4	107.0	93.2
1953	102.0	79.7	122.5	114.6	89.8	115.2	199.3	87.9	109.1	93.4
1954	101.9	81.5	123.5	108.3	102.5	110.6	228.2	87.6	112.7	95.4
1955	103.9	76.0	125.0	116.2	100.7	106.0	247.6	94.8	114.2	93.6
1956	104.2	72.1	124.8	112.7	121.1	109.2	274.5	97.5	120.2	93.7
1957	102.7	69.4	124.3	114.3	114.4	111.4	297.6	90.8	117.8	91.3
1958	107.3	66.7	123.1	132.0	139.4	120.6	318.9	89.9	126.1	93.5
1959	109.6	65.0	124.4	140.6	139.2	132.6	342.6	98.2	128.8	94.0
1960	110.8	63.4	126.4	138.4	136.0	134.4	354.4	101.2	129.1	93.5
1961	111.9	63.2	123.1	143.9	131.3	154.5	369.3	108.8	128.3	93.4
1962	114.2	61.3	128.7	139.8	131.5	168.0	403.0	108.8	131.5	93.9
1963	114.4	60.2	133.2	149.7	141.9	188.5	421.8	118.5	139.3	96.0
1964	114.0	58.5	136.9	158.3	150.2	225.4	435.3	123.0	146.2	97.2
1965	115.6	55.2	141.2	142.0	164.7	243.2	458.3	118.9	151.6	97.6

*Includes interest on investment, depreciation and repairs on buildings, and property taxes, all for both owned and rented real estate.

†Total farm labour force (farm operators, unpaid family labour, and hired labour).

‡Includes fuel and other purchased items associated with machinery operation plus interest on investment and depreciation.

§Interest on investment in livestock and purchased livestock.

‖Includes fruit and vegetable containers, nursery stock, veterinary, twine, irrigation charges, pesticides, fencing, breeding fees, and other miscellaneous purchased goods and services.

inputs. His data are presented in Table XVII. They show labour input to have been reduced nearly 50 percent since the first postwar quinquennium. Total capital inputs rose by a similar proportion over the same period. Among the capital inputs, fertilizer increased about 165 percent. This is one of the most significant structural changes in Canadian agriculture. While the percentage increase in the input of electricity is considerably greater, this particular input still accounts for a very small part of total inputs. The study cited shows that labour now accounts for about 30 percent of total inputs, down from 50 percent in the 1945–49 period. On the other hand, total capital inputs now represent about one-half of all inputs, up from 30 percent in 1945–49. This switch in relative importance of these groups of inputs, paralleling that of the United States, measures the modernization of the farm industry. This trend will continue, its rapidity depending on the rate of growth of the non-farm economy. As it proceeds, agriculture will become more commercial in character and less oriented to the labour of the family farm.

The increased importance of capital inputs, especially fertilizer, has resulted in apparent increases in yields per acre. The relevant data are presented in Table XVIII. However, one must take account of the fact

TABLE XVIII

YIELDS PER ACRE, SELECTED CROPS,
ANNUAL AVERAGES, 1926–55 AND 1956–64
(bushels per acre)

Crop	1926–55	1956–64
Wheat	16.6	20.0
Oats	30.6	40.7
Barley	23.8	28.2
Rye	13.2	16.5

Source: DBS, *Handbook of Agricultural Statistics* and *Quarterly Bulletin of Agricultural Statistics*

that weather conditions were more favourable in the latter period. In fact, one is surprised by the relatively smaller yield increases in Canada, compared with those of the United States. This clearly reflects on the relative strength of the agriculture of the two countries and represents a major challenge to Canadian farmers and equally to the scientific programs on which they depend for higher yields.

W. M. Drummond and William MacKenzie[18] found, for the period

[18]*Progress and Prospects for Canadian Agriculture*, Ottawa, Queen's Printer, 1958, p. 84.

1935–39 to 1955, an increase of about 24 percent in output per hog and of about 26 percent for beef. In the present research, it has been impossible to secure fully comparable data. However, preliminary work suggests a continuation of productivity gains, but at a slightly lower rate (see Table XIX).

TABLE XIX

CANADA, PRODUCTIVITY IN
AGRICULTURE, 1953–64
(constant 1949 dollars per man-hour)

Year	Productivity
1953	0.98
1954	0.76
1955	0.99
1960	0.91
1961	0.82
1962	1.13
1963	1.30
1964	1.25

Source: 1953–55 data: Hood and Scott, *Output, Labour and Capital in the Canadian Economy*, p. 399; 1960–64 data: rough extension of Hood and Scott data by authors of present study (see text).

William Hood and Anthony Scott, in their constant-dollar estimates (1949 dollars) of gross domestic product in Canadian agriculture over the period 1926–55, found that productivity measured in constant 1949 dollars per man-hour rose from $0.58 to $0.99 over the years 1946–55.[19] This is a good measure of the results of the sweeping structural changes in Canadian agriculture over these years. We have attempted an extension of this measure, although the result must necessarily be rough, since data on hours of work per week or per man-year are not available. We have arbitrarily estimated that farm labour works fifty-five hours per week, fifty weeks per year. The results are shown in Table XIX.

A generally comparable measure for the United States was presented earlier in this study. It showed a 168 percent increase in product per man-hour from 1949 through 1965. Over those years American agriculture became relatively more capital-intensive. This in part accounts for the

[19]*Output, Labour and Capital in the Canadian Economy*, Royal Commission on Canada's Economic Prospects, Ottawa, 1955, chap. v, Appendix F.

above results. Further, the U.S. industry was only partially exposed to the forces of world competition. In terms of over-all productivity Canadian agriculture shows up very well. Furniss shows that in terms of value output per unit of composite input, Canadian farm productivity increased at a compound rate of more than 2 percent per year over the past fifteen years, while that of the United States increased at a rate of less than 2 percent per year. The low rate of gain reflects more than anything else the fact that farm product prices in both countries were unresponsive to economic development.

In any assessment of Canada's prospective position in international markets, wheat is naturally of major importance. This fact has both favourable and unfavourable features. Each of the last five crops was extremely large and would normally result in marketing difficulties. However, these large crops coincided with the very large-scale entry of the USSR, China, and eastern European countries into the Canadian market. In fact, in Canada's booming export trade in 1964, wheat was our largest export, and most of that went to the areas named above. Thus, year-end carry-over has not developed into a serious problem. It would have been extremely serious were it not for purchases by the Communist countries.

The trend of exports to traditional markets in western Europe and Japan has been slowly declining for the past five years. This is a serious matter, since the prospect is that the decline may continue and even be accelerated by technological developments in milling that apparently will detract from the advantage of Canada's high-protein wheat. In these markets, Canada has been faced with competition of subsidized American wheat, with surpluses of French wheat looking for a home, and with governmental pressures on western European and British millers to use a smaller proportion of Canadian wheat in flour mixes.

In addition, the Communist countries are under tremendous pressure to reach a state of self-sufficiency in food grains, and they clearly have the land resources to realize this. The prospect is that over the next five to ten years most of these countries will reach self-sufficiency, or at least will not provide the very large markets they have in recent years. Thus, over the longer period, Canada may face increasing difficulties in marketing large wheat crops.

Canada's shipments of wheat to the developing countries, both in an external-aid and in a commercial-sales context, have increased sharply. The prospect is that the demand for food grains in both spheres will increase rapidly. On the one hand, nothing could stimulate commercial wheat exports more rapidly than well-based economic development. On the other, if these countries fail to secure economic development and at the same time experience rapid population growth, the need for foreign aid will increasingly take the form of food-grain shipments. Both will assuredly be of great importance over the next decade or two. Further, oilseed crops are coming to occupy an increasingly important role in Canadian agriculture. The 1966 acreage of 3.7 million was the highest on record, and there is evidence that the improvement in production technology in Canada will make these crops increasingly competitive in international trade. With a moderate expansion of the demand for livestock products on this continent, it is our judgment that the wheat area of Canadian agriculture can make the prospective adjustments (favourable or unfavourable) which may face this sector of agriculture.

The only other important sector of Canadian agriculture which faces possible significant adjustment in the light of international trade considerations is the dairy industry. Of course, the fluid sector of the industry, which uses nearly 40 percent of the milk leaving farms, is protected by a tangle of provincial and municipal restraints. Butter production, which takes up more than 30 percent of total milk production, is exceedingly inefficient, and returns to labour and capital are generally very low despite a butter price roughly twice that in competitive world markets. In cheddar cheese, on the other hand, Canada has a clear and large comparative advantage but is restrained by the virtual prohibition on exports to the United States and by restraints imposed by other countries. However, with some relaxation of trade barriers and the resultant diversion of manufacturing milk from butter to cheese, most of the difficulties would disappear. Judging by the cost of present producer and consumer subsidies to manufacturing milk, Canada could afford to make substantial concessions to secure wider markets for cheddar cheese.

Certainly the present maze of municipal, provincial, and federal restraints and subsidies, whose incidence can be seen only dimly, is neither conveying adequate returns to farmers nor assisting in the needed adjustments of the industry. It is significant that the United States, faced with a similar market situation and an equally inelastic supply, has increasingly (and with success) turned these problems over to the market.

The development of Canadian agriculture reflects in no small degree the types of farm policy which have been embraced by the country. In its historical context, policy was largely concerned with the conquest and settlement of the Prairie frontier area, with the provision of rail transport services involving special tariffs for export grains, and with the restricting influences on agricultural development of the national (tariff) policy beginning in 1879.

In the first four decades of the present century—until the Second World War—emphasis in farm policy was on (1) maintaining a market economy in the agricultural sector, (2) education, extension, and research—all in the public sector, (3) public provision of farm credit, with the purpose of strengthening the family farm, (4) grading and inspection services and public assistance in the provision of warehousing and processing facilities, and (5) aids to the cooperative movement and authorization of the creation of provincially oriented marketing boards.

Such policies made only limited contributions to raising or stabilizing farm incomes. Thus, policies of the 1930s and the post-1939 period put emphasis on these areas. In 1935 the monopoly Canadian Wheat Board was created, a modest crop-insurance scheme for Prairie farmers was inaugurated, and, after the war, price supports on an increasing range of products were introduced. To these measures has been added the Agricultural Rehabilitation and Development program (ARDA), the purpose of which is to lead the way in land and human-resource adjustment in the chronically low-income areas of Canadian agriculture.

As in the United States, farm income has not responded to the fairly rigorous policies employed. In fact, the real income of the industry fell substantially throughout more than a decade of the 1950s and into the 1960s. The consequences were moderated when viewed on the basis of the farm family and entirely overcome when considered on a per worker basis. But at the same time real incomes of non-farm workers were rising substantially. However, as noted earlier, when incomes of farm people from non-farm sources are included, the situation of farm families is shown to be significantly improved.

Canadian agriculture has clearly suffered from the restrictive Canadian trade policies and those of actual and potential importers. Even the most protected sector, the dairy industry, produces very low incomes per worker. And typically incomes have been highest in the export sectors of the Canadian farm industry. On the cost side, the industry's comparative-advantage position is worsened by the tariff on some types of agricultural equipment, on corn, and on other feeds. This suggests that revision of tariff policy would be to the advantage of Canadian agriculture—even if the adjustments were made on a unilateral basis.

We must accept the judgment of Dr. John A. Dawson[20] that, compared to other major agricultural countries, the performance of Canadian agriculture has been very satisfactory. Dawson's main point is that Canadian policy, with relatively minor supports for farm prices and income, has permitted rapid structural adjustments, essentially in a market context. At the same time he is aware that the low incomes in large sectors of Canadian agriculture represent an important policy problem.

[20]"The Performance of Canadian Agriculture," *Agricultural Institute Reviewer*, XXI, May–June 1966, p. 18.

IV. Possibilities and Strategy for Freer Trade

In this exceedingly difficult area, consideration must be given to the prospects for achieving freer trade in farm products by any of the following means, or by combinations of means: (1) multilateral GATT negotiations; (2) the development of additional blocs, or groups such as the EEC, EFTA, Comecon, or the Latin American Free Trade Area; (3) the prospect that the continuing improvement in cost-price relationships, especially in North American agriculture, will make possible, or even require, relaxation of quantitative import controls and make domestic farm aid programs less needed and less costly; (4) further erosion of British preferences; (5) unilateral tariff reduction by individual countries; (6) reductions in barriers of a non-tariff, non-quota character; (7) the development of a commodity approach to aiding in the expansion of exports from the less developed countries; (8) commodity agreements; and (9) the use of appropriate transition periods. These will be considered in order.

1. There is little doubt that the EEC was the most important negotiating party in the Kennedy round of negotiations in agriculture. Neither can we doubt that negotiations concerning grain were crucial to the success of the Kennedy round. The United States, Canada, and other grain exporters were anxious to secure the opportunity to continue to supply similar quantities of grain to the major importing countries. However, their efforts were thwarted. The Common Agricultural Policy of the EEC, which was then being arranged, set target prices on many commodities, including grains, above world market prices. In addition, Britain's precarious balance of payments position and attempted entry into the EEC militated against acceptance of any access-to-markets proposals.

No real progress was made in the Kennedy round negotiations on grain and other agricultural products with respect to domestic agricultural policy. Nevertheless, a substantial proportion of Canada's agricultural trade has been affected. The conclusion of the cereals agreement, significant reductions in tariffs on Canadian-U.S. agricultural trade, and a new anti-dumping code all have significant implications for Canadian agriculture. The Kennedy round, at the very least, brought into focus the nature of the problem of agricultural trade liberalization, which centres on acceptance by the major trading nations of some limitation on their freedom of action in domestic agricultural policies. Without this, future negotiations are futile.

2. We should not rule out the prospect for the development of further trading blocs involving two or more Atlantic countries, or among other regions whose integration might concern Canada's agricultural trade. Already, we have the example of the British-Irish arrangement, under

which free trade will extend to all commodities by 1975. There is increasing interest in the development of a Canada–United States free trade area. The possible contribution that such an agreement might make to the rate of Canada's economic growth is emphasized. It is most important that this opportunity be continually studied. It has been suggested that the Caribbean area might be included. The writers present the opinion that, given adequate time for adjustment—ten to fifteen years—Canadian agriculture could make an almost complete adjustment to free trade with the United States, but that if the Caribbean area were included, the area might require a twenty-year adjustment period.

3. The fact that farm prices in Canada showed a sharp increase of over 10 percent during a recent period of two to three years[1] is of the greatest importance. Farm prices in the United States increased similarly over the years 1964–66. The prospect that this improvement will continue over a decade is equally important, since it would provide a very favourable climate in which these countries might address themselves to the many constructive possibilities for expansion of trade in farm products.

The increase in farm prices has come about by (a) an expansion in exports, particularly to Russia, China, and the developing countries, (b) the structural changes in agriculture, and (c) the farm programs of the United States, which, after showing little in the way of price and income improvement over many years, have in the past four years increasingly affected supply and demand relationships for an increasing number of important commodity groups. This has resulted partly from the industrial prosperity of the 1960s, which accelerated the adjustments within agriculture. The war in Viet Nam is also a factor.

It is most significant that wheat stocks in the United States at the end of the 1965–66 crop year were well below the strategic reserve levels established by the Secretary of Agriculture. The following year, American wheat acreage allotments were expanded more than 30 percent. But growers, fearful of possibly declining prices, increased their seeded acreage by only 20 percent. This can be taken as evidence that, within the context of the still government-supported prices, wheat farmers are consciously attempting to plant an acreage of wheat that maximizes their returns. Acreage restrictions still exist, but they do not restrict. It is also most significant that American surpluses of dairy products have disappeared and probably will not recur. In addition, the livestock and fruit and vegetable sectors of American agriculture have for many years operated in an essentially free market climate.

[1]The increase was 11 percent between the average for 1964 and the month of July, 1966, and since this increase was greater than the rise in farm costs, the result was a reversal of the unfavourable terms of trade.

Here, then, we have in this greatest agricultural country, and the country whose domestic farm programs were the greatest barrier to increased trade, a new situation—and one much more favourable to pursuing the objectives with which this study is concerned.

4. The GATT encourages dismantling of the British preferential system. These preferences apply to only about 5 percent of Canada's farm exports to Britain. Their disappearance would make little difference, apart from providing a better atmosphere for embracing opportunities for a more constructive and positive negotiation on more fundamental issues. For Canada, the loss of British preferences on farm products would be far more than offset if the British were in a position to remove quantitative and other restrictions on food imports.

5. The scope for unilateral tariff reductions should not be underestimated. There are surely situations where a tariff reduction (without reciprocal action) is clearly to the advantage of a country. Canada recently took such action in regard to sugar imports from the West Indies. The freeing of Canadian farmers from farm-machinery tariffs—one of the most constructive trade measures of the past twenty-five years—was unilateral. And there remains considerable scope for such action. The clearest cases today are for the removal of the 22½ percent duty on dairy, poultry, and other equipment and for removal of the import duty of 8 cents per bushel on corn. Rather than being likely to worsen Canada's balance of payments difficulties, the removal of the above-mentioned duties would seem likely to have the opposite effect. These duties (and there are others) tend to worsen Canada's comparative-advantage position. For instance, Canada's farm exports to the United States are still at about 1950–54 levels, while her imports of farm products from the United States have increased by 65 percent. And only to a moderate degree is this due to increased American restrictions on imports over these years. Removal of restrictions might include unilateral concessions for tropical products entering the more developed countries. Recent literature suggests that this might be an important one of the several approaches available for aiding the developing countries through trade.

6. There is also scope for attacking trade barriers other than tariffs and quotas. As noted elsewhere, the EEC negotiators may be prepared to negotiate on the basis of freezing domestic subsidies at present levels. This would at least put the question of domestic subsidies to agriculture on the bargaining table. This would represent a considerable advance, since although they represented the basis for restraints on trade, they have not as yet been regarded as an area for international negotiation. Even between Canada and the United States there are many real barriers to trade (apart

from tariffs and quotas), largely in the areas of health and transportation regulations. These must be subject to continuing negotiation, and, in the case of Canada, there must be an improvement in health regulations applicable to food.

7. The more developed countries are under strong pressure to open their markets on a wider basis to the export crops of the less developed countries. Limited progress has been made through UNCTAD, but much remains to be achieved. It is quite possible that, for some developing countries and for some products, unilateral action by the more developed countries is the *least expensive* means for providing economic development assistance.

8. Commodity agreements, by providing a measure of price and output stability, represent a useful supplement to other means of expanding trade in some farm products. Opportunities in this area should be explored, but it should be noted that, thus far, agreements have applied only to commodities subject to extremely erratic fluctuations in price, e.g., wheat, sugar, coffee. They also require very strong support from producers in the exporting countries, and it is unlikely that this would be forthcoming for livestock products and even for feed grains.

The International Wheat Agreement (IWA) is most important to Canada, since it is the only agreement in which Canada participates as an exporter. The IWA obliges exporters to sell (and importers to take) specific quantities of wheat at the negotiated maximum (minimum) prices if market prices move outside the negotiated range of prices. Only in the first of the five agreements (which covered the period 1949–52) did market prices move outside the negotiated range—and on that occasion in favour of the importers. The United States has carried out its vast PL480 subsidized export program from 1955 to the present without reference to the IWA. In fact, the inability to include production restraints in any agreement is often cited as the major weakness of the IWA. Largely because of the large contracts negotiated between Canada and mainland China and because of Canada's reduced stocks, it was possible to secure an increase in the price range under the 1962 agreement.

The new wheat agreement should come into effect in August, 1968. It covers the principal grades of wheat grown in the leading wheat-exporting countries and will provide for higher price ranges for ten of the major grades. The increase in the negotiated range of prices is often wrongly read as automatically assuring an increase in the price of wheat. While an increase in the IWA range has a somewhat bullish effect on market prices, it does no more than confirm prospective supply-demand conditions existing at the time of the negotiations.

Perhaps the most important contribution of the IWA is to provide a continuing forum for discussion of wheat-marketing problems. In its price and guaranteed-quantities provisions, it has largely reflected what a group of tough bargainers representing importer and exporter countries consider would happen in the absence of an agreement. It has almost entirely avoided any approach to restructuring the world wheat industry on a more economic basis.

9. In any review of strategy considerations respecting the opportunity to expand trade in agricultural products, the concept of a transition period must occupy a central place. Only with such periods—and in some cases they may seem long—could progress be made in facing the realities of expanding trade. This reflects the nature of resources presently employed in agriculture, many of which would become redundant in a world seeking the gains of international specialization. This could be illustrated with the adjustments which would be required of the wheat industry in Britain and Europe, of sugar beet production everywhere, of parts of the Canadian dairy and fruit and vegetable industries. But land resources are substitutable, and other fixed investments can be adjusted out of (economic) existence in periods of five, ten, and very seldom more than fifteen years. A profitable area for farm policy, and particularly for farm-policy research, is to assess the most economic means for making such adjustments in each country concerned.

Uniting agriculture: negotiation, accommodation, and harmonization

Agriculture will continue to represent the most serious barrier to Atlantic economic unity. But with the completion of the Kennedy round and with the imminence of the full implementation of the CAP, we now, for the first time in ten years, face a somewhat stabilized situation. The task now is to provide the analysis of that new situation and to proceed to studies of the gains that might be realized from integration of agriculture in the North Atlantic area. The new situation will be difficult. After a ten-year struggle to shape the CAP, there is understandable reluctance by the EEC to discuss the gains from freer trade.

However, the situation of American agriculture in the context of trade-policy discussions is more promising than it has been for forty years. It should be possible to accommodate American insistence on expanding agricultural trade—a policy on which the United States now places the highest priority. Canada has not been particularly vocal on the issue of trade, but after observing the obviously great benefit of expanded wheat sales, she may seriously consider trade-policy changes which would lead at once to strengthening her domestic agriculture and expanding her exports.

Perhaps of all groups in the North Atlantic, the EFTA countries would be the ones most willing to negotiate on agricultural trade. Certainly Britain's willingness to face the prospect of membership in the Common Market would suggest her readiness to negotiate on the basis of a wider trading group. This study has stressed the very high costs Britain would have to face in joining the EEC. Any conceivable North Atlantic arrangement would be far less costly.

One of the most promising bases for considering freer trade in a North Atlantic area is food aid for developing countries. The need for this aid is already great and will doubtless increase over the next two decades. Again the advantages of an intergovernmental approach are obvious. Further, the UNCTAD represents a most advantageous platform from which to launch the idea of an intergovernmental approach. Under such a plan, with the North Atlantic countries leading and providing most of the required resources, the problem of farm surpluses (which have led to most of the barriers to trade in farm products) could be handled in an appropriate manner. The countries of the North Atlantic, and others, could very well, within the context of foreign aid, commit themselves to providing food in kind and/or foreign exchange resources for the purchase of food. In fact, the EEC Agricultural Guidance and Guarantee Fund in some respects provides a guideline to the approach required. Because of the priority given to grains in food aid, this program would be directed particularly to the sector of agriculture where surpluses have been largest over the postwar years. The scale of food aid requirements is of an order that would exhaust surplus production. In fact, they are of a scale that would probably require conscious production decisions to meet these needs. The ending of a surplus situation would provide a climate in which reduction of trade barriers could realistically be faced. And the systematic diversion of farm products into the aid channel would encourage an adjustment of agricultural production patterns in a manner consistent with an economic use of resources. In such a climate the harmonization of presently divergent farm policies would be possible.

The foregoing paragraphs have considered the climate, largely political and institutional, which would render certain strategies for expanding trade not only necessary from the standpoint of overcoming economic difficulties or achieving economic benefits, but also necessary from the standpoint of hoping to win acceptance at a political level. Postwar trade negotiations are replete with examples of how important it is to develop strategies that take account of the realities of political, historical, and institutional barriers to trade. When the very substantial gains in returns to resources and to consumers from a more rational pattern of resource use are widely known, there will probably arise a strong and effective desire to press ahead with strategies for achieving these gains.

V. Implications of Freer Trade in Farm Products

We proceed now to bring this study together by examining the implications of freer trade in agricultural products among North Atlantic countries. The case for the obvious gains has already been suggested, largely in our references to two recent authoritative studies[1] on comparative advantage.

In summary terms, the advantage rests in wheat, oilseeds, live cattle, cheddar cheese, some fruits and vegetables, and, at times, meats. Thus, if a move towards freer trade were made, we should observe adjustments which would lead to increased resources being employed in these areas, and fewer in butter, some fruits and vegetables, mutton, lamb and wool, and of course sugar beets (in which perhaps no resources would be retained). Because of the readiness with which land can undertake substitutions of one crop for another, the transition to a new agriculture is not as difficult as might be expected. Of course, there are the problems of skills and of the "set ways" of the farmer. It is to meet these problems that a transition period is suggested. Canada would expand wheat production in the Prairies by millions of acres at the expense of feed grains, hogs, and dairy products. According to comparative-cost studies, Canadian wheat would expand until a point was reached where the marginal cost would make further expansion uneconomic. Oilseeds would follow a similar trend.

In eastern Canada, livestock production would increase significantly, as would feed-grain production. Cheese output would double to treble in a few years, employing resources presently used in butter. Production of some fruits and vegetables would expand significantly, while for other products in this group there would be large reductions. Such reductions might leave local or regional problems of a fairly serious nature—and these would have to be dealt with on a special basis. Maritime agriculture would probably continue to decline, whether or not trade were freed. But if it were, there would be very large gains for apple and potato producers and for producers of other fruits and vegetables. The vigorous economic development programs for the non-farm sector of the Atlantic area will surely expand total demand in the region's domestic markets, and this would greatly ease the restructuring and rationalization of agriculture during a transition to freer trade. On the whole, farm incomes should rise considerably under the circumstances suggested above.

[1]The study by G. I. Trant in the present volume; and MacEachern and MacFarlane, "The Relative Position of Canadian Agriculture in World Trade."

Canada's comparative-advantage position has clearly worsened over the past ten years. This makes it imperative to consider domestic and foreign trade policies which would at least allow us to recapture the position of the mid-1950s. The most striking evidence of our worsening position is to be seen by comparing recent data with data for 1950–54. Canadian agricultural exports to the United States in 1950–54 averaged some $290 million annually and exceeded imports from that country. By 1966 Canadian exports to the United States had declined to about $240 million, while imports from that country had risen to $480 million. A part of this widening of the gap, but no more than one-quarter to one-third, was due to arbitrary import restrictions imposed by the United States. The balance represents a genuine loss of comparative advantage and should be regarded with major concern by Canadians. An equally striking measure of the worsening position of agriculture is that, whereas in 1950 more than 40 percent of Canadian exports to the United States were farm products, by 1966 this proportion had dropped almost to 20 percent. Of course, as has already been suggested, some of this decline was due to quantitative restrictions of farm imports into the United States.

In the United States perhaps the largest expansion of output would be in feed grains. This, in turn, would come about largely by freeing land now held in the Soil Bank. It is also possible that wheat acreage in some high-cost areas in the country would decline. Soybean acreage might decline as export subsidies on that crop were removed or reduced. Cotton, tobacco, and peanuts, important in the southern United States, would be little affected if the freer trade area were limited to North Atlantic countries.

The income effects of freer international trade are difficult to project for the United States because the effects of such a move on government payments to farmers and on other bases of support are difficult to assess. Again we must think in terms of a transition period, since it would be unrealistic to think of dismantling the vast American farm programs in a short period. However, we have already been heartened by the increasing proportion of American agriculture that has moved into a market context. Freeing trade would clearly speed that process. We are also impressed with the general optimism of American specialists, not only about the expected expansion of world food exports, but also about the capacity of the United States to realize rapid gains in exports on a commercial basis.

Studies of comparative costs in agriculture in the EEC and EFTA countries are not available. But there is a basis for fairly well-informed judgments. A rapid rationalization of the agriculture of most of these areas is essential if their agricultural efficiency is not to fall increasingly behind that of North America. While there are programs for structural improvement of agriculture in both cases, these programs are generally accompanied by other farm policies (price and income supports) which discourage the needed changes. However, the actual programs and market forces have combined to effect substantial rationalization. Some writers feel that in choosing to import unskilled and semi-skilled industrial workers from Mediterranean countries into the EEC, the Community passed up an opportunity to improve the efficiency of its agriculture through the substitution of capital for labour.

But the agriculture of western Europe and Britain is not to be written off. The land resources are fairly good to very good. The difficulty lies (understandably) in more than one hundred years of policies that have, in effect, been contrived to prevent a more economic organization of the farm industry. And the CAP continues such policies. In a competitive context, EEC production of fruits, vegetables, and other specialty crops would be fully viable, and so would a large livestock industry. Again in a free market there would be less, but still very substantial, wheat production in France. We are not suggesting an immediate free market—but rather that, with an adequately long transition, such changes could be effected satisfactorily, from the standpoint of the EEC agricultural industry. And considering the cost to consumers of the CAP arrangements, there would seem to be the greatest advantage to the EEC countries' seriously considering greater freedom of trade in farm products.

Moves towards unification of agricultural policies do not imply the abolition of distinctively national farm policies. It is quite proper for any country to have a national farm policy, even under free trade arrangements. This is particularly true in the area of stabilizing farm prices and incomes—a very proper area for national farm policy. Again policies for promoting structural changes in agriculture must reflect the divergent political and social goals being pursued by various countries. It is therefore desirable that any further round of general trade-policy negotiations over the next few years should include in its terms of reference the removal of barriers to trade in farm products.

At the farm-policy level this implies moving into a suitably long transition away from supported agricultural price levels that are well in excess of world prices. It implies permitting agriculture to adjust at least in moderate measure to the forces of the market. It is scarcely necessary to state again that the generally constructive changes in agriculture that have already occurred in the North Atlantic area have been in response to market forces rather than to domestic farm policies.

The pursuit of social and income objectives is quite proper. But this pursuit is a matter more appropriate to social policy than to agricultural price policy. The Scandinavian countries and the Netherlands have already provided constructive leadership in this area.

The timing for a serious review of agricultural policy in the North Atlantic area is now propitious. The agriculture of the North American continent is moving towards viability in an economic or market sense. Significant structural improvements in the agriculture of Britain and Europe have already been made, despite their farm policies, and as this process continues, the segment of their agriculture that has achieved or approached economic viability will expand. The agriculture of Britain and western Europe has characteristics revealing economic strength. It is most desirable from the standpoint of farmers, consumers, and governments that the efficient or potentially efficient sectors be encouraged to expand and thus claim resources presently used less efficiently. Just as Professor Heady sees American agriculture fully adjusted to a market climate by 1980, so we can visualize at some later date the agriculture of western Europe and Britain reaching a similar position. Such a situation, entirely new in the history of agriculture, provides an encouraging climate for moving aggressively into further negotiations aimed at expanding international trade in farm products.

Specifically, on the issue of whether an adequate degree of harmonization of agricultural policies could be achieved if a move towards freer trade were made, we point again to the belated success of the EEC in achieving harmonization when confronted with a far more difficult task; belated or not, the significant fact is that the harmonization has been achieved. As Professor Harry Johnson points out, harmonization on the level of the CAP is "far beyond the objectives and possibilities of a free trade arrangement. . . ." By comparison, harmonization of farm policy in an area moving towards freer trade, while still very difficult, would be easier. At the same time, we must remember that agriculture in general was exempted from the EFTA arangements, so that we do not have an actual example of how necessary or difficult it might be to harmonize agricultural policies in a free trade area.

On the importance of the issues considered in this study, we cannot do better than to express our agreement with John Coppock:

The real point is that an Atlantic Community, if it is to become an economic reality, should not exclude agriculture. The exclusion would not be very serious economically. But it almost certainly would become a political sore, a point of debilitating infection spreading to areas of the political body far beyond itself.[2]

---

[2]*Atlantic Agricultural Unity: Is It Possible?*, p. 207.

VI. Summary

The peculiar difficulties of agriculture in facing the large adjustments necessary to secure the gains from international specialization have been stressed. They centre on the slow growth of demand, price inelasticity, and the exceedingly rapid progress in agricultural technology. Put in very blunt terms, it is these factors plus an inherent conservatism of farm people that have led farm leaders to exercise a political influence against facing any serious examination of the gains (to themselves and to consumers) from freer trade. Rather, farm spokesmen have employed this conservatism to lead governments to establish an incredible jungle of restraints on trade, production, and marketing, to employ very large subsidies, and so on. And by the nature of the problem, these "solutions" cannot solve the difficulties, cannot give farmers the incomes they (perhaps rightfully) demand. Thus agriculture has come to be regarded as a sick industry, in chronic maladjustment to its market.

An important theme of this study is that events of the present decade have provided a climate in which the historical tendency of farmers to look to protective policies for a way out of their economic difficulties is now less necessary. Export demand, particularly for the leading farm exports, has risen sharply during the recent period. And the prospect is that the rapid rise will continue, owing to urgent food needs for famine relief and to expansion of the commercial demand for farm products, especially food grains, in the developing countries as the pace of economic activity increases. (Canada may thank the United States for converting large populations in the developing countries from other cereal foods to wheat by their twelve-year give-away and subsidized export programs.) For either or both of these reasons, the prospect for Canadian wheat exports and, indirectly, for almost the whole of Canadian agriculture is improved. In fact, it is now becoming common to assert that even if the developing countries do not succeed in achieving industrial development, but even more so if they do, their requirements would overtax the land resources of those countries which are efficient in the production of food grains.

The second change in attitude which makes more propitious a serious facing of the implications of freer trade results from the (long delayed) success which now appears to attend American efforts to bring their agriculture into a competitive economic context. Who would have believed that by 1966 the U.S. government would, in the face of small wheat stocks, increase its wheat acreage allotments by 30 percent? By now 70 to 80 percent of American agriculture produces essentially in a market context. And the proportion is increasing. It is not so much that American farm programs have been a great success, as that adjustments in the industry, largely resulting from market forces operating in a full-employment economy, have led to a vast restructuring of inputs. According to Professor Heady, we may expect by 1980 to have achieved (of all things) the two-man farm with labour returns fully equal to those in non-farm industries. American agriculture, if not yet strong in all economic respects, is very sophisticated. As it becomes stronger economically, it will surely be able to apply its sophistication to the speeding up of its national and international adjustments—much to its own profit. The greatest barrier to such development, apart from trade restrictions, is the large acreage of U.S. farm land held idle in reserve.

A statistical measure of the change in the economic climate in which Canadian agriculture operates is shown in Table XX. The greatest significance which can be attached to these data is that Canada has in recent years passed from a plateau of cash receipts below $3,500 million annually to a level above that. We expect recent levels of both cash and net income to be maintained.

TABLE XX

GROSS CASH RECEIPTS AND NET FARM
INCOMES, 1961–66
(millions of dollars)

Year	Cash receipts	Net income
1961	2,890	935
1962	3,102	1,492
1963	3,198	1,495
1964	3,491	1,281
1965	3,806	1,565
1966	4,232	1,978

Source: DBS, *Farm Net Income*, various years.

While the structural changes in Canadian agriculture have been more substantial, they have in most areas lacked the glow of sophistication observable in the United States. But the changes have been accompanied by larger gains in productivity. And this implies that there is more to be gained by Canadian than by American farmers from an attempt to achieve the gains available through freer trade.

Data of the FAO support those presented above for Canada and the United States. That organization's index of international prices of food and feed exports was up nearly 18 percent in 1963 over 1962. It was up a further 11 percent in 1965. The volume of world agricultural imports has risen each year since 1955, and in 1965 was about 40 percent higher than in 1955.[1]

Other studies have established the fact that Canada has a significant comparative advantage in wheat, oilseeds, live cattle, cheddar cheese, and in some fruits and vegetables. Thus a move towards freer trade would lead to a significant expansion of the output of the above products; these increases would be to some extent at the expense of feed grains, butter, poultry meat, mutton, lamb, and wool. While Canada has a clear comparative advantage in several products, there has been a deterioration in this respect compared to the United States over the past ten to fifteen years. Thus while Canadian farm exports to the United States have declined by some $50 million over the past fifteen years, farm imports from the United States have increased very sharply—by some 65 percent. The deterioration in comparative advantage reflects Canada's agricultural and trade policies, and it is a matter of urgent importance that this trend be reversed. Part of the reversal could be secured by freeing the farm industry from import duties on corn and on some types of agricultural equipment not already freely traded.

With the imminence of full implementation of the Common Agricultural Policy of the European Economy Community and with the completion of the Kennedy round negotiations, a new and more stable situation faces the agriculture of the North Atlantic area in coming years. This more stabilized situation, and particularly the improved agricultural market climate which will continue to prevail, provides a most useful opportunity for a review of agricultural policies and for initiatives aimed at improving the allocation of resources in the industry to the benefit of consumers and of government— and with opportunities for improvement of agricultural incomes.

A large part of American agriculture now operates in a market context. By 1980 the industry will be entirely rationalized or adjusted to the economic climate which will exist by that date. This will also probably apply to a very large part of Canadian agriculture. European and British agriculture is undergoing rapid structural adjustments, so that there too the need for highly protective policies is decreasing.

Trade in agricultural products has increased rapidly over the postwar years despite policies which have discouraged this trend. There is reason for optimism regarding exports of agricultural products over the next decade or two. The last few years have witnessed the disappearance of surpluses of major agricultural products. Furthermore, two factors related

[1]See United Nations, Food and Agriculture Organization, *The State of Food and Agriculture, 1966*, Rome, pp. 34–8.

to the developing countries—their need for food aid whether they achieve development or not, and the further stimulation of their agricultural-import needs if they make significant progress in development—lead to the conclusion that the demand for farm products will rise sufficiently to encourage the further restructuring of agriculture in the developed countries and to make this restructured industry viable. Such a prospect affords great incentive for further discussions or negotiations directed towards expansion of trade and towards resolving the agricultural-policy difficulties discussed earlier. In fact, such a resolution of policy difficulties would in itself speed the full rationalization of the agricultural industry and so is the major challenge in the farm-policy area over the next decade or two. If an integrated Atlantic economy is to become a reality, it should not and could not exclude agriculture.

RELATED PUBLICATIONS BY THE
PRIVATE PLANNING ASSOCIATION OF CANADA

CANADIAN TRADE COMMITTEE PUBLICATIONS

THE WORLD ECONOMY

The World Economy at the Crossroads: A Survey of Current Problems of Money, Trade and Economic Development, by Harry G. Johnson, 1965.
The International Monetary System: Conflict and Reform, by Robert A. Mundell, 1965.
International Commodity Agreements, by William E. Haviland, 1963.

CANADA'S TRADE RELATIONSHIPS

Canada's International Trade: An Analysis of Recent Trends and Patterns, by Bruce Wilkinson, 1968.
Canada's Trade with the Communist Countries of Eastern Europe, by Ian M. Drummond, 1966.
Canada's Role in Britain's Trade, by Edward M. Cape, 1965.
The Common Agricultural Policy of the E.E.C. and its Implications for Canada's Exports, by Sol Sinclair, 1964.
Canada's Interest in the Trade Problems of Less-Developed Countries, by Grant L. Reuber, 1964.

CANADA'S COMMERCIAL POLICY AND COMPETITIVE POSITION

Prices, Productivity, and Canada's Competitive Position, by N. H. Lithwick, 1967.
Industrial Structure in Canada's International Competitive Position: A Study of the Factors Affecting Economies of Scale and Specialization in Canadian Manufacturing, by H. Edward English, 1964.
Canada's Approach to Trade Negotiations, by L. D. Wilgress, 1963.

CANADIAN-AMERICAN COMMITTEE PUBLICATIONS

CANADA-U.S. ECONOMIC RELATIONS

Constructive Alternatives to Proposals for U.S. Import Quotas (a Statement by the Committee), 1968.
U.S.-Canadian Free Trade: The Potential Impact on the Canadian Economy, by Paul Wonnacott and Ronald J. Wonnacott, 1968.
The Role of International Unionism in Canada, by John H. G. Crispo, 1967.
A New Trade Strategy for Canada and the United States (a Statement by the Committee), 1966.
Capital Flows between Canada and the United States, by Irving Brecher, 1965.
A Possible Plan for a Canada-U.S. Free Trade Area (a Staff Report), 1965.
Invisible Trade Barriers between Canada and the United States, by Francis Masson and H. Edward English, 1963.
Non-Merchandise Transactions between Canada and the United States, by John W. Popkin, 1963.
Policies and Practices of United States Subsidiaries in Canada, by John Lindeman and Donald Armstrong, 1961.

Canada in the Atlantic Economy

CANADA IN THE ATLANTIC ECONOMY

Published:

Forthcoming:

Trade Liberalization
and the Canadian Pulp and Paper Industry

W. E Haviland, N. S. Takacsy, E. M. Cape

Published for the
Private Planning Association of Canada by University of Toronto Press

To William E. Lambert

These studies of "Canada in the Atlantic Economy" are dedicated with respect and gratitude to the late William B. Lambert, Chairman of the Board of the Private Planning Association of Canada from 1965 to 1967, who played a vital role in the development and supervision of the Atlantic Economic Studies Program, on which the publications are based.

His interest went far beyond his formal responsibility; he held a deep conviction concerning the importance of international cooperation among the North Atlantic nations. His untimely death came when the first draft studies had entered the early stages of publication.

Foreword

There have been two outstanding developments in international trade policy during the past twenty years—the multilateral dismantling of trade barriers under the General Agreement on Tariffs and Trade, which has been the agency for several rounds of successful tariff negotiations since its inception in 1947, and the establishment of the European Economic Community and the European Free Trade Association in the late 1950s. In a period of reconstruction and then sustained growth, these policies have helped the participating nations of the Atlantic area to experience the benefits of international specialization and expanding trade. The wealth generated by trade and domestic prosperity has also made possible external aid programs to assist economic growth in the developing countries.

Whatever the trade and economic development problems of the future, it is widely acknowledged that the industrially advanced countries of the North Atlantic region must play an important role. It is also generally conceded that the ability of these countries to maintain their own economic growth and prosperity and to contribute to that of the less advanced nations will be greatly enhanced if they can reduce or remove the remaining trade barriers among themselves. Cooperation among Atlantic countries is now fostered by the GATT and by the Organisation for Economic Co-operation and Development. But the success of these and other approaches depends on the assessment by each country of the importance of international trade liberalization and policy coordination for its domestic economy and other national interests. This is particularly true for countries such as Canada which are heavily dependent upon export markets.

The Atlantic Economic Studies Program of the Private Planning Association of Canada was initiated to study the implications for Canada of trade liberalization and closer economic integration among the nations bordering the North Atlantic. It is planned to issue at least twelve paperbound volumes, incorporating over twenty studies by leading Canadian and foreign economists. Despite the technical nature of much of the subject matter, the studies have been written in language designed to appeal to the non-professional reader.

The directors and staff of the Private Planning Association wish to acknowledge the financial support which made this project possible—a grant from the Ford Foundation and the contributions of members of the Association. They are also appreciative of the help that has been provided by very many individuals in the preparation and review of all the studies—in discussions and correspondence with authors, at the Association's November, 1966, conference on "Canada and the Atlantic Economy," and on other occasions.

H. E. ENGLISH
Director of Research
Atlantic Economic Studies Program

Contents

1. Introduction

The purpose of this study is to assess the economic impact upon the Canadian pulp and paper industry of free or freer trade among North Atlantic countries. Its purpose does not include the passing of judgment for or against freer trade. But it cannot avoid expressing some judgment implicitly in its assessment of the probable impact of freer trade and the possible ameliorative role of government policy.

The study is one of several industry-impact studies which were undertaken between 1965 and 1967 as part of the Atlantic Economic Studies Program of the Private Planning Association of Canada. The terms of reference for the PPAC program of studies were provided in the form of the following trade-policy alternatives:
1. Free trade among all Atlantic countries, with allowance for the possibility of delayed EEC participation, for special arrangements for agriculture, for inclusion of Japan, and for special concessions to the developing countries;
2. Free trade between Canada and the United States in all products, with the probable initial exception of agricultural products;
3. Free trade between Canada and the United States in particular products or industry sectors. For the above three alternatives, appropriate transitional arrangements were to be given explicit consideration.
4. Linear cuts of 25 to 33 percent in the tariff levels that existed before the Kennedy round settlements, with no further initiative ensuing.

In point of fact, the bulk of the analysis in this study was conducted, explicitly or implicitly, in the context of alternatives 1 and 2—complete free trade among Atlantic countries or between Canada and the United States. Alternatives 3 and 4—on the one hand, sectoral free trade covering the industry's outputs but not necessarily all its inputs, and, on the other hand, partial reduction of trade barriers—were generally treated as divergences from, or incomplete approximations to, the first two alternatives.

The authors structured their investigations as follows. Part A describes the Canadian pulp and paper industry and examines its existing trends and prospects. Part B examines the probable impact on the industry of assumed conditions of free trade among North Atlantic countries. Some of the cost data developed for this analysis are to be found in the appendix. Part C discusses the policy implications of the impact findings. A short chapter of summary and conclusions for the study as a whole is provided at the beginning for the convenience of readers.

Part A of the study was mainly the responsibility of W. E. Haviland. The responsibility for Part B was shared among N. S. Takacsy, E. M. Cape, and W. E. Haviland. The cost study which forms the basis of Chapter 6 and the appendix was done by Mr. Cape. Part C was the joint responsibility of Messrs. Takacsy and Haviland. The latter wrote the coordinating draft of the report.

To obtain a preliminary impression of some actual industry operations, the authors visited paper mills at Cornwall, La Tuque, and Hull. One of the authors later visited pulp and paper people in Scandinavia and western Europe.

The method employed in Part A of the study was mainly statistical. Part B utilized an extensive opinion survey among industry leaders, as well as an independent analysis of production costs and marketing factors. The cost analysis was based on published data and on questionnaires and discussions with various people in the industry at the appropriate technical levels. Part C brings together the conclusions reached by the authors on the basis of all these approaches.

Published sources, where applicable, are noted in the text or in footnote references. The authors also benefited from the work of other people involved in the Atlantic Economic Studies Program and from the related International Conference on Canada and the Atlantic Economic Community held at the Seigniory Club, Montebello, Quebec, in November 1966. Beyond that, much essential information was supplied by numerous people throughout the industry. Although these people must remain anonymous, we wish to acknowledge the key contribution they made, individually and collectively. The authors, however, assume responsibility for the findings and opinions presented in this report.

2. Summary and Conclusions

The purpose of this study is to assess the impact upon the Canadian pulp and paper industry of free or freer trade among the countries of the North Atlantic.

Part A describes the industry and examines its trends and prospects under existing tariffs. For purposes of this study, the "Canadian pulp and paper industry" refers to production within Canada, excluding products (such as envelopes or boxes) manufactured from paper or paperboard. In 1966 the value of the total production from 136 pulp and/or paper mills was $2.3 billion. Quebec, Ontario, and British Columbia are the main producing provinces. The varieties of pulp and paper produced are many. The tariff-protected papers account for 26 percent of the total value of the industry's output. Ontario and Quebec account for a large share of the production of tariff-protected papers. These papers are produced mainly for the home market and therefore in smaller volumes and with higher labour content than pulp and newsprint, which are generally traded tariff-free. Prior to 1968 Canada levied MFN tariffs on paper and paperboard imports, these tariffs varying up to 25 percent, with the level often being 22½ percent. Canada's leading export markets for pulp and paper are the United States and the United Kingdom, but sales are also made in many other countries.

The industry's volume of production has been expanding since 1945 at a compound annual rate of just over 4½ percent. Both the number and average size of pulp and/or paper mills have grown. The relative importance of the tariff-protected grades of paper has been increasing, and their output value now amounts to about 26 percent of total pulp and paper production, compared with about 23 percent after the Second World War.

The volume of pulp and paper exports has been expanding at a compound rate of just under 4½ percent per year in the postwar period, while imports have been increasing at just over 7 percent per year. A Dominion Bureau of Statistics study of productivity trends between 1947 and 1961 revealed that productivity in the U.S. industry increased more than twice as fast as in Canada. Rapid rates of increase in exports since 1945 took place in the book and writing (including fine), sanitary, and paperboard groups of protected papers. The rapid rates of increase in imports took place in the paperboard, tissue (excluding sanitary), book and writing, special industrials, and wrapping paper groups. Exports of book and writing (fine) papers and sanitary papers have been expanding faster than imports. Imports of paperboard, wrapping paper, special industrial papers, and tissue papers (excluding sanitary) have been expanding faster than exports since 1945. As for ownership trends, although U.S. and U.K. capital continues to be invested in the Canadian industry, there has been a tendency in recent years towards more widespread international financial participation.

World demand for paper is expected to at least double every fifteen years. The countries with the highest per capita consumption in 1966 were the United States (530 pounds), Sweden (353 pounds), and Canada (310 pounds). The most rapidly growing markets among industrialized countries are Japan and the EEC. Canada ranks second to the United States among countries producing pulp and paper. Under the tariff pattern existing prior to 1968, the prospective increase to 1975 in total demand for Canada's pulp and paper was estimated at a compound annual rate of 4.8 percent. Total paperboard production was expected to increase at 5¾ percent per year. Production of fine papers was expected to increase at a 6 percent rate. Production of wrapping paper and building papers and boards was expected to continue expanding at 3½ percent per year. Sanitary and tissue paper production was expected to continue expanding at a compound rate of 6¾ percent per year.

Part B assesses the probable impact of free North Atlantic trade on industry production and marketing. The rationale of free trade lies in producing countries' achieving economies of scale by specializing in products in which they possess a competitive advantage. For paper production in Canada to survive under free trade, it must be competitive with imports; for it to thrive, it must be competitive in export markets. If paper-making were to thrive in Canada, employment opportunities would probably be created for the rapidly expanding labour force. Could the presently tariff-protected grades of paper survive and thrive under free trade? If this sector of the industry were to be restructured during a transition period, would it then be cost-competitive? To explore this basic question, hypothetical mills of specified efficient size, producing each of four representative grades of paper (linerboard, groundwood paper, bond paper, and toilet tissue) were located in certain Canadian and U.S. regions and were compared regionally. Mill costs and the costs of transporting the products to selected U.S. markets were taken into detailed account in Chapter 6.

Using 1964 data, we found that the U.S. South (really Southeast) had a mill-cost advantage over eastern Canada in linerboard, groundwood paper, and bond paper. If competitive rail rates could be negotiated, the South's advantage would be reduced or eliminated in those U.S. markets which were relatively close to eastern Canadian producers. In toilet tissue, the eastern Canadian producer had a mill-cost advantage over producers in Maine and Wisconsin; if competitive rail rates were assumed, the advantage over Maine was reduced in only such north-easterly markets as Boston, while the advantage over Wisconsin was reduced in only such "westerly" markets as Chicago. B.C. producers, compared with those in Washington or Oregon, should be competitive in most papers in west coast North American and Pacific overseas markets.

Updating from 1964 to the present, and looking ahead about five years, it appeared that the relative mill-cost situation was characterized by more-rapidly rising wood costs in the South slightly outweighing more-rapidly rising wage rates in eastern Canada. Beyond about five years ahead, we foresee the possibility of the relative cost situation beginning to change moderately in favour of the South, as the wood-cost rise decelerates.

These comparative-cost findings suggest that for eastern Canada the best lines of specialization in the now-protected grades under free trade would be: first, sanitary tissues, because the U.S. South is out of the competition owing to coarse wood and the amount of electricity required; second, groundwood papers, which also use a lot of electricity; third, bond paper, where the substantial use of hardwood narrows the density gap between Canadian and southern wood; and fourth, linerboard (and probably kraft paper and paperboards generally), for which the U.S. South is particularly well suited.

There are two ways of expanding a company's sales to justify longer production runs—by specializing a company's product lines for the domestic market and/or by doing so for export markets. At first glance, the opportunities that would be opened up for Canadian papers in U.S. and other markets look very good. Effective penetration of these export markets, however, would not be simple. Achieving competitive costs under free trade conditions would be a necessary but not a sufficient condition for success. In addition to problems of restructuring their production in order to achieve economies of scale, most Canadian-owned producers of hitherto tariff-protected papers would face formidable, although not necessarily insuperable, marketing obstacles in both the domestic and export markets. Because of the importance of tied sales, converting facilities and marketing outlets would often have to be acquired. This and various other marketing problems are examined in Chapter 7. Since trade generally is already free in pulp and newsprint, no gains for these products *attributable to freer trade* would result for purposes of offsetting impact losses or for financing expensive adjustments in other grades.

The general conclusion we draw from all the evidence of the study is that the Canadian pulp and paper industry could compete in domestic and export markets under conditions of free trade *provided its production and marketing were reorganized and related public policies were conducive.* Restructuring the industry would imply greater product specialization by companies and much longer runs on wider and faster machines in the present tariff-protected sector. One of the results would probably be that production of some grades of paper would be discontinued in Canada. The net impact of restructuring on the volume of pulp exports is impossible to forecast.

In certain instances, paper mills might have to be relocated. Some small companies would probably be absorbed by larger ones with greater financial resources, and perhaps a few companies would go out of business entirely. Mill relocations or shut-downs would cause serious unemployment and other social dislocations in small mill towns. The impact of free trade would have regional disparities, with the major adjustments being required in Ontario and Quebec, where production of tariff-protected papers for the domestic market has been concentrated. Which grades of paper and which companies would be forced out of business would be determined mainly by cost competitiveness and marketing aggressiveness, neither of which is immutable. The outcome can be influenced by qualities of ownership, management, and research.

It was not a purpose of the study to pass judgment for or against free trade, but to assess its impact on the pulp and paper industry. Part C explores the policy implications of our impact conclusions. Since most employees and all consumers would benefit from freer trade, equity requires that the impact costs be shared among the beneficiaries rather than that the whole brunt of the shift be borne by particular companies and the employees who would be dislocated. This general case for adjustment assistance applies with special force to pulp and paper because so many of the mills are located in single-industry communities which would be highly vulnerable to dislocations resulting from tariff cuts. These single-industry communities are often located in provinces which tend to suffer from above-average rates of unemployment. Specific forms of adjustment assistance are suggested in Chapter 9. In a capital-intensive industry such as pulp and paper, there is an important time dimension to restructuring production and marketing. Firms need to know well in advance what kinds and amounts of aid they can count on.

A program of trade liberalization would have policy implications extending far beyond adjustment assistance. If it became a national goal to lower the costs of products by reducing tariffs, then various other policies should contribute to this achievement, or at least not be incompatible with it. If monetary and fiscal policies are used to help maintain an expansionary economy with reasonable price stability, the problem of adjusting to freer trade would be lessened, the time required for transition would be shortened, and the amount of adjustment assistance needed would be reduced. If the tax burden of Canadians gets out of line with that of foreign competitors, the competitiveness of Canadian products will suffer. It is in the long-run interest of the industry for the new anti-dumping code to be applied similarly in Canada and in the United States. This is not to deny that diligence is needed in the legitimate application of the code to dumped imports, especially sporadic dumping of odd lots, side runs, and start-up tonnage.

Other federal policies and programs needed or requiring reconciliation with trade liberalization include reform of rail-rate structures, particularly in eastern Canada, to conform with a shift towards a north-south continental flow of trade; avoidance of an exchange rate policy that would weaken the competitive position of Canadian producers; equivalent export sales promotion; relaxation of anti-combines provisions to permit restructuring of the industry; and fiscal or financial incentives to encourage faster mechanization and pollution abatement. The fact that there is federal jurisdiction over international trade but provincial jurisdiction over resources means that federal-provincial cooperation is needed to prevent conflicts in policy. Achieving the main goal of trade liberalization—lower costs—could be helped or hindered by provincial policies with respect to tenure of timber limits, reforestation, forest fire and insect control, access roads, and the nature and timing of industrial development programs.

This study has been made, for the most part, within the assumed context of free trade in all products among North Atlantic countries, but it also applies, although to a lesser extent, to a general free trade arrangement between Canada and the United States. With reference to the paper industry, the main reason for preferring Atlantic-wide to Canada–U.S. free trade is that the former would provide access to wider markets for papers in which the Canadian industry could become competitive after restructuring. If free trade between Canada and the United States were confined to the papers sector, excluding industry inputs, the competitiveness of the Canadian industry would be weakened to that extent.

A. The Industry
and Its Trends and Prospects

3. Description of the Industry

No single definition of the Canadian pulp and paper industry would suit all purposes. Since the main purpose of the present study is to isolate the probable impact on the industry of free trade among North Atlantic countries, the study is essentially forward-looking and comparative. It is also concerned with the transition to free trade and with appropriate adjustment policies.

For our purposes, then, the "Canadian pulp and paper industry" should refer to production within Canadian territory. This does not mean that a producing company must be Canadian-owned or that it may not also produce pulp and paper outside Canada. The industrial collectivity involved in the definition is closely but not identically represented by the membership of the Canadian Pulp and Paper Association. However, since resources are under the jurisdiction of the provinces, which formulate regional production and "export" policies, the statistical entity "Canada" is not the same as the policy-making entity "Canada."

In any event, the definition of the industry obviously covers pulp and paper production. To this extent the DBS industrial classification, with reporting by establishment, and the classification used in the annual DBS publication *Pulp and Paper Mills* are appropriate. However, there are still some economic complications. Many Canadian pulp and paper comanies are multi-establishment producers widely dispersed geographically. Several firms convert some of their pulp and paper into paper products. Some firms also produce lumber and other wood products. Statistically these paper products and non-paper products are excluded from our study, but they have economic implications which must be considered.

The application of a "primary-secondary" industrial classification would not be helpful for present purposes. The logging operations of the pulp and paper industry may be primary, but the pulping and paper-making processes are not. "Resource-based" would be a more appropriate designation.

In 1966 there were 136 pulp and/or paper mills in Canada. Quebec, Ontario, and British Columbia are the main producers. The sizes of the mills in 1965, as indicated by average value of manufactures and average number of employees, by province, are shown in Table II. Newfoundland mills average largest, and Prairie mills smallest.

In the two-year period 1963–64, the average output of mills was 85,000 to 86,000 tons in Ontario and Quebec, 188,000 tons in British Columbia, and 124,000 tons in "other provinces." The lower output per mill in Quebec and Ontario, compared with British Columbia and "other provinces," is mainly due to the fact that the two big eastern provinces account

TABLE I
PULP AND PAPER MILL LOCATIONS, 1966

	Pulp mills	Pulp and paper mills	Paper mills	Total
Newfoundland	—	2	—	2
Nova Scotia	2	2	—	4
New Brunswick	5	4	1	10
Quebec	9	35	12	56
Ontario	4	21	13	38
Manitoba	—	3	—	3
Saskatchewan	—	1	—	1
Alberta	1	2	—	3
British Columbia	9	8	2	19
Canada	30	78	28	136

Source: Canadian Pulp and Paper Association (hereafter cited as CPPA), *Reference Tables*, 1967

TABLE II
AVERAGE VALUE OF MANUFACTURERS AND NUMBER OF
EMPLOYEES* PER PULP AND PAPER MILL, BY PROVINCE, 1965

	Selling value per mill	Employees* per mill
	($000)	
Newfoundland	37,058	1,485
Nova Scotia	10,076	421
New Brunswick	14,108	467
Quebec	13,613	482
Ontario	15,531	569
Man., Sask., and Alta.	7,434	179
British Columbia	29,754	722
Canada	15,943	530

Source: CPPA, *Reference Tables*.
*Excluding wood workers.

for a large share of the industry's production of the tariff-protected grades of paper, which are produced in smaller volumes than pulp and newsprint. For example, Ontario and Quebec accounted for 90 percent of Canada's production of fine paper.

Higher labour-output ratios in the tariff-protected papers than in pulp and newsprint are general in the industry. This would explain, in part at least, the higher labour-output ratio for Ontario mills than for Quebec mills in 1963–64. Although the average output tonnages of mills in the two provinces were about the same, Ontario mills employed 529 persons per mill, and Quebec mills averaged 483 persons. Ontario accounted for 65 percent of Canada's production of fine paper, Quebec for 25 percent.

The Canadian pulp and paper industry manufactures diverse products— about 150 product lines. These are grouped in summary categories and listed alphabetically in Table III. A more detailed list of products is contained in Table V.

The total volume and value of production and exports in 1966 are shown in Table IV. Volume of production amounted to 15.9 million tons of pulp and paper, valued at about $2.3 billion. This was a greater value of output

TABLE III

MAIN PRODUCT GROUPS

Blotting papers	Groundwood printing and specialty papers
Bond, ledger, and writing papers	Hardboard
Book, litho label, offset, and text papers	Kraft papers—bleached, semi-bleached,
Boxboard—folding paperboard	unbleached
Boxboard—non-folding paperboard	Miscellaneous papers
Boxboard—other grades	Miscellaneous boards
Bristols—index and printing	Newsprint
Building papers—felts, roofing, sheathing,	Rigid insulating board
etc.	Sanitary papers
Coated papers	Specialty papers
Containerboards	Tissue papers
Envelope papers	Wood pulp

Source: CPPA, *Pulp and Paper from Canada*, 1966, p. 11.

TABLE IV

VALUE OF CANADIAN PULP AND PAPER PRODUCTION AND EXPORTS, 1966

	Production		Exports	
	000 tons	$000	000 tons	$000
1966	15,931	2,300,000*	12,615	1,579,054*

Source: CPPA, *Reference Tables*.
*Approximate.

than from any other manufacturing industry. Exports represented 79 percent of the tonnage produced.

Among the exports, by far the largest are pulp and newsprint, as shown for 1966 in Table V. The table also indicates that the two leading export markets for Canadian pulp and paper are the United States and Britain. The tariff-protected papers are sold mainly in the domestic market. The two largest groups of paper exports among the protected grades are book and writing paper and paperboard.

Canada imports a small amount of pulp and some tariff-protected grades of paper, in quantities summarized for 1966 in Table VI.

In 1965, the manufacturing and related operations of the industry employed almost 70,000 people, whose total salaries and wages amounted to $423.7 million. Pulp and paper ranked first among manufacturing industries in terms of number of employees and total salaries and wages (as well as in terms of value of production). The distribution of these employees by kind of work is shown in Table VII for 1964.

The total cost of materials and energy used in manufacturing pulp and paper in 1964 amounted to $984.9 million. The distribution of this and other input expenses is shown in Table VIII.

New capital expenditures by the pulp and paper industry in 1966 were $514 million, and revised investment intentions for 1967 totalled $396 million. Capital-asset figures are less readily available; but for 1964, seventy-five pulp and paper companies reported to the Department of National Revenue assets of $4,574 million, including inventories and cash. The Canadian Pulp and Paper Association publication *Reference Tables* estimates the corresponding figure for 1965 at $4,958 million.

The cost of transporting pulp and paper products to markets in 1965 was estimated by the Canadian Pulp and Paper association at $320 million. This would have amounted to an average out-transport cost of $21.90 per ton of product. One large, centrally located company shows transport costs of $19.28 per ton of product in 1966.

Except for newsprint, pulp, and certain types of book and coated paper for periodicals, which are tariff-free, Canada has levied on paper and paperboard imports MFN tariffs ranging up to 25 percent. The rate was most frequently 20–22½ percent. Pre- and post-Kennedy round tariffs of Canada, the United States, Britain, and the EEC are summarized in Table IX.

Roughly speaking, Canadian concessions under the Kennedy round will reduce existing tariff rates of 20–22½ percent to 15–17½ percent. Existing rates of up to 7½ percent will be either left unchanged or eliminated. Practically all U.S. paper tariffs, including coated and uncoated printing papers

TABLE V

PULP AND PAPER EXPORTS BY MAIN GRADES AND MARKETS, 1966

	Total exports		To United States		To United Kingdom		To other countries	
	Tons	Value ($000)	Tons	Value ($000)	Tons	Value ($000)	Tons	Value ($000)
PULP								
Dissolving and special alpha (sulphite and sulphate)	364,451	65,034	283,214	51,280	13,831	2,365	67,406	11,389
Sulphate—paper grades:	2,614,701	333,243	1,906,112	249,713	116,718	14,359	591,871	69,171
Bleached	1,986,728	266,352	1,529,426	209,573	81,772	10,522	375,530	46,257
Semi-bleached	233,616	27,420	100,812	12,462	19,010	2,202	113,794	12,756
Unbleached	394,357	39,471	275,873	27,678	15,935	1,635	102,549	10,158
Sulphite—paper grades:	851,735	103,963	625,967	78,648	118,454	14,033	107,314	11,282
Bleached	605,290	78,989	511,394	67,143	52,767	6,782	41,129	5,064
Unbleached—strong	209,106	20,933	113,969	11,442	32,630	3,631	62,507	5,860
Unbleached—news grade	37,338	4,041	604	63	33,057	3,620	3,677	358
Total chemical	3,830,887	502,240	2,815,293	379,641	249,003	30,757	766,591	91,842
Mechanical:	253,867	17,260	151,030	10,552	74,763	4,831	28,074	1,877
Bleached	5,608	453	5,608	453	—	—	—	—
Unbleached	248,259	16,807	145,422	10,099	74,763	4,831	28,074	1,877
Other pulps	36	4	36	4	—	—	—	—
Screenings:	11,487	563	11,487	563	—	—	—	—
Chemical	990	49	990	49	—	—	—	—
Mechanical	10,497	514	10,497	514	—	—	—	—
Total miscellaneous	265,390	17,827	162,553	11,119	74,763	4,831	28,074	1,877
Total pulp	4,096,277	520,067	2,977,846	390,760	323,766	35,588	794,665	93,719
NEWSPRINT PAPER								
Standard	7,821,148	968,224	6,652,270	823,664	384,034	48,883	784,844	95,677
Mutilated	58,897	3,875	34,313	2,269	933	54	23,651	1,552
Total newsprint	7,880,045	972,099	6,686,583	825,933	384,967	48,937	808,495	97,229

OTHER PAPER

Wrapping paper:	46,510	8,182	16,747	3,762	26,130	3,779	3,633	641
Bleached sulphite and sulphate	15,419	3,646	13,727	3,185	1,349	364	343	97
Unbleached sulphite and sulphate	26,824	3,792	2,635	426	21,416	2,908	2,773	458
Wrapping—n.o.p.	4,268	744	384	151	3,366	507	518	86
Book and writing paper:	171,418	32,932	117,896	19,968	26,627	5,912	26,895	7,052
Groundwood printing—n.o.p.	129,694	21,738	108,990	17,564	12,905	2,416	7,799	1,758
Book—n.o.p.	11,297	2,509	6,171	1,254	4,497	1,083	629	172
Writing and reproduction	28,313	8,115	2,735	1,147	8,431	2,202	17,147	4,766
Fine paper—n.o.p.	2,114	570	*	3	793	211	1,321	356
Paperboard:	257,546	30,875	8,585	1,476	178,066	21,051	70,895	8,348
Liner board	182,468	22,033	455	48	132,203	15,840	49,810	6,145
Container board—n.o.p.	57,715	5,369	685	57	37,659	3,687	19,371	1,625
Solid bleached and folding boxboard	7,114	1,327	12	3	7,097	1,322	5	2
Set-up boxboard—n.o.p.	4,354	683	4,076	638	71	9	207	36
Wet machine board	3,314	1,143	1,979	598	55	48	1,280	497
Paperboard—n.o.p.	2,581	320	1,378	132	981	145	222	43
Building board:	39,059	4,436	32,977	3,496	2,249	442	3,833	498
Rigid insulating board	12,546	1,517	9,923	1,097	798	167	1,825	253
Hardboard	24,943	2,690	21,951	2,261	1,381	266	1,611	163
Building board—n.o.p.	1,571	229	1,103	138	70	9	398	82
Building paper	19,040	1,686	8,173	903	907	67	9,960	716
Tissue paper, except sanitary	106	27	3	4	—	—	103	23
Sanitary paper	13,962	3,166	2,285	468	5,942	1,404	5,735	1,294
Hanging paper	26	4	26	4	—	—	—	—
Special industrial paper	771	185	49	13	554	115	168	57
Coated paper, except machine-coated	1,869	781	644	288	532	182	693	311
Waste paper—n.o.p.	88,603	4,614	87,849	4,559	—	—	754	55
Total other paper	638,910	86,888	275,234	34,941	241,007	32,952	122,669	18,995

Source: CPPA, *Reference Tables*.
*Less than 1 ton

TABLE VI

QUANTITY OF IMPORTS OF PULPS
AND PROTECTED GRADES OF
PAPER BY CANADA, 1966

(tons)	
Pulps	57,988
Protected grades	160,238
Total	218,226

Source: CPPA, *Reference Tables*.

TABLE VII

DISTRIBUTION OF PULP AND PAPER MILL
EMPLOYMENT, BY BROAD CATEGORIES OF WORK,
1964

(percentages)	
Production and related workers	85.1
Administration and office	14.6
Sales and distribution	0.3
Total	100.0

Source: Dominion Bureau of Statistics,
Pulp and Paper Mills, 1964.

TABLE VIII

DISTRIBUTION OF MATERIALS AND ENERGY
EXPENSES IN MANUFACTURING PULP AND
PAPER, 1964

(percentages)	
Fuel and electricity	14.1
Pulpwood	40.8
Wood residue	7.0
Waste papers, other stock, etc.	2.1
Wood pulp	8.9
Chemicals and other supplies	13.0
Container and other packaging materials	2.3
Other materials, operating and repair supplies, and payment to others for work done on materials supplied	11.8
Total	100.0

Source: DBS, *Pulp and Paper Mills*, 1964.

and wrapping paper, will be cut in half. The U.S. tariff on hanging paper and certain building paper and paperboard items will be eliminated. Papers from Commonwealth countries will continue to enter the United Kingdom free of duty. UK tariffs on papers from non-EFTA countries will be reduced from levels of 12½–20 percent to levels of 10–18 percent. U.K. pulp imports remain duty-free. EEC paper tariffs, except for the 7 percent rate on newsprint which remains in effect on imports above a duty-free quota of 625,000 tons, will be reduced to 12 percent from 16 percent. The 6 percent tariff on pulp will be reduced to 3 percent, except for the duty-free quota of 1,935,000 tons.

The value of production of the tariff-protected papers accounts for just over one-quarter of the total value of Canada's pulp and paper production. In 1963–64, the value share of the protected grades was 26 percent.

About half of the sixty companies producing pulp and paper in Canada produce tariff-protected grades. Approximately two-thirds of the thirty companies producing the tariff-protected grades produce 40,000 tons or more per year. The smaller companies are mainly in the paperboard and specialty board fields.

Among companies producing the paperboard grades, eight (in descending order—Consolidated-Bathurst, Domtar, CIP, MacMillan-Bloedel, Continental Can, Price, Abitibi, and Beaver Wood Fibre) produce about 80 percent of the industry's output. Among companies producing book and writing (including fine) papers, four (Domtar, Abitibi-Provincial, Rolland, and Eddy) produce about 90 percent of the industry's output. A fifth company (MacMillan-Bloedel) produces an additional few percent, with the balance produced by a few other companies. Among companies producing wrapping papers, six (Domtar, Prince George, Consolidated-Bathurst, Crown-Zellerbach, Dryden, and Price) produce about 80 percent of the industry's output. Among companies producing sanitary and tissue papers, four (Scott, Kimberly-Clark, Eddy, and CIP) produce about 80 percent of the industry's output. Among companies producing building papers and boards, the four largest are thought to be (in alphabetical order), Building Products, CIP, Domtar, and MacMillan-Bloedel.

The tendency in foreign ownership in the Canadian pulp and paper industry as a whole (not just in the tariff-protected sector) over the years has been for non-Canadian capital to come into the industry from the United States and United Kingdom. Financial participation in the rapid expansion of recent years has been more widespread, however. U.S. and British capital continues to flow into the industry, but considerable new capital also has come from Scandinavia, western Europe, and Japan. This

TABLE IX

SUMMARY OF EXISTING AND FORTHCOMING TARIFFS ON PULP AND PAPERS,
CANADA, U.S., U.K., AND EEC, AND VALUE OF CANADA'S EXPORTS TO THESE COUNTRIES
IN 1966

Products	Base rate of duty	Kennedy round rate of duty	Imports from Canada in 1966 ($000 U.S.)
CANADA			
Wallpapers, wrapping paper, coated paper, paper n.o.p.	22½%	15%	
Paperboard; roofing and shingles of saturated felt, paper sacks, fibreboard shipping containers	20%	15%	
Printing papers	22½	12½%	
Book or coated paper for magazines, newspaper, and periodicals	0	0	
Manifold paper and duplicating paper, uncut	7½%	7½%	
Liner for gypsum or plaster board	5%	0	
Shoe board, item 19235-1	7½%	0	
Shipping and distribution containers, paper and paperboard, item 19945-1	7½%	0	
Various specialty papers, and toilet paper	22½%	15%	
Certain carbonizing and condenser tissues and insulating papers	7½%	7½%	
UNITED STATES			
Building papers	5%	free	84
Beer mat board	4%	free	146
Shoe board	6.75%	3%	424
Other paperboard	4.75%	free	792
Book paper and printing paper	0.17¢ per lb. +4%	0.08¢ per lb. +2%	20,530
Sulphate wrapping paper	8.5%	4%	3,475
Vegetable parchment paper	1¢ per lb. +3%	0.5¢ per lb. +1.5%	219
Greaseproof paper	1¢ per lb. +5%	0.5¢ per lb. +2.5%	655
Coated printing paper	2¢ per lb. +4.5%	1¢ per lb. +2%	202
Paper impregnated, coated, not litho-printed, not gummed	2¢ per lb. +4.5%	1¢ per lb. +2%	156

TABLE IX—*continued*

Products	Base rate of duty	Kennedy round rate of duty	Imports from Canada in 1966 ($000 U.S.)
Wallpaper	0.5¢ per lb. +10%	5%	1,176
Other paper and paperboard cut to size or shape	15%	7.5%	460
Boxes of paper, of paperboard, of papier mache, n.e.s.	14%	7%	511
Tubes of paper, tapered	1.5¢ per lb. +16.5%	0.7¢ per lb. +8%	132
Printed catalogs of foreign authorship	3%	1.5%	1,306
Printed catalogs—other	7%	3.5%	253
Maps, atlases, charts	8.5%	free	140
Architectural drawings and plans	8.5%	4%	246
Greeting cards	15%	7.5%	103
Lithographs on paper	12¢ per lb.	6¢ per lb.	130
Photographs, engravings, etchings, etc.	8.5%	4%	377
Printed matter, printed by a lithograph process	12¢ per lb.	6¢ per lb.	258
Other printed matter	15%	7.5%	429
UNITED KINGDOM			
Kraft wrapping paper	13½%	10%	3,300*
Linerboard	12½%	10%	15,900*
Groundwood printing paper	16⅔%	15%	2,400*
Writing and reproduction paper	16⅔%	15%	2,200
Corrugated containerboard	12½-20%	10-18%	3,700*
EUROPEAN ECONOMIC COMMUNITY			
Wood pulp	6% (duty-free for 1,935,000 metric tons)	3% (duty-free for 1,935,000 metric tons)	26,668
Newsprint	7%	7% (625,000 tons duty-free)	1,539
Kraft paper (linerboard)	16%	12%	1,579
Other papers (building paper; wet machine board; writing and reproduction paper)	16%	12%	1,385
Corrugated container board	21%	14%	
Paper and paperboard, cut to size	13-16%	6.5-12%	94

Source: Department of Trade and Commerce, reprint from *Foreign Trade*, July 1967.
*$000 Canadian, not U.S.

development reflects the fact that Canada is one of the world's few remaining large sources of softwood fibre.

Within the tariff-protected sector of the industry, the companies marketing branded products through retail grocery outlets tend to be subsidiaries of United States firms, in contrast with producers of printing, writing, and packaging grades, which tend to be Canadian-owned.

A concurrent development has been the outflow of some capital from Canadian producers into foreign pulp and paper production and marketing situations. In short, there is a trend towards larger companies, more fully integrated internationally.

4. Industry Trends, 1945–66

Trends in the Canadian pulp and paper industry over the last two decades have a special significance for the present study. Since one of the main purposes of the study is to appraise the impact upon the industry of free trade among North Atlantic countries, it is important not to attribute to the free-trade assumptions changes which were already taking place in the industry under the existing tariff structure.

At the same time, it is necessary to recognize the possibility that some changes occurred owing to the anticipation of freer trade under the Kennedy round. Although the Kennedy round was not concluded until mid-1967, and although it was not certain until then what, if any, reductions in paper tariffs might be made, some precautionary adjustments in production and marketing may have been undertaken by some pulp and paper companies in recent years. An attempt was made in the preparation of this chapter to screen out recent changes that may have been influenced by the anticipation of reductions in tariffs under the Kennedy round.

LOCATION AND SIZE OF MILLS

Trends in the location and size of pulp and paper mills since 1945 are shown, by province, in Table X. At the end of the Second World War, Quebec accounted for 51 percent of the total Canadian tonnage of pulp and paper production, Ontario for 29 percent, and British Columbia for about 8 percent. Almost two decades later, Quebec's share of total production had dropped to 35 percent and Ontario's to 25 percent; British Columbia's share, however, had increased to 20 percent.

The total number of pulp and paper mills in Canada increased from 111 at the end of the Second World War to 136 in 1966. The number of mills in Quebec and Ontario declined slightly over the 1945–64 period, but in

TABLE X

TRENDS IN PRODUCTION, NUMBER OF MILLS, OUTPUT PER MILL, AND
EMPLOYEES PER MILL, CANADA AND PRODUCING PROVINCES, 1945–64

	Two-year averages		
	1945–46	1954–55	1963–64
CANADA			
Production (000 tons)	6,280	10,098	13,274
Percent of total production	100	100	100
Number of mills	111	125	128.5
Average output per mill (000 tons)	57	80	103.4
Average number of persons employed per mill	383	492	517
QUEBEC			
Production (000 tons)	3,197	4,433	4,633
Percent of total production	50.9	43.9	34.9
Number of mills	49.5	55.0	54.5
Average output per mill (000 tons)	64.6	80.1	85.0
Average number of persons employed per mill	419	479	483
ONTARIO			
Production (000 tons)	1,827	2,706	3,332
Percent of total production	29.1	26.8	25.1
Number of mills	41.5	41	38.5
Average output per mill (000 tons)	44.0	66.0	86.5
Average number of persons employed per mill	315	464	529
BRITISH COLUMBIA			
Production (000 tons)	521	1,313	2,642
Percent of total production	8.3	13.0	19.4
Number of mills	7	12	14
Average output per mill (000 tons)	74.4	109.4	188.7
Average number of persons employed per mill	591	564	612
OTHER PROVINCES			
Production (000 tons)	735	1,645	2,667
Percent of total production	11.7	16.3	20.0
Number of mills	13	17	21.5
Average output per mill (000 tons)	56.5	96.7	124.0
Average number of persons employed per mill	346	548	475

Source: DBS, *Pulp and Paper Mills*, various issues.

British Columbia and "other provinces" the number of mills increased. In all provinces, however, the size of the mills increased over the period as a whole, in terms of both tonnage produced and number of persons employed. The average output per mill in 1945–46 was 57,000 tons, but by 1963–64 it had nearly doubled. The average number of persons employed per mill increased over the period from 383 to 517.

PRODUCTION AND TRADE

Postwar trends in volume of production, exports, and imports of pulp and paper are shown in Table XI. The volume of exports in 1963–64 represented 79 percent of Canadian production, slightly down from 81 percent at the end of the Second World War. Imports amounted to 1.6 percent of Canadian production in 1963–64, up from 1.0 percent two decades earlier.

TABLE XI

VOLUME OF CANADIAN PULP AND PAPER PRODUCTION,* EXPORTS, AND
IMPORTS IN 1945–46, 1955–56, AND 1965–66
(000 tons, two-year averages)

	Production	Exports	Imports†
1945–46	6,280	5,092	61
1955–56	10,602	8,879	212
1965–66	15,324	12,108	240

Source: CPPA, *Reference Tables*, various issues.
*To avoid double counting, pulp and paper production is derived by adding pulp exports to paper production.
†Approximate.

Volume of production since 1945 has grown at a compound annual rate of just over 4½ percent. Volume of exports has increased at a rate of just under 4½ percent compounded annually, and the growth in volume of imports has been at a compound rate of just over 7 percent per year. Trends in volume of production, exports, and imports by nine pulp and paper product groups are shown in Table XII.

It is worthwhile for our study to emphasize more clearly than does Table XII the trends since 1945 in exports and imports of the tariff-protected groups of papers. These are shown as compound annual rates of growth in Table XIII. This table reveals that rapid rates of increase in exports have taken place in the book and writing, sanitary, and paperboard groups. Rapid rates of increase in imports have taken place in the paperboard, tissue (excluding sanitary), book and writing (including fine papers), building paper and boards, special industrial paper, and wrapping paper groups.

Paperboard is the largest of the tariff-protected groups of papers. The containerboard line of the paperboard group has been expanding at a somewhat faster rate than the boxboard grades. Although paperboard production is oriented to the domestic market, exports, especially to the United Kingdom, have increased rapidly during the last decade. Exports of paperboard to the United States have been declining, however.

TABLE XII

VOLUME OF CANADIAN PULP AND PAPER PRODUCTION, EXPORTS,
AND IMPORTS IN 1945–46, 1955–56, AND 1965–66, BY NINE PRODUCT GROUPS
(000 tons, two-year averages)

Product group	Production			Exports			Imports		
	1945–46	1955–56	1965–66	1945–46	1955–56	1965–66	1945–46	1955–56	1965–66
Wood pulp	6,108	10,442	15,289	1,118	2,370	3,974	14	62	76
Newsprint	4,657	6,330	8,181	3,490	5,882	7,460	0	0	0
Paperboard	579	920	1,606	62	54	222	15	77	87
Book and writing	169	321	560	26	43	151	8*	17*	24*
Wrapping papers	169	276	394	26	17	38	2.5	3.8	6.4
Building papers and boards	125	267	389 }	35	56	66	12	37	31
Special industrial papers	8	8	20	2.4	3.9	1.6	2.7	5.2	7.9
Sanitary papers	39	97	187			13	4.8	4.1	3.8
Tissue papers	15	16	20	0.4	0.8	0.2	2.0	5.5	7.2

Source: CPPA, *Reference Tables*, various issues.
*Import group entitled "fine papers."

TABLE XIII

RATES OF GROWTH IN VOLUMES OF CANADIAN EXPORTS AND IMPORTS
OF TARIFF-PROTECTED GROUPS OF PAPERS, 1945–46 TO 1965-66,
EXPRESSED AS COMPOUND ANNUAL RATES
(percentages)

Paper group	Exports	Imports
Paperboard	6.5	9.1
Book and writing	9.1	5.6*
Wrapping	1.9	4.8
Building papers and boards and special industrial papers	3.3	4.9
Sanitary	8.8	−1.1
Tissue papers	−3.5	6.6

Source: Computed from data in CPPA, *Reference Tables*, various issues.
*Import group entitled "fine papers."

Imports of paperboard have been increasing faster than exports. The rate of increase in imports of paperboard was faster during the first decade following the Second World War than in the second decade.

The book and writing papers group (including fine papers) ranks second to paperboard in production and exports. Exports have been expanding at a rapid rate, about twice as fast as production. Exports to the United States have been expanding, but not as rapidly as exports to Britain. Imports of fine papers, mostly from the United States, have been expanding since 1945, but at a diminishing rate. The average value per ton of imports of fine papers substantially exceeds the average value per ton of exports.

Exports of wrapping papers have been expanding at an increasing rate over the past two decades, while imports have been increasing at an even faster rate.

For statistical reasons, special industrial papers have been grouped here with building papers and boards. Exports of the combined group have been expanding since 1945, but not as fast as imports. Imports of special industrial papers amount to a substantial percentage of domestic production. The rate of expansion of exports of building papers and boards has slowed over the past two decades. Imports of building papers and boards increased rapidly in the first decade after 1945, but declined in absolute amount during the second decade.

Exports of sanitary paper increased rapidly over the past two decades, while imports declined in absolute amount.

The production and export of tissue papers (excluding sanitary) are small. Exports expanded in the first decade after 1945, but declined thereafter. The trade in tissue papers is unique in that Canada imports more than it exports. The rate of increase in imports of tissue papers declined in the second decade after 1945, however, compared with the first decade. The average value per ton of imports of tissue papers greatly exceeds the average value per ton of exports.

RELATIVE IMPORTANCE OF PROTECTED GRADES

Table XIV indicates trends in relative importance of tariff-protected papers as a whole. By expressing the value of tariff-protected groups of papers as percentages of the value of all pulp and paper in 1945–46 and 1963–64, the table also shows the relative importance of each group of protected papers. The production of protected grades of paper has become more important since 1945. In 1963–64, the value of production of the protected grades amounted to 26.0 percent of the value of total pulp and paper production, compared with 23.3 percent in 1945–46. In terms of value of exports, protected grades hold about the same relative position as in 1945–46.

TABLE XIV

TRENDS IN VALUES OF PRODUCTION OF PROTECTED PAPERS RELATIVE TO
VALUE OF PRODUCTION OF ALL PULP AND PAPER
(percentages)

Paper group	1945–46	1963–64
Paperboard	8.8	10.5
Book and writing	6.1	7.6
Wrapping	4.3	4.3
Building papers and boards and special industrial papers	2.3	2.5
Sanitary	1.0	0.9
Tissues	0.8	0.2
Subtotal	23.3	26.0
All pulp and paper*	100.0	100.0

Source: Computed from data in DBS, *Pulp and Paper Mills*, various issues.
*To avoid double counting, pulp and paper production is derived by adding pulp exports to paper production.

Paperboard and book and writing papers have increased in relative importance. Wrapping papers, building papers and boards, special industrials, and sanitary papers retained about the same relative position over the period. The relative importance of tissue papers (excluding sanitary) has declined.

PRODUCTION COSTS

Dominion Bureau of Statistics data on production costs are for the Canadian pulp and paper industry as a whole. The absolute levels of component costs, therefore, are not very significant. Trends in the relative importance of the main cost items, however, are relevant to the present study. Table XV shows these as percentages of the mill value of the product[1] for the two-year periods 1945–46, 1954–55, and 1963–64.

TABLE XV

TRENDS IN PULP AND PAPER COSTS RELATIVE TO AVERAGE MILL VALUE
OF PRODUCTION
(percentages)

Cost item	1945–46	1954–55	1963–64
Wood and wood residue	30.9	28.3	24.7
Salaries and wages	20.0	20.9	16.8
Fuel and electricity	9.5	7.1	7.3
Chemicals	2.8	3.3	6.6
Other materials and supplies	12.1	11.3	12.8
Other costs plus profit or loss	24.7	29.1	31.8
Total	100.0	100.0	100.0

Source: Computed from data in DBS, *Pulp and Paper Mills*, various issues.

Although the cost of pulpwood per cord has been rising since 1945, and although the cost of wood per ton of product rose during the first decade after 1945, the relative importance of wood costs declined from 31 percent of the mill value of the product in 1945–46 to 28 percent in 1954–55 and 25 percent in 1963–64. The relative shift from mechanical pulping to chemical pulping, which has a lower wood yield, would have worked in the direction of raising the relative importance of wood costs, but this influence was outweighed by increased productivity in logging, the sharp increase in the amount of wood residue used, the shift towards more highly processed and expensive products, and the rapid increases in certain other costs. In 1945, wood residues accounted for less than 1 percent of the total wood used in pulping, compared with over 16 percent in 1964, when wood residue had an average value per cord of $19.63, compared with $25 per cord of roundwood.[2]

[1]To avoid double counting, the product is taken as the sum of pulp exports plus the output of all papers and paperboards.
[2]According to DBS, *Pulp and Paper Mills*.

The relative importance of labour costs remained about the same between 1945–46 and 1954–55, but then declined. This was mainly due to decreased labour-output ratios.

There has been a downward trend in the relative importance of fuel and electricity costs since 1945 and a sharp upward trend in chemical costs. Costs of other materials and supplies have maintained their relative importance. All remaining costs,[3] including profits and losses, have increased in relative importance.

PRODUCTIVITY

The only study available on productivity trends in the Canadian pulp and paper industry was published in 1966 by the Dominion Bureau of Statistics.[4] It related mill output to labour input over the fifteen-year period 1947–61 and made comparisons with the U.S. industry. Some findings of the DBS study are shown in Table XVI. This table suggests that there was

TABLE XVI

COMPARISON OF TRENDS IN OUTPUT PER WORKER IN
CANADIAN AND U.S. PULP AND PAPER MILLS OVER THE
PERIOD 1947–61
(index numbers, 1949 = 100)

	Real gross output per production and related worker	
	Canada	U.S.
1947	95.6	98.3
1954	106.4	121.9
1961	127.5	168.5
Average yearly rate of change, 1947–61	1.6%	3.6%

Source: DBS, *Productivity Trends in Industry*, Report no. 1.

substantial disparity between Canada and the United States in productivity gains over the period. Real gross output per production and related worker increased at a compound annual rate of 1.6 percent in Canada, compared with 3.6 percent in the United States.

The rate of increase in number of production workers in Canada between 1947 and 1961 was 1.9 percent per year, while the number of "persons employed," which includes office and administrative staff as well as production workers, increased at an annual rate of 2.2 percent.

[3]Including taxes, depreciation, maintenance, selling and advertising, etc., but excluding cost of transportation of the product, about which little information is published.
[4]*Productivity Trends in Industry*, Report no. 1.

Changes in output per unit of labour are attributable, not just to labour, but to other inputs as well. Prominent among these other inputs, particularly in pulp and paper production, is capital. The rate of capital formation in the pulp and paper industry has been substantial over the last two decades. Capital expenditures over the three-year period 1948–50 averaged over $73 million a year. Over the three-year period 1964–66, capital expenditures in the industry averaged $286 million per year.

The total amount of capital employed in the industry in 1948 has been estimated at $1.4 billion, compared with $4.8 billion in 1964. In 1948, the amount of capital per employee was approximately $27,000, compared with $69,000 in 1964—an increase of over 150 percent. Output per man-year increased from 148 tons in the 1945–46 period to 200 tons in 1963–64.

Mention was made earlier in this chapter of the fact that there has been a trend towards using more wood per ton of output because of the shift towards chemical pulps, which use more wood than mechanical pulps. In the 1945–46 period, an average of 1.33 cords of wood was used per ton of product, compared with 1.39 cords in 1954–55 and 1.41 cords in 1963–64.

PROFITS

The profit record of firms in the pulp and paper industry for the past decade has been mixed. However, the firms which are both integrated and concentrated on newsprint and pulp production have been able to maintain, with few exceptions, rates of return on equity at 10 percent or above (until 1966). On the other hand, the producers who have a larger stake in protected grades have generally experienced a poorer profit record: their return on equity has fluctuated between 3 and 9 percent during the past ten years. Only in the production of book and writing papers—the protected product for which Canadian producers have shown greatest relative strength in export markets—have rates of return at times exceeded 10 percent.

Clearly, protection has not proved as strong a base for financial success as export orientation. Whether the now-protected grades could, under free trade, match pulp and newsprint as a basis for financially successful production is, of course, another question.

THE PRESENT STATUS OF THE INDUSTRY

In Chapters 3 and 4, the industry's record of recent years has been described. To interpret this record is not the main purpose of our study, but it is important to identify those aspects of development and organization which might be called upon to explain the current status of the industry and its likely reaction to trade liberalization.

There are three most important features of the industry's record: its rapid growth, its sharp division between export-oriented and domestic-oriented production, and the predominance among the latter group of about ten principal producers with widely varying product patterns. The rapid growth of the industry has always meant that the stimulus to new investment has been high and that the timing of new capacity has been an important feature of competitive activity in the industry. Because of the large capital expenditures required in each addition to productive capacity, there have been times when capacity has outstripped demand and profit levels consequently depressed.

The substantial differences between export-oriented pulp and newsprint production on the one hand and tariff-protected grades of paper on the other have apparently bequeathed a legacy of practices and attitudes. It has been comparatively easy to produce and market the large volume of newsprint required on this continent. The standardized nature of the product and, in some instances, the proprietary interest of large publishers have enabled Canada's producers to obtain the large orders required to assure long runs, and elaborate distribution facilities have not been needed in the foreign market. The principal problem has centred on efforts to ensure that those major interests in the publishing world would not be able to play off against one another the newsprint producers in the principal supplying countries.

For the other grades of paper, the situation is very different. While Canadian suppliers do not have to face the bargaining strength of major buyers, they do have the challenges of distribution to overcome, and in such major markets as those of the United States this means not only a need to absorb the U.S. tariff, but also the necessity of competing with American producers who supply a full line of paper products through distribution outlets which are often an integral part of the manufacturing firm. A related factor is the great diversity of the product range covered in the non-newsprint sector, a factor which under the circumstances cited makes the penetration of foreign markets appear a formidable task.

Under the circumstances, the activities of the dominant firms in the protected sector of the industry can be better understood and interpreted. Behind a Canadian tariff generally 20–22½ percent (before the Kennedy round) on the categories of paper other than newsprint, there has been a frustrating search for efficient supply conditions. With substantial economies of scale to be enjoyed in production, the number of firms producing any product line (often four or five of the ten firms which dominate the protected sector) has been too many for any one to achieve the lengths of run possible on modern paper-making machines. Furthermore, there was not available in this industry the opportunity to win a larger market share by differentiating products through elaborate style change or advertising activity (tissues being an exception). In such circumstances, because each firm recognizes the impact of its price and selling decisions on other producers, there is a tendency either to severe price competition or to efforts towards stabilization of markets through agreements among the manufacturers. In the past this latter tendency appeared at times in this sector of the paper industry. Even in the absence of explicit agreement, it is not difficult to achieve a measure of pricing stability in industries of this kind in Canada, because of the clear possibility of setting a price just below that at which imports could reach the Canadian market—that is, just under the foreign (usually U.S.) price plus the Canadian tariff.

The difficulty is that stabilization of price at or near this level is no guarantee of comfortable profits or efficient operation. Not only is there a tendency to compete in the building of new capacity in a growing market, but in an industry sector in which a wide variety of products is in demand, each firm attempts to diversify in order to supply a full line of products and to discover a line in which it can gain unusual advantage over its rivals. This would appear to have happened among the Canadian producers, as the uneven profit record for manufacturers of protected grades (as well as other evidence) clearly suggests.

Some have been tempted to prescribe a more fully "organized" industry in order to ensure specialization by firm, but if such a solution were further to concentrate production of particular product lines without exposing Canadian producers to import competition, it would be likely to arouse the opposition of government and the consumer. Perhaps the only alternative is to face the adjustment to reduction of trade barriers and to adopt at the same time policies designed to enable the achievement of longer runs through effective penetration of continental and world markets and specialization by individual firms where required.

It is within this context that the industry itself has moved in recent years to consider more seriously the implications of free trade for its future development.

5. Demand Levels and Prospects

The "16th Annual World Review" of *Pulp & Paper*, issued in 1966, stated that it is now generally accepted by FAO and other international forecasters that world demand for paper and paperboard will at least double every fifteen years. This would mean a compound rate of growth of at least 4¾ percent per year. World production of paper and paperboard increased by 7.5 percent in 1966, compared with an increase of 6.2 percent in 1965.

FAO's estimates of world consumption of paper and paperboard in 1965 and 1980 were 109 and 230 million tons, respectively. For 1965 and 1980, North America's share of world consumption was estimated for FAO at 45.3 percent and 41.2 percent, respectively.

World consumption per capita of paper and paperboard in 1966 was estimated at 69 pounds. The country with the highest per capita consumption was the United States (530 pounds), followed by Sweden (353 pounds), and Canada (310 pounds). It was not until 1962 that the world reached the level of per capita consumption which the United States had reached at the turn of the century. The populations of 135 countries in 1966 and their per capita consumption of paper in 1956, 1960, 1965, and 1966 are shown in Table XVII.

It is relevant to compare particularly the more developed countries, especially those of the OECD, in their increases in per capita paper consumption. This can be done with the aid of Chart 1, which shows per capita paper consumption in the OECD countries in 1955 and 1965. The most rapidly growing markets among industrialized countries are Japan and the EEC. The U.S. share of world consumption is expected to continue declining slowly. Canada's share of world consumption in 1980 may also be slightly smaller than it is at present.

Canada ranks second to the United States among countries producing pulp and paper. Sweden and Finland are the third and fourth largest pulp producers in the world, while Japan and the USSR rank third and fourth as paper producers. Tables XVIII and XIX list the pulp and paper producing countries in descending order of importance.

DEMAND PROSPECTS FOR CANADA'S PULP AND PAPER

For estimates of the prospective demand for Canada's pulp and paper, we have relied mainly on a study, *Demand For Canada's Wood Fibre in 1975 and 2000*, prepared for the National Forestry Conference in February, 1966, by W. E. Haviland, I. B. Chenoweth, and E. T. Owens, all of the Canadian Pulp and Paper Association. Referring to the usual hazards of forecasting, the authors of the demand study also pointed out that overseas exports "are especially difficult to forecast at this time, due to uncertainties caused by tariff negotiations, apparent wood shortages in western Europe and Japan, emphasis on local production in many countries, and Russia's supply-demand prospects."

The CPPA demand study selected four mutually exclusive categories of pulp and paper: wood-pulp exports, dissolving pulp for domestic

TABLE XVII

PER CAPITA PAPER AND BOARD CONSUMPTION OF COUNTRIES

(by rank)

#	Country	Population 1966 (000)	Per capita consumption in lbs			
			1956	1960	1965	1966
1	United States	196,502	432	431	501	530
2	Sweden	7,800	208	265	363	353
3	Canada	20,000	280	280	310	310
4	Switzerland	5,950	163	195	256	266
5	U.K.	54,744	180	236	260	265
6	Denmark	4,745	154	198	255	265
7	Netherlands	12,442	117	185	231	246
8	Norway	3,767	159	180	216	243
9	W. Germany	59,700	129	174	239	225
10	New Zealand	2,682	141	177	233	224
11	Australia	11,448	156	176	223	222
12	Belgium/Luxembourg	9,830	110	137	180	217
13	Finland	4,639	131	156	198	208
14	Japan	99,060	60	103	162	176
15	France	49,230	106	127	159	175
16	Iceland	197	93	92	157	155
17	Ireland	2,880	81	90	134	142
18	Austria	7,291	72	103	124	133
19	Puerto Rico	2,660	70	98	109	127
20	E. Germany	17,500	82	92	131	119
21	Hong Kong	3,800	43	49	99	116
22	Czechoslovakia	14,210	74	36	100	106
23	Italy	53,000	43	63	97	105
24	Bahamas	15,500	46		53	103
25	Israel	2,600	53	57	84	83
26	Costa Rica	1,497	14	15	82	81
27	South Africa	18,298	51	59	70	76
28	Argentina	22,800	43	64	57	73
29	Spain	32,000	19	26	51	73
30	Hungary	10,197	24	40	68	68
31	Singapore	1,900		42		63
32	Poland	31,800	76	47	57	61
33	Ecuador	4,900		8	2	59
34	Honduras	2,400	4	8	25	58
35	Chile	9,144	24	21	50	55
36	Venezuela	10,170	10	44	49	55
37	Yugoslavia	19,857	15	20	51	53
38	Greece	8,500	17	26	40	52
39	Jamaica	1,859	9		36	50
40	Bulgaria	8,200	22	18	36	50
41	Uruguay	2,500	48	42	58	48
42	Lebanon	2,300	18	24	46	46
43	USSR	234,000	24	33	44	46
44	Surinam	400		18	46	45
45	Panama	1,221	20	21	35	44
46	Taiwan	13,473	14	39	41	44
47	Cuba	7,500	69	73	40	44
48	Portugal	9,600	17	23	29	43
49	Trinidad/Tobago	1,000	40		45	42
50	Mexico	43,400	26	32	38	41
51	Rumania	19,143	37	42	32	40
52	Cyprus	603	20	14	32	33
53	Colombia	18,620	12	11	37	26
54	Guiana, Fr.	39			5	25
55	Brazil	84,000	19	21	24	23
56	Albania	1,900		17	21	23
57	Peru	12,000	7	14	19	22
58	Kuwait	460			12	22
59	Malaysia	8,400			10	19
60	UAR	30,000	10	16	11	17
61	Br. Honduras	114	34	11	13	17
62	Nicaragua	1,600	8	35	10	16
63	Rhodesia	4,210		8	10	16
64	Algeria	12,550	6	8	8	15
65	Guyana	650	26	27	14	15
66	So. Vietnam	15,800	4	5	14	15
67	Philippines	34,500	8	9	14	15
68	South Korea	29,208	5	5	11	14
69	Jordan	2,077			10	14
70	Turkey	32,000	8	6	9	12
71	Tunisia	4,600	8		9	12
72	Guatemala	4,300	8	8	42	12
73	Syria	5,200			9	12
74	Libya	1,560	5	8	12	11
75	Domin. Rep.	3,700	5	6	11	11
76	Malta	300			3	10
77	El Salvador	2,900	8	8	10	10
78	Mainland China	786,000				10
79	Kenya	9,300	3	4	10	10
80	Thailand	31,500	6	5	8	9
81	Iraq	8,300	2	8	8	9
82	Zambia	3,790			7	9
83	Congo Rep.	850			12	9
84	Morocco	13,500	6	6	8	9
85	Iran	25,800	2	6	8	9
86	Ceylon	11,500	5	6	8	8
87	Mongolia	1,100			6	8
88	Senegal	3,440			7	7
89	Ivory Coast	3,800			6	7
90	Ghana	8,000		7	6	6
91	Paraguay	2,100	5	4	5	6
92	Somalia	4,500			5	5
93	Sierra Leone	2,250		.5	4	5
94	Bolivia	4,325	3	1	4	4
95	Swaziland	375		6	3	4
96	Malagasy	6,336			4	4
97	Gabon	470			4	4
98	Angola	5,012			2	3
99	N. Korea	11,000			3	3
100	India	490,000	2	2	3	3
101	Tibet	1,400			3	3
102	Cameroon	5,100			3	3
103	Liberia	2,700	5		.6	3
104	Laos	3,000		4	3	3
105	Sudan	13,000	2	2	3	3
106	Uganda	7,600	2	2	2	3
107	Tanzania	10,250		2	2	3
108	Nepal	9,400				2
109	Burundi	2,800				2
110	Nigeria	56,500	2	2	3	2
111	Pakistan	100,000				2
112	Guinea	3,500			2	2
113	N. Vietnam	16,200		1	2	2
114	Cambodia	6,000	3	3	3	2
115	Burma	24,200	2	2	2	2
116	Yemen	5,000				2
117	Congo Dem. Rep.	15,700			2	1
118	Malawi	4,024			1	1
119	Trucial States	313				1
120	Lesotho	900				1
121	Togo	1,500			1	1
122	Botswana	550				1
123	Mozambique	6,900			2	1
124	Indonesia	105,000	4	4	2	1
125	Saudi Arabia	8,000	4		2	1
126	Cent. African Rep.	1,465	1		2	1
127	Haiti	4,600	4	3	2	1
128	Rwanda	3,200			2	1
129	Ethiopia	22,500		.5	.7	1
130	Gambia	2,320	.5		.6	.5
131	Dahomey	2,500			.3	.5
132	Mauretania	900			.3	.5
133	Chad	3,500				.4
134	Upper Volta	5,000			.3	.4
135	Niger	3,250				.3
136	Mali	2,300	.2		.4	.3
137	Afghanistan	13,494			.2	.1
	World except U.S.A.	3,189,445	28.1	32	40	42
	Total world	3,385,947	50.4	55	66.6	69

Source: Reprinted with permission of the magazine PULP & PAPER from the 17th [...]

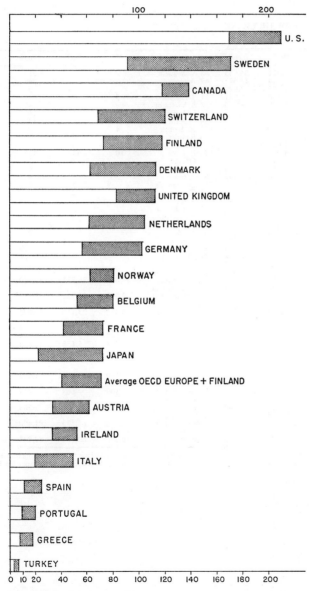

Chart 1. Approximate Consumption of Paper and Board in OECD Member Countries (in kilograms: 1 kilo = 2.2 pounds). The white part of bar shows consumption in 1955, the shaded part the increase to 1965.

Source: OECD, *Pulp and Paper*, September 1966.

TABLE XVIII

ALL NATIONS PRODUCING PULP AND HOW THEY RANK
(thousand tons)

		1956	1960	1965	1966
1	United States	22,131	24,154	33,921	35,635
2	Canada	10,543	11,183	14,244	15,673
3	Sweden	4,512	5,480	7,163	7,020
4	Finland	3,131	4,071	6,145	6,291
5	Japan	2,427	3,893	5,680	6,260
6	USSR	2,871	3,568	5,016	5,350
7	Mainland China	600	850	2,200	2,300
8	Norway	1,378	1,669	2,012	1,982
9	France	886	1,365	1,621	1,708
10	W. Germany	1,437	1,718	1,557	1,567
11	Italy	461	596	774	851
12	India	57	90	711	743
13	Austria	631	699	736	739
14	E. Germany	636	812	678	694
15	Poland	421	505	621	678
16	Czechoslovakia	530	761	671	671
17	Brazil	210	343	574	633
18	Netherlands	491	601	592	577
19	Spain	147	180	424	534
20	New Zealand	214	293	460	481
21	Yugoslavia	134	193	416	448
22	U.K.	149	150	359	428
23	Rumania	104	130	322	392
24	Mexico	174	260	372	388
25	S. Africa	85	128	327	381
26	Australia	208	241	350	368
27	Chile	22	115	225	351
28	Switzerland	209	227	295	293
29	Belgium, Luxembourg	117	160	248	284
30	Portugal	53	95	218	257
31	Taiwan	23	174	227	229
32	Argentina	88	97	199	209
33	Bulgaria	28	34	121	124
34	Swaziland			93	109
35	Denmark	15	25	82	100
36	Colombia			56	100
37	Hungary	25	49	91	99
38	Turkey	32	54	88	91
39	Pakistan	31	62	77	88
40	Philippines	5	7	63	64
41	Peru	15	21	55	44
42	UAR		5	33	44
43	Morocco	4		40	39
44	S. Korea	7	11	30	39
45	Cuba	20	25	33	33
46	Puerto Rico	12	32	30	30
47	Tunisia			30	28

		1956	1960	1965	1966
48	Venezuela			21	23
49	Angola			26	23
50	Sudan			15	15
51	Thailand	3	3	11	15
52	S. Vietnam			14	15
53	Indonesia		5	16	15
54	Algeria	20		13	13
55	N. Korea	4		10	10
56	Rhodesia		4	7	8
57	Uruguay	8	9	8	8
58	Ireland	10	11	17	8
59	Greece		8	2	7
60	Israel			6	6
61	Albania	3	3	4	4
62	Guatemala	.9	1	4	4
63	Ceylon		2	2	4
64	Syria			3	3
65	Cambodia			3	3
66	N. Vietnam			3	3
67	Iran			3	3
68	Jordan			2	2
69	Bolivia		.4	.4	.4
70	El Salvador			.3	.3
71	Malaysia		.2	.1	.1
	U.S. & Canada (short tons)	32,674	36,337	47,540	51,308
	U.S. & Canada (metric tons)	29,641	32,964	43,127	46,546
	Europe (short tons)	18,412	23,110	32,005	31,191
	Europe (metric tons)	16,703	20,965	29,034	28,959
	Asia (short tons)	3,580	5,684	9,879	16,655
	Asia (metric tons)	3,248	5,156	8,962	15,109
	Latin America (short tons)	551	905	1,547	1,829
	Latin America (metric tons)	500	821	1,403	1,659
	Africa (short tons)	109	663	428	663
	Africa (metric tons)	99	601	388	601
	Total world (short tons)	55,326	66,173	91,400	95,646
	Total world (metric tons)	50,296	60,031	82,935	86,253

Source: Reprinted with permission of the magazine PULP & PAPER from its 17th Annual World Review number for 1967.

TABLE XIX

ALL NATIONS PRODUCING PAPER AND BOARD AND HOW THEY RANK
(thousand tons)

		1956	1960	1965	1966
1	United States	31,428	34,282	43,600	46,567
2	Canada	8,504	8,617	10,319	11,256
3	Japan	2,831	4,974	7,487	9,014
4	USSR	2,839	3,549	5,158	5,796
5	United Kingdom	3,618	4,562	5,102	5,088
6	W. Germany	2,955	3,787	4,670	4,781
7	Finland	1,684	2,180	3,533	3,815
8	France	2,141	2,884	3,490	3,804
9	Mainland China	1,729	2,110	3,300	3,600
10	Sweden	1,733	2,371	3,440	3,508
11	Italy	1,023	1,619	2,428	2,795
12	Netherlands	931	1,223	1,424	1,496
13	Norway	651	870	1,001	1,164
14	E. Germany	680	867	1,220	1 041
15	Poland	437	705	898	920
16	Brazil	378	512	772	880
17	Australia	397	556	827	834
18	Spain	287	360	670	830
19	Austria	557	652	796	813
20	Czechoslovakia	485	674	773	799
21	Switzerland	407	529	672	693
22	Mexico	346	450	651	696
23	India	217	380	704	667
24	Belgium	371	453	561	598
25	Argentina	289	361	513	577
26	Yugoslavia	129	193	524	527
27	S. Africa	130	225	411	481
28	Rumania	123	154	305	400
29	New Zealand	121	203	391	397
30	Chile	60	122	210	251
31	Taiwan	68	156	205	234
32	Denmark	160	200	230	232
33	Hungary	100	153	192	213
34	Venezuela	14	44	167	187
35	S. Korea	10	35	157	184
36	Colombia	46	46	210	160
37	Portugal	81	120	167	171
38	Bulgaria	60	59	138	146
39	Greece	50	94	145	132
40	UAR	22	60	122	119
41	Turkey	53	75	108	117
42	Cuba	80	150	107	115
43	Pakistan	34	77	112	111
44	Peru	36	55	93	104
45	Philippines	20	43	100	95
46	Ireland	71	92	110	71
47	Israel	20	30	58	59
48	Puerto Rico	24	40	52	55
49	Thailand	4	4	22	50
50	Morocco	5	9	52	45
51	Uruguay	39	37	43	41
52	Algeria	30		31	35
53	Rhodesia	7	8	18	22
54	S. Vietnam	2		17	18
55	Indonesia	7	7	18	17
56	Lebanon	1	2	14	15
57	N. Korea	5	5	12	12
58	Albania	5	8	11	11
59	Iran	3	6	6	11
60	Ceylon	.2	5	8	10
61	Guatemala	.9	3	8	9
62	W. Malaysia		.3	3	8
63	Angola			8	7
64	Libya	1	2	3	5
65	Tunisia			5	5
66	N. Vietnam	1		5	4
67	Sudan		2	4	4
68	Cambodia	1		3	3
69	Kenya			3	3
70	Costa Rica			3	3
71	Dominican Rep.	.1	.6	3	3
72	Jordan			2	2
73	Ghana	.3	.3	2	2
74	Paraguay	.4	.4	1	1
75	Congo, Dem. Rep. of		.6	1	1
76	Syria			5	1
77	Panama			1	1
78	Ecuador	1	5	6	.5
79	Mongolia	.4		.5	.5
80	Ethiopia	.2	.3	.5	.5
81	Bolivia	.8	.4	.5	.5
82	Nepal			.4	.4
83	El Salvador	.2	.2	.3	.3
84	Tibet	.2		.2	.2

	1956	1960	1965	1966
TOTALS	68,541	81,963	108,739	116,941
U.S. & Canada (short tons)	39,933	42,899	53,919	57,823
U.S. & Canada (metric tons)	36,226	38,917	48,914	52,456
Europe (short tons)	21,629	28,257	37,864	39,962
Europe (metric tons)	19,621	25,634	34,349	36,253
Asia (short tons)	5,469	8,665	13,456	15,347
Asia (metric tons)	4,961	7,861	12,207	13,922
Latin America (short tons)	1,314	1,825	2,839	3,080
Latin America (metric tons)	1,192	1,656	2,575	2,794
Africa (short tons)	196	317	661	729
Africa (metric tons)	178	288	600	661
Total world (short tons)	68,541	81,963	108,739	116,941
Total world (metric tons)	62,310	74,355	98,646	106,087

Source: Reprinted with permission of the magazine PULP & PAPER from its 17th Annual World Review number for 1967.

non-paper uses, newsprint for domestic and export markets, and other papers (excluding newsprint) and paperboards for domestic and export markets. The wood-pulp exports were subdivided into sulphate (kraft), sulphite, mechanical, and dissolving. Other papers and paperboards were subdivided into paperboard, fine papers, wrapping papers, building papers and boards, and tissue and sanitary papers.

Annual production and shipments data for the selected products were plotted on semi-logarithmic paper for the two decades 1945–64. Such paper allowed constant annual rates of change to be represented by straight trend lines, which were fitted to the postwar time series. Allowance was made for the abnormal recovery of markets in satisfying pent-up demand at the end of the Second World War. By anchoring the other end of the trend lines to 1964, the study chose to emphasize the high level of output in recent years. The postwar rates of change are shown in column 2 of Table XX.

The most important and difficult step in the exercise was estimating the prospective rates of change in output for the 1965–75 decade (column 3). The prospective rates of change (compound annual rates) were the result of balancing various considerations such as the industry's past performance, present practices and development plans, and market outlook for the future. The projected levels of demand for product groups for 1975 (column 4) were derived arithmetically from the prospective rates of change over the 1965–75 decade.

The CPPA study warned that since the estimates were based on existing demand conditions and known production plans, they would be too low if a massive shift were to develop towards North American sources of supply for meeting the growing demand of European and other overseas markets. Otherwise, the prospective increase in the total demand for Canada's pulp and paper between 1964 and 1975, expressed in terms of a simple percentage change (row 15 of Table XX), was 67.8 percent; expressed as a compound annual rate (row 16), it was 4.8 percent. With respect to the product composition of the prospective demand for papers, the relative importance of newsprint is declining, and the relative importance of other papers and paperboards is increasing.

Pulp exports for the first decade after 1945, although irregular, trended upward at a 5 percent annual rate. Based on the seven years since 1958, the CPPA demand study forecast a 7 percent rate of growth for the 1965–75 decade, reaching the impressive level of over 7.5 million tons in 1975.

Pulp exports to the United States, the major export market, increased during the first two postwar decades at a 4 percent rate and were expected to expand at a faster rate during the next decade. Postwar pulp exports to

TABLE XX

DERIVATION OF PROSPECTIVE LEVELS OF PRODUCTION AND/OR EXPORTS OF PULPS AND PAPERS
(all quantities except rates of change are in thousands of tons)

Group or subgroup	(1) 1964	(2) Estimated postwar annual percentage change	(3) Prospective annual percentage change 1965–75	(4) Level in 1975
1. Pulp exports:	3,603	5 (1948–64)	7	7,545
2. Sulphate pulp*	2,029	5½ (1961–64)	11	6,060
3. Sulphite pulp	885	8½ (1961–64)	−1	800
4. Dissolving pulp	403	7 (1961–64)	⅔	435
5. Mechanical pulp	286	½ (1948–64)	−1¼	250
6. Dissolving pulp for domestic non-paper market	67	4½ (1950–64)	4¾	110
7. Newsprint exports and domestic	7,310	2⅔ (1948–65)	3⅓	10,500
8. Other papers and paperboards, domestic and exports:	2,821	4⅔ (1948–64)	5⅓	4,998
9. Paperboard	1,376	4½ (1948–64)	5⅔	2,515
10. Fine papers†	561	5½ (1948–63)	6‡ (1964–75)	1,064
11. Wrapping paper	343	3½ (1948–65)	3½	516
12. Building papers and boards	350	3½ (1948–64)	3½	511
13. Tissue and sanitary	191	6¾ (1948–64)	6¾	392
14. Total	13,734			23,043
15. Increase in demand, 1975 over 1964				67.8%
16. Compound annual rate of change 1964–75				4.8%

*Includes a small amount of soda pulp and screenings.
†Includes groundwood printing paper.
‡Upward discontinuity in 1964.
Source: W. E. Haviland, I. B. Chenoweth, and E. T. Owens, *Demand for Canada's Wood Fibre in 1975 and 2000*, prepared for the National Forestry Conference of February, 1966.

the United Kingdom expanded at a 4½ percent rate, which was expected to be maintained. Pulp exports to overseas markets, other than the United Kingdom, had been expanding faster than 10 percent a year, a rate of growth that was expected to continue.

The forecasts of pulp exports were in large part derived from forecasts for the four main component groups discussed below. Pulp exports are predominantly chemical pulps, which accounted for almost 80 percent of pulp exports in 1945–46 and 92 percent in 1964. As mentioned previously, the trend towards chemical-pulp exports and away from mechanical-pulp exports is expected to continue in the 1965–75 period.

(1) In 1964, sulphate (kraft) pulp exports exceeded 2 million tons, accounting for 55½ percent of all pulp exports. Having regard to current increases in sulphate-pulp capacity, the demand study expected these

exports to expand at an annual rate of 11 percent over the next decade, reaching a level of approximately 6.1 million tons in 1975.

(2) In 1964, sulphite-pulp exports accounted for almost 24½ percent of all pulp exports. A slight decline in sulphite-pulp exports was forecast for the next decade, to a level of 800,000 tons in 1975.

(3) In 1964, dissolving-pulp exports accounted for about 12 percent of all pulp exports. With little new capacity coming in, only a slight increase in exports was forecast for the next decade, to a level of 435,000 tons in 1975.

(4) In 1964, mechanical-pulp exports accounted for 7½ percent of all pulp exports. Economic pressures appear to be inhibiting the export of ground-wood pulp (as well as pulpwood and chips). The demand study expected to see mechanical-pulp exports decline by over one percent per year, reaching a level of about 250,000 tons in 1975.

(5) Over the 1950–64 period, domestic shipments of dissolving pulp for non-paper uses in Canada increased irregularly at an annual rate of 4½ percent. Although little new capacity was expected for the early future, production for the domestic market was expected to continue increasing at about the same rate, reaching a level of 110,000 tons in 1975.

The United States is the major market for Canadian newsprint. In 1965 and 1966, newsprint exports to the United States accounted for 79 percent of Canadian production. Newsprint consumption in the United States is determined mainly by circulation and amount of advertising, the latter in turn being determined by income growth and competition of other media. Shipments to the United States tend to be residual to production capacity there. In the postwar period 1948–65, newsprint exports to the United States increased by about 2½ percent a year. Exports to overseas markets over the period 1954–65 expanded at a rate of 4½ percent. Domestic shipments since 1948 have increased at a rate of 3¾ percent, and total production for all markets has been expanding at a rate of 2⅜ percent. Production was expected to expand at a rate of 3⅛ percent, to a level of 10.5 million tons in 1975. This estimate was based on the optimistic assumption that shipments to the United States and overseas markets will increase more rapidly than they have in past decades.

In the period since the Second World War, the production of papers (excluding newsprint) and paperboards for the domestic and export markets has trended upward at an annual rate of 4⅜ percent. The dominant component here is the domestic market, which has grown at a rate of 4½ percent. Since 1955, exports have increased at a rate of nearly 8½ percent, owing largely to a rapid rate of increase in exports to the United Kingdom.

The 4½ percent domestic rate of growth was expected to continue during the 1965–75 decade. Sales, however, could be influenced substantially by the outcome of tariff developments. Export changes in the component subgroups, which were already under way before the Kennedy round settlement, are discussed below. The CPPA demand study estimated a 5⅛ percent rate of growth in total production for the coming decade, reaching a level of close to 5 million tons in 1975.

Paperboard is the largest component of the "other papers and paperboards" group. Postwar production in Canada has been mostly for the domestic market and has been growing at a rate of 4½ percent per year. Production for the domestic market was expected to continue expanding at this rate. Exports declined during the first postwar decade but have been growing at a rapid rate since then, notably to the United Kingdom. Exports were expected to jump during 1966–67, owing to increased capacity, and to expand thereafter at a rate of 3¾ percent. Total paperboard production was expected to increase at a rate of 5⅝ percent, reaching a level of 2.5 million tons in 1975.

The fine papers subgroup (including groundwood printing) is the second largest component of the "other papers and paperboards" group. Postwar production has been growing at an annual rate of 5½ percent. Production has been mainly for the domestic market, which has been expanding at a rate of 5 percent. Exports expanded at a 7½ percent rate until 1963, largely owing to continuing increases in exports of groundwood printing papers to the United States. In 1964, however, exports increased sharply, mainly because of an expansion of shipments to the United Kingdom.

The domestic market for fine papers was expected to continue to grow at an annual rate of 5 percent, and the export market was expected to grow at a rate of 7½ percent from a new 1964 level. The net effect would be an increase in total production of 6 percent per year, reaching a level of about 1.1 million tons in 1975.

Wrapping paper production in the postwar period expanded at an annual rate of 3½ percent. This production was largely for the domestic market, and the rate of growth of the domestic market has been tapering off. The demand study expected the domestic market to grow at a 1¾ percent rate during the coming decade.

Total production of wrapping paper has maintained its growth owing to expanding exports in recent years. A jump in exports in 1966 was expected, because of new capacity, and growth thereafter at a 5⅛ percent rate per year. Total production of wrapping papers was expected to continue expanding at a 3½ percent rate, reaching a level of 516,000 tons in 1975.

Production of building papers and boards during the postwar period expanded at an annual rate of 3½ percent. This production was largely for the domestic market, which expanded at a 3 percent rate per year. Exports, mostly to the United States, increased irregularly at a rate of 6 percent per year. These rates were expected to continue through to 1975, with total production reaching a level of 511,000 tons.

Production of tissue and sanitary papers expanded during the postwar period at an annual rate of 6¾ percent. Production was dominated by the domestic market, which grew at an annual rate of 6½ percent. Exports of sanitary papers, especially to the United Kingdom, have been expanding during the last decade. It was expected that the production of tissue and sanitary papers would continue to expand at a 6¾ percent rate per year, reaching a level of 392,000 tons in 1975.

COMPARISONS OF DEMAND ESTIMATES

These findings of the CPPA demand study made in 1966 were compared with related forecasts previously made by others. For example, a comparison was made with the forecasts of the Royal Commission on Canada's Economic Prospects (the Gordon Commission). The Gordon Commission's forecasts were made eleven years ago, and so one can begin to see for what groups of pulps and papers the forecasts are, or are not, being vindicated.

The tonnage estimates of the CPPA study are about 22 percent higher than those of the Gordon Commission. The estimates for paperboard, fine papers, wrapping, building, and sanitary papers are 37 percent, 97 percent, 10 percent, 5 percent, and 115 percent higher, respectively. The newsprint estimate is about 5 percent lower than that of the Gordon Commission, however, with the estimate for overseas shipments being 43 percent lower and the estimates for the U.S. and domestic shipments being 13 percent and 2 percent higher.

Professor Udell of Wisconsin estimated in 1965 that total U.S. newsprint consumption will expand at an annual rate of 3 to 4 percent, reaching a level of 11.4 million tons in 1975.[5] The CPPA estimate of Canadian newsprint shipments to the United States in 1975 was 7,850,000 tons—69 percent of Udell's estimate for the total U.S. market. Canada's share in 1964 was 70 percent, compared with 80 percent in 1954. Canada's share in 1965 and 1966 was 72 percent, and in the first nine months of 1967 it was 69 percent.

In 1960, FAO published *World Demand for Paper to 1975,* containing estimates of consumption in Canada. Four levels of consumption estimates (depending on different assumed rates of growth in income per capita) were given for each of the main papers and paperboards and for all of

[5]J. G. Udell, *1975 U.S. Newsprint Consumption,* New York, American Newspaper Publishers Association, 1965.

them together. FAO's highest total was just over 4.2 million tons, which is 13 percent lower than the CPPA figure of 4.9 million tons. FAO's highest newsprint and fine papers figures are 4½ percent and 17½ percent lower than those of the CPPA study. FAO's highest paperboard figure, however, is quite close to that of the CPPA study.

In 1965, Canada's Department of Forestry completed a review draft, "Timber Trends and Prospects in Canada." Among other things it contains projections of domestic demand for all papers and paperboards. If the Department's figures for 1975 are compared with those done for the CPPA study, one finds that the Department's are 10 percent lower for the group as a whole. The estimates of the CPPA study for newsprint, fine papers, and wrapping papers are lower than those of the Department, but the estimates of the CPPA study for paperboards and tissue and sanitary papers are higher.

Finally, comparison can be made between the CPPA estimate of a 4.8 percent compound rate of growth in over-all demand for Canada's pulp and paper to 1975 and the historical rate of 4.3 percent achieved over the past forty years.

B. Probable Impact
of North Atlantic Free Trade

6. Comparative Costs*

A. METHOD OF INVESTIGATION

The comparative-cost analysis undertaken as part of this study attempted to determine the relative costs of producing certain now-protected grades of paper and paperboard, under comparable conditions of large scale and high degree of specialization, in different regions of Canada and the United States. It also examined probable costs of delivering the products to major U.S. markets. It tried, in other words, to answer the question: If a North Atlantic free trade area were established, covering all inputs as well as outputs of the industry, and if the now-protected sector of the Canadian industry were restructured, would the restructured industry be competitive from a cost standpoint?

The cost study itself did not try to answer certain closely related questions: *Whether* the industry could restructure, and *whether* it could obtain markets large enough to enable it to operate at the levels of scale and specialization on which the cost estimates were based, were questions examined in Chapters 7 and 8 and Part C. All that the cost study tried to say was that *if* the industry restructured, and *if* it operated at the designated levels of scale and specialization, its resulting relative cost position might be as presented here.

The Nordic countries were not included in the cost comparisons shown. A preliminary investigation indicated that average wood-related costs in the Nordic countries were at least $20 higher per ton of paper or paperboard than in eastern Canada, that this difference was likely to widen with time, and that the ocean freight rate between the eastern seaboard of North America and the western seaboard of Europe was about $20 per ton.

*The cost study assembled a large amount of data from published and private sources. Correspondence was carried on with U.S. trade associations, government agencies, and university departments that specialize in forest products. But the most important source of data were managerial and technical personnel in Canadian companies and in the Canadian Pulp and Paper Association. None of these people necessarily agree or disagree with our methods, figures, or interpretations.

Therefore, it seemed evident that, in the absence of tariffs, the efficient producers in eastern Canada would be cost-competitive in Europe, while the Nordic producers could not be significant competitors in North America, except for some specialties. The more intensive type of investigation of costs proceeded under the assumption that the main markets involved were in Canada and the United States and that Canada's leading competitors in these markets would be U.S. producers.

The method used in developing the cost comparisons involved creating a hypothetical mill for each of four representative grades of paper or paperboard and then locating these mills in certain producing regions of Canada and the United States. By "hypothetical mill" is meant, basically, a specified efficient size of plant and rate of output. Interregional differences in cost per unit of each type of input were then the essential subject matter for study.

The comprehensive cost comparisons were based on figures for 1964, the latest year for which sufficient comparable data could be obtained or developed. All value figures were expressed in Canadian dollars. An attempt was then made to assess the significance of changes that had occurred since 1964 and of the problems and prospects that appeared to lie ahead (see final section of this chapter).

The four representative grades examined were kraft linerboard (to represent paperboards), newsprint (to represent groundwood papers), bond paper (to represent fine papers), and toilet tissue (to represent sanitary tissues). The section on linerboard will be longer than those on any of the other grades, but only because the linerboard section occurs first. Whichever product was taken up first would raise information that would also apply to others.

B. KRAFT LINERBOARD

The mill-cost data for the kraft linerboard comparison are set out in Table XXI. The hypothetical mill was assumed to have a single linerboard machine fully integrated with large-scale pulp facilities. Capacity was assumed as 750 tons of linerboard per day and 345 days per year.[1] The largest actual linerboard machine in the United States has a capacity of about 1,500 tons per days, compared with about 600 tons per day in Canada. Average production in Canada on diversified machines is less than 200 tons per day. But if a new linerboard mill were being built in

[1]This assumes seven-day (continuous) operation, which is general in the United States but not yet in Quebec. Continuous operation saves on cessations, wash-up, start-ups, and so on. A shift to continuous operation before or during the transition to free trade would bring an important improvement in the competitiveness of some Canadian mills.

TABLE XXI

HYPOTHETICAL MILL—KRAFT LINERBOARD*
COSTS PER TON OF PRODUCTION IN VARIOUS LOCATIONS,
CAPACITY 750 TONS PER DAY AND 345 DAYS PER YEAR,
UNDER HYPOTHETICAL FREE TRADE IN 1964
(all value figures in Canadian dollars)
For wood requirements and costs, and total mill cost,
two-figure range represents "low", "average"

	Quebec	Georgia	British Columbia	Washington–Oregon
Wood				
Cunits roundwood/ton	0.98–1.27	0.83–0.94	0.55–0.83	0.55–0.83
Basic cost/cunit	$18–26	$23–25	$17–18	$18–20
Cunits chips/ton†	0.43–0.14	0.35–0.24	0.83–0.55	0.83–0.55
Basic cost/cunit	$15–18	$19	$10–15	$10–17
Total cunits/ton	1.41	1.18	1.38	1.38
Basic cost/cunit	$17.09–25.21	$21.81–23.78	$12.81–16.80	$13.21–19.10
Basic cost/ton	$24.10–35.55	$25.74–28.06	$17.68–23.18	$18.23–26.36
Mill management of roundwood				
Expense/cunit roundwood	$2.00	$2.00	$2.00	$2.00
Cunits roundwood/ton	0.98–1.27	0.83–0.94	0.55–0.83	0.55–0.83
Cost/ton	1.96–2.54	1.66–1.88	1.10–1.66	1.10–1.66
Forest main roads				
Amortization/cunit roundwood	$0.50	‡‡‡	$0.50	‡‡‡
Maintenance/cunit roundwood	$0.50	‡‡‡	$0.50	‡‡‡
Cost/ton	0.98–1.27	‡	0.55–0.83	‡
Stocks of roundwood				
Months of supply	3	1	2	2
Interest rate	6%	5.2%	6%	5.2%
Carrying cost/ton	0.26–0.44	0.08–0.10	0.08–0.15	0.09–0.14
WOOD-RELATED COSTS				
Per cunit roundwood	$21.75–29.35	$25.10–27.11	$20.17–21.18	$20.16–22.17
Per cunit chips	$15.00–18.00	$19.00	$10.00–15.00	$10.00–17.00
Per ton of product	$27.30–39.80	$27.48–30.04	$19.41–25.82	$19.42–28.16

Wages				
Manhours/ton	2.8	2.8	2.8	2.8
Wage/hour	$2.80	$3.35	$3.25	$3.45
Cost/ton	7.84	9.38	9.10	9.66
Salaries				
Salaried people	80	80	80	80
Average annual salary	$7,400	$9,400	$8,200	$9,800
Cost/ton	2.29	2.91	2.54	3.03
Fringe benefits				
% of wages	15–17	18–20	15–17	18–20
% of salaries	6–8	7–9	6–8	7–9
Cost/ton	1.41	2.01	1.64	2.08
Electricity				
Kwh/ton	780	820	780	780
Cost/kwh	$0.0040–0.0060	$0.0060–0.0080	$0.0040–0.0050	$0.0035–0.0040
Cost/ton	3.90	5.74	3.51	2.93
Fuel	4.00	3.00	3.50	3.50
Chemicals and additives	5.50	5.50	5.50	5.50
Other materials, overheads, and contingencies	15.00	15.00	15.00	15.00
Mill fixed capital§	$55 million	$52 million	$53 million	$53 million
Depreciation at 5%	10.63	10.05	10.24	10.24
Mill working capital	$8 million	$8 million	$8 million	$8 million
Interest rate	6%	6%	6%	5.2%
Cost/ton	1.86	1.61	1.86	1.61
MILL COST	$79.73–92.23	$82.68–85.24	$72.30–78.71	$72.97–81.61

Source: Private Planning Association of Canada, work with private and published sources. Sources and methods are discussed more fully in text and in appendix tables.

*Single linerboard machine fully integrated with large-scale kraft sulphate pulp mill. Assumed to be producing the same grade of linerboard continuously at 90 percent efficiency.

†For chips, the two-figure range of cunit quantities is stated as "high": "average" (a high proportion coinciding with a low cost). As a proportion of all wood used in chemical-pulp furnish, the use of chips has been assumed to be ("average","high") 10–30 percent in the East, 20–30 percent in the South, and 40–60 percent in the West.

‡Main roads are financed by the counties and states.

§Capital investment estimates assume zero tariffs on Canadian imports of machinery. Regional differences in initial outlay are entirely attributable to differences in climate and resulting differences in facilities and construction-labour productivity

Canada nowadays, it would probably have a capacity somewhere between 500 and 1,000 tons per day; if in the United States, probably 750 tons per day or higher. Factors that limit the capacity that is feasible in any region include the availability of wood, as well as the availability of markets. The machine was assumed to be producing the same grade of linerboard continuously at 90 percent efficiency—standard linerboard having a thickness of 0.0115 inches, 20 percent top stock and 80 percent base stock, and a weight of 42 pounds per thousand square feet.[2]

Four regions are shown in the table, but essentially two separate comparisons are involved: one between the province of Quebec and the state of Georgia, the other between British Columbia and the U.S. Northwest. This discussion will first concentrate on the Quebec-Georgia comparison, then briefly draw attention to some of the interesting features in the western comparison.

The types of softwood in eastern Canada are softer and lighter in weight than those in the U.S. South, and therefore a larger volume of wood is required to get the given weight of fibre needed per ton of linerboard. It was estimated in this study that a ton of linerboard required 1.41 cunits of wood in Quebec and 1.18 cunits in Georgia (a cunit is 100 solid cubic feet of wood). The Quebec requirement is thus seen to be almost 20 percent higher.

Although the U.S. South is a relatively high-wage area for *mill* workers, it is a relatively low-wage area for woodcutters. These are mainly Negroes, non-unionized, and working in small crews not yet covered by the Fair Labour Standards Act. Mechanization is at a rudimentary level. In 1964, the size of crew that did not have to be reported under the Fair Labour Standards Act was any number under twelve. Since the beginning of 1967, it has been any number under eight, and the upper limit is expected to continue dropping until all workers have to be reported.

In eastern Canada, wage rates of woodcutters are slightly higher than in the U.S. South, but some operations are among the most highly mechanized in the world. Because the degree of mechanization varies considerably in Quebec, the range of wood costs is wider than in the South. Although the most efficient woods operations in Quebec probably match the lowest-cost operations in the South, on the average there appears to

[2]Actually, in recent years there has been somewhat faster growth in markets for thinner grades, such as 26-pound linerboard. The thickness of the grade affects production costs (per ton) in various minor ways. But since our choice of thickness did not appear likely to affect the relative regional standings, and since markets for the 42-pound grade have also been growing quite rapidly, we chose that grade, which was the one the industry people usually had the most experience with.

be a considerable advantage in wood-related costs—about $10 per ton of linerboard—in favour of the South.

There may be a natural tendency on the part of some readers to attach more significance to the "low" figures than to the "average" and to conclude that wood costs in eastern Canada are "just as low" as in the South. But such an interpretation would be unwarranted; only a minority of producers, in a minority of their several logging operations, are so efficient and so fortunately located as to be able to achieve anything like the "low" of the range. A more appropriate interpretation would be based on the "averages," which indicate that wood-related costs in eastern Canada are higher than in the U.S. South.

For building and maintaining forest main roads in eastern Canada, $1.00 was added per cunit roundwood or $1.27 per ton of linerboard. Nothing was added for the U.S. regions, where main roads are largely or entirely built and maintained by the counties and states. For inventories of roundwood at the mill, an average three-month supply was assumed for Quebec, carried at 6 percent, and an average one-month supply for Georgia, carried at 5.2 percent.

Wages and salaries in pulp and paper mills in the United States are highest in the South and West. The specific figures developed by this study for Quebec and Georgia are not precisely those given by any private or published source, but in the light of a good deal of evidence from such sources these are the figures that seem appropriate. Average hourly earnings were estimated at $2.80 for Quebec and $3.35 for Georgia—these figures being conceived to include all premium pay for work on Sundays, holidays, overtime, and night shifts. Average annual salaries were estimated at $7,400 for Quebec and $9,400 for Georgia.

To illustrate the impact that restructuring the Canadian industry might have on manpower costs, reference might be made to a cost survey for 1961. For the average kraft linerboard operation in Canada at that time, the combined cost of wages, salaries, and fringe benefits was found to be about $30 per ton of linerboard. The hypothetical-mill estimates reduce this figure to $11.54—even though higher estimates were used for hourly wages and annual salaries in 1964 than were found by the other study for 1961. The reduction is due, essentially, to a more than tripling of output, without any significant increase in number of workers.

Electricity costs are lower in Quebec than in Georgia because water and water power are more abundant and the wood is finer. Some companies in eastern Canada entered long-term purchase contracts many years ago and are getting some of their electricity at rates below what could be negotiated today. These exceptionally low rates may not cover all their present-day power needs, but even present-day rates for purchased power would rarely exceed $0.0055 per kilowatt hour. Companies that generate some of their own power usually do so with the help of natural water potential.

In Georgia, virtually all mills must generate their own electricity and must do so without water power. For mill-generated electricity, a normal rate of profit must be included in the "cost," because capital invested in the generating facilities could be profitably employed elsewhere. Probably none of the Georgia mills use much, if any, power purchased from electric utilities, but if they did, they might be expected to have to pay about $0.008 per kilowatt hour.

On the assumption that no heating is done by electricity (i.e., that all heating is done by fuel), the kilowatt hours required per ton of linerboard were estimated at 780 in Quebec and 820 in Georgia and the resulting electricity costs at $3.90 in Quebec and $5.74 in Georgia—a difference of $1.84.

Any of the various fuels (coal, oil, or gas) can, of course, be used by pulp and paper mills. Some mills are also able to fill a portion of their fuel needs by burning slabs, bark, or other sawmill waste, but this consideration was ignored since it did not seem to give rise to any "representative" difference between these two regions. Many southern mills are located right over, or very near, a natural gas well and can tap it directly. Although oil is also relatively economical in the South, the lowest-cost fuel—for conveniently located mills—would be natural gas. In eastern Canada, most of the mills use oil, though some use coal. In 1964, natural gas was available to southern mills at costs ranging from $0.25–$0.35 per MCF (thousand cubic feet) and oil was available to eastern Canadian mills at costs ranging from $2.00 to $3.00 per barrel. The estimated fuel costs per ton of linerboard were $4.00 for Quebec (1.6 barrels at $2.50 per barrel) and $3.00 for Georgia (10 MCF at $0.30 per MCF).

The group of chemicals and additives includes saltcake, limestone, alum, size, starch, and miscellaneous chemicals such as sulphuric acid. Different mills use surprisingly different amounts of any particular item: for example, according to information from the companies, one mill uses twice as much saltcake as another (per ton of linerboard), one uses twice as much limestone as another, one uses twice as much size as another, and so on. However, there does not seem to be any basis for assuming a "representative" difference between regions in the quantity of any item used per ton of linerboard.

Prices seem to vary slightly within each region, but again there does not seem to be any significant representative difference between regions. California saltcake is used in the U.S. South at a delivered price of about $33 per ton. While Quebec mills sometimes use saltcake from Saskatchewan at a delivered price of about $36 per ton, they can also get saltcake from Britain at a delivered price of about $34 per ton. Since the amount of saltcake assumed per ton of linerboard is 100 pounds, a dollar per ton of saltcake means only $0.05 per ton of linerboard.

In any event, the figures assumed per ton of linerboard for all regions were 100 pounds of saltcake at $33 per ton = $1.65; 30 pounds of limestone at $7.50 per ton = $0.10; 30 pounds of alum at $70 per ton = $1.05; 10 pounds of size at $240 per ton = $1.20; and 10 pounds of starch at $200 per ton = $1.00. These costs add up to $5.00 per ton of linerboard, and $0.50 was added for miscellaneous chemicals.

In regard to the residual, "other materials, overheads, and contingencies," several industry people suggested a figure of $15, and none could provide any basis for assuming a representative difference between regions. No claims are made here about the content or probable validity of the figure, except what has already been said about the method of arriving at it.

In the analysis of capital costs, an attempt was made to exclude those major facilities that not all linerboard mills in all regions would build or acquire.[3] The fixed-capital investment required in Quebec was estimated at $55 million: $10 million for the installed linerboard machine and its housing and $45 million for the pulp mill. The $55 million can also be broken down in the following way: machinery and equipment, 55 percent; labour to install machinery and equipment, 7 percent; construction material, 13 percent; labour for construction, 6 percent; construction overhead, 10 percent; engineering services, 5 percent; contingencies, 4 percent.

The estimate of fixed capital for Quebec might have been the same regardless of whether or not free trade had been assumed for machinery. Some industry people claimed, though others disagreed, that machinery and equipment for the industry is less costly in eastern Canada than in the United States. Most eastern Canadian mills do not import any more than about 10 to 15 percent of their machinery and equipment. The

[3]Thus, for example, major power-generating facilities were excluded, but a feeder from the region's hydro system was included, as were main transformation and switching equipment, an internal distribution system, and unit substations in the various mill departments. Excluded, for example, were docks or harbours, but included were such essential facilities as a railroad siding. The following items were excluded: mill-site acquisition, woodlands acquisition, logging and hauling equipment, executive and guest housing, employee housing or mortgage loans, hospital and recreation facilities, and sales and distribution facilities.

industry has had the benefit of long years of specialization on the part of eastern Canadian equipment producers and engineering firms. The market is said to be much more competitive in eastern Canada than in the United States, with Canadian, British, and European, as well as American, suppliers competing and keeping prices at least as low as in the United States, where most pulp and paper firms tend to confine themselves to American-made equipment.[4]

The estimated $55-million fixed-capital investment for Quebec is about 6 percent higher than the corresponding figure of $52 million estimated for Georgia, the entire difference being attributable to climate. The Quebec mill would have to be better protected against winter weather, and costs would also be higher for that part of construction done during winter.[5] At a 5 percent rate of depreciation, the fixed-capital cost per ton of linerboard worked out to $10.63 in Quebec and $10.05 in Georgia, a difference of about $0.60.

A figure of $8 million was allowed for working capital in both regions. This may have been an overestimate, since carrying charges on pulpwood inventories had already been included in the wood-related costs. A 6 percent interest rate was used for Canada, compared with a 5.2 percent rate for the United States, which resulted in a difference of merely $0.25 per ton of linerboard.

The total mill cost of producing a ton of linerboard in 1964 worked out to $92.23 for Quebec and $85.24 for Georgia—a difference of about $7.00. Several industry people felt that the mill cost for Quebec should have worked out to about $95. However, among those who seemed knowledgeable about operations in the South as well, there were some who felt that the mill cost for Georgia too should have worked out to something higher than was estimated—perhaps to $90. The latter tended to believe that wood-related costs in the U.S. South are quite a bit higher than people in eastern Canada are inclined to suppose. (In this connection, the reader might find it interesting to examine Table A-6 in the appendix.)

If free trade brought about specialization and long runs in Canada, this

---

[4]The discussion in the above paragraph does not apply nearly as fully to western Canada. Canadian-made pulp and paper machinery is produced almost entirely in eastern Canada; mills in western Canada import a much higher proportion of their machinery needs, purchase from the United States a higher proportion of their imports, and pay higher delivered prices for eastern Canadian, British, or European machinery. Nevertheless, the estimate of fixed capital was slightly lower for British Columbia than for eastern Canada, because of the milder winters and because machinery *was* assumed to be tariff-free.

[5]But we have probably overestimated the difference. A southern mill requires some support facilities (for its various installations) that are unnecessary in Canada, where the building is more solid. But being relatively exposed, the southern mill has higher maintenance costs.

would reduce not only production costs but also unit selling costs. Industry people suggested that selling costs for linerboard would be no higher than $3 per ton, even if a company's markets were widely dispersed, and might be lower if the markets were concentrated.

Laid-down costs of linerboard in selected U.S. markets—Boston, New York, Pittsburgh, Cincinnati, and Chicago—were estimated as shown in Table XXII. Rail rates for the Georgia shipments are from Savannah and are incentive rates for at least 50 tons at a time. Rail rates for the Quebec shipments are from La Tuque and are hypothetical "commodity" rates that

TABLE XXII

HYPOTHETICAL LAID-DOWN COSTS, KRAFT LINERBOARD
(Canadian dollars per ton)
Two-figure range represents "low"–"average."

	Quebec	Georgia
Mill cost, 1964	79.73– 92.23	82.68– 85.24
Selling cost	3.00	3.00
Rail rate to:	(probable from La Tuque)	(actual from Savannah)
Boston	(520 mi.) 11.56	(1,057 mi.) 17.71
New York	(620 mi.) 12.64	(830 mi.) 15.34
Pittsburgh	(795 mi.) 15.12	(868 mi.) 15.77
Cincinnati	(975 mi.) 16.20	(714 mi.) 13.72
Chicago	(1,000 mi.) 16.42	(989 mi.) 17.06
Laid-down cost at:		
Boston	94.29–106.79	103.39–105.95
New York	95.37–107.87	101.02–103.58
Pittsburgh	97.85–110.35	101.45–104.01
Cincinnati	98.93–111.43	99.40–101.96
Chicago	99.15–111.65	102.74–105.30

Sources and methods: Mill costs are as derived in Table XXI. Selling costs are from suggestions by industry informants. Actual rail rates are from U.S. railway companies and are for shipments of 50 tons. Probable rail rates are those that Canadian railway companies think would be likely to be approved by U.S. railway companies if an application were made.

Canadian railway companies suggested to us as probably obtainable in negotiations with U.S. railway companies. The assumed La Tuque rates are slightly higher on a ton-mile basis than the actual Savannah rates for comparable distances. An important question for policy, as discussed in Chapter 10, is whether such Canadian rates could be brought about and the remaining differentials removed.[6]

[6]Eastern Canadian newsprint, which has long moved in volume to the United States, has been unable to negotiate freight rates as favourable as those for U.S. competitive movements, and the persistence of such differentials under free trade could be more undermining competitively for the now-protected grades that might be struggling for U.S. markets under many difficult circumstances.

The study indicates, then, that the hypothetical "average" Quebec mill would be competitive in the local market and in such nearby U.S. markets as Boston and perhaps New York, but not in the other U.S. markets shown. An exceptionally efficient Quebec mill—which might be roughly represented by the "lows" in the table—could possibly compete in all five of the U.S. markets. Moreover, the more westerly of the markets shown, Cincinnati and Chicago, could perhaps be served more economically from Ontario mills than from Quebec.

Western comparison. Wood-related costs, and therefore total mill costs, are lower on the West Coast than in the East or South. The advantage of the West Coast results mainly from the abundance of chips and sawmill residue from lumber operations that are often affiliated with the pulp and paper companies. In addition, compared with the East, the larger-diameter woods in the West lend themselves better to mechanization, and relatively full mechanization is typical. Compared with the South, the labour in the West is more suitable to efficient mechanization.

There is not much difference in wood-related costs between British Columbia and Washington or Oregon, but the B.C. producers do seem to have a modest advantage for several reasons. B.C. stumpage rates are lower than in Washington and Oregon, and B.C. wood hauls are somewhat shorter on the average. In addition, B.C. chips and sawmill residue are generally more available relative to demand than in the U.S. Northwest; the state of Washington quite often imports chips, and even pulpwood, from British Columbia.

One advantage that the U.S. Northwest has over British Columbia is in forest main roads. A difference of $0.83 per ton was estimated in this study, based on the assumption that the B.C. roads were entirely privately financed. Actually, a more representative difference would probably be about half that, because the B.C. government is quite active in constructing development roads.

A second advantage in favour of the U.S. Northwest is in electricity rates. A U.S. government agency, the Bonneville Power Administration, operates a series of very large generating stations on the Columbia river, and only 50 percent of the capital costs of any power development are charged against power generation (the balance being charged to irrigation, navigation, and fisheries). The result is a subsidized power rate about 15–25 percent below rates in British Columbia. The system goes back to the era of President Franklin Roosevelt, when efforts were made to encourage industry in the U.S. Northwest. Some B.C. producers believe or hope that free trade would tend to equalize their power rates with those in the U.S. Northwest.

The study's assumptions regarding the use of chips need a little explanation. It was assumed that the "average" producers in the West were using 40 percent chips and were buying them at market prices—estimated at $15 per cunit-equivalent in British Columbia and $17 in the U.S. Northwest. The "low"-cost western producers were assumed to be using 60 percent chips, all obtained from sawmill affiliates at a transfer price arbitrarily estimated at $10 per cunit-equivalent. The estimates of "average" wood-related costs were, per cunit roundwood, $21.18 in British Columbia and $22.17 in the U.S. Northwest ($27.11 in Georgia and $29.35 in Quebec). On a per-ton-of-linerboard basis, average wood-related costs were estimated at $25.82 in British Columbia and $28.16 in the U.S. Northwest ($30.04 in Georgia and $39.80 in Quebec). Total mill cost, for the "average" producer, was calculated at $78.71 in British Columbia and $81.61 in the U.S. Northwest ($85.24 in Georgia and $92.23 in Quebec).

Rail rates to California from points on the B.C. coast (or at least from points not too far north of the border) are about the same as from points on the Washington coast—to San Francisco about $14 and to Los Angeles about $18. Rates from Oregon to California are somewhat lower. It seems reasonable to conclude that B.C. linerboard would be cost-competitive in California markets. The same would apply to Pacific (and perhaps also to Atlantic) overseas markets.

C. NEWSPRINT (AS INDICATIVE OF GROUNDWOOD PAPER)

In selecting newsprint as one of the representative grades, the study sought to throw light, not so much on the comparative costs of newsprint itself (which already trades freely with the United States) as on the great variety of tariff-protected groundwood papers. It was realized, of course, that the scale of machinery and degree of specialization that would be assumed for newsprint would not be "realistic" for the other groundwood papers. But it was felt that a large-scale, highly specialized newsprint operation, on which accurate data might be obtained, would throw more light on the *relative* regional costs for the other grades than would the technique of conceiving a hypothetical mill for a particular one of those other grades. Of course, if a groundwood-paper producer in Canada could not achieve the same scale and specialization as his competitor in the United States, his relative position would not be as favourable as the newsprint comparisons might suggest.

The mill-cost data for newsprint are set out in Table XXIII. The hypothetical mill was assumed to have two machines, one with a capacity of 425 tons per days, the other with a capacity of 255 tons per day. Actual

TABLE XXIII

HYPOTHETICAL MILL—NEWSPRINT*

COSTS PER TON OF PRODUCTION IN VARIOUS LOCATIONS,
CAPACITY 680 TONS PER DAY AND 345 DAYS PER YEAR,
UNDER HYPOTHETICAL FREE TRADE IN 1964
(all value figures in Canadian dollars)

For wood requirements and costs, and total mill cost,
two-figure range represents "low" - "average"

	Quebec	Alabama	British Columbia	Washington-Oregon
Wood				
Cunits/roundwood/ton	0.94–1.02	0.78–0.82	0.79–0.88	0.79–0.88
Basic cost/cunit	$18–26	$22–24	$17–18	$18–20
Cunits chips/ton†	0.13–0.05	0.11–0.7	0.26–0.17	0.26–0.17
Basic cost/cunit	$15–18	$18	$10–15	$10–17
Total cunits/ton	1.07	0.89	1.05	1.05
Basic cost/ton	$17.62–25.63	$21.62–23.61	$15.27–17.51	$16.02–19.51
	$18.85–27.42	$19.24–21.01	$16.03–18.39	$16.82–20.
Mill management of roundwood				
Expense/cunit roundwood	$2.00	$2.00	$2.00	$2.00
Cunits roundwood/ton	0.94–1.02	0.78–0.82	0.79–0.88	0.79–0.88
Cost/ton	1.88–2.04	1.56–1.64	1.58–1.76	1.58–1.76
Forest main roads				
Amortization/cunit roundwood	$0.50	‡	$0.50	‡
Maintenance/cunit roundwood	$0.50	‡	$0.50	‡
Cost/ton	0.94–1.02	‡	0.79–0.88	‡
Stocks of roundwood				
Months of supply	3	1	2	2
Interest rate	6%	5.2%	6%	5.2%
Carrying cost/ton	0.25–0.36	0.08–0.08	0.13–0.16	0.13–0.15
WOOD-RELATED COSTS				
Per cunit roundwood	$21.27–29.35	$24.10–26.10	$20.17–21.18	$20.16–22.17
Per cunit chips	$15.00–18.00	$18.00	$10.00–15.00	$10.00–17.00
Per ton of product	$21.92–30.84	$20.88–22.73	$18.53–21.19	$18.53–22.40

Wages				
Manhours/ton	3.7	3.7	3.7	3.7
Wage/hour	$2.80	$3.50	$3.25	$3.45
Cost/ton	10.36	12.95	12.03	12.77
Salaries				
Salaried people	80	80	80	80
Average annual salary	$7,400	$9,800	$8,200	$9,800
Cost/ton	2.29	3.03	2.54	3.03
Fringe benefits				
% of wages	15–17	18–20	15–17	18–20
% of salaries	6–8	7–9	6–8	7–9
Cost/ton	1.82	2.70	2.10	2.67
Electricity				
Kwh/ton	1,600	1,850	1,600	1,600
Cost/kwh	$0.0040–0.0060	$0.0045	$0.0040–0.0050	$0.0035–0.0040
Cost/ton	8.00	8.33	7.20	6.00
Fuel	4.00	3.00	3.50	3.50
Chemicals and additives	2.50	2.50	2.50	2.50
Other materials, overheads, and contingencies	15.00	15.00	15.00	15.00
Mill fixed capital§	$50 million	$47 million	$48 million	$48 million
Depreciation at 5%	10.66	10.02	10.23	10.23
Mill working capital	$8 million	$8 million	$8 million	$8 million
Interest rate	6%	5.2%	6%	5.2%
Cost/ton	2.05	1.78	2.05	1.78
MILL COST	$78.60–87.52	$80.19–82.04	$75.68–78.34	$76.01–79.88

Source : Private Planning Association of Canada, work with private and published sources. Sources and methods are discussed more fully in text and in appendix tables.
*Two newsprint machines fully integrated with large-scale groundwood and kraft sulphate pulp mills. Assumed to be producing the same grade of newsprint continuously at 90 percent efficiency.
†For chips, the two-figure range of cunit quantities is stated as "high", "average" (a high proportion coinciding with a low cost). As a proportion of all wood used in chemical-pulp furnish, the use of chips has been assumed to be ("average"–"high") 10–30 percent in the East, 20–30 percent in the South, and 40–60 percent in the West. The chemical-pulp is assumed to be 25 percent of the total-pulp furnish.
‡Main roads are financed by the counties and states.
§Capital investment estimates assume zero tariffs on Canadian imports of machinery. Regional differences in initial outlay are entirely attributable to differences in climate and resulting differences in facilities and construction-labour productivity.

production per newsprint machine in Canada averaged about 165 tons per day in 1966, while the maximum was about 500 tons per day.

Wood requirements per ton of output are lower for newsprint than for kraft linerboard because wood yields are much higher in groundwood pulping than in chemical pulping. (See the appendix tables, particularly Table A-3.) The pulp furnish in the newsprint operation was assumed to be 75 percent groundwood and 25 percent kraft sulphate. For both newsprint and linerboard, the wood requirements would be about 20 percent higher in eastern Canada than in the U.S. South.

In wood-related costs per ton of output, the study indicated that the disadvantage of eastern Canada compared with the U.S. South would narrow to about $8 for newsprint, compared with almost $10 for linerboard. Total mill cost per ton of newsprint worked out to $87.52 for Quebec and $82.04 for Alabama—a difference of about $5.50, compared with a difference of about $7 between Quebec and Georgia in linerboard.

The main reason for choosing Alabama rather than Georgia to represent the South in newsprint production was that power costs are much lower in Alabama with the availability of electricity from the Tennessee Valley Authority. Mechanical pulping requires much more electricity than chemical pulping, and the hypothetical southern situation was set up to be as competitive as possible with that in eastern Canada. The electricity cost per ton of newsprint was estimated at $8.33 for Alabama and $8.00 for Quebec. Had the rate previously used for Georgia been applied to Alabama, the cost of electricity would have worked out to $12.95 and would have given Quebec a $5 advantage.

Alabama appears to have slightly lower wood costs, but slightly higher wage rates and salaries, than Georgia.

The average laid-down costs shown in Table XXIV suggest that the Quebec mill would be cost-competitive in such U.S. markets as Boston and New York, but not in such markets as Cincinnati and Chicago. As with linerboard, it should be added that Cincinnati and Chicago could perhaps be served more economically from Ontario mills than from Quebec. For other groundwood papers, if mills in eastern Canada could achieve the same scale and specialization as in the South, the same relative-cost conclusions would presumably apply.

Little needs to be said by way of describing the study's newsprint comparison for the West. The West Coast of both Canada and the United States can produce newsprint more cheaply than the East or South, though the margin of advantage is somewhat narrower with newsprint than with linerboard, owing to the smaller role that chips and mill residue play in newsprint. (Chips and mill residue are not used in the groundwood-

TABLE XXIV

HYPOTHETICAL LAID-DOWN COSTS—NEWSPRINT
(Canadian dollars per ton)
Two-figure range represents "low"–"average."

	Quebec	Alabama
Mill cost, 1964	78.60– 87.52	80.19– 82.04
Selling cost	1.50	1.50
Rail rate to:	(actual from Three Rivers)	(actual from Coosa Pines)
Boston	(372 mi.) 14.45	(1,218 mi.) 23.00
New York	(538 mi.) 15.45	(991 mi.) 20.40
Pittsburgh	(714 mi.) 18.65	(801 mi.) 18.00
Cincinnati	(919 mi.) 20.25	(502 mi.) 11.75
Chicago	(945 mi.) 20.25	(694 mi.) 15.20
Laid-down cost:		
Boston	94.55–103.47	104.69–106.54
New York	95.56–104.47	102.09–103.94
Pittsburgh	98.75–107.67	99.69–101.54
Cincinnati	100.35–109.27	93.44– 95.29
Chicago	100.35–109.27	96.89– 98.74

Sources and methods: Mill costs are as derived in Table XXIII. Selling costs are from suggestions by industry informants. Rail rates are from Canadian and U.S. railway companies and are for shipments of 50 tons.

pulp furnish, but only in the 25 percent that is chemical-pulp furnish.) In terms of the "averages," the mill cost of producing a ton of newsprint works out to $78.34 in British Columbia and $79.88 in the U.S. Northwest ($82.04 in Georgia and $87.52 in Quebec.)

D. BOND PAPER

In the mill-cost comparisons for bond paper (set out in Table XXV), Wisconsin and Maine are brought into the picture, and Ontario is used to represent eastern Canada, as these are important regions for production of fine papers. Costs in Wisconsin and Maine are shown to be somewhat higher than in Ontario. The South's advantage over eastern Canada appears to be about the same for bond paper as for newsprint, but not as great as for linerboard. The West Coast now shows, not a cost advantage, but a cost disadvantage, compared with eastern Canada or the South.

The hypothetical mill consists of two identical machines, each producing 200 tons of bond paper per day and fully integrated with large-scale kraft sulphate pulp facilities. The largest single fine-paper machine in the United States reportedly has a capacity of about 400 tons per day, but some smaller machines are still being installed with capacities of 150 tons or less per day. The hypothetical operation includes finishing and the loading of packaged sheets.

TABLE XXV

HYPOTHETICAL MILL—BOND PAPER*
COSTS PER TON OF PRODUCTION IN VARIOUS LOCATIONS,
CAPACITY 400 TONS PER DAY AND 345 DAYS PER YEAR,
UNDER HYPOTHETICAL FREE TRADE IN 1964
(all value figures in Canadian dollars)
For wood requirements and costs, and total mill cost,
two-figure range represents "low"–"average"

	Ontario		Wisconsin		Maine	
Wood						
Cunits roundwood/ton	0.88–1.12		0.89–1.14		0.89–1.14	
Basic cost/cunit†	$18–25		$20–27		$19–25	
Cunits chips/ton†	0.37–0.13		0.38–0.13		0.38–0.13	
Basic cost/cunit	$14–16		$14–19		$14–18	
Total cunits/ton	1.25		1.27		1.27	
Basic cost/cunit	$16.74–24.19		$18.41–25.09		$17.71–23.16	
Basic cost/ton		$20.93–30.24		$23.38–32.75		$22.49–30.?
Mill management of roundwood						
Expense/cunit roundwood	$2.00		$2.00		$2.00	
Cunits roundwood/ton	0.88–1.12		0.89–1.14		0.89–1.14	
Cost/ton		1.96–2.24		1.78–2.28		1.78–2.?
Forest main roads						
Amortization/cunit roundwood	$0.50		‡		‡	
Maintenance/cunit roundwood	$0.50		‡		‡	
Cost/ton		0.88–1.12		‡		‡
Stocks of roundwood						
Months of supply	3		3		3	
Interest rate	6%		5.2%		5.2%	
Carrying cost/ton		0.24–0.36		0.23–0.39		0.22–0.?
WOOD-RELATED COSTS						
Per cunit roundwood	$21.27–28.32		$22.26–29.73		$21.25–27.70	
Per cunit chips	$14.00–16.00		$14.00–19.00		$14.00–18.00	
Per ton of product		$24.01–33.96		$25.39–35.42		$24.49–32.9
Wages						
Manhours/ton	8.0		8.0		8.0	
Wage/hour	$2.90		$3.25		$3.10	
Cost/ton		23.20		26.00		24.8
Salaries						
Salaried people	60		60		60	
Average annual salary	$7,600		$9,200		$8,600	
Cost/ton		3.30		4.00		3.7
Fringe benefits						
% of wages	15–17		18–20		18–20	
% of salaries	6–8		7–9		7–9	
Cost/ton		3.94		5.26		5.0
Electricity						
Kwh/ton	920		920		920	
Cost/kwh	$0.0040–0.0060		$0.0060–0.0090		$0.0060–0.0090	
Cost/ton		4.60		6.90		6.9
Fuel		5.00		5.00		4.5
Chemicals and additives		30.00		30.00		30.0
Other materials, overheads, and contingencies		30.00		30.00		30.0
Mill fixed capital§	$54 million		$54 million		$54 million	
Depreciation at 5%		19.57		19.57		19.57
Mill working capital	$10 million		$10 million		$10 million	
Interest rate	6%		5.2%		5.2%	
Cost/ton		4.35		3.77		3.77
MILL COST		$147.97–157.92		$155.89–165.92		$152.78–161.2?

Source: Private Planning Association of Canada, work with private and published sources. Sources and methods are discussed more fully in text and in appendix tables.
*Two identical fine-paper machines, capacity of each 200 tons per day at 90 percent efficiency, fully integrated with large-scale kraft sulphate pulp mill. Assumed to be producing the same grade of bond paper continuously. Finished and loaded as packaged sheets.
†For chips, the two-figure range of cunit quantities is stated as "high"–"average" (a high proportion coinciding with a low cost). As a proportion of all wood used in chemical-pulp furnish, the use of chips has been assumed to be ("average"–"high") 10–30 percent in the

Alabama		British Columbia		Washington-Oregon	
81–0.92		0.66–0.99		0.66–0.99	
.1–23		$17–20		$18–22	
34–0.23		0.99–0.66		0.99–0.66	
5		$9–14		$9–16	
15		1.65		1.65	
8.94–21.10		$12.88–19.33		$12.88–19.33	
	$21.78–24.27		$21.25–31.89		$21.25–31.89
.00		$2.00		$2.00	
81–0.92		0.66–0.99		0.66–0.99	
	1.62–1.84		1.32–1.98		1.32–1.98
		$0.50		‡	
		$0.50		‡	
	‡		0.66–0.99		‡
%		2		2	
		6%		5.2%	
	0.09–0.11		0.11–0.20		0.11–0.19
23.11–25.12		$20.17–23.20		$20.16–24.19	
15.00		$9.00–14.00		$9.00–16.00	
	$23.49–26.22		$23.34–35.06		$22.68–34.06
.0		8.0		8.0	
3.50		$3.25		$3.45	
	28.00		26.00		27.60
0		60		60	
9,800		$8,200		$9,800	
	4.26		3.57		4.26
8–20		15–17		18–20	
–9		6–8		7–9	
	5.66		4.41		5.58
,010		900		900	
0.0045		$0.0040–0.0050		$0.0035–0.0040	
	4.55		4.05		3.38
	3.50		4.00		4.00
	27.75		29.50		30.00
	30.00		30.00		30.00
$51 million		$52 million		$52 million	
	18.48		18.84		18.84
$10 million		$10 million		$10 million	
5.2%		6%		5.2%	
	3.77		4.35		3.77
	$149.46–152.19		$148.06–159.78		$150.11–161.49

East, 20–30 percent in the South, and 40–60 percent in the West. The hardwood:softwood pulp-furnish ratios are assumed to be 70:30 in the East and South and 50:50 in the West.
‡Main roads are financed by the counties and states.
§Capital investment estimates assume zero tariffs on Canadian imports of machinery. Regional differences in initial outlay are entirely attributable to differences in climate and resulting differences in facilities and construction-labour productivity.

The specific type of fine paper selected was a white bond having a basis weight of 20 pounds for a ream of 500 sheets of 17 inches by 22 inches. Other qualities include a brightness of over 80 degrees and an opacity of over 80 percent. The paper would be smooth, fairly stiff, suitable for ink writing, have good erasure properties, and be suitable for printing by high-speed offset and letterpress. The various mills, in achieving this group of high qualities, seem to use greatly differing amounts of each of many chemicals and additives.

Economy and quality in fine papers are achieved more readily with a high admixture of hardwood. Some fine-paper mills use pulp furnish of which 80 percent or more is derived from hardwood. For the hypothetical operations, it was assumed that the mills in the East and South would use pulp furnish derived 70 percent from hardwood, while the mills in the West, where hardwood is quite scarce, would use pulp furnish derived 50 percent from hardwood.

In eastern Canada, average hardwood density (3,200 pounds) is much higher than average softwood density (2,450 pounds) and is almost as high as average hardwood density in the U.S. South (3,300 pounds). In the West, the hardwood available in meaningful amounts is quite low in average density (2,200 pounds). (Compare Table A-4 with Tables A-1 and A-2.) In all regions, hardwoods tend to be somewhat cheaper than softwoods, owing to lower demand and lower intensity of past cutting.

Wood requirements in eastern Canada, which were estimated to be about 20 percent higher than in the South for linerboard and newsprint, were estimated to be only about 8 or 9 percent higher than in the South for bond paper, owing to the high admixture of hardwood. Estimated wood requirements in the West, which are slightly lower than those in eastern Canada for linerboard and newsprint, are almost one-third *higher* than in eastern Canada for bond paper.

The number of manhours required to produce a ton of bond paper in the hypothetical mill was estimated at 8.0. This can be broken down into 2.5 for the pulp up to the slush state, 2.5 for the paper up to the large-roll state, and 3.0 for the converting into small sheets and the loading of packaged sheets. For wages, salaries, and fringe benefits together it was estimated that Ontario had about a $7.50 advantage per ton over Alabama and about a $5.00 advantage over Wisconsin.

Chemicals and additives represent a much larger cost component in bond paper than in any of the other representative grades in this study. Analysis of regional differences in this component is difficult and quite vulnerable to errors that could amount to a significant total. Five paper companies each submitted a long list of the chemicals and additives required for a ton of bond paper, the properties of which had been defined very specifically in advance. Each of the lists contained some items that were not included in other lists, and important items contained in all lists were each used in greatly differing quantities by the different mills. No inherent regional reasons could be determined for the quantity differences.

As for price differences, the preliminary possibility of significant ones appeared to be related to four items—clay, sulphur, soda ash, and saltcake —and the analysis therefore concentrated on them. In order to establish a basis for regional comparisons, it was assumed that, for each item, a uniform quantity was used per ton of bond paper in all regions: 200 pounds of clay, 200 pounds of sulphur, 100 pounds of soda ash, and 100 pounds of saltcake. And it was assumed that each of these products would be purchased in large bulk volumes that would economize prices and rail rates.

Clay is used in fine-paper production as a coating and as a filler. The only North American source of coating clay is the city of Macon in central Georgia. Filler clays are produced a little more widely in the same region. At the points of origin, the coating clays range in price from about $25 to $40 per ton in bulk, and are about $5 higher per ton in bags,[7] while the filler clays range in price from about $15 to $17 in bulk. Mills generally use about twice as much clay for coating as for filler, though they use different total amounts ranging from under 150 pounds to over 300 pounds per ton of fine paper. Rail rates are higher for coating clay, even in bulk, than for filler clay.

To simplify the explanation and yet enable readers to calculate the regional differentials, it is sufficient to provide the weighted average freight rates per ton of both types of clay, under assumed free trade. These rates, from Georgia, are estimated as $17 to Ontario, $19 to Maine and Wisconsin, and $9 to Alabama. (Rail rates to British Columbia would be about $30, compared with about $28 to the U.S. Northwest.) These figures can be converted at $1.00 per ton of clay = $0.10 per ton of bond paper.

Sulphur is produced in Alberta and British Columbia as a by-product of natural gas, and natural sulphur is produced in Texas. Under hypothetical free trade rail rates, Ontario could probably obtain Texas, as well as Alberta, sulphur at a delivered price of about $64 per ton. Texas sulphur would be used at a delivered price of about $53 in Alabama, $68 in Maine, and $62 in Wisconsin. (The U.S. Northwest would probably use mainly Texas sulphur

---

[7]There seems to be controversy at some fine-paper mills concerning the quality of coating clay needed and whether it must necessarily be purchased in bags.

TABLE XXVI

HYPOTHETICAL LAID-DOWN COSTS, BOND PAPER
(Canadian dollars per ton)
*Two-figure range represents "low"–"average."

	Southern Ontario	Eastern Ontario	Wisconsin
Mill cost, 1964	147.97–157.92	147.97–157.92	155.89–165
Selling cost	4.00	4.00	4
Rail rate to:	(probable from London)	(probable from Cornwall)	(actual from Neenah)
Buffalo	(156 mi.) 6.50	(320 mi.) 9.80	(525 mi.) 13
Detroit	(116 mi.) 6.06	(500 mi.) 12.88	(338 mi.) 10.
Boston	(775 mi.) 16.94	(380 mi.) 11.90	(996 mi.) 19.
New York	(556 mi.) 13.76	(440 mi.) 12.00	(925 mi.) 18.
Baltimore	(610 mi.) 14.42	(580 mi.) 13.98	(914 mi.) 18.
Cincinnati	(370 mi.) 10.90	(740 mi.) 16.28	(463 mi.) 12.
Chicago	(383 mi.) 11.12	(760 mi.) 16.72	(183 mi.) 7.
Laid-down cost at:			
Buffalo	158.47–168.42	161.77–171.72	172.96–182.
Detroit	158.03–167.98	164.85–174.80	169.93–179.
Boston	168.91–178.86	163.87–173.82	178.90–188.
New York	165.73–175.68	163.97–173.92	178.25–188.
Baltimore	166.39–176.34	165.95–175.90	178.25–188.
Cincinnati	162.87–172.82	168.25–178.20	172.31–182.
Chicago	163.09–173.04	168.69–178.64	166.91–176.

Sources and methods: Mill costs are as derived in Table XXV. Selling costs are from su
gestions by industry informants. Actual rail rates are from U.S. railway companies and a
for shipments of 25 tons. Probable rail rates are those that Canadian railway compani
think would be likely to be approved by U.S. railway companies if an application were ma

at a delivered price of about $53, while British Columbia would probably use mainly local by-product sulphur at a delivered price of about $45.) These figures can be converted at $1.00 per ton of sulphur = $0.10 per ton of bond paper.

Soda ash is produced in Ontario and in the states of New York, Louisiana, and California. Under free trade, delivered prices per ton in bulk, from the obvious sources, would be about $41 in Ontario and Maine, $47 in Wisconsin (from either Ontario or the present sources, New York or Louisiana), and $36 in Alabama. (In Washington and British Columbia, delivered prices would be about $47 and $49, respectively.) Saltcake is available from Saskatchewan, California, and Britain. Ontario could get either Saskatchewan or British saltcake for about $34 per ton, Maine would probably use British saltcake at about $34, Wisconsin would use Saskatchewan saltcake at about $33, and Alabama would use California saltcake at about $33. (Washington could get either California or Saskat-

Maine	Northern Alabama	Southern Alabama
52.78–161.21	149.46–152.19	149.46–152.19
4.00	4.00	4.00
actual from Westbrook)	(actual from Birmingham)	(actual from Mobile)
547 mi.) 13.82	(900 mi.) 17.93	(1,157 mi.) 20.74
778 mi.) 16.42	(734 mi.) 15.98	(991 mi.) 19.01
112 mi.) 6.05	(1,217 mi.) 21.17	(1,443 mi.) 23.11
346 mi.) 10.80	(990 mi.) 19.01	(1,216 mi.) 21.17
529 mi.) 13.18	(809 mi.) 16.85	(1,035 mi.) 19.44
963 mi.) 18.58	(480 mi.) 12.42	(737 mi.) 15.98
045 mi.) 19.20	(644 mi.) 15.12	(837 mi.) 17.06
170.60–179.03	171.39–174.12	174.20–176.93
173.20–181.63	169.44–172.17	172.47–175.20
162.83–171.26	174.63–177.36	176.57–179.30
167.58–176.01	172.47–175.20	174.63–177.36
169.96–178.39	170.31–173.04	172.90–175.63
175.36–183.79	165.88–168.61	169.44–172.17
175.98–184.41	168.58–171.31	170.52–173.25

chewan saltcake for about $33, and British Columbia would use Saskatchewan saltcake at about $31.) These figures can be converted at $1.00 per ton of soda ash or saltcake = $0.05 per ton of bond paper.

If the above figures for the four chemicals and additives are computed per ton of bond paper, Ontario is found to have an advantage of $0.60 over Maine and $0.25 over Wisconsin, but a disadvantage of $2.10 compared with Alabama. In the light of other considerations for the chemicals and additives viewed as a whole, it was decided to eliminate Ontario's marginal advantages over Maine and Wisconsin and to increase its disadvantage over Alabama to $2.25. Total cost of chemicals and additives per ton of bond paper was estimated as $30 in Ontario, Maine, and Wisconsin, and as $27.75 in Alabama. (Calculations that can be made with the data given here for the West show the U.S. Northwest as $0.25 higher, and British Columbia as $0.40 lower, than Ontario.)

The laid-down-cost estimates in Table XXVI suggest that Ontario would be quite competitive compared with Wisconsin and Maine in all the U.S. market centres shown. Compared with Alabama, Ontario should be competitive in Buffalo, Detroit,[8] Boston, and New York, but perhaps not in Baltimore, Cincinnati, and Chicago. The more easterly U.S. market centres, such as New York and Boston, should be within competitive range of Quebec.

What are the economies of an integrated fine-paper operation compared with a non-integrated operation? In approaching this question, one might assume a single company which could have an integrated operation in Ontario, of the sort indicated by the hypothetical-mill data, or could have its pulp mill in Ontario and ship the pulp to its paper mill in a U.S. market area. What would this fact of non-integration add as an extra cost per ton of bond paper? A first approximation is that the extra cost would be at least $20 per ton—$17 for drying the slush pulp at the pulp mill and then re-slushing at the paper mill, and $3 for extra handling and double loading.

However, if the paper plant could not operate as economically in the U.S. market area as in Ontario—as would seem to be the typical case—the cost of non-integration would be more than $20 per ton. Some industry people have suggested figures as high as $30 per ton. There are some obvious marketing advantages in having a paper plant right in the heart of a major U.S. market area; and possibly, as one industry informant suggested, the drying of the pulp helps to improve the quality of the paper. But it is doubtful that such advantages could conceivably outweigh a production-cost disadvantage of $20 or more per ton.

As for the West Coast, the main general problem that affects both British Columbia and Washington-Oregon is the scarcity of hardwoods. However, some B.C. producers may be able to obtain sufficient hardwood—or sufficient pulp derived from hardwood—to be able to produce fine papers competitively. Or they may do so quite well without hardwood.

E. TOILET TISSUE

The mill-cost data for toilet tissue are presented in Table XXVII. The hypothetical mill consists of large-scale kraft and groundwood pulp facilities supplying two identical tissue machines, each producing 100 tons per day of white, dry-crepe, single-ply tissue having a basis weight of 13.5 pounds per ream of 500 sheets 24 inches by 36 inches. At the present time, the shortest runs in eastern Canada are as low as 15 tons, which is about one shift's output. The hypothetical mill cost estimates include packaging and loading of the finished rolls.

[8]Buffalo can also represent, for example, Rochester, while Detroit can represent, for example, Toledo, Akron, and Cleveland. In general, there are numerous U.S. cities of considerable size within apparent competitive range of southern Ontario.

Ontario was compared with Wisconsin and Maine, and British Columbia was compared with Washington-Oregon. Very little sanitary tissue is produced in the U.S. South because the wood is in high demand and is more suitable for other grades. The South is unlikely ever to become a significant producer of tissue.

Estimated laid-down costs in the selected markets are presented in Table XXVIII. The Ontario mill appears to be quite competitive. Ontario's advantage over Wisconsin and Maine is not primarily due to the somewhat higher density and lower cost of the Ontario wood; moreover, this advantage is partly offset by the road costs that were included for Ontario but not for the other regions. In wood-related costs per ton of tissue, the Ontario mill seemed to have only a negligible advantage over the mill in Maine, though it had, according to the estimates, a $3.50 advantage over the mill in Wisconsin.

The chief advantages of Ontario as a region for producing toilet tissue appeared to be in electricity and in wages, salaries, and fringe benefits.

As to electricity, a ton of toilet tissue requires even more kilowatt hours than a ton of newsprint—1900 compared with 1600.[9] At estimated average electricity rates of $0.0050 in Ontario and $0.0075 in both Wisconsin and Maine, the cost per ton of tissue worked out to $9.50 in Ontario and $14.25 in Wisconsin and Maine, for an advantage of almost $5 in favour of Ontario.

Wages, salaries, and fringe benefits, on a per-ton basis, came out to $33.31 in Ontario, $38.64 in Wisconsin, and $36.75 in Maine, giving Ontario an advantage of about $5.50 over Wisconsin and about $3.50 over Maine. The number of manhours required to produce a ton of tissue in the hypothetical operation was estimated at 8.5. This can be broken down into 2.5 up to the slush pulp, 3.0 up to the jumbo rolls of paper, and 3.0 for the converting into packaged rolls and loading.

Total mill costs per ton of tissue add up, then, to $148.97 for Ontario, $162.13 for Wisconsin, and $156.69 for Maine. The Ontario mill would thus have a production-cost advantage of about $13 or $14 over the mill in Wisconsin and about $7.50 over the mill in Maine.

The laid-down-cost estimates given in Table XXVIII indicate that the Ontario mill's production-cost advantage is usually maintained, and

9This is mainly because tissue is very light in weight and has a great deal of surface area per ton, so that a relatively large amount of electricity is required to power the machinery to turn out a ton of tissue. In addition, the proportion of groundwood pulp used in the furnish for toilet tissue is sometimes quite substantial, and, as pointed out for newsprint, mechanical pulping requires more power than chemical pulping.

TABLE XXVII

HYPOTHETICAL MILL—TOILET TISSUE*
COSTS PER TON OF PRODUCTION IN VARIOUS LOCATIONS,
CAPACITY 200 TONS PER DAY AND 345 DAYS PER YEAR,
UNDER HYPOTHETICAL FREE TRADE IN 1964
(all value figures in Canadian dollars)

For wood requirements and costs, and total mill cost,
two-figure range represents "low"–"average"

	Ontario		Wisconsin	
Wood				
Cunits roundwood/ton	1.11–1.33		1.16–1.39	
Basic cost/cunit	$18–27		$21–29	
Cunits chips/ton†	0.34–0.12		0.35–0.12	
Basic cost/cunit	$15–18		$15–21	
Total cunits/ton	1.45		1.51	
Basic cost/cunit	$17.30–26.27		$19.61–28.36	
Basic cost/ton		$25.09–38.09		$29.61–42.
Mill management of roundwood				
Expense/cunit roundwood	$2.00		$2.00	
Cunits roundwood/ton	1.11–1.33		1.16–1.39	
Cost/ton		2.22–2.66		2.32–2.
Forest main roads				
Amortization/cunit roundwood	$0.50		‡	
Maintenance/cunit roundwood	$0.50		‡	
Cost/ton		1.11–1.33		‡
Stocks of roundwood				
Months of supply	3		3	
Interest rate	6%		5.2%	
Carrying cost/ton		0.30–0.48		0.31–0.
WOOD-RELATED COSTS				
Per cunit roundwood	$21.27–30.36		$23.27–31.35	
Per cunit chips	$15.00–18.00		$15.00–21.00	
Per ton of product		$28.72–42.56		$31.08–46.
Wages				
Manhours/ton	8.5		8.5	
Wage/hour	$2.90		$3.25	
Cost/ton		24.65		27.
Salaries				
Salaried people	40		40	
Average annual salary	$7,600		$9,200	
Cost/ton		4.41		5.
Fringe benefits				
% of wages	15–17		18–20	
% of salaries	6–8		7–9	
Cost/ton		4.25		5.
Electricity				
Kwh/ton	1900		1900	
Cost/kwh	$0.0040–0.0060		$0.0060–0.0090	
Cost/ton		9.50		14.
Fuel		5.00		5.
Chemicals and additives		12.00		12.
Other materials, overheads, and contingencies		25.00		25.
Mill fixed capital§	$25 million		$25 million	
Depreciation at 5%		18.12		18.
Mill working capital	$4 million		$4 million	
Interest rate	6%		5.2%	
Cost/ton		3.48		3.
MILL COST		$135.13–148.97		$147.11–162.

Source: Private Planning Association of Canada, work with private and published sources. Sources and metho
are discussed more fully in text and in appendix tables.
*Two identical tissue machines, capacity of each 100 tons per day at 90 percent efficiency, fully integrated wi
large-scale kraft sulphate and groundwood pulp mills. Assumed to be producing the same grade of toilet tissu
continuously. Finished and loaded as packaged rolls.
†For chips, the two-figure range of cunit quantities is stated as "high"–"average" (a high proportion coincidir
with a low cost). As a proportion of all wood used in chemical-pulp furnish, the use of chips has been assumed

Maine		British Columbia		Washington-Oregon	
1.16–1.39		0.77–0.98		0.77–0.98	
$20–27		$17–18		$18–20	
0.35–0.12		0.65–0.44		0.65–0.44	
$15–19		$10–15		$10–17	
1.51		1.42		1.42	
$18.84–26.36		$13.80–17.07		$14.34–19.07	
	$28.45–39.81		$19.59–24.24		$20.36–27.08
$2.00		$2.00		$2.00	
1.16–1.39		0.77–0.98		0.77–0.98	
	2.32–2.78		1.54–1.96		1.54–1.96
‡		$0.50		‡	
‡		$0.50		‡	
	‡		0.77–0.98		‡
3		2		2	
5.2%		6%		5.2%	
	0.30–0.46		0.13–0.18		0.12–0.17
$22.26–29.33		$20.17–20.18		$20.16–22.17	
$15.00–19.00		$10.00–15.00		$10.00.17.00	
	$31.07–43.05		$21.26–27.36		$22.02–29.21
8.5		8.5		8.5	
$3.10		$3.25		$3.45	
	26.35		27.63		29.33
40		40		40	
$8,600		$8,200		$9,800	
	4.99		4.75		5.68
18–20		15–17		18–20	
7–9		6–8		7–9	
	5.41		4.75		6.02
1900		1900		1900	
$0.0060–0.0090		$0.0040–0.0050		$0.0035–0.0040	
	14.25		8.55		7.13
	4.50		4.00		4.00
	12.00		12.00		12.00
	25.00		25.00		25.00
$25 million		$24 million		$24 million	
	18.12		17.39		17.39
$4 million		$4 million		$4 million	
5.2%		6%		5.2%	
	3.02		3.48		3.02
	$144.71–156.69		$128.81–134.91		$131.59–138.78

be ("average"–"high") 10–30 percent in the East and 40–60 percent in the West. The chemical-pulp is assumed to be 60 percent of the total pulp furnish.
‡Main roads are financed by the counties and states.
§Capital investment estimates assume zero tariffs on Canadian imports of machinery. Regional differences in initial outlay are entirely attributable to differences in climate and resulting differences in facilities and construction-labour productivity.

TABLE XXVIII

HYPOTHETICAL LAID-DOWN COSTS, TOILET TISSUE
(Canadian dollars per ton)
Two-figure range represents "low"–"average."

	Ontario	Wisconsin	Maine
Mill cost, 1964	135.13–148.97	147.11–162.13	144.71–156.69
Selling cost	5.50	5.50	5.50
Rail rate to:	(Probable from Merriton)	(Actual from Green Bay)	(Actual from Winslow)
Buffalo	(50 mi.) 4.74	(520 mi.) 14.69	(626 mi.) 16.85
Detroit	(220 mi.) 8.70	(333 mi.) 11.12	(857 mi.) 19.44
Boston	(520 mi.) 14.96	(991 mi.) 21.17	(191 mi.) 8.86
New York	(420 mi.) 12.88	(920 mi.) 20.30	(425 mi.) 14.04
Baltimore	(440 mi.) 12.28	(909 mi.) 20.30	(608 mi.) 16.63
Cincinnati	(460 mi.) 12.54	(478 mi.) 13.72	(1,042 mi.) 21.38
Chicago	(500 mi.) 14.20	(197 mi.) 8.10	(1,124 mi.) 22.46
Laid-down cost at:			
Buffalo	145.37–159.21	167.30–182.32	167.06–179.04
Detroit	149.33–163.17	163.73–178.75	169.65–181.63
Boston	155.59–169.43	173.78–188.80	159.07–171.05
New York	153.51–167.35	172.91–187.93	164.25–176.23
Baltimore	152.91–166.75	172.91–187.93	166.84–178.82
Cincinnati	153.17–167.01	166.33–181.35	171.59–183.57
Chicago	154.83–168.67	160.71–175.73	172.67–184.65

Sources and methods: Mill costs are as derived in Table XXVII. Selling costs are from suggestions by industry informants. Actual rail rates are from U.S. railway companies and are for shipments of 18 tons. Probable rail rates are those that Canadian railway companies think would be likely to be approved by U.S. railway companies if an application were made.

sometimes increased, as a delivered-cost advantage in the U.S. market areas shown. It appears that production of tissues would probably expand in eastern Canada under free trade and that the important uncertainties are really about ownership, control, management, and marketing affiliations.

British Columbia, for toilet tissue as for most other grades, seems to be in a good competitive position compared with the U.S. Northwest.

Non-integration between a pulp mill in Canada and an affiliated tissue plant in one of the U.S. market areas would add, as was pointed out with reference to bond paper, at least $20 per ton to the production and delivered cost of toilet tissue. But another kind of non-integration, in which an integrated tissue mill in eastern Canada might ship jumbo rolls to be converted into packaged rolls at a U.S. finishing plant, would involve only a small addition to the cost—unless operating expenses happened to be substantially higher in the U.S. market area—and might represent a feasible prospect in some instances.

F. UPDATING AND LOOKING AHEAD

The comparative-cost estimates based on 1964 data suggest that, for Canada, the most competitive lines of specialization in the now-protected grades would be, under free trade: first, sanitary tissues, because the U.S. South is out of the competition and because a lot of electricity is required; second, groundwood papers, which also require a lot of electricity; third, fine papers, where the substantial use of hardwood narrows the density gap between Canadian and southern wood; and fourth, linerboard (and probably kraft paper and paperboards generally), for which southern wood is particularly suitable.

To simplify the updating and projecting of the position from 1964, this final section will concentrate on bond paper and on the comparison between eastern Canada and its strongest prospective competitor, the U.S. South.

The estimates based on 1964 data showed that, per ton of bond paper, Ontario had an advantage over Alabama of $7.50 in wages, salaries, and fringe benefits, but a disadvantage of $7.75 in wood-related costs. Since these roughly offset one another, Alabama's over-all mill-cost advantage of $5.75 can be attributed, for the sake of simplicity, to the other items: advantages of $2.25 in chemicals, $1.50 in fuel, and $2.00 in capital costs. Further, it can be said that this $5.75 was offset, at least in some important U.S. markets, by lower rail rates from Ontario than from Alabama. The whole crux of the question, then, appears to be whether Ontario's advantage in wages, salaries, and fringe benefits has narrowed, or is likely to narrow, more than its disadvantage in wood-related costs.

Between 1964 and 1968, mill wage rates appear to have increased somewhat faster in Ontario than in Alabama, but the extent and significance of this development have sometimes been exaggerated. To clarify the situation, let us make an extreme assumption: that wages, salaries, and fringe benefits in Ontario have all risen to domestic-currency parity[10] with Wisconsin and that the gap between Wisconsin and Alabama has remained constant in absolute terms. This would mean that Ontario will have lost $2.40 (Can.) of its 1964 advantage of $7.50 per ton of bond paper over Alabama. For the future as well, the most by which one can reasonably expect the gap to narrow is about $2.40 compared with 1964—and all the evidence points to a widening of the gap between soaring wage rates in Alabama and those in both Wisconsin and Ontario.

Although eastern Canadian producers are inclined to express alarm over the increase in wood costs since 1964, there is no doubt that the increase

[10]By "domestic-currency parity" is meant numerical equality between one figure expressed in U.S. dollars and another figure expressed in Canadian dollars.

has been even greater in the South. Admittedly, the information available for 1968 is not as ample or precise as the evidence for 1964, but it appears to be entirely reliable concerning the direction in which the regional wood-cost gap is changing. In any event, a reasonable estimate seems to be that wood-related costs per ton of bond paper, which were estimated for 1964 as $33.96 in Ontario and $26.22 in Alabama, are now about $39 in Ontario and $35 in Alabama. In other words, Alabama appears to have lost about $3.75 of its 1964 advantage of $7.75 over Ontario.

Thus, while we would not want to make too much out of these figures in any precise sense, it certainly looks as though Ontario producers in 1968 would not be any worse off relative to the South than they appeared to be in the comparison based on 1964 data. For the future, the wood-cost gap between Ontario and Alabama seems likely to change in Ontario's favour for about the next five years, but then to start changing in Alabama's favour.

A highly interesting article on the pulpwood outlook in the South was recently presented by Albert Wilson, Editor-in-Chief of the periodical, PULP & PAPER, in the July 3, 1967, issue of that periodical. He was commenting on views presented by two noted authorities on the southern pulpwood situation, Dr. Bruce Zobel and Mr. Robert Kellison. Mr. Wilson's own summary of these views is so pertinent and concise that it is worth reproducing directly:

1. In the long run, economically available sources of timber will become increasingly critical.
2. In some areas, usable hardwoods already are in short supply, especially on the Gulf and southeast Atlantic Coast. Despite statistics indicating a large supply, the hardwoods in many areas are too inferior to be worth logging or are growing in swampy areas where logging costs are prohibitive.
3. There will be more opportunity for small mobile machinery than gigantic mechanized units because of small scattered holdings and small timber.
4. Many factors such as various new manufacturing plants are creating a shortage of wood workers, especially the better educated or trained people.
5. Forest land, especially on the Southeast and Gulf coasts, is being turned back to agriculture at an accelerating rate and this appears to be an irreversible trend.
6. Tax rates will unquestionably rise: already there is a tendency to tax forest lands as agricultural lands in certain areas.
7. Stumpage prices in some areas are very high and higher rates tend to spread rapidly over the South.
8. Plywood, once welcomed to balance wood use, is now competing strongly for Southern pine, taking trees formerly considered so small that they would be of use for pulpwood only.
9. There is a movement to try supplementary fiber sources with some companies trying Kenaf and sileage sycamore.

10. Most companies do not plan to obtain more than 40 to 50 percent of wood requirements off their own lands, so industry must continue to rely on thousands of small woodlot owners for the bulk of its raw material.

Of course, industry people in any region are naturally most aware of their own region's problems. The South has its swampy areas, and eastern Canada has its hilly areas. The South has a faster growth rotation, but eastern Canada has incomparably more untapped wood. The South has small woodlots, but the woodlands in eastern Canada are farther away from the mills or transportation centres. The South has higher land taxes, and eastern Canada has higher road-financing costs. Southern labour is scarce and sometimes difficult to educate, and eastern Canadian labour, particularly when well educated, is difficult to induce into remote areas.

For the next five years or so, however, it appears likely that wood labour costs, and wood costs, will rise more rapidly in the South than in eastern Canada. Mechanization of logging is almost certain to proceed far more rapidly in eastern Canada than in the South, and in about five years' time productivity in eastern Canadian woods is apt to be considerably higher than it is now, though it is doubtful that labour costs per unit of output will be prevented from rising. Mechanization in the South, even though it proceeds slowly, or particularly because it proceeds slowly, is likely to be accompanied by rapidly rising labour costs per unit of output. As soon as the industry brings in mechanization in the South, it inevitably brings in unionization, social security, and fast-rising wage rates, and these factors tend to spread also into areas in which mechanization has not occurred. Wood costs will almost certainly rise more rapidly in the South than in eastern Canada for about the next five years.

The reason why these comparative trends between eastern Canada and the South seem likely to be reversed in about five years' time is that there appears to be an underlying potential in favour of the South that should eventually come to the surface. Southern trees and pulpwood logs are considerably thicker than those in eastern Canada, on the average. Given the height of tree or length of log, the volume of wood is proportional to the *square* of the diameter. The movement of a machine when it lifts a tree or log is essentially the same whether the trunk is thick or thin, but the productivity of the movement is much greater to the extent that the log is thicker. This applies more strongly to the extent that southern wood is also denser.

Before concluding this chapter, we might mention a dilemma that fine-paper producers have faced in trying to decide on the kind of new machines to install. In recent years, all the major fine-paper producers in eastern Canada have installed larger machines than previously, perhaps in anticipation of larger markets via the Kennedy round, perhaps in anticipation of complete free trade sooner or later. Under the circumstances, such machines were necessarily designed to have considerable versatility. It should be noted that long production runs on versatile machines do not achieve the full cost efficiences of long runs on machines *designed* for highly specialized operation.

On the other hand, in the absence of free trade, these machines must operate for many years at considerable undercapacity, and greater efficiency might have been achieved with smaller machines operating closer to capacity. The dilemma, in other words, is that the large and versatile machines are too large in the absence of free trade and would be too versatile in the event of free trade. Therefore, if free trade is, in fact, to come eventually, perhaps it would be best if it came before further such major investments were made in machines of only intermediate effectiveness.[11]

7. Market Opportunities and Obstacles

Part A contained information on markets and on demand trends and prospects under existing tariff conditions. A brief recapitulation here may be helpful. The tariff-protected papers, which account for 26 percent of the value of the industry's production, are sold mainly in the domestic market. The tariffs have encouraged producers to cater to a full range of product lines. Prior to 1968, the starting date for the Kennedy round tariff cuts, Canada's MFN tariffs on paper and paperboard imports ranged up to 25 percent, with the rate usually 20–22½ percent. The two leading export markets are the United States and Britain. Paperboard and book and writing (fine) papers are the leading exports among tariff-protected papers. Exports of book and writing papers and sanitary papers have been expanding faster than imports. Imports of paperboard, wrapping paper, special industrial papers, and tissue papers (excluding sanitary) have been expanding faster than exports. World demand for paper is expected to increase at almost 5 percent per year. The three leading countries in per capita consumption are the United States, Sweden, and Canada. The most rapidly growing markets among industrialized countries are Japan and the European Economic Community. Under the tariff pattern existing prior to 1968,

[11]A policy issue raised is whether it would not be reasonable for the adjustment-assistance program to offer modest compensation to producers for being "stuck" for many years with relatively new machines of intermediate effectiveness. The simple fact is that these producers have not had any fully satisfactory option open to them in their choice of machinery for necessary additions to capacity.

the prospective increase to 1975 in total demand for Canada's pulp and paper was estimated at 4.8 percent per year. Paperboard production was expected to increase at a rate of 5% percent per year, fine paper production at 6 percent, wrapping paper and building paper and boards at 3½ percent, and sanitary and tissue paper at 6¾ percent.

It was concluded in Chapter 6 that restructuring the Canadian pulp and paper industry in order to achieve competitive production and selling costs under free trade conditions would involve, among other adjustments, longer production runs for each product. There are two ways of expanding company sales to justify the longer runs—companies can specialize their product lines for the domestic market and/or they can export.

At first glance, the market opportunities that would be opened up for Canadian papers by free trade among North Atlantic countries look very good. The U.S. market alone is many times greater, incomes are higher there than in Canada, and there should be markets in other North Atlantic countries as well. The U.S. market is, of course, regionalized. Nevertheless, there are substantial centres of consumption close to the Canadian border.

Effective penetration of these markets, however, would not be easy for most Canadian producers. And even if the penetrating of export markets were easy, would not the opportunity be reciprocal? Would not existing sales by Canadian producers in the domestic market be highly vulnerable to imports?

The answer to such questions might seem to depend simply on comparative costs. Other things being equal, low-cost producers would be best able to compete in domestic and export markets. In fact, achieving competitive costs under free trade conditions would be a necessary, but not a sufficient, condition for successful competition. In addition to restructuring their production in order to achieve low costs, small and medium-sized independent Canadian producers of hitherto tariff-protected papers would face formidable, although not necessarily insuperable, marketing obstacles. Such obstacles would not arise for Canadian subsidiaries of U.S. corporations and would be less pronounced for those large Canadian-owned companies which have already begun to integrate forward in the United States (or other foreign markets). These obstacles, which are both financial and institutional in nature, are appraised in this chapter, and certain policy implications are discussed in Part C.

NATURE OF THE PRODUCTS

A characteristic of the pulp and paper industry has been its resource orientation, that is, its tendency to locate close to abundant supplies of wood and water. On the other hand, converters of paper into paper products, particularly of the more highly processed and expensive "white" papers, have been relatively more market-oriented.

The consumption of papers (excluding newsprint) and paperboards is sensitive to changes in disposable personal income. Economists would say that the demand is "income-elastic." In particular, the consumption of fine papers, sanitary and tissue papers, containerboard, and buildingboard tends to respond strongly to changes in personal income. Papers and paperboards in general have been withstanding the inroads of substitutes because of favourable prices (enabled, for example, by making thinner paper of equal or better quality), to some extent by utilizing the substitutes in improving the quality and usefulness of paper products, and by developing new uses for paper products.

The influence of technology on the unfolding world supply-demand pattern must be emphasized. Just as paper in certain forms competes with other products (e.g., metal, glass, and plastics) in industrial and consumer uses, so various fibre sources (raw wood, waste paper, rags, etc.) vie with each other on the bases of availability, cost, and quality for papermaking. Dramatic developments are taking place in the regeneration and utilization of forest resources, such as fast-growing hybrids, improvements in hardwood technology, and the spectacular growth in pulping of southern pine. It is against this background of change in consumer preference, product development, improved processing, and raw-material utilization that Canada's longer-run prospects as a supplier of pulp and paper must be viewed.

With few exceptions, the paper products concerned in this study tend to be more highly processed and hence more expensive than pulp and newsprint. Indeed, some of them are branded (that is, sold under brand names) and exhibit quite different marketing characteristics than the more standardized ones. Perhaps most prominent of these characteristics are watermarks, differentiated packaging, and advertising. There are also specialty grades in which quality innovations for purposes of penetrating new markets would imply small-volume rather than large-volume sales. In any case, substantial "threshold" marketing costs would be involved.

It is sometimes argued that impact losses suffered by producers of protected grades of paper could be offset by gains in pulp and newsprint sales. This assumes that all pulp and paper companies are fully integrated and diversified, which is certainly not so now and might not become so even after the transition period. But even if this were the result of restructuring the industry, there is another flaw in the argument. Since trade generally is already free in pulp and newsprint, no gains for these products *attributable to freer trade* would result for the purposes of offsetting impact losses, or financing adjustments, in other grades. This argument, therefore, would amount to an arbitrary and compulsory income transfer rather than an impact offset. The cases for or against restructuring the protected sector of the industry should be made on their own merits. This is not to deny that the large, diversified companies are likely to command greater resources for financing the expensive restructuring of their production and marketing operations in the protected grades or for riding out temporarily depressed paper markets.

DOMESTIC MARKET

As is well known, the population of Canada is concentrated in urban centres strung across the country close to the U.S. border. The greatest concentration is along the Quebec City-Windsor axis, where a population of twelve million is located over a distance of 730 miles. Under free trade, some Canadian markets would be closer to existing U.S. paper mills than to Canadian mills. This might not be serious if the reverse were equally true, thereby permitting a trade-off of customers, or if Canadian mills were lower-cost producers. We do not pretend to know with certainty what the net impact of all this would be on Canadian suppliers of the domestic markets, but it is a potential threat not to be dismissed lightly. Current overcapacity is greatest in the tariff-free pulp and newsprint lines, not in the tariff-protected ones. In 1967, Canadian pulp and newsprint were operating at 85 to 87 percent of capacity, compared with 92 to 95 percent in 1966. Other papers were operating at 88 to 90 percent of capacity in 1967, compared with 86 to 91 percent in 1966.

Imports of the protected grades as a whole have been increasing faster than exports. Under freer trade, U.S. suppliers would begin with a better-prepared position. Their initial position would be better not only because of lower-cost production but because of established subsidiaries and market contacts in Canada. Market outlets in Canada are still, for the most part, independent merchants who could readily be tied up financially by aggressive U.S. suppliers.

Some branded paper products are highly advertised on television and in journals in the United States. This advertising spills readily over the border, and under freer trade the advertised products might find a preconditioned and popular acceptance in Canada. It might even be feasible at times for U.S. suppliers to bypass Canadian paper merchants and sell directly to large-scale retailers such as the supermarket chains.

U.S. suppliers are used to lower prices at home than have prevailed in Canada, and this could be a compelling sales advantage. They could price aggressively in Canada without dumping. (For discussion of anti-dumping, see Chapter 10.) Even after prices settle to uniform levels in both countries, established marketing connections would tend to persist.

Canadian suppliers would be better prepared to meet such competition if they could merge, integrate forward, and specialize in anticipation of freer trade. This would require changes in the combines law, however (see Chapter 10).

U.S. MARKET

The U.S. market appears to hold the main opportunities for increased Canadian exports. The EEC effectively discouraged Canadian paper exports by refusing to make substantial tariff concessions on papers in the Kennedy round. The possibility of the United Kingdom's joining the EEC at some future date raises the possibility that Canada will lose free or preferential access to this important market. Also there is the probability that Scandinavian producers will extend their hold on U.K. and western European markets. On the other hand, the United States made substantial tariff cuts in the Kennedy round of negotiations.

There are basic production and marketing similarities in the pulp and paper industry between eastern Canada and the U.S. Northeast, between central Canada and the U.S. North Central, and between British Columbia and the U.S. Rocky Mountain and Pacific Coast states. An important regional exception is the U.S. South, which has no counterpart in Canada. Production in the United States is more evenly balanced by product lines for domestic consumption in contrast with the dominant pulp-newsprint export bias of the Canadian industry. More specifically, trends since 1945 in the major U.S. producing regions have been:

1. The South and West have experienced substantial growth in over-all production, while the northeast and north-central regions have declined relatively.

2. The fastest growing products in the South have been coarse papers, containerboard, special foodboard, and newsprint, with gains in the first two reflecting a shift in production from the North Central and Northeast. The West has concentrated on containerboard, coarse papers, and sanitary papers. The north central region has emphasized sanitary tissue, ground-wood, and printing papers. Similarly, the Northeast has shown considerable growth in sanitary tissue, printing, and fine papers.

Although there are similarities between counterpart regions in the United States and Canada, there are also important differences. Some of these were mentioned above. The pulp and paper companies in the United States are more highly integrated. The latest stage in the integration process from raw material through to consumer has tended to be the purchase of converters and wholesalers and, in some cases, new fibre supplies in Canada. The trend towards tied outlets has been accompanied by a broadening of product lines produced and marketed by the integrated companies. The highly capitalized, integrated, and diversified companies enjoy economies of large-scale production and marketing. They have specialized sales personnel and conduct costly advertising campaigns. Such producers are well prepared not only to meet competition in their own markets from Canadian exports, but to export aggressively to Canada and to third countries which are of potential interest to Canadian producers.

In spite of the importance of pulp and newsprint exports to the United States, Canada remains very much a "residual supplier" of these products. Tied sales have a great advantage when slack develops in a market. The amount of capital and know-how required to put Canadian suppliers of other papers on a competitive and secure basis in U.S. markets would be substantial. The more highly processed the papers, the greater the marketing obstacles tend to be. There are other problems to overcome as well. Paper prices in the United States are relatively low and would be difficult for Canadian producers to meet, especially during the transition period, without dumping. It has been estimated that price reductions in Canadian fine papers of 8 to 14 percent would be needed to meet U.S. competition.

On the cost side, inflation has been less rapid in the United States than in Canada. This has eroded the advantage gained by the 1962 devaluation of the Canadian dollar. It is also fair to say that relevant U.S. freight rates tend to be more favourable than Canadian, although the differential might be narrowed by securing more favourable Canadian rates for larger volume exports.

OTHER MARKETS

After Canada and the United States, the main markets among North Atlantic countries can be grouped into the EFTA and the EEC. The European Free Trade Association includes Austria, Denmark, Finland, Norway, Portugal, Sweden, Switzerland, and the United Kingdom. The European Economic Community includes Belgium, France, West Germany, Italy, Luxembourg, and the Netherlands. EFTA has a larger export surplus in paper than North America, while the EEC has a large import surplus. Finland and Sweden supply more than two-thirds of EFTA's exports. After Canada, Finland is the largest exporter of paper in the world.

During the 1960s, there has been an increased concentration in paper trade among EFTA members. This can be ascribed largely to the lowering of tariffs among EFTA countries. The EFTA Secretariat has estimated[1]

[1]European Free Trade Association, *EFTA Bulletin*, February 1968.

that paper exports within EFTA had risen by over $100 million by 1965 as a result of the tariff reductions. There was not only an increased volume of paper trade among EFTA countries, but also greater emphasis on producing higher-grade paper and importing lower-grade and semi-finished products.

Following a tour of western Europe and the United Kingdom, one of the authors of the present study concluded that those countries are not anxious to see completely free trade in papers. EEC fears of Scandinavian imports are lessening as demand in Europe expands faster than the supply of fibre, but the fear of imports from North America remains strong. It is acknowledged that a long-run shift to North American sources of fibre supply is under way, but there is great resistance to a rapid shift. European producers fear that they would be unable to compete with North American producers under free trade, except in a few specialized grades.

The EEC market is vital to the Scandinavians, and they tend to regard it as primarily theirs. This attitude is reinforced by the product up-grading, restructuring of the industry, and vertical integration which are under way throughout Europe. Producers are shifting into differentiated product lines that require closer market connections. Interestingly, it is the medium-size European mills, not the small ones, which seem to be hardest pressed, because the small ones are close to both wood and customers and the large ones have economies of scale and forward integration.

The United Kingdom is the fourth most important paper producer in the world, after the United States, Canada, and Japan. U.K. production is far from adequate for home consumption, and substantial imports of both pulp and paper are required. The United Kingdom was described earlier as a leading export market for Canadian pulps and papers. Prior to the elimination of EFTA's internal tariffs, Canadian exports to the United Kingdom enjoyed Commonwealth preference. Elements of the British paper industry would welcome entry into the EEC for the sake of the common external tariff because they have had no tariff protection against EFTA imports since the end of 1966.

A practical problem for Canadian overseas exports has been how to get over and around European tariffs, in order to supply as much of the growth market as possible. Forward financial integration is the most obvious answer. Forward integration might not alter the pulp-newsprint bias of the Canadian industry, however. Free North Atlantic trade might accomplish that. Presumably, a deficit European market area and a surplus North American supply area cannot be kept apart indefinitely by high tariffs. Another hurdle facing paper exports to Europe has been differences in consumer preferences.

In exporting to third-country markets, the U.S. companies referred to in the previous section have available to them a battery of governmental export-promotion services. Although similar services are available, or could be made available, to Canadian exporters, U.S. companies are also under pressure to expand exports as a contribution to the chronic U.S. balance of payments problem.

A stepped-up overseas export drive by Canadian producers under free trade conditions presumably would include several of the formerly protected grades of paper. The comparative wood-cost figures in Chapter 6 are not sufficiently favourable to the Canadian industry to warrant a policy of sitting and waiting for the world to come to us to satisfy its rapidly expanding needs for wood fibre, pulps, and papers. With the possible exception of B.C. producers in relation to Pacific overseas markets, there is no margin for complacency concerning the competitiveness of Canadian producers *vis-à-vis* rival suppliers and substitute products.

Other things being equal, companies with superior management, research, and sales expertise will have greater success in expanding their market shares. The large international companies that increasingly characterize the industry will seek to match demand with supply, *wherever they find it*, in the most economical way, having regard for the trading and industrial development policies of nations. The less developed countries, for example, can be expected to play an increasing role in supplying their expanding markets for papers. For this they have greater need for investment of capital and know-how from North America than for paper.

8. Impact Conclusions

It is a human failing for people involved in enforced change to see the attendant difficulties more clearly than the opportunities. There is also a tendency for people not closely involved to see the opportunities more clearly than the difficulties. So it is in the present instance. Even within the large, diversified pulp and paper companies, pulp and newsprint personnel, accustomed as they are to free trade conditions, tend to see the opportunities more readily than the difficulties which would result from restructuring the tariff-protected sector of the industry. It is not surprising, therefore, that policy-makers and the general public, who are less well-informed, should stress the gains to be expected from freer trade but are largely unaware of the accompanying difficulties and dangers. The results of such unbalanced views, however, are often unexpected and occasionally disastrous. The purpose of our previous two chapters was to explore and clarify both sides of the issue and not to exaggerate either.

The general conclusion that we draw from all the evidence gathered and from the findings of our cost analysis is that the Canadian pulp and paper industry could compete under conditions of free or freer trade among North Atlantic countries *provided that its production and marketing were reorganized and that related government policies were helpful.* This qualified conclusion has a corollary. As presently structured, the sector of the Canadian industry which has been protected by tariffs and whose diversified production is oriented to small domestic markets could not compete in North American markets with U.S. competitors under free trade conditions. As shown in Chapter 4, productivity in the U.S. industry increased more than twice as fast as in Canada between 1947 and 1961, and imports of the protected grades as a group into Canada since the Second World War have been expanding faster than exports.

The basic restructuring required of the Canadian pulp and paper industry would imply greater product specialization by companies and much longer runs on wider and faster machines in the presently tariff-protected sector. This specialization would be very likely to result in cessation of production in Canada of some grades of paper. In certain other instances, the mills would have to be relocated. Except for newsprint and pulp, where there is a long tradition of free trade, market orientation would have to shift from domestic towards export in order to achieve adequate volumes of sales at lower North American price levels. This also implies competing successfully with imports in the domestic market. The net impact of restructuring on the volume of pulp exports is impossible to forecast.

Restructuring of the industry probably would involve some small companies being absorbed by larger ones with greater financial resources and perhaps a few companies going out of business entirely. The impact of free trade on the industry would have regional disparities, with the major adjustments being required in Quebec and Ontario, where production of tariff-protected papers for the domestic market has been concentrated. Which grades of paper and which paper companies are forced out of production will be determined mainly by their cost competitiveness and marketing aggressiveness. Neither of these determinants is immutable. The outcome can be influenced by qualities of ownership, management, and research.

If production and marketing could be restructured, and if competitive freight rates could be negotiated with the railways, our findings in Chapter 6 suggest that the best lines of specialization in the now-protected grades for eastern Canada under free trade would be (in descending order): first, sanitary tissues, because of the coarse woods and higher costs of electricity used in the U.S. South; second, groundwood papers, which also require a lot of electricity; third, bond paper, where the substantial use of hardwood narrows the density gap between Canadian and southern wood; and fourth, linerboard (and probably kraft paper and paperboards generally), for which the U.S. South is particularly well suited. British Columbia should be competitive in most papers in West Coast and Pacific overseas markets.

The restructuring and reorientation of the Canadian pulp and paper industry would require large amounts of capital, not only for financing the transition to specialized production, but also for acquiring converting facilities and marketing outlets. The importance of tied outlets is demonstrated by the current overcapacity in Canadian newsprint resulting from Canadian producers being residual suppliers in a slack U.S. market. During the transition period for restructuring Canadian production and marketing, there would be attendant employment and other social dislocations in some small mill towns in Canada.

The policy implications of the foregoing impact conclusions are explored in Part C.

C. Policy Implications

9. Adjustment Assistance

THE CASE FOR FREE TRADE AND FOR ADJUSTMENT ASSISTANCE

The general case made for free trade is that people enjoy a higher level of living when they specialize in producing goods in which they have the greatest advantage and trade them freely for other goods produced elsewhere. A pejorative version of this is that tariffs are an indirect system of taxing the general public through higher prices of products in order to subsidize the protected producers. The only economic exception to free trade theory is the familiar "infant-industry" or "infant-economy" kind of argument, which becomes less applicable to Canada after one hundred years and more of economic development.

The general case made for adjustment assistance is that, since most workers and virtually all consumers benefit from freer trade, equity requires that the impact costs be shared among the beneficiaries rather than that the whole burden be borne by particular companies and sometimes their employees. No one can doubt that genuine cases of difficulty would arise in adapting an economy such as Canada's to substantially freer trade.

The general cases both for freer trade and for adjustment assistance also apply to the Canadian pulp and paper industry. Canadian consumers and most workers would benefit from producers achieving economies of scale in the present tariff-protected grades of paper. The case for adjustment assistance applies with special force because so many of the pulp and paper mills are located in single-industry communities which would be highly vulnerable to dislocations resulting from tariff cuts. Frequently these single-industry communities are located in provinces that tend to suffer from above-average rates of unemployment. On the other hand, some communities, as well as the general public, would benefit from any local increases in production and income resulting from greater specialization. In short, adjustment assistance can be justified on three grounds—equitable sharing of the costs as well as of the benefits of tariff cuts, encouragement of more efficient and competitive industrial organization, and community welfare.

PRECEDENTS

There are good precedents, both general and specific, for provision of adjustment assistance. The principle of general provision of adjustment assistance probably originated with the European Common Market. A European investment bank was created for the purpose of financing (among other things) projects for modernizing or converting plants as necessitated by the establishment of the Common Market, if these could not be financed elsewhere. A social fund was established with purposes including reimbursement of half of member countries' costs of retraining and resettling workers and paying temporary unemployment benefits during conversion of plants.

Provision for adjustment assistance was incorporated in the U.S. Trade Expansion Act of 1962. It was felt to be unfair for those workers and companies injured by tariff cuts to bear the full brunt of these cuts, since benefits would be so widespread among the nation as a whole. The Trade Expansion Act provides for technical, financial, and tax assistance to eligible firms and for trade readjustment, training, and relocation allowances for eligible workers.

In its *Second Annual Review*, the Economic Council of Canada recommended a general program of adjustment assistance as follows:

In anticipation of possible adjustments in the structure of production resulting from future reductions in trade barriers, [we recommend that] immediate steps be taken to establish a general programme under which adequate and effective assistance would be available to particular industries and groups of workers which may be adversely affected by any such reductions. The basic purpose of such a programme would be to bring about an effective and speedy transfer of productive resources from less efficient to more efficient lines of production. The resulting improvements in the productivity of the economy would amply justify the costs involved.

In terms of dislocations and adjustments resulting from lower tariffs under the Kennedy round, the need for some form of adjustment assistance was recognized in Canada. For example, the Minister of Finance said in Moncton on July 10, 1967, that the government realized that there might be genuine cases of difficulty in adapting to these changes and was working on measures to assist firms to make the necessary changes in production and marketing. The Minister of Industry invited suggestions about the kind of assistance that would be most useful in such situations.

On December 27, 1967, the Prime Minister announced a three-point program to help companies badly hit by the Kennedy round tariff cuts. The announcement stated that:

The principal feature of the program will be the offer by the Government of insurance of the major share of the risk of loss on . . . industrial adjustment assistance loans made by private lenders. A second element will be direct Government loans in case of carefully defined hardship up to a total of $10 million in the first year of the program. An important third feature of the program will be the extension of technical assistance to manufacturers in preparing adjustment proposals for the purpose of improving their production, managerial, marketing and financial operations. The program will be built on the experience gained from the automotive adjustment assistance program but it will be administered by a separately constituted board. In essence the program, as a whole, is designed to help accelerate the mobilization of resources in the private sector for the purpose of attaining our important national economic objective of an expanded and more productive secondary industry.

To be eligible for insured loans firms must, as a first step, establish that they have either been seriously injured or threatened with serious injury as a result of the Kennedy Round tariff reductions made by Canada or that they have significant export opportunities arising out of the Kennedy Round. There are also three further tests which have to be met by a firm in order to qualify for an insured loan. First, a firm must present a comprehensive plan involving a restructuring of its operations in order to improve its competitive position. Second, its comprehensive plan must be judged to be sound by the adjustment assistance board. Third, it must be clearly established that sufficient financing cannot be obtained on reasonable terms from other sources. The government will charge a fee for insuring loans and the private lenders, in agreement with the borrowers, will set the terms of the loans subject, of course, to competitive forces in the financial markets.

For firms that have been seriously injured or threatened with serious injury as a result of reductions in the Canadian tariff and who are unable to borrow the funds they require to re-adjust from the private sector under the insured loan program, the Government will be prepared to provide direct loans providing the firm undertakes to seek a viable solution to its problems in co-operation with the Board. It is expected that very few firms will experience these conditions and consequently only limited use will be made of direct Government loans.

Since many of the applicants for financial assistance under the program will be small and medium-sized firms which may not have the resources within their own organizations to formulate fully sound adjustment proposals, a provision for technical assistance is being included in this program. Where necessary, applicant firms will be assisted in finding competent technical and professional advice in the private sector. The proposal is that the Government share the cost of such consulting services with the firm to the extent considered appropriate in each case, but the Government's share would not exceed 50 percent.

SUGGESTED FORMS OF ASSISTANCE FOR COMPANIES AND EMPLOYEES

For Industry. As already concluded, necessary and desirable adjustments to freer trade by pulp and paper companies would in most cases involve specialization and much longer runs in the currently protected grades (with some relocation of mills and some producers going out of business) and the acquisition of expertise, facilities, and outlets for purposes of penetrating export markets.

In making his announcement of the adjustment assistance program, the Prime Minister said that the government would be prepared to consider, if necessary, further appropriate and workable programs consistent with the program outlined above. The kinds of adjustment assistance to be made available to companies under the announced program should be included in an extended program in the event of freer trade beyond the results of the Kennedy round, subject to the following comments:

For small and medium-sized companies the program covers two of the major obstacles that might prevent adjustment to changed conditions by providing technical assistance to a company in formulating its plan to transform its facilities and enter new markets and, once such a plan has been worked out, by helping to assure the means of financing it. The majority of pulp and paper companies, because of their size, will be aided only insofar as they can qualify for government guarantees of loans. Clarification is needed as to what loan purposes will be considered eligible for government guarantee. Loans for marketing purposes could be as important as those to promote production adjustments. In some cases, the justification for restructuring production may depend on successful marketing adjustments. The danger is that just when additional financing is needed for adjustment purposes, a company will find its borrowing powers reduced by low earnings and reduced cash flow caused by lower prices and disrupted markets.

For Employees. Intensified manpower retraining and relocation measures would be appropriate forms of government assistance for employees to encourage their adjustment and to alleviate attendant problems.

ELIGIBILITY

In order for the general public to derive maximum benefit from restructuring industry to lower tariffs (that is, transferring resources from less efficient to more efficient lines of production), firms need to know what kinds and amounts of adjustment assistance they can count on in overcoming transitional bottlenecks. Therefore, forms of adjustment assistance and eligibility rules for each have to be devised by the government or its dispensing agency, and announced well in advance. Such rules must be flexible enough to enable the assistance to be tailored to specific company situations and at the same time to offer aid adequate to accomplish the basic public objectives of the program. One of the basic objectives is to promote industries that can be competitive in domestic and export markets at lower tariff levels. People who are inclined to take a harder line concerning the eligibility for assistance of marketing, compared with production, adjustments, and towards assistance for large, compared with small, companies, should remember that there is under way a trend towards large, international firms in the pulp and paper business. In view of Canada's large forest resources and pulp and paper industry, should not at least a few of these be Canadian-owned? Canadian ownership would be endangered if the only sources of adequate financing for expensive restructuring were foreign.

The distinction which is sometimes made between providing transitional assistance to firms restructuring and modernizing their production and denying any indemnity to firms and their employees ceasing production altogether is also invalid. No such distinction can be drawn on grounds of public interest, since it is as desirable for firms *rendered hopelessly uncompetitive by freer trade* to cease production promptly as it is for other firms quickly to adjust their production by specializing in order to achieve economies of scale. If there were no indemnity available for quitting at the outset of free trade, the doomed firms would surely press, perhaps irresistibly, for continuing forms of adjustment or other assistance which, if granted, would constitute a more expensive public subsidy of hopelessly uneconomic businesses. The cynical view that such firms are doomed under freer trade with or without indemnity can be overruled by the widely accepted equity and community-welfare arguments which were stated earlier in the chapter. This is not an argument for indemnifying firms rendered uneconomic for sundry reasons other than large cuts in tariff. Conventional business expansion also does not qualify as "adjustment" and therefore does not deserve special assistance.

TRANSITIONAL PERIOD

In a capital-intensive industry such as pulp and paper, there is an important time dimension to restructuring. Planning, financing, and constructing modern new production facilities take years. The market research, raising of funds, and financial negotiations involved in the acquiring of distribution outlets (including sometimes warehousing and converting facilities) for purposes of expanding exports also are time-consuming.

Adequate advance notice of intended future reductions in tariffs is needed, therefore, or else the reductions should be phased over a period of several years. Moreover, a direct relationship is implied between the speed of reduction in tariffs and the intensity of appropriate adjustment assistance. If one is accelerated, then the other should be also.

10. Other Policy Implications

A program for achieving free or freer trade would have far-reaching policy implications extending beyond adjustment assistance. To avoid wasteful

conflicts in policy and maximize resulting opportunities, a free trade program should be viewed against the whole fabric of the Canadian economy
as well as against the social and political goals of Canadians. If it becomes
a national goal to lower the costs of products in domestic and export
markets by reducing or eliminating tariffs and non-tariff barriers, then
various other policies should contribute to this achievement or at least not
be incompatible with it. For example, if monetary and fiscal policies are
used to help maintain an expansionary economy with reasonable price
stability, the problems of adjusting to freer trade would be lessened, the
transition period would be shortened, and the amount of adjustment assistance required would be reduced. Another general example is the tax burden
borne by companies and individuals in Canada relative to that borne in rival
trading countries. If the tax burden of Canadians gets out of line with that
of foreign competitors, the competitiveness of Canadian products will suffer
in both the domestic and export markets. Certain other critical areas where
policies are needed, compatible with or reinforcing the discipline of lower
tariffs, are discussed briefly in this chapter.

ANTI-DUMPING

Anti-dumping duties can be applied or threatened in order to serve not
only as a legitimate protection against dumped imports but also as a
harassment to other imports. When tariffs were reduced under the Kennedy
round, a new anti-dumping code, based on Article VI of the GATT, was
agreed upon by the signatory countries, which permits the levying of anti-
dumping duties on dumped imports only where these cause or threaten
material injury to the domestic industry. The new code probably will
protect Canadian industry from continuous dumping without being incompatible with the freer trade spirit of the Kennedy round. How it actually
works will depend considerably on how each country translates it into
enforcing legislation and regulations, to be introduced, in Canada's case,
by July 1, 1968. This is important for the present study because the new
code may well determine anti-dumping policy under any tariff cuts for
some years beyond the Kennedy round.

    In view of the crucial importance to the Canadian pulp and paper
industry of becoming competitive in both domestic and U.S. markets under
freer trade, it is in the long-run interest of the industry for the code to be
applied similarly in both countries, short-run considerations to the contrary
notwithstanding. Anti-dumping harassment almost certainly would become
retaliatory, if it were not reciprocal from the outset.

    Although during the transition period it may prove difficult to avoid
dumping Canadian exports in the United States because of traditionally

higher costs in Canada, Canadian exports would be unlikely to cause material injury to a much larger U.S. industry. Although it may prove easier for U.S. exports to Canada to avoid being dumped, any U.S. exports which are dumped are likely to cause material injury to a smaller Canadian industry. If, because of shorter production runs and higher cost levels, the Canadian industry faces more severe adjustment problems during the transition period than its U.S. counterpart, then some more appropriate remedy than the preferential application of anti-dumping duties by Canada should be found.

This is not to say that diligence is unnecessary in the legitimate application of the code to dumped imports, regardless of the tariff level. It is to recognize, rather, that the diligence will in all probability, be reciprocal.

Diligence will be needed to prevent sporadic dumping of odd lots, side runs, and start-up tonnage by U.S. producers on Canadian markets. Because of the relatively small scale of Canadian producers, at the outset and during the transition period, and the seasonal nature of sales, such sporadic dumping could be crippling. To guard against sporadic dumping, adequate information about dumped imports must be communicated promptly to the industry by some governmental "early-warning system" in order to enable the industry to gather the evidence of injury required *before* provisional anti-dumping measures can be applied. Exceptional care will be needed in the definition and application of the term "material injury," as well as "like product" and "industry," to make these appropriate both for a transitional period involving major restructuring and for the longer-run future.

TRANSPORTATION

Canadian transportation policy also would require reappraisal in the light of a national policy of trade liberalization. Transportation policy and rate structures, especially for railways, developed within the context of protectionism, called the "national policy," and an east-west flow of goods. Under freer trade, the flow of goods would shift towards a north-south continental pattern, and transportation policy and freight rates should be altered to conform with this change. It is recognized that some alterations may need to be negotiated reciprocally with transportation authorities in the United States.

The transporting of pulp and paper products to market accounts for a substantial share of delivered costs. Rate structures inconsistent with the policy of freer trade would undermine the competitiveness of Canadian pulp and paper in both domestic and export markets. This applies particularly to eastern mills.

EXPORT SALES PROMOTION

Governments of leading trading countries such as Canada provide a widening range of services (such as trade missions, fairs, exhibits, lists of foreign distribution outlets, reports on foreign business conditions and practices, export credit insurance, etc.) to help promote exports. Although some of these services may not be needed by relatively sophisticated exporters such as most pulp and newsprint producers, the services could be very helpful to most producers of the hitherto protected grades of paper under freer trade conditions, especially during the transition period. Marketing for these producers has been oriented to the domestic market, and acquiring expertise for aggressive export selling would be both time-consuming and expensive. ESP (export sales promotion) advice on sales opportunities, and assistance with initial contacts in foreign markets, could be quite valuable in surmounting some of the threshold marketing problems encountered in exporting. This also applies to opportunities for investing in converting facilities and distribution outlets in other countries, which are sometimes a prerequisite to expanding exports.

Knowledge of the export sales promotion services available to foreign competitors could also become important. This would apply not only to paper exporters, but also to producers who hope to continue to concentrate on the domestic market, in order to help them to compete with imports.

WAGE PARITY

Wage parity between Canada and the United States has become a subject of increasing interest and controversy. Unless wage parity is preceded or accompanied by parity of productivity, the international competitiveness of Canadian industry would be undermined.

In certain jobs, wage parity already exists in the pulp and paper industry. There is a tendency for wage-parity pressures to spread throughout the industry, however, not only to product lines where Canadian productivity is comparable to that of the United States, but to the protected grades of paper where it is not. If, in the absence of wage restraint, wage parity were to spread too fast during the transition to freer trade, it would anticipate the productivity gains from the adjustment process and prevent some Canadian producers of the presently protected grades from becoming competitive in domestic and export markets. It would seem important in this connection to avoid an exchange rate policy which could weaken the competitive position of Canadian producers.

ANTI-COMBINES

In its *Second Annual Review*, the Economic Council of Canada stated that where reduced trade barriers resulted in increased foreign competition, thereby safeguarding the interest of consumers, specialization agreements or mergers among producers in order to increase efficiency and eliminate excessive duplication might well be appropriate. Relaxation of some provisions of combines and restrictive trade practices legislation would be needed under freer trade to permit Canadian producers of formerly protected grades of paper to achieve quickly longer runs of fewer grades. Indeed, the producers should be given advance assurance that such measures would be permitted as tariffs are cut, since restructuring is in the public interest. The permission should cover specialization in both production and marketing without prejudging whether or not it might be necessary for the sales organizations of the specialized producers to continue to handle a full line of products. Specialization agreements would avert dangerous trial-and-error adjustments by companies working largely in the dark concerning their comparative costs for particular grades of paper. Otherwise each producer would be completely dependent on breaking into export markets in order to obtain the volume of sales needed to justify longer runs.

It has been said that the present Combines Act would not be a serious obstacle to restructuring an industry under freer trade because it already permits joint action among exporters. This viewpoint is unconvincing, in the case of the pulp and paper industry at least, because of the technical and economic difficulties of separating structural adjustments as between export and domestic markets. Indeed, even if such a separation were possible, it would be inconsistent with the public purpose in opting for freer trade in the first place.

The question has been raised whether legal permission would be enough to ensure agreement among rival companies on product specialization under free trade conditions. We think that fear of business failure under a cut-throat trial-and-error process would be compulsion enough and that government directives on specialization should be a last resort.

INCENTIVES FOR POLLUTION ABATEMENT
There is increasing public recognition of the need for abatement of air and water pollution caused by industries and municipalities. The benefits to society of expenditures on pollution abatement exceed the benefits to industry, and the benefits to industry are usually less than the cost. In addition to imposing higher standards and stricter enforcement, governments are providing incentives for expenditures on pollution abatement. In Canada, an accelerated (two-year) write-off is provided for federal income tax purposes. In the United States, various incentives are offered, and new kinds are being tried. This recognizes both the urgency of the pollution

problem and the technical fact that as higher abatement requirements are met, further improvements become increasingly costly in relation to the gains.

Pulp and paper processing requires large amounts of fresh water. The capital and operating costs of pollution abatement in older mills, which are found in eastern Canada especially, are considerably greater than in newly constructed mills for which higher abatement can be designed from the outset. Under conditions of freer trade it would become increasingly important that the mounting costs of mandatory pollution abatement not place Canadian companies at a competitive disadvantage vis-à-vis U.S. and European rivals.

FORESTRY AND LOGGING

The fact that there is federal jurisdiction over international trade but provincial jurisdiction over resources means that federal-provincial coopera- tion is needed to prevent conflicts in policy. Achieving the main goal of lower tariffs, i.e., lower costs, could be helped or hindered in the pulp and paper industry by provincial forestry programs. This is not an exaggeration, because wood is a major cost of production. If the Canadian pulp and paper industry is to succeed in becoming and remaining competitive under freer trade conditions, then the costs of important inputs such as wood fibre must also be competitive. Our analysis of comparative costs in Chapter 6 indicates that, with the possible exception of British Columbia, wood costs in Canada are not reassuringly competitive. The existence of forest resources is no guarantee that Canadian wood fibre will not price itself out of world markets or encourage substitutes.

Although the degree of mechanization in Canadian logging compares favourably with that in the United States, there are other respects in which comparison is unfavourable to Canada. In the United States there are much more extensive and competitive rail and road networks which result in relatively favourable costs of transporting wood to the mills. The milder climate there facilitates year-round hauling, and the higher growth rate of trees means that the wood yield per mile of road is high. Owing to severe frost and snow conditions during Canadian winters, the costs of year- round roads are high. Local access roads to wood limits in Canada are financed by industry, while in the United States their construction and maintenance are mainly the responsibility of local, state, or federal govern- ments. The industry in Canada is also faced with the mounting problem of maintaining an adequate woods labour force. Logging operations, especially in eastern Canada, are increasingly remote from settlements where the workers can live with some amenities and to and from which they may have to be transported on a weekly or even a daily basis by their employers.

At present rates of expansion in utilization of Canada's forests, the limits of available cut on a continuous-yield basis may be reached in about fifteen years. While private and public costs of more intensive silvicultural practices may be about the same, corporate benefits on Crown lands with insecure tenure fall far short of public benefits, which encompass multiple uses over a much longer period of time. The better the quality of the timber and the closer it is to present and prospective mills, the more likely is the forest to be of interest for public purposes as well, and so to justify correspondingly more intensive silviculture. It is sound policy, therefore, for governments to invest increasingly along such lines as access roads, fire and insect protection, and reforestation.

Meanwhile, the hauls of pulpwood to the mills are getting longer. The trend towards year-round hauling reduces the investment required in reserve wood piles at the mill. Mechanical logging promises to contain rapidly rising labour costs where there are large enough forest tracts with hospitable terrain. The increasing capital being committed to the foregoing and related mechanization would need to be expedited in the event of freer trade, and faster tax write-offs (accelerated capital-cost allowances) would encourage mechanization promptly by increasing corporate cash flows.

This does not mean that subsidizing high-cost mills, such as some provinces are doing in various ways in order to attract industry, is consistent with the main purpose of freer trade—lower-cost production. There is some danger that interprovincial rivalry for industrial development will escalate inefficiencies. It can contribute at times to excess capacity by encouraging too rapid utilization of new timber concessions. This aggravates the historic tendency for rival pulp and paper companies to overexpand periodically in an effort to maintain their shares of an expanding market. A greater degree of federal-provincial cooperation could help to moderate such cyclical excesses.

One source of inefficiency in logging has been cross-hauling of pulpwood from Crown-land limits to mills. This may not yet be a serious problem, but it might become so under freer trade conditions requiring relocation of some mills.

Although all provinces have legislated against the export of raw wood from Crown lands, some provinces make exceptions for wood cut in localities suffering from unemployment or cut from trees which would otherwise be wasted. The threat which such exports pose for pulp and paper exports should not be exaggerated for two reasons. First, the total volume of raw-wood exports is not large and is unlikely to increase (and probably will decline) because long-distance shipping of bulky wood is uneconomic. The other reason is that pulpwood exports have been declining from eastern Canada to the United States, the area of most serious competition for eastern Canadian paper producers under conditions of freer trade.

SECTORAL APPROACH TO FREE TRADE

Most of the analysis in this study has been within the assumed context of free trade in all products among North Atlantic countries, but the findings are also applicable, although to a lesser extent, to an assumption of bilateral free trade in all products between Canada and the United States (see terms of reference in Chapter 1). The main reason for preferring Atlantic-wide to Canada–U.S. free trade is that the former approach would provide access to wider markets for those papers in which the Canadian industry could become competitive after restructuring.

Members of the Canadian government have spoken of post-Kennedy round initiatives for freer trade along multi-nation, industry-sector lines, and the forest industries were cited as being highly eligible. However, free trade in paper alone would be less attractive than free trade in all products. As has been shown, the Canadian pulp and paper industry is a large consumer of machinery, chemicals, and other purchased supplies, the prices of which include a tariff component (actual or imputed). Obviously, if tariffs were retained on such inputs while being removed or reduced on the industry's output, the industry's competitive position could be worsened. Whether this happened or not would depend on the relative levels of tariffs on these inputs in Canada and in rival producing countries, notably the United States. Since tariffs on these inputs tend to be higher in Canada than in the United States (even after the Kennedy round reductions), liberalizing trade only in papers could worsen the competitiveness of the Canadian pulp and paper industry. This would be serious for marginal grades of paper and marginal producers during the transition period. If the sector approach were adopted for Canada–U.S. trade alone, there would be an additional difficulty arising out of the fact that single-industry arrangements not on a "most-favoured-nation" basis would be contrary to GATT.

MULTILATERAL TARIFF REDUCTIONS

Further reduction of trade barriers by the traditional GATT approach should also be assessed as a possibility. There are serious doubts concerning the prospects for significant new negotiations in the near future now that many of the tariffs of the United States and the EEC are at or below 10 percent. Furthermore, one can cite reservations on the part of industry itself as to whether the traditional gradual dismantling of tariffs is well suited to the investment planning and adjustment needs of Canadian industry. When adjustment to international competitive pressures is necessary, industries tend to prefer a clear-cut treaty commitment to the freeing of trade, with staged reductions, and appropriate policies for adjustment assistance. The traditional method is more likely to leave residual tariffs and the uncertainty associated with possible backsliding by the U.S. Congress when concessions offered by the administration are not covered in a general treaty obligation. For this reason, now that trade barriers have been reduced to levels where further cuts are likely to require major adjustments to the challenges—and opportunities—of international competition, the free trade association approach seems better suited to the needs of Canadian manufacturers than other approaches to trade liberalization.

Appendix: Twelve Tables on Wood Requirements and Costs in the Production of Kraft Linerboard, Newsprint, Fine Paper, and Toilet Tissue

TABLE A-1

SOFTWOOD DENSITIES IN EASTERN AND WESTERN CANADA AND UNITED STATES
(pounds per 100 solid cubic feet or cunit, oven-dry weight and green volume)

	Density	Average of four species	Average used in model-mill computations*
Quebec, Ontario, and U.S. Lake States			
Black Spruce	2500		Quebec & Ontario
White Spruce	2250	2368	2450
Balsam Fir	2100		U.S. Lake States
Jack Pine	2620		2350
B.C., Wash., & Ore. Coastal Strip			
Western Hemlock	2620		
Douglas Fir	2780	2520	
Sitka Spruce	2180		2500
Lodgepole Pine	2500		

Sources and commentary: Sources are numbered to facilitate the explanation of when they were used or how their figures differ from those used. (1) Forest Branch of Forest Products Laboratories Division, Department of Resources and Development, *Canadian Woods: Their Properties and Uses*, Ottawa, 1951. (2) Forest Service, Department of Agriculture, *Western Wood Density Survey: Report Number 1*, FPL 27, Madison, Wis., July 1965. (3) Irving H. Isenberg, *Pulpwoods of United States and Canada*, second edition, Appleton, Wis., Institute of Paper Chemistry, 1951. (4) Forest Products Laboratory of the Forest Service, Department of Agriculture, "Wood Data and Yield," Data Sheet A-3, Madison, Wis., June 1954, still the latest in this series. Other sources consulted include several good papers in *Proceedings of the Symposium on Density*, May 1965, and *Proceedings of the Third Forestry Biology Conference of the TAPPI*, November 1865, both issued by Forest Products Laboratory of the Forest Service, Department of Agriculture, Madison, Wis. Estimated average densities are given as follows. Black Spruce: Source (1) 2500; (3) 2500. White Spruce: (1) 2180; (3) 2200. Balsam Fir: (1) 2020; (3) 2100; (4) 2100. Jack Pine: (1) 2620; (3) 2400; (4) 2400. Western Hemlock: (1) 2560; (2) 2620; (3) 2400; (4) 2400. Douglas Fir (Coast): (1) 2870; (2) 2780; (4) 2800. Sitka Spruce: (1) 2180; (3) 2200. Lodgepole Pine: (1) 2500; (3) 2400.
*The figures in this column have been adjusted from those in the previous column, in the light of the following considerations: Various published sources (see below) sometimes give somewhat different figures as the estimated average density for a particular species and region. Species other than those shown above are also of some importance in each region, although the groups shown are thought to be the most representative for the purposes at hand. Industry respondents have provided density figures, often based on their own experiences, which sometimes differ from those in the published sources. The higher-density species tend to occur with greater prevalence in Quebec and Ontario than in the U.S. Lake States. In any event, the figures adopted for the model-mill computations are the results of an effort to take the best possible account of the evidence and suggestions available.

TABLE A-2

SOFTWOOD DENSITIES IN SOUTHERN UNITED STATES
(pounds per 100 solid cubic feet or cunit, oven-dry weight and green volume)

	Northern Georgia and Alabama		Southern Georgia and Alabama		Average used in model-mill computations
	Natural trees*	Planted trees*	Natural trees*	Planted trees*	
Loblolly Pine	2780	2630	2930	2880	2828‡ for fine
Shortleaf Pine	2930	2880	2870	2720	paper & tissue
Longleaf Pine	†	†	3350	3200	2925‡ for
Slash Pine	†	†	3280	3130	linerboard & newsprint

Sources and commentary: A comprehensive study of wood densities in the U.S. South has been under way since the late 1950s. It is part of a U.S. nationwide survey of all commercially important coniferous species. A progress report was issued by the Forest Products Laboratory of the Forest Service, Department of Agriculture, *Southern Wood Density Survey: 1965 Status Report*, FPL 26, Madison, Wis., May 1965; and at about the same time some findings were reported by Harold L. Mitchell, Chief, Division of Wood Quality Research, FPL, "Highlights of Results of the Souther Wood Density Survey," *Proceedings of Symposium on Density*, Madison, FPL, May 1965. Completion of findings is not expected until 1970 or later. Density figures shown in the present table—with reference to natural trees—are derived through conversion of specific-gravity figures given in the above-cited reports. These reports indicate a positive relationship between density and tree age, and an inverse relationship between density and growth rate: that is, older trees and slower-growing trees tend to have higher densities than younger trees and faster-growing trees. Although no attempt has yet been made through the reports themselves to quantify these relationships precisely, an effort to do so has been made in the present study in consideration of the fact that plantation trees are a significant and increasing part of the wood resources of the South. From the evidence in the two reports cited, and from other published and unpublished evidence, it has been assumed for purposes of the present table that the densities of plantation trees (which in the South are being grown and planned in rotations of 25 or 30 years) are lower by 150 pounds per cunit than the densities of natural trees of the same species and region. The underlying principles involved in this assumption are commonly accepted in the recent literature, but the figure itself should not be attributed to any source other than the present study.
*See source note.
†Longleaf Pine is very sparse, and Slash Pine rarely occurs in a natural state, in the northern halves of Georgia and Alabama.
‡Only the lighter-weight pines—Loblolly and Shortleaf—are suitable for use in fine paper and tissue. The density figure 2828 is an average of the eight figures in the top two rows. The heavier pines, as well as the lighter pines, are suitable for linerboard and newsprint. The density figure 2925 is derived by taking an average of the four figures in the first two columns, an average of the eight figures in the second two columns, and an average of these two averages.

TABLE A-3

SOFTWOOD YIELDS IN VARIOUS PULPING PROCESSES
(pounds per 100 solid cubic feet or cunit, oven-dry weight and green volume)

Densities Used in Model-Mill Computations*	Yield†				
	Percent of density = pounds of oven-dry wood fibre				
	High-yield sulphate (57.5%)	Low-yield sulphate (47%)	Semi-bleached sulphate (44.5%)	Bleached sulphate (42%)	Groundwood (92%)
Quebec & Ontario 2450 for:					
linerboard base	1409	†	—	—	—
linerboard top	—	1152	—	—	—
newsprint	—	—	1090	—	2254
fine paper	—	—	—	1029	—
tissue	—	—	—	1029	2254
U.S. Lake States 2350 for:					
linerboard base	1351	—	—	—	—
linerboard top	—	1105	—	—	—
newsprint	—	—	1046	—	2162
fine paper	—	—	—	987	—
tissue	—	—	—	987	2162
U.S. South 2925 for:					
linerboard base	1682	—	—	—	—
linerboard top	—	1375	—	—	—
newsprint	—	—	1302	—	2691
2828 for:					
fine paper	—	—	—	1188	—
tissue	—	—	—	1188	2602
B.C., Wash., & Ore. Coastal Strip 2500 for:					
linerboard base	1438	—	—	—	—
linerboard top	—	1175	—	—	—
newsprint	—	—	1113	—	2300
fine paper	—	—	—	1050	—
tissue	—	—	—	1050	2300

*As derived in preceding two tables.
†The yield in unbleached sulphate pulping has been adjusted to allow for 2 percent loss of wood substance in barking, 2 percent loss of wood in chipping, and 2 percent loss of fibre in white water. Further successive losses of 2.5 percentage points each have been allowed for partial bleaching and full bleaching. The yield in groundwood pulping has been adjusted to allow for 2 percent loss of wood substance in barking, 3.5 percent water soluble loss, and 2.5 percent loss in white water.
‡Figures are not included in spaces not relevant to the model mills.
Sources: Sources of density figures are cited in previous two tables. Sources of yield figures are, for the most part, industry informants. For a published source of yield figures, see

TABLE A-4

HARDWOOD YIELDS IN FULLY BLEACHED SULPHATE PULPING FOR FINE PAPER

	Oven-dry density of cunit green wood	Average used in model-mill computations	Average yield	Oven-dry wood fibre per cunit green wood
	(lbs.)	(lbs.)	(%)	(lbs.)
Quebec, Ontario, and U.S. Lake States				
Sugar Maple	3500			
White Elm	2900			
Red Beech	3900			
White Birch	3000	3200	45	1440
Yellow Birch	3400			
Poplar (Aspen)	2300			
Average of six	3167			
U.S. South				
Black Gum	2900			
Red Gum	2700			
White Elm	2900			
Red Beech	3900	3300	45	1485
White Oak	3700			
Red Oak	3600			
Average of six	3283			
B.C., Wash., & Ore. Coastal Strip				
Red Alder	2310			
Poplar (Aspen)	2080			
Bigleaf Maple	2930	2200	45	990
White Birch	3180			
Average of four	2625			

Sources and note: Density figures for the Central-East (Quebec, Ontario, and the U.S. Lake States) and the South are from Irving H. Isenberg, *Pulpwoods of United States and Canada*, second edition, Appleton, Wis., Institute of Paper Chemistry, 1951. Density figures for the West are from Forest Branch of Forest Products Laboratories Division, Department of Resources and Development, *Canadian Woods: Their Properties and Uses*, Ottawa, 1951. Since the two sources give somewhat different figures, it might be noted in regard to the Central-East that the two sources do not lead to substantially different averages for the six species shown. The average from Isenberg is 3167 (as shown above), and the average from *Canadian Woods* is 3278. Discussion with industry people led to the feeling that average hardwood density in the Central-East is about 3 percent lower than in the South and that average figures of 3200 and 3300 are appropriate for representing the regional comparison. The figure of 2200 adopted for the West is considerably lower than the arithmetic average of 2625 and is based on the fact that Poplar and Alder are the more available hardwoods in the region; the other two species are, in fact, quite scarce.

Forest Products Laboratory of the Forest Service, Department of Agriculture, "Wood Data and Yield," Data Sheet A-3, Madison, Wis., June 1954, still the latest in this series; this data sheet has been endorsed by the Engineering Data Sheet Committee, Technical Section, Canadian Pulp and Paper Association. See also FPL, *Pulping Characteristics of Lake States and Northeastern Woods*, Madison, revised 1955, reviewed and reaffirmed 1960; includes discussion of experimental efforts to improve pulpwood yields.

TABLE A-5

CUNITS WOOD REQUIRED PER TON FINISHED PRODUCT

	Type of pulp furnish	Oven-dry wood fibre required*	Yield per cunit†	Cunits required
Linerboard		(lbs.)	(lbs.)	
Que. & Ont.	80% high-yield sulphate	1520	1409	1.08
	20% low-yield sulphate	380	1152	0.33
		1900		1.41
U.S. Lake	80% high-yield sulphate	1520	1351	1.13
	20% low-yield sulphate	380	1105	0.34
		1900		1.47
South	80% high-yield sulphate	1520	1682	0.90
	20% low-yield sulphate	380	1375	0.28
		1900		1.18
West	80% high-yield sulphate	1520	1438	1.06
	20% low-yield sulphate	380	1175	0.32
		1900		1.38
Newsprint				
Que. & Ont.	75% groundwood	1425	2254	0.63
	25% semi-bleached sulphate	475	1090	0.44
		1900		1.07
U.S. Lake	75% groundwood	1425	2162	0.66
	25% semi-bleached sulphate	475	1046	0.45
		1900		1.11
South	75% groundwood	1425	2162	0.53
	25% semi-bleached sulphate	475	1302	0.36
		1900		0.89
West	75% groundwood	1425	2300	0.62
	25% semi-bleached sulphate	475	1113	0.43
		1900		1.05
Bond Paper				
Que. & Ont.	70% hardwood fully bleached	1120	1440	0.78
	30% softwood fully bleached	480	1029	0.47
		1600		1.25

TABLE A-5—*continued*

	Type of pulp furnish	Oven-dry wood fibre required*	Yield per cunit†	Cunits required
		(lbs.)	(lbs.)	
U.S. Lake	70% hardwood fully bleached	1120	1440	0.78
	30% softwood fully bleached	480	987	0.49
		1600		1.27
South	70% hardwood fully bleached	1120	1485	0.75
	30% softwood fully bleached	480	1188	0.40
		1600		1.15
West	50% hardwood fully bleached	800	990	0.89
	50% softwood fully bleached	800	1050	0.76
		1600		1.65
Toilet Tissue				
Que. & Ont.	60% fully bleached sulphate	1140	1029	1.11
	40% groundwood	760	2254	0.34
		1900		1.45
U.S. Lake	60% fully bleached sulphate	1140	987	1.16
	40% groundwood	760	2162	0.35
		1900		1.51
South	60% fully bleached sulphate	1140	1188	0.96
	40% groundwood	760	2602	0.29
		1900		1.25
West	60% fully bleached sulphate	1140	1050	1.09
	40% groundwood	760	2300	0.33
		1900		1.42

*A ton (2000 pounds) of finished linerboard, newsprint, or tissue consists approximately of 95 percent oven-dry wood fibre, 5 percent moisture, and negligible retained additives; the amount of oven-dry wood fibre required per ton of finished product is therefore 1900 pounds. A ton of finished bond paper consists approximately of 80 percent oven-dry wood fibre, 5 percent moisture, and 15 percent retained additives; the amount of oven-dry wood fibre required per ton of finished product is therefore 1600 pounds.
†As derived in Tables A-3 and A-4.

TABLE A-6

PULPWOOD COSTS AS COMPUTED FROM PUBLISHED DATA
ON AGGREGATE QUANTITIES AND VALUES,*
CANADIAN DATA FOR 1964, U.S. DATA FOR 1963

	Computed value per rough cord	Converted to Can. $ per cunit†
	(Can. $)	(Can. $)
Quebec		
Roundwood, mainly softwood	26.91	31.66
Chips, softwood	25.11	29.54
Chips, hardwood	17.74	20.87
Ontario		
Roundwood, mainly softwood	27.61	32.48
Chips, softwood	25.60	30.12
Chips, hardwood	20.45	24.06
British Columbia		
Roundwood, mainly softwood	17.64	20.75
Chips, softwood	17.74	20.87
Chips, exported†	—	14.64‡
Indefinite U.S. regions	(U.S. $)	(Can. $)
Spruce and True Fir for paper mills	30.89	39.25
Spruce and True Fir for paperboard mills	19.66	24.98
Hemlock for pulp mills	20.67	26.26
Jack Pine for paper mills	25.00	31.76
Southern Pine for paper mills	25.98	38.97
Southern Pine for paperboard mills	25.84	38.76
Western softwood for paper mills	22.19	28.19
Western softwood for paperboard mills	12.78	16.24
Chips, softwood, for paper mills	19.50	24.78
Chips, softwood, for paperboard mills	15.45	19.63
Northern hardwood for paper mills	22.01	27.97
Aspen and Popple for paper mills	22.19	28.19
Southern hardwood for paperboard mills	16.97	25.46
Western hardwood for paper mills	20.90	26.56
Chips, hardwood, for paper mills	20.77	26.39

Sources: DBS, Annual Census of Manufactures, *Pulp and Paper Mills*, 1964, Tables 12A and 12B; U.S. Bureau of the Census, Census of Manufactures 1963, *Industry Statistics: Pulp, Paper and Board Mills*, MC63(2)-26A, published 1966, Table 7A.

*Caution is advisable in interpreting the figures in this table. Very little is known about their composition or validity. No claim is made here about them, and they are presented merely by way of saying: "These are the results of doing computations with published aggregate quantities and values—for whatever interest or usefulness these results may hold." They do not in any way enter subsequent estimates of wood costs.

†To convert from cord to cunit (100 solid cu. ft.), it was assumed that one cord = 85 solid cu. ft. for all woods other than southern roundwood, for which the assumption was one cord = 72 solid cu. ft.

‡Pacific Northwest Experiment Station, Forest Service, Department of Agriculture, *Production, Prices, Employment, and Trade in Pacific Northwest Forest Industries*, fourth quarter 1965, Table 10, gives figure as $7.49 (U.S.) per short ton (for over a million tons).

TABLE A-7

PULPWOOD PRICES AS GIVEN IN PUBLISHED SOURCES,
VARIOUS REGIONS OF THE UNITED STATES, 1964

	As given: U.S.$ per rough cord*	Converted to Can.$ per cunit*
Wisconsin		
Roundwood, Spruce	24.00–27.50	30.49–34.94
Roundwood, Balsam Fir	18.00–23.00	22.86–29.21
Roundwood, Aspen	13.00–14.50	16.52–18.42
Roundwood, hardwood	15.50	19.69
New Hampshire		
Roundwood, Hemlock	16.00–20.00	20.33–25.41
Southeast (includes Georgia)		
Roundwood, Pine	17.00	25.50
Roundwood, hardwood	13.60	20.40
Chips, Pine	6.50†	18.36
Chips, hardwood	5.25†	14.83
Midsouth (includes Alabama)		
Roundwood, Pine	15.92	23.88
Roundwood, hardwood	13.17	19.76
Chips, Pine	6.21†	17.54
Chips, hardwood	4.60†	13.00
Northwest		
Roundwood, softwood	19.53	24.80
Chips, mainly softwood	15.65	19.88

Sources: Wisconsin University, Extension Service College of Agriculture, *Wisconsin Forest Products Price Review* (semi-annual); New Hampshire University, Cooperative Extension Service, *New Hampshire Forest Market Report* (annual); Forest Service, U.S. Department of Agriculture, *Pulpwood Prices in the Southeast* (annual) and *Pulpwood Price Trends in the Midsouth* (annual); Northwest Pulp and Paper Association, *Annual Economic Review*; Forest Service, U.S. Department of Agriculture, *Production, Prices, Employment, and Trade in Pacific Northwest Forest Industries* (quarterly). A comprehensive and summary source is Forest Service, U.S. Department of Agriculture, *The Demand and Price Situation for Forest Products* (annual)—though it does not contain as much varied detail as the sources for each region.
*Delivered at the mill. To convert from cord to cunit (100 solid cu.ft.), it was assumed that one cord = 85 solid cu. ft. for all woods other than southern roundwood, for which the assumption was one cord=72 solid cu. ft.
†For southern chips, prices in this column are per ton of green chips. To convert U.S. $/ton into Can. $/cunit, the following conversion multiplier was used: green weight of cunit of Southern Pine × 1/2000 × 0.96 × 1.08; i.e., 5450 × 1/2000 × 0.96 × 1.08. The 0.96 figure is a price-lowering adjustment for other computations on yields which assume that all cunits lose 4 percent in barking and chipping.

TABLE A-8

BASIC* COST OF WOOD PER CUNIT, 1964, AS DEVELOPED FOR PURPOSES OF THE MODEL MILLS
(Canadian dollars per cunit)
Single figure represents "average"; two-figure range represents "low–average."

	Softwood, roundwood	Market chips	Transfer or contract chips†	Hardwood, roundwood	Market chips	Transfer or contract chips†
Quebec	18–26	18	15	18–23	15	13
Ontario	18–27	18	15	18–24	15	13
B.C.	17–18	15	10	17–21	13	9
Wisconsin	21–29	21	15	20–25	18	13
Maine	20–27	19	15	19–23	17	13
Georgia	23–25	19	19	20–22	15	15
Alabama	22–24	18	18	20–22	13	13
Wash.-Ore.	18–20	17	10	18–23	15	9

Sources and method: Figures in the present table have been developed and presented in such a way as to allow comparisons among regions and with the published data. Roundwood figures have been built up from estimates of component costs. It was assumed, for all regions, that the harvesting and hauling of roundwood is done by independent contractors who own their own equipment and trucks. The above estimates for roundwood thus include estimates of the following components: contract logging and hauling (including equipment depreciation, bush-road construction, and contractors' administration and profit), scaling, and stumpage and land acquisition. The figures for chips are based on market prices of chips and on arbitrary values assigned to company transfers. *Neither the figures for roundwood nor those for chips include the following additional costs to the mill, which are shown separately in subsequent tables: supervision and overhead related to wood supply, charges related to forest main roads (not applicable to the U.S. regions, where the counties and states pay for the main roads), and carrying charges on wood inventories.* The differences in estimated costs between Canadian and U.S. regions relate mainly to the greater distances over which wood must be hauled in the U.S. regions, where wood has become somewhat less accessible. For a published illustration of the components of wood costs, see C. R. Silversides, "Pulpwood Harvesting Requirements, Eastern Canada, 1967–1975," *Theme Papers*, 49th Annual Meeting, Woodlands Section, Canadian Pulp and Paper Association, March 1967; and same author, *Developments in Logging Mechanization in Eastern Canada*, Vancouver, University of British Columbia, 1964.

*This "basic" cost is not meant to represent the total wood cost or total of wood-related costs. Other cost elements are shown in subsequent tables. See emphasized portion of source note to present table. Figures in this table are not derived from, and are not comparable with (except as a matter of interest), those in Table A-6.

†The term "transfer chips" is relevant mainly to the West Coast and pertains to situations in which a pulp mill has a company affiliation with a sawmill operation. The term "contract chips" is meant to cover situations in which a pulp mill is favourably located near a sawmill with which it has no company affiliation, but with which it can arrange a special contract price.

TABLE A-9

WOOD COSTS PER TON OF KRAFT LINERBOARD, 1964,

AS USED IN THE MODEL MILL

(all value figures in Canadian dollars)

Two-figure range represents "low"–"average."

	Quebec	Georgia	B.C.	Wash.-Ore.
Wood requirements				
Cunits roundwood	0.98–1.27*	0.83–0.94	0.55–0.83	0.55–0.83
Basic cost/cunit	$18–26	$23–25	$17–18	$18–20
Cunits chips*	0.43–0.14	0.35–0.24	0.83–0.55	0.83–0.55
Basic cost/cunit	$15–18	$19	$10–15	$10–17
Total cunits	1.41	1.18	1.38	1.38
Basic cost/cunit	$17.09–25.21	$21.81–23.78	$12.81–16.80	$13.21–19.10
Basic cost/ton	$24.10–35.55	$25.74–28.06	$17.68–23.18	$18.23–26.36
Mill management of roundwood				
Expense/cunit roundwood	$2.00	$2.00	$2.00	$2.00
Cunits roundwood/ton	0.98–1.27	0.83–0.94	0.55–0.83	0.55–0.83
Cost/ton	$1.96–2.54	$1.66–1.88	$1.10–1.66	$1.10–1.66
Forest main roads				
Amortization/cunit roundwood	$0.50	†	$0.50	†
Maintenance/cunit roundwood	$0.50	†	$0.50	†
Cost/ton	$0.98–1.27	†	$0.55–0.83	†
Stocks of roundwood				
Months of supply	3	1	2	2
Interest rate	6%	5.2%	6%	5.2%
Carrying cost/ton	$0.26–0.44	$0.08–0.10	$0.08–0.15	$0.09–0.14
WOOD-RELATED COSTS				
Per cunit roundwood	$21.75–29.35	$25.10–27.11	$20.17–21.18	$20.16–22.17
Per cunit chips	$15.00–18.00	$19.00	$10.00–15.00	$10.00–17.00
Per ton of product	$27.30–39.80	$27.48–30.04	$19.41–25.82	$19.42–28.16

*For chips, the two-figure range of cunit quantities is stated as "high"–"average" (a high proportion coinciding with a low cost). As a proportion of all wood used in the chemical-pulp furnish, the use of chips has been assumed to be ("average"–"high") 10–30 percent in the East, 20–30 percent in the South, and 40–60 percent in the West.

†Main roads are financed by the counties and states.

TABLE A-10

WOOD COSTS PER TON OF NEWSPRINT, 1964,

AS USED IN THE MODEL MILL

(all value figures in Canadian dollars)

Two-figure range represents "low"–"average."*

	Quebec	Alabama	B.C.	Wash.-Ore.
Wood requirements				
Cunits roundwood	0.94–1.02	0.78–0.82	0.79–0.88	0.79–0.88
Basic cost/cunit	$18–26	$22–24	$17–18	$18–20
Cunits chips*	0.13–0.05	0.11–0.07	0.26–0.17	0.26–0.17
Basic cost/cunit	$15–18	$18	$10–15	$10–17
Total cunits	1.07	0.89	1.05	1.05
Basic cost/cunit	$17.62–25.63	$21.62–23.61	$15.27–17.51	$16.02–19.51
Basic cost/ton	$18.85–27.42	$19.24–21.01	$16.03–18.39	$16.82–20.49
Mill management of roundwood				
Expense/cunit roundwood	$2.00	$2.00	$2.00	$2.00
Cunits roundwood/ton	0.94–1.02	0.78–0.82	0.79–0.88	0.79–0.88
Cost/ton	$1.88–2.04	$1.56–1.64	$1.58–1.76	$1.58–1.76
Forest main roads				
Amortization/cunit roundwood	$0.50	†	$0.50	†
Maintenance/cunit roundwood	$0.50	†	$0.50	†
Cost/ton	$0.94–1.02	†	$0.79–0.88	†
Stocks of roundwood				
Months of supply	3	1	2	2
Interest rate	6%	5.2%	6%	5.2%
Carrying cost/ton	$0.25–0.36	$0.08	$0.13–0.16	$0.13–0.15
WOOD-RELATED COSTS				
Per cunit roundwood	$21.27–29.35	$24.10–26.10	$20.17–21.18	$20.16–22.17
Per cunit chips	$15.00–18.00	$18.00	$10.00–15.00	$10.00–17.00
Per ton of product	$21.92–30.84	$20.88–22.73	$18.53–21.19	$18.53–22.40

*For chips, the two-figure range of cunit quantities is stated as "high"–"average" (a high proportion coinciding with a low cost). As a proportion of all wood used in the chemical-pulp furnish, the use of chips has been assumed to be ("average"–"high") 10–30 percent in the East, 20–30 percent in the South, and 40–60 percent in the West. The chemical pulp is assumed to be 25 percent of the total pulp furnish.

†Main roads are financed by the counties and states.

TABLE A-11

WOOD COSTS PER TON OF BOND PAPER, 1964,
AS USED IN THE MODEL MILL
(all value figures in Canadian dollars)
Two-figure range represents "low"–"average."

	Ontario	Wisconsin	Maine
Wood requirements			
Cunits round softwood	0.33–0.42	0.34–0.44	0.34–0.44
Basic cost/cunit	$18–27	$21–29	$20–27
Cunits softwood chips*	0.14–0.05	0.15–0.05	0.15–0.05
Basic cost/cunit	$15–18	$15–21	$15–19
Cunits round hardwood	0.55–0.70	0.55–0.70	0.55–0.70
Basic cost/cunit	$18–24	$20–25	$19–23
Cunits hardwood chips*	0.23–0.08	0.23–0.08	0.23–0.08
Basic cost/cunit	$13–15	$13–18	$13–17
Total cunits	1.25	1.27	1.27
Basic cost/cunit	$16.74–24.19	$18.41–25.79	$17.71–23.85
Basic cost/ton	$20.93–30.24	$23.38–32.75	$22.49–30.29
Mill management of roundwood			
Expense/cunit roundwood	$2.00	$2.00	$2.00
Cunits roundwood/ton	0.88–1.12	0.89–1.14	0.89–1.14
Cost/ton	$1.96–2.24	$1.78–2.28	$1.78–2.28
Forest main roads			
Amortization/cunit roundwood	$0.50	†	†
Maintenance/cunit roundwood	$0.50	†	†
Cost/ton	$0.88–1.12	†	†
Stocks of roundwood			
Months of supply	3	3	3
Interest rate	6%	5.2%	5.2%
Carrying cost/ton	$0.24–0.36	$0.23–0.39	$0.22–0.35
WOOD-RELATED COSTS			
Per cunit	$21.27–28.32	$22.26–29.73	$21.25–27.70
Per cunit chips	$14.00–16.00	$14.00 19.00	$14.00–18.00
Per ton of product	$24.01–33.96	$25.39–35.42	$24.49–32.92

*For chips, the two-figure range of cunit quantities is stated as "high"–"average" (a high proportion coinciding with a low cost). As a proportion of all wood used in the chemical-pulp furnish, the use of chips has been assumed to be ("average"–"high") 10–30 percent in the East, 20–30 percent in the South, and 40–60 percent in the West. The hardwood:softwood pulp-furnish ratios are assumed to be 70:30 in the East and South and 50:50 in the West.

†Main roads are financed by the counties and states.

Alabama	B.C.	Wash.,Ore.
.28–0.32	0.30–0.46	0.30–0.46
$22–24	$17–18	$18–20
.12–0.08	0.46–0.30	0.46–0.30
$18	$10–15	$10–17
.53–0.60	0.36–0.53	0.36–0.53
$20–22	$17–21	$18–23
0.22–0.15	0.53–0.36	0.53–0.36
$13	$9–13	$9–15
1.15	1.65	1.65
$18.94–21.10	$12.48–17.33	$12.88–19.33
$21.78–24.27	$20.59–28.59	$21.25–31.89
$2.00	$2.00	$2.00
0.81–0.92	0.66–0.99	0.66–0.99
$1.62–1.84	$1.32–1.98	$1.32–1.98
†	$0.50	†
†	$0.50	†
†	$0.66–0.99	†
1	2	2
6%	6%	5.2%
$0.09–0.11	$0.11–0.20	$0.11–0.19
$23.11–25.12	$20.17–23.20	$20.16–24.19
$15.00	$9.00–14.00	$9.00–16.00
$23.49–26.22	$23.34–35.06	$22.68–34.06

TABLE A-12

WOOD COSTS PER TON OF TOILET TISSUE, 1964,
AS USED IN THE MODEL MILL
(all value figures in Canadian dollars)
Two-figure range represents "low"–"average".*

	Ontario	Wisconsin
Wood requirements		
Cunits roundwood	1.11–1.33	1.16–1.39
Basic cost/cunit	$18–27	$21–29
Cunits chips*	0.34–0.12	0.35–0.12
Basic cost/cunit	$15–18	$15–21
Total cunits	1.45	1.51
Basic cost/cunit	$17.30–26.27	$19.61–28.36
Basic cost/ton	$25.09–28.09	$29.61–42.83
Mill management of roundwood		
Expense/cunit roundwood	$2.00	$2.00
Cunits/roundwood/ton	1.11–1.33	1.61–1.39
Cost/ton	$2.22–2.66	$2.32–2.78
Forest main roads		
Amortization/cunit roundwood	$0.50	†
Maintenance/cunit roundwood	$0.50	†
Cost/ton	$1.11–1.33	†
Stocks of roundwood		
Months of supply	3	3
Interest rate	6%	5.2%
Carrying cost/ton	$0.30–0.48	$0.31–0.49
WOOD-RELATED COSTS		
Per cunit roundwood	$21.27–30.36	$23.27–31.35
Per cunit chips	$15.00–18.00	$15.00–21.00
Per ton of product	$28.72–42.56	$31.08–46.10

*For chips, the two-figure range of cunit quantities is stated as "high"–"average" (a high proportion coinciding with a low cost). As a proportion of all wood used in the chemical pulp furnish, the use of chips has been assumed to be ("average"–"high") 10–30 percent in the East and 40–60 percent in the West. The chemical-pulp is assumed to be 60 percent of the total pulp furnish.
†Main roads are financed by the counties and states.

Maine	B.C.	Wash.-Ore.
6–1.39	0.77–0.98	0.77–0.98
)–27	$17–18	$18–20
5–0.12	0.65–0.44	0.65–0.44
5–19	$10–15	$10–17
51	1.42	1.42
8.84–26.36	$13.80–17.07	$14.34–19.07
8.45–39.81	$19.59–24.24	$20.36–27.08
.00	$2.00	$2.00
16–1.39	0.77–0.98	0.77–0.98
.32–2.78	$1.54–1.96	$1.54–1.96
	$0.50	†
	$0.50	†
	$0.77–0.98	†
	2	2
2%	6%	5.2%
.30–0.46	$0.13–0.18	$0.12–0.17
2.26–29.33	$20.17–20.18	$20.16–22.17
5.00–19.00	$10.00–15.00	$10.00–17.00
1.07–43.05	$21.26–27.36	$22.02–29.21

RELATED PUBLICATIONS BY THE
PRIVATE PLANNING ASSOCIATION OF CANADA

CANADIAN TRADE COMMITTEE PUBLICATIONS

THE WORLD ECONOMY

The World Economy at the Crossroads: A Survey of Current Problems of Money, Trade and Economic Development, by Harry G. Johnson, 1965.

The International Monetary System: Conflict and Reform, by Robert A. Mundell, 1965.

International Commodity Agreements, by William E. Haviland, 1963.

CANADA'S TRADE RELATIONSHIPS

Canada's International Trade: An Analysis of Recent Trends and Patterns, by Bruce Wilkinson, 1968.

Canada's Trade with the Communist Countries of Eastern Europe, by Ian M. Drummond, 1966.

Canada's Role in Britain's Trade, by Edward M. Cape, 1965.

The Common Agricultural Policy of the E.E.C. and Its Implications for Canada's Exports, by Sol Sinclair, 1964.

Canada's Interest in the Trade Problems of Less-Developed Countries, by Grant L. Reuber, 1964.

CANADA'S COMMERCIAL POLICY AND COMPETITIVE POSITION

Prices, Productivity and Canada's Competitive Position, by N. H. Lithwick, 1967.

Industrial Structure in Canada's International Competitive Position: A Study of the Factors Affecting Economies of Scale and Specialization in Canadian Manufacturing, by H. Edward English, 1964.

Canada's Approach to Trade Negotiations, by L. D. Wilgress, 1963.

CANADIAN-AMERICAN COMMITTEE PUBLICATIONS

CANADA-U.S. ECONOMIC RELATIONS

Constructive Alternatives to Proposals for U.S. Import Quotas (a Statement by the Committee), 1968

U.S.–Canadian Free Trade: The Potential Impact on the Canadian Economy, by Paul Wonnacott and Ronald J. Wonnacott, 1968

The Role of International Unionism in Canada, by John H. G. Crispo, 1967.

A New Trade Strategy for Canada and the United States (a Statement by the Committee), 1966.

Capital Flows between Canada and the United States, by Irving Brecher, 1965.

A Possible Plan for a Canada-U.S. Free Trade Area (a Staff Report), 1965.

Invisible Trade Barriers between Canada and the United States, by Francis Masson and H. Edward English, 1963.

Non-Merchandise Transactions between Canada and the United States, by John W. Popkin, 1963.

Policies and Practices of United States Subsidiaries in Canada, by John Lindeman and Donald Armstrong, 1961.

Canada in the Atlantic Economy

CANADA IN THE ATLANTIC ECONOMY

Published:

1. David W. Slater, *World Trade and Economic Growth: Trends and Prospects with Applications to Canada*
2. H. Edward English, *Transatlantic Economic Community: Canadian Perspectives*
3. Harry G. Johnson, Paul Wonnacott, Hirofumi Shibata, *Harmonization of National Economic Policies under Free Trade*
4. Gerald I. Trant, David L. MacFarlane and Lewis A. Fischer, *Trade Liberalization and Canadian Agriculture*
5. W. E. Haviland, N. S. Takacsy, E. M. Cape, *Trade Liberalization and the Canadian Pulp and Paper Industry*
6. David E. Bond and Ronald J. Wonnacott, *Trade Liberalization and the Canadian Furniture Industry*

Forthcoming:

7. Jacques J. Singer, *Trade Liberalization and the Canadian Steel Industry*
8. John Munro, *Trade Liberalization and Transportation in International Trade*
9. John F. Earl, *Trade Liberalization and the Atlantic Provinces Economy*
10. G. David Quirin, *Trade Liberalization and the Mineral Industries*
11. R. A. Shearer, G. R. Munro, and J. H. Young, *Trade Liberalization and the British Columbia Economy*
12. Richard E. Caves and Grant L. Reuber, *Canadian Economic Policy and the Impact of International Capital Flows*
13. Jacques J. Singer and Eric C. Sievwright, *Trade Liberalization and the Canadian Primary Textiles Industry*
14. Hirofumi Shibata, *Harmonization of Fiscal Policy under Freer Trade*
15. R. A. Matthews, *Easing the Adjustment to Freer Trade: A Program of Transitional Policies for Canada*
16. Eric Hehner, *Non-Tariff Barriers Affecting Canada's Trade*
17. David W. Slater, Bruce W. Wilkinson, and H. Edward English, *Canada*

Trade Liberalization and the Canadian Furniture Industry

David E. Bond and Ronald J. Wonnacott

Published for the
Private Planning Association of Canada by University of Toronto Press

To William B. Lambert

These studies of "Canada in the Atlantic Economy" are dedicated with respect and gratitude to the late William B. Lambert, Chairman of the Board of the Private Planning Association of Canada from 1965 to 1967, who played a vital role in the development and supervision of the Atlantic Economic Studies Program, on which the publications are based.

His interest went far beyond his formal responsibility; he held a deep conviction concerning the importance of international cooperation among the North Atlantic nations. His untimely death came when the first draft studies had entered the early stages of publication.

Foreword

There have been two outstanding developments in international trade policy during the past twenty years—the multilateral dismantling of trade barriers under the General Agreement on Tariffs and Trade, which has been the agency for several rounds of successful tariff negotiations since its inception in 1947, and the establishment of the European Economic Community and the European Free Trade Association in the late 1950s. In a period of reconstruction and then sustained growth, these policies have helped the participating nations of the Atlantic area to experience the benefits of international specialization and expanding trade. The wealth generated by trade and domestic prosperity has also made possible external aid programs to assist economic growth in the developing countries.

Whatever the trade and economic development problems of the future, it is widely acknowledged that the industrially advanced countries of the North Atlantic region must play an important role. It is also generally conceded that the ability of these countries to maintain their own economic growth and prosperity and to contribute to that of the less advanced nations will be greatly enhanced if they can reduce or remove the remaining trade barriers among themselves. Cooperation among Atlantic countries is now fostered by the GATT and by the Organisation for Economic Co-operation and Development. But the success of these and other approaches depends on the assessment by each country of the importance of international trade liberalization and policy coordination for its domestic economy and other national interests. This is particularly true for countries such as Canada which are heavily dependent upon export markets.

The Atlantic Economic Studies Program of the Private Planning Association of Canada was initiated to study the implications for Canada of trade liberalization and closer economic integration among the nations bordering the North Atlantic. It is planned to issue at least twelve paperbound volumes, incorporating over twenty studies by leading Canadian and foreign economists. Despite the technical nature of much of the subject matter, the studies have been written in language designed to appeal to the non-professional reader.

The directors and staff of the Private Planning Association wish to acknowledge the financial support which made this project possible—a grant from the Ford Foundation and the contributions of members of the Association. They are also appreciative of the help that has been provided by very many individuals in the preparation and review of all the studies—in discussions and correspondence with authors, at the Association's November, 1966, conference on "Canada and the Atlantic Economy," and on other occasions.

H. E. ENGLISH
Director of Research
Atlantic Economic Studies Program

Contents

1. Introduction

*Introduction**

Furniture-making is Canada's fifteenth-largest manufacturing industry. It employs more than thirty-three thousand people, with a payroll in excess of $121 million.

The furniture industry[1] is characterized by a high degree of dependence on domestic markets; less than 3 percent of total production is normally exported.[2] Despite the high existing tariff (25 percent), Canadian imports continue to rise in dollar volume and in percentage of total retail sales; the share of domestic market held by Canadian manufacturers is currently 94 percent, but it is declining by almost one percent per year. Both rising imports and limited exports suggest that with any reduction in the tariff the Canadian furniture industry would be highly vulnerable to import competition.

Five broad questions are addressed in this study: (1) Why are prices and costs now higher in Canada than in competing countries? (2) What are the prospects of the industry in a North American free trade area, and what would be the major impediments to its reorganization? (3) What are industry prospects under a broader North Atlantic free trade scheme? (4) What have been the costs to Canada of protecting this industry? (5) If

*Our major debt is to Paul Wonnacott, who in cooperation with one of the authors of this study first formulated the cost and price analysis of chapter 2. See Ronald J. Wonnacott and Paul Wonnacott, *Free Trade between the United States and Canada*, Cambridge, Mass., Harvard University Press, 1967.

During the course of this study, many people familiar with the industry were good enough to talk to us. Although our policy conclusions do not necessarily reflect their views (which were indeed quite varied), we are indebted to them for the insights they provided. We also wish to thank Donald Angevine for his assistance in collecting and evaluating much of the empirical evidence presented here.
[1]Furniture is defined as the movable articles in a dwelling, place of business, or public building. This definition therefore excludes some articles frequently considered to be furniture, e.g., kitchen cabinets, built-in bookcases. For a classification of furniture and the relative importance of each sector of the industry, see Appendix A.
[2]Data taken from Dominion Bureau of Statistics bulletins on the furniture industry, 1962, nos. 35–211, 35–212, and 35–213.

free trade is viewed as a long-term objective, which interim policy measures would be preferable in achieving this goal?

The changes induced in the furniture industry by freer trade will depend on a number of factors. The proximity of foreign sources of supply will determine the pressure on the industry to contract in the face of import competition, while the nearness of potential export markets for Canadian producers will operate as an incentive to Canadian producers to expand. The trade-off of these two conflicting influences cannot be determined without examining how free trade costs would compare in Canada and elsewhere. But one thing is clear: the importance of space in determining trading patterns. Furniture is a bulky item, frequently involving a low ratio of weight to value. Hence transport costs often prohibit its shipment over great distances. This is reflected in current Canadian imports, with more than 75 percent originating in the United States.[3] Hence Canada's ability to compete with the United States becomes a far more critical issue than the Canadian ability to compete with Europe.

There is another reason why the Canadian industry would be more sensitive to U.S. than to European competition: furniture is a taste item. Present Canadian tastes run towards U.S. styles and designs, as evidenced by the fact that Canadian manufacturers often copy designs from U.S. furniture shows; furthermore, the brand names that have wide acceptance in the United States (e.g., Simmons and Kroehler) are also familiar names to Canadian consumers. (Clearly the influences of distance and taste are not independent. Canadian tastes follow U.S. tastes because the Canadian public is subjected to the advertising of U.S. firms in the various media of communication. Furthermore, Canadian tastes are influenced by imported items on display, and most of these come from the United States, largely because it is the nearest source of supply.)

Taste factors would influence export potential as well as import competition. Canadian export sales to the United States might require some, but not excessive, styling changes, and the resulting product would sell easily in the domestic Canadian market as well. However, selling in Europe might demand a complete dichotomy between domestic and export production, with higher production costs as a direct consequence. Furthermore, Canadian development of sales organizations and distribution facilities would be easier in the United States than in Europe because of the common language and similarity in business methods.

It may be concluded that the prime issue for the Canadian industry is its ability to compete with U.S. producers; competition with Europe is of secondary importance and will be examined later.

[3]DBS, *Trade of Canada, Imports by Commodity*, 1964.

2. Present Canadian
and U.S. Prices and Costs

1. *How Do Canadian Furniture Prices Compare with Those in the United States?*

Price comparisons are particularly difficult in furniture. Two articles may have the same outward appearance but be built of components of entirely different quality. For example, one may be solid wood, while the other may be a veneer. Two sofas may have the same shape, but the upholstering may be different in grade and composition.[1]

In an effort to minimize this source of error, price comparisons were limited to products of two companies, manufacturing identical items on both sides of the border. Executives of these companies indicated that they used similar engineering specifications and wood finishes; to the best of their knowledge they knew of no quality differences in the items compared. (Because of the desirability of this sort of rigid quality control, this survey had to be limited to only two types of furniture, case goods and mattresses.)

The data are presented in Table I. On average, for this sample, Canadian prices exceed U.S. prices by 18 percent. It should be recognized that this estimate may be subject to substantial error because of the (admitted) limitations of this sample. Only seventeen Canadian-produced items are examined out of a total of more than a hundred thousand items produced by more than two thousand establishments. Furthermore, only Canadian subsidiaries are represented, rather than domestically owned Canadian companies, and pricing policies of these two groups may vary. However, fragmentary information suggests that a broader sample would exhibit price differences of at least the same magnitude. Indeed, there are several reasons for expecting that a broader sample would indicate an even greater excess in Canadian price. The two firms represented in this sample are two of the largest firms in Canada and hence may have lower costs of production than

[1]It is extremely difficult to control for quality differences in upholstery. One Canadian manufacturer indicated that a grade *A* fabric in Canada is at best a grade *B* fabric in the United States. In most cases there are differences in thread, the count per square inch, or the fibre used.

TABLE I

FACTORY PRICE COMPARISONS OF FURNITURE, UNITED STATES AND CANADA
NET OF TAXES, SEPTEMBER 1, 1965
(all prices converted into Canadian dollars)

	(1) U.S. price	(2) Canadian price	(3) Percentage Canadian price exceeds U.S. price
	($)	($)	
Case goods			
Headboard with heavy-duty metal frame	39.96	45.00	13.1
Headboard with heavy-duty metal frame	66.60	75.00	12.6
5-drawer chest on chest	121.47	145.00	19.4
9-drawer triple dresser	132.23	155.00	17.2
Night table	47.30	55.00	16.5
Headboard panel bed	27.95	36.00	28.8
Night table	25.75	26.00	1.0
5-drawer chest	66.11	72.00	8.9
9-drawer triple dresser	83.85	111.00	32.4
Panel bed	20.37	28.00	37.5
4-drawer chest	39.24	47.00	19.8
3-drawer chest	37.03	39.00	5.3
6-drawer double dresser	54.93	76.00	38.3
Bedding			
Mattress—tufted	50.26	54.00	7.4
Mattress—quilted	50.26	55.25	9.9
Mattress	36.28	37.00	2.0
Mattress	32.20	43.50	35.4
Average difference in price			18.0

many smaller Canadian companies. As international firms, their pricing practices may be more sensitive to international influences. Finally, their Canadian products are almost identical to U.S. items. Hence they receive no "protection" from imports based on real or supposed differences in quality.[2]

A wide variation in the excess Canadian price (in column 3) is one of the most striking characteristics of Table I. Of the many possible explanations for this variance, three have been emphasized by authorities in the industry: (1) there may be large differences in the size of runs, reflecting

[2]A final reason that our 18 percent estimate may understate true price differences is the more liberal payment terms offered in the United States. One manufacturer offered thirty days net in Canada, but a discount of 2 percent if paid in ten days in the United States i.e. prices of the U.S. items for fast-pay purchasers should be reduced 2 percent below the figures quoted in Table I.

large economies of scale, (2) some of the pieces may be imported by the manufacturer, and (3) the amount of wood that is visible may vary, and much of this wood is imported into Canada. In any case, there is no indication that Canadian price is determined by applying a rigid formula to a U.S. price base. From the very limited evidence, it appears that the tariff may have a mildly progressive effect on the price: more often than not, the more expensive the product, the greater is the percentage excess in Canadian price. On *a priori* grounds this is not surprising: it seems less likely[3] that Canadian producers can capture (U.S.) economies of scale in expensive items with small markets.

It must be recognized that price is an inadequate indicator of the degree to which the consumer is less well-off in Canada than in the United States. In addition to a higher price, the Canadian consumer faces a narrower range of choice. For example, in September, 1965, Kroehler offered forty-seven different items in its "Del Morro" suite in the United States but only six items in Canada. In such circumstances, the Canadian consumer can enjoy the style selection of the U.S. consumer only if he is prepared to import selected items. This involves both a personal cost of shopping in the United States and an eventual landed Canadian price which exceeds the U.S. price by substantially more than the 18 percent indicated in Table I.

2. *Why Are Canadian Prices Higher?*

There are two necessary conditions for a higher Canadian price: (1) the industry must be insulated from foreign price competition by a Canadian tariff (or similar impediments to the free international flow of furniture); and (2) Canadian costs or profits must be higher. Both must be examined in any explanation of Canadian price.

A. THE CANADIAN TARIFF

The Customs Act of Canada, section 519, imposes a duty upon "furniture: house, office, cabinet, or store; of wood, iron or other material; and parts thereof not to include forgings, castings, and stampings of metal in the rough." The Commonwealth preference rate is 15 percent, the most-favoured-nation rate is 25 percent, and the general rate is 45 percent. For our Canadian-U.S. comparisons, the appropriate rate is the 25 percent MFN rate imposed on U.S. imports; this appears to be the maximum degree to which the tariff allows a higher Canadian price.

[3]This is by no means certain. One can easily postulate a counter example.

However, the existence of Canadian protection indirectly allows an even greater excess Canadian price. Notice from Table I that Canadian producers succeed in pricing certain items in Canada substantially above the U.S. price plus the 25 percent Canadian tariff. This implies that other restrictions on the free international flow of furniture are important. These include lack of information by the Canadian public on comparative prices and model availability in the United States. In addition, extra service costs are involved for a Canadian importing through a Canadian dealer; alternatively, shopping directly in the United States involves personal cost, inconvenience, and problems in avoiding the payment of sales or excise taxes in both countries.

Since the 18 percent higher Canadian price falls short of the 25 percent Canadian tariff, imported items are more expensive in the Canadian market than similar items produced in Canada. (This may be explained by price competition among domestic Canadian producers, or as a conscious attempt by these producers to divert Canadian consumption from imports to lines that are domestically produced, or as an attempt to discourage competition from other U.S. firms that might export into Canada.) But even though Canadian prices are not as high as the tariff might allow, they are still substantially above U.S. domestic prices. Consequently, Canadian unit costs and/or profits must be higher. It is appropriate at this point to examine comparative costs and profits in some detail.

B. LABOUR COSTS

These vary in the two countries because of wage and productivity differences.

Average labour productivity in Canada falls short of that in the United States.[4] There are indications that this does not occur because labour is inherently less productive, but rather because production for the smaller Canadian market involves inefficiencies in the allocation and execution of tasks. The difference in labour productivity therefore can be viewed as one component in a broader category of "inefficiency of limited scale," which is evaluated below.

This assumption of equal "inherent" productivity of the Canadian and U.S. labour forces is sufficiently critical to deserve further examination. In a survey of firms employing labour in similar tasks on both sides of the border, Young[5] found that Canadian labour was preferred in some respects ("more cooperative, less pampered") but inferior in others ("more

[4]This is generally true; exceptions are noted below.
[5]John H. Young, "Some Aspects of Canadian Economic Development;" an unpublished Ph.D. dissertation, Cambridge University, 1955.

leisurely, less responsive to incentives").[6] He concluded that lower observed productivity of Canadian labour was not due to a difference in inherent efficiency but was primarily because of the size of the market and resulting lower volume output.[7] A recent survey by Laurence Daignault of Dufresne, McLagan and Daignault showed that output per worker is now approximately equal in the most efficient plants in Quebec and the United States. (This suggests not only that inherent labour productivity is comparable in the two countries, but also that scale effects on labour efficiency have been overcome in some Quebec plants.) This and other supporting evidence[8] suggest that Canadian production workers would be equally productive in a free trade North American economy.[9] On the basis of this conclusion, only two differences in labour cost need be considered—the difference in labour productivity due to Canadian scale (discussion of which is deferred to Section G(b) below) and the difference in wage payments, to which we now turn.

Computing the impact of different wages on total costs involves two steps—comparing wage rates in Canada and the United States and deflating this by the importance of wages in total costs.[10] A problem arises in comparing wage rates because hourly wages vary greatly among regions within each country. Rather than take a national average, we used rates paid in principal regions of production, thus highlighting centres of strongest wage competition.

In Canada, two regions were selected—Quebec (centred in Montreal) and Ontario (centred in Toronto). Together these two provinces account

[6]*Ibid.*, pp. 77–3. Another possible advantage of the U.S. labour force is its greater degree of education. See *Towards Sustained and Balanced Growth, Second Annual Review*, Economic Council of Canada, Dec. 1965, p. 58. The most significant educational effects are likely to occur at the management and professional levels rather than at the production-worker level considered here. Thus the major complaint of Canadian management was the shortage of trained engineers familiar with modern production techniques. There is nothing in Canada comparable to the furniture-engineering course at the University of North Carolina.

[7]*Ibid.*, p. 86.

[8]Mordechai Kreinin, "The Leontief Scarce-Factor Paradox," *American Economic Review*, March 1965, p. 131; and National Industrial Conference Board, *Costs and Competition: American Experience Abroad*, p. 54.

[9]Even some of the "inherent" differences in productivity listed above may be indirectly related to the tariff. For example, labour may be less leisurely in U.S. plants simply because management, under the pressure of a more competitive market, expects more of its labour force.

[10]The specific formula used was: [(U.S. hourly wage — Canadian hourly wage) / U.S. hourly wage] × (Total Canadian wage bill / Value of furniture shipped by Canadian manufacturers). Value of shipments is used as a proxy for total costs. The only difference in the two figures is profits. For many analytical purposes, (normal) profits may be usefully viewed as part of costs; even if they are not, value shipped is still the best available indicator of total costs.

for about 85 percent of total furniture production in Canada.[11] The remainder of the industry is scattered over the other eight provinces. While British Columbia has a growing and important furniture industry (6 percent of Canadian production in 1962), it still lags far behind both Quebec and Ontario and was therefore not included in our study. The two provinces selected lie close to the largest U.S. markets and production centres. Consequently, they would be in a stronger position than the other provinces to export as tariffs fell: they would also be very sensitive to import competition. An examination of their competitive position will highlight the strengths and weaknesses of the Canadian industry under free trade.

Three areas were selected in the United States—the Middle Atlantic (centred in New York City), the East North Central (centred in Chicago), and the South Atlantic (centred in High Point, North Carolina).[12] More than 75 percent of total U.S. production is concentrated in these three regions.[13]

Wage comparisons between the two Canadian provinces and three U.S. regions are shown in Table II.[14] Ontario and the U.S. South have similar wages. Quebec wages are roughly 10 to 15 percent lower, while the two northern U.S. regions have wages roughly 30 to 40 percent higher.

The impact of these wage differences on total costs is shown in Table III. (Estimates for 1958 and 1960 did not differ appreciably and therefore were not included.) Except for the comparison of Ontario with the U.S. South, Canadian manufacturers (and especially those in Quebec) enjoy a substantial wage advantage over their American counterparts. If this were the only difference in costs, Canadian furniture could sell for *less*, not more, than American furniture.

Wage costs depend not only on nominal hourly rates but also on fringe benefits, e.g., vacations with pay. In Canada, the average worker gets 6.3 paid holidays per year, a benefit similar to that enjoyed by the labour force in the U.S. East North Central and Middle Atlantic regions. However, in the U.S. South, 70 percent of the employees get no paid holidays;[15]

---

[11]48.2 percent in Ontario and 36.2 percent in Quebec in 1962.

[12]The Middle Atlantic states are New York, New Jersey, and Pennsylvania. The East North Central states are Ohio, Indiana, Illinois, Michigan, and Wisconsin. The South Atlantic states are Maryland, Virginia, West Virginia, North Carolina, South Carolina, Georgia, and Florida.

[13]20.7 percent in the Middle Atlantic, 28.7 percent in the East North Central, and 24.9 percent in the South Atlantic. New England and California are the only other significant centres of U.S. production.

[14]For a more detailed breakdown of comparative wages, see Appendix B.

[15]Department of Labour, Ottawa, *Working Conditions in Canadian Industry*, 1962, p. 39; and "Earnings in Wood Household Furniture, July 1962," *Monthly Labor Review*, Department of Labor, Washington, July 1963, pp. 814–16.

TABLE II

AVERAGE HOURLY WAGES FOR PRODUCTION WORKERS IN THE
FURNITURE INDUSTRY, UNITED STATES AND CANADA
(in domestic dollars)

| | Canada | | United States | | |
	Ontario	Quebec	East North Central	Middle Atlantic	South
1958	1.39	1.22	2.05	1.98	1.44
1960	1.51	1.31	2.11	1.98	1.48
1962	1.58	1.38	2.16	2.13	1.58

Sources: Canada: DBS, *General Review of the Furniture and Fixture Industries*, 1960, *Miscellaneous Furniture Industries*, 1962, *Office Furniture Industry*, 1962, *Household Furniture Industry*, 1962. The Dominion Bureau of Statistics defined production workers to exclude workers paid on a piecework basis only. Production workers were 71 percent of the labour force of the firms responding to the annual DBS survey.

United States: Department of Commerce, *Census of Manufacturing*, 1958, and the *Annual Survey of Manufacturers*, 1960 and 1962. Hourly wage rates were obtained by dividing total wages paid production workers by the total hours worked by production workers.

TABLE III

ESTIMATED PERCENTAGE THAT TOTAL COSTS ARE LOWER IN CANADA
DUE TO LOWER CANADIAN WAGE RATES, 1962

	East North Central	Middle Atlantic	Southern Atlantic
Ontario	6.3	6.1	0.0
Quebec	8.5	8.3	3.0

accordingly, southern wage figures should be lowered by 2½ to 3 cents per hour prior to comparison with other regions. In Canada and the U.S. North, virtually all employers provide at least one week of paid vacation. But in the southern states 12 percent of the employees do not enjoy this benefit. In comparative terms, this lowers southern wages by an insignificant amount, i.e., about ⅛ cent per hour. Both these considerations improve the relative position of the U.S. South, reducing its disadvantage vis-à-vis Quebec and placing it in a slightly preferred position vis-à-vis Ontario.

These and subsequent cost calculations are based on the assumption of a parity rate of exchange ($1 U.S. = $1 Canadian). It is difficult to project exchange rates into the future, especially in the face of the substantial changes in commercial policy considered in this study. Our estimates are therefore on the conservative side; they apply even if the Canadian dollar rises to parity. If it remains at its present level, then the Canadian industry would enjoy the additional competitive advantage of paying wages in less expensive dollars. This would be equivalent (in 1962) to 10 to 12 cents per hour, or 2–2½ percent of total costs.

Wage differences and their resulting effect on total costs are brought into perspective in Table IV.

TABLE IV

WAGE DIFFERENCES AND THEIR IMPACT ON TOTAL COSTS, 1962

Wage differences (from Table II)		Cost differences (from Table III)
30 to 40% above Ontario ——	U.S. Middle Atlantic and East North Central	—— 6% above Ontario
0 ——	Ontario U.S. South	—— 0
15% below Ontario ——	Quebec	—— 3% below Ontario

Sources: Tables II and III

C. TRANSPORT COSTS ON INPUTS

Input costs of U.S. and Canadian producers may vary for three reasons. First, inputs may be subject to different government taxes or tariffs in the two countries; these influences are considered in section F below. Second, inputs may vary in price at different sources; information on this is exceedingly difficult to acquire. Finally, input costs may vary because some furniture producers are closer to input sources than others; transport cost differences of this kind are examined in this section.

Major furniture inputs were identified, along with the major sources of supply.[16] Not surprisingly, it turned out that Canadian producers were

[16]Inputs for the industry are listed in the DBS sources cited for Table I above.

closer to important input supplies than U.S. producers. Rail rates were applied to these data to determine the total cost advantage of Toronto and Montreal over the three U.S. locations.[17] The results are displayed in Table V.

TABLE V

ESTIMATED PERCENTAGE THAT TOTAL COSTS ARE LOWER IN CANADIAN LOCATIONS BECAUSE OF PROXIMITY TO INPUT SUPPLIES (T_m)

	Chicago	New York	High Point
Toronto	2.01	1.92	.41
Montreal	1.74	1.65	.15

Proximity to input supplies (like favourable wage rates) is a reason why Canadian prices might be *lower* than those in the United States. Since our original objective was to explain Canadian price that is observed to be *higher*, we seem to be making progress in the wrong direction. A consideration of our strategy is therefore in order.

D. A DIGRESSION: A GRAPHIC PRESENTATION OF COMPARATIVE COSTS

Our price and cost estimates are assembled in Figure 1. For purposes of illustration only, the Toronto-Chicago comparison is shown in this diagram. (Similar comparisons of Toronto with the other two U.S. regions, and Montreal with all three U.S. regions, are presented later.)

The heavy horizontal reference line in this figure is the factory price of U.S. furniture. Higher or lower Canadian prices and costs are measured, respectively, above or below this U.S. base line. Reading from left to right, the first bar (D) represents the Canadian tariff of 25 percent—an index of the direct price protection provided to the furniture industry. Percentage P is our best estimate of the amount of this protection the industry in fact

[17]The formula for estimating T_m in the jth column and kth row of Table V was:
$$\sum^n_{i=1} (Z_{ij} - Z_{ik}) R_i A_i$$
in which:
Z_{ij} refers to the distance in miles of U.S. centre of furniture manufacturing j ($j =$ High Point, Chicago, or New York) from its most likely source of input i.
Z_{ik} refers to the distance in miles of Canadian centre of furniture manufacturing k ($k =$ Toronto or Montreal) from its most likely source of supply of input i.
Sources of supply were obtained from U.S. *Census of Manufacturing 1958*, U.S. *Annual Survey of Manufacturing*, 1960, 1961, and 1962, and DBS industry surveys.
R_i refers to the cost of shipping $1 worth of input i for one mile as determined from waybill statistics.
A_i refers to the proportion of costs of furniture manufacture devoted to the purchase of input i.

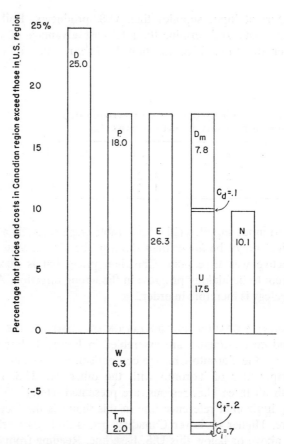

Figure 1. Comparison of Prices and Costs, 1962:
Ontario (Toronto) *vs.* East North Central (Chicago)

uses—i.e., the 18 percent higher price charged, on average, in the Canadian market.

There are two other advantages (in addition to their higher price) that Canadian producers enjoy. Their total costs are lower by 6.3 percent because of lower wages (W), and lower by 2 percent because of proximity to input supplies (T_m). Since both represent lower Canadian costs, they are entered in this diagram below the U.S. reference line. Terms P, W, and T_m all represent advantages enjoyed by Canadian producers selling in the Canadian market. Their sum ($E = 26.3$ percent) represents the margin that must be explained—in terms of other costs that are higher in Canada and/or higher Canadian profits. Canadian costs are shown in the next column in Figure 1; to their evaluation we now turn.

E. HIGHER CANADIAN CAPITAL COSTS

Higher interest rates in Canada increase the cost of borrowing; the impact on total manufacturing costs (C_i) was estimated in several steps.[18]

First, the total amount of bank loans, mortgage debt, and capital stock outstanding was calculated.[19] Each of these elements was multiplied by the differential between the relevant Canadian and U.S. rates.[20] These figures were then summed and divided by the total value of furniture shipped. The results of these calculations are displayed in Table VI.[21] Only a single Canadian-U.S. comparison is shown. A regional breakdown of this cost (like many of the others that follow) is unnecessary, since firms in various regions in either country have access to the same capital market.

TABLE VI

ESTIMATED PERCENTAGE THAT CANADIAN TOTAL COSTS WERE HIGHER
THAN IN THE UNITED STATES BECAUSE OF HIGHER CAPITAL COSTS

	1958	1960	1962
Effect of higher interest rate and return on equity (C_i)	0.84	0.81	0.68

Another higher Canadian capital cost has received a great deal of attention recently—the 11 percent sales tax on buildings and machinery (C_t). The effect of this tax was computed by applying the 11 percent tax to the industry's total expenditure on machinery and part of its spending on new plant[22] in 1962.[23] The estimated differential was only about 0.2 percent

[18]The rationale of our estimating procedure has been discussed at length in Wonnacott and Wonnacott, *Free Trade*, chap. VIII, and is consequently not reproduced here.
[19]From information taken from tax data published by the Department of Revenue.
[20]The appropriate rate for bank loans was the difference between the Canadian and U.S. prime rates. For bond debt, we used the average rate of return on ten Canadian industrial bonds (compiled by McLeod, Young, Weir) less the equivalent U.S. rate of return on Moody's AAA bonds. This differential was doubled before being applied to equity. (It was assumed that *after-tax* returns to equity in Canada would exceed U.S. levels by the Canadian-U.S. interest differential. With a corporate profit tax of 50 percent, the excess in *before-tax* returns would have to be double this.)
[21]These estimates are very tentative. While the prime rate is applicable to the loans of the large firms in the United States, the small, family-owned firms in the Canadian industry may not be able to obtain funds at the prime rate. Hence the cost of bank-loan capital in Canada may be understated. On the other hand, the required rate of return on equity capital in Canada may be overstated. Frequently family fortunes are locked into Canadian firms. The inability or unwillingness of the owners to exit from the industry may induce them to accept a lower rate of return than the average industrial enterprise.
[22]Only part of building costs (i.e., building materials) is subject to this tax; labour and many other costs of construction are not.
[23]Cf. n. 30, for reasons why this procedure is not the ideal procedure for estimating cost differences on capital inputs. Any bias in our method, however, is more likely than not to overstate cost effects, which are insignificant in any case.

of total costs; it is evident that the limited capital requirements of this industry prevent this tax from being a major influence on costs. Moreover, with the abolition of a portion of this tax on machinery in the 1966 budget, over one-fourth of this cost will disappear, and the removal of the remaining tax on building materials is certain.[24]

F. HIGHER CANADIAN FURNITURE COSTS DUE TO PROTECTION ON INPUTS
There are two reasons why furniture costs may be raised because of Canadian tariff protection on material inputs (e.g., foam rubber). First, foam rubber that is actually imported will be more costly by the amount of the tariff. Second, the price of domestically produced rubber may be higher because of the protection it receives; this will occur if the Canadian rubber industry takes advantage of this tariff when pricing its product.

Two different measures were used to determine how much the cost of furniture is raised by protection. One, a minimum estimate, assumed that Canadian input prices were higher only on goods that were in fact imported. Each furniture input listed in the DBS publications was taken separately. The ratio of imports of this good to total Canadian consumption was determined, and this figure was assumed also to apply to purchases by the furniture industry. Thus, if one-ninth of total foam rubber used in Canada was imported, it was assumed that one-ninth of the foam rubber used by the furniture industry was imported. Appropriate tariff rates were applied to all such computed imports[25] of the furniture industry, yielding an estimate of the total increased cost of inputs resulting from all tariffs. This figure, expressed as a percentage of total furniture costs, is shown in the first row of Table VII.

Interviews with manufacturers led us to believe that these minimum estimates were far too low.[26] For the maximum estimate, it was assumed that prices of all inputs—whether imported or domestically produced— fully reflected the protection they received. Many firms in the industry indicated that this was the case, particularly for textiles, plastic laminates, and plastic covers for dinette suites. The higher (protected) price was applied to all inputs regardless of their source; this yielded an estimate of the total increase in costs resulting from protection. This figure, expressed as a percentage of total furniture costs, is shown in the second row of

[24]See budget speech of Honourable Mitchell Sharp, March 29, 1966, *House of Commons Debates*, p. 3386.
[25]There was a problem in assigning the correct tariff to each input. For example, import data refer to "plastic sheeting," yet the Customs Act refers not to plastic sheeting in general but to a wide variety of specific types of sheeting varying in width, composition, and use.
[26]On theoretical grounds, the assumptions involved are inconsistent with competitive markets: similar products are assumed to sell in the Canadian market at differing prices (i.e., imports are higher priced than domestic products).

TABLE VII

ESTIMATED PERCENTAGE THAT TOTAL COSTS ARE HIGHER IN CANADA
DUE TO PROTECTION ON INPUTS

	1958	1960	1962
Effect of protection on material inputs (D_m): minimum	0.48	0.52	0.66
maximum	6.72	6.68	7.79
Effect of protection on machinery (C_d)	0.10	0.12	0.11

Table VII. Since our interviews with manufacturers indicated that this maximum estimate was closer to the mark than the minimum estimate, it is used throughout for comparative purposes.[27] It is used for another reason. Canadian protection not only has a price effect; it also restricts variety. Our maximum estimate of the price effect is used as a proxy for both disadvantages facing Canadian manufacturers.

In passing, it is interesting to note that the Canadian case-goods industry imports a high percentage of the hardwoods it uses on exterior surfaces. This includes not only exotic woods like teak and pecan, but also woods native to Canada, such as birch and maple. There are two reasons. First, in many parts of Canada woods are marred by a mineral streaking that is almost impossible to remove. Second, forestry management in Canada often favours the pulp and paper industry at the expense of hardwood lumbering. Pulp and paper companies with exclusive cutting rights to northern forests generally cut all wood within their region, regardless of size.[28]

Machinery is another input of the industry which is more expensive in Canada because of protection. Only a maximum estimate (in the last row of Table VII) was computed for this item; because this is so small, it was unnecessary to consider a minimum. An average tariff rate for machinery imports[29] was applied to the total expenditure by the furniture industry on (domestic and imported) machinery.[30] Since even our low estimate has an

[27]The choice of this maximum estimate is not critical in analyzing the impact of a general movement towards free trade. It becomes important only if single-industry schemes are considered.
[28]Recent events in Quebec suggest a change in this policy.
[29]Derived from *Trade of Canada: Imports*, 1958. A tariff rate was computed by comparing the imports by the furniture industry with the tariff revenue collected on these same imports. (The latter figure was available only for 1958; hence, the 1958 tariff rate computed in this way was also used in the 1960 and 1962 calculations.)
[30]Since machinery is a capital, rather than a material, input, it should ideally be treated differently—i.e., the higher price (in the year in which each machine was purchased) should be applied to its depreciation in the year studied. Our method, however, is a good approximation—although in a period of growth it will tend to overstate true costs.

upward bias, it must be concluded that this cost is normally a relatively insignificant influence in this industry.

Both these higher input costs (D_m and C_d) help to explain how the total Canadian advantage (E) is dissipated. Moreover, like the higher protected Canadian price (P), these elements of higher Canadian cost would disappear in any general move to across-the-board free trade. Hence these items are entered in Figure 1, opposite P. The net protection that the furniture industry uses is now evident and is graphically represented by N: this is simply the higher output price charged because of the furniture tariff (P) less the higher cost the industry faces because of protection on its inputs (D_m and C_d). Even though nominal protection for the industry is a 25 percent tariff, the net protection producers actually use is only 10 percent.

G. INEFFICIENCIES OF MARKET SIZE

When E (the sum of all Canadian advantages) has been reduced by all the Canadian disadvantages identified above, a large residual (U) remains. This can be explained only by higher Canadian profit or by some higher Canadian cost as yet unidentified.

(a) *Are Canadian profits higher?* Specifically, do manufacturers exercise more market power in Canada and quote a high price in order to raise profit levels above those in the United States?

The large number of small establishments in the industry does not suggest a concentration of market power. Nor is this indicated by concentration ratios of the industry.[31] While there are some two thousand establishments in Canada producing furniture, eighty-three of them do more than 42 percent of the total business. Each of these eighty-three establishments had sales in 1962 between $1 million and $5 million. Any effective collusion by such a large number of firms of roughly equal size would be unlikely to escape the notice of the Restrictive Trade Practices Commission.

The exercise of market power in Canada can also be tested by examining profit rates. While there are some very profitable firms in the industry, average profits are low. The return on equity (total common and preferred stock and retained earnings) in 1961 was 4.5 percent. The comparable return on equity for all manufacturing enterprise in Canada was 6.2 percent.[32] Since the industry return is below average for Canada, it may be concluded that excessive profits do not accrue to furniture-makers. Nor does their profit exceed that in the United States. In 1960, after-tax profit,

[31]I.e., the percentage of business held by the largest firms.
[32]Department of Industry and the *Canadian Handbook*.

expressed as a return on equity, was 6.4 percent in U.S. furniture-making,[33] compared with 4.5 percent in Canada.

(b) *Effects of a restricted market on costs.* Since there is no evidence of higher profit in Canada, our residual U is attributed to the one remaining explanation: inefficiencies of a small market. This can reflect either a lower degree of management efficiency and labour productivity (because management directly and labour indirectly are not subjected to the external discipline of the more competitive U.S. market) or technical scale effects (because of the duplication of labour tasks[34] and capital equipment involved in fragmented production runs).

There is ample evidence of technical scale effects. Instances are frequently cited of how short production runs induce frequent changeovers, idle capital, and costly inventories. Canadian manufacturers expressed the opinion that they could reduce costs in the range of 15 to 20 percent if they could operate at U.S. scale. This confirms our independent estimate of U of 17½ percent in Figure 1.[35] A further implication is that U represents restricted scale, rather than management or labour inefficiency *per se*. No one familiar with the industry will be surprised by our estimate that scale effects are the major present competitive cost problem of the Canadian industry. When furniture manufacturers (or almost any other manufacturers, for that matter) are asked why their costs are higher than in the United States, their first reply is almost invariably: "the size of the Canadian market."

Consider in detail how scale effects raise Canadian costs.

(i) Excessive duplication of capital equipment. While many U.S. casegoods plants increasingly concentrate on the assembly of precut subcontracted parts, the Canadian industry by and large continues to have fully integrated plants. Each plant has its own breakout department (for preliminary cutting), kilns (for drying the wood), and dimension stock shops

[33]Quarterly financial reports of corporations, Federal Trade Commission.

[34]Since the restricted Canadian market prevents the efficient allocation of labour (and capital), observed labour productivity in Canada will be lower. This follows even though the Canadian labour force is inherently as productive—i.e., even though a Canadian worker performs any given task equally efficiently. Cf., the discussion in 2B above.

[35]Since U could not be estimated directly, it had to be estimated as the residual left unexplained after all other influences were accounted for. The major problem in this sort of estimating technique is that all errors in prior estimates accumulate in U. This, however, is not as serious a problem as it sounds. If errors in prior estimates are randomly distributed with a mean of zero, they will tend to be self-cancelling—i.e., there will be no bias in the estimating procedure.

Curiously, our estimate of U is almost exactly equal to our estimate of the higher Canadian price (P). There is no analytical reason for expecting this; as far as one can judge, it is pure coincidence.

(for final cutting to specific dimensions). In the bedding industry the situation is similar. Several intermediate-size firms have their own coilers even though their volume of sales does not warrant such an investment. Similarly, chrome-furniture manufacturers often bend their own steel (and in some instances even do their own plating) rather than specialize in the assembly and marketing of prebent forms. The result is that this machinery is frequently idle.[36] When industry spokesmen were questioned on this apparently irrational investment, it was justified on the grounds that suppliers were unable to provide components of the desired degree of "quality." This is a simple variation on an earlier theme: components of equal quality cost more in Canada. This suggests that the Canadian tariff structure may protect inefficient scale in supplying industries.

(ii) Research, design and development. Sales in Canada are not large enough for many firms to support these overhead expenditures. As an example, consider design. Because most Canadian firms cannot afford first-class design, various options come into play.

An extreme measure was at one time suggested for the auto industry; the large companies, it was argued, should form a consortium to produce a "Canadian car," carefully designed to service the northern climate and to satisfy Canadian tastes. The Canadian market, the argument went, would be sufficient to allow the industry to achieve full economies of scale and hence price at internationally competitive levels. The intractable problems posed by such an auto scheme would be even more pronounced in furniture. The large number of furniture firms would increase the difficulties of arriving at a consortium agreement. Further, if an agreement were feasible, a monopoly-like concentration would result, with little assurance that efficiency gains would go to the consumer and not to the industry.

The big problem, however, is one of taste. Even though a dining-room suite may be a masterpiece of design and craftsmanship, it will be resisted by a consumer if every third house in his neighbourhood—and in the country—sports an identical suite. (Even if consumers could be induced into large-scale purchases, it is hard to justify this type of policy on aesthetic grounds.) As consumers able to afford variety turned to imports, the large Canadian markets (on which this policy was predicated) would not materialize. Hence the industry could not afford its quality design and development, nor could it reduce price by longer runs. The argument that the Canadian market is large enough to support one or a few producers of optimum scale is insufficient. In such a taste item as furniture, economies of scale can be achieved only in a market many times the optimal level of output of a single firm.

[36]The Department of Industry encourages the use of dimension stock and precut or bent components, but the industry has been slow to change.

The present situation of the industry is almost at the other extreme, with a proliferation of inexpensive designs produced for a fragmented Canadian market. To keep design costs at a minimum, pieces are often copied from U.S. furniture shows. The design is, of course, modified slightly.[37] In the process the Canadian manufacturer often bows to market pressure by adding a feature to attract an entirely new group of consumers. The result is not always a happy one. As one manufacturer said in a candid moment, "Usually we copy an American design and somehow manage to foul it up slightly." The problem is not bad taste; this is simply the reaction of a producer cornered in a limited market who attempts to cater to widely divergent tastes. In these circumstances, economic success is often aesthetic disaster.

(iii) Economies of scale in distribution. Canadian manufacturers are often restricted in their marketing methods by the small domestic market. All but the largest firms rely on commission salesmen. These salesmen are normally paid a retainer plus commission—or commission only—and often represent four or five firms. As a consequence, they may be unable to do full justice to the products of each firm. Furthermore, the Canadian market is not only small; it is also spread out over space. The long distance between factory and outlying population makes it difficult and expensive to adequately service lines in terms of inventory, repairs, etc. A further complication is the lengthy delay in delivery. Manufacturers typically defer cutting a piece until sufficient orders are on hand to justify the necessary changeover. Because of their shortage of liquid capital, most producers are unwilling to cut and make up items in anticipation of orders. (There are, however, a few exceptions in Quebec.) Another distribution problem in a limited market is illustrated in a rule of thumb used by the industry: once a firm reaches 12 percent of the market in a particular type of furniture, it must diversify its lines in order to enlist additional retail outlets.

(iv) Obsolete plant and equipment. It is difficult to analyze the problem of obsolescence, since it is almost certainly both a cause and an effect of higher Canadian costs. Many firms continue to manufacture in plants long since outdated, using machinery long since obsolete; as a consequence their costs are higher. The ancient buildings with poor production layout are wasteful of time and capital. With a few exceptions, the case-goods industry continues to use inefficient plants in rural areas that were once close to the forests but are now far from both timber supplies and markets.

But why does the industry not modernize and relocate? At least part of the answer is the difficulty of raising funds, because of the problems the

---

[37]Many U.S. firms also design in this way. And it must be recognized that it is exceedingly difficult to draw a line between copies and designs that are original. For example, are any of the "new" French Provincial designs original?

industry faces. Thus the higher costs of the industry (discussed above) become a cause (as well as an effect) of continued obsolescence.

3. *An unanswered question: Why have not economies of scale induced industry nationalization?*

Since economies of scale are the major explanation of higher Canadian cost, why do not large firms expand, in the process reducing costs and eliminating competition? A Canadian firm might expand by capturing a larger share of the domestic market and/or by exploiting export markets.

A. WHY HAVE FIRMS NOT EXPANDED IN THE DOMESTIC CANADIAN MARKET? Manufacturers are of the opinion that available economies of scale can be achieved in case goods or upholstery by a firm with an output of $15–$20 million per year. (Such a firm would have a separate breakout and dimension plant, one plant for chairs, one for case goods, one for occasional pieces, and one for upholstered goods. It would be able to centralize bookkeeping and maintain its own sales force.) [38]

It is evident that the Canadian market is sufficiently large[39] to support several case-goods firms of this optimum size. Instead, there are over two thousand establishments, with the output of the largest limited to the $6 million range. Expansion of firms in the Canadian market has been deterred for two reasons.

First, competitive pressures have not been allowed to operate to squeeze out the inefficient. Special government programs (tax concessions, loans, etc.) have helped not only the efficient but also the inefficient. Even more important is the Canadian tariff, which has provided a price cover for furniture firms. While there is no evidence that the higher Canadian price has allowed higher Canadian profits, it has allowed continuing higher costs. But the nagging question remains: why has one farsighted Canadian manager not seized the initiative and, by increasing volume, reduced cost and price?

Once again, the answer is that furniture is a taste item. And consumers prefer variety to lower cost. This is the critical trade-off. Industry spokesmen recognize that a large Canadian firm ($6 million sales) could decrease its costs and prices by 15 to 20 percent by increasing its output to three to

[38]Estimates of optimal bedding plants varied greatly but ranged around a figure of $1 million in sales per year. Such an operation would include coilers, garneters, etc.
[39]Canadian sales of domestic case goods in 1962 were $126 million.

five times its present level.[40] This policy is not undertaken, because this price reduction would be insufficient to attract such a large increase in sales.

B. WHY NOT EXPANSION BASED ON EXPORT SALES?

Because of its proximity, the United States provides by far the most promising export market. Even a limited probe into this market would greatly increase Canadian output and provide scale economies. But Canadian firms have not been able to market there at an attractive enough price. Even if full economies of scale were to be achieved by an expanding Canadian firm, its potential cost reduction ($U = 17\frac{1}{2}$ percent in Figure 1) would allow a reduction in its prices only to about the U.S. factory price level.[41] Even assuming that it could overcome initial design and distribution difficulties, the Canadian industry would be barely competitive.[42] In a tariff-ridden world this is not sufficient. Sales in the United States have been blocked by the 10 percent U.S. import duty[43] on wooden furniture and 35 percent on upholstered furniture.[44] There are also non-tariff barriers such as labelling requirements or "inspections" which involve slashing open a mattress to discover its contents.

In summary, there are two major reasons Canadian firms have not expanded to optimal scale. The domestic market is too small, given consumer preference for variety over price, and export markets have been blocked by foreign protection.

[40]I.e., we were told that a fully integrated firm could achieve full economies of scale at $20–$30 million sales (see above). Industry spokesmen estimate that this would involve a cost reduction of 15–20 percent; our estimate (U) is $17\frac{1}{2}$ percent.

[41]I.e., reduce P in Figure 1 to almost zero.

[42]Its Canadian advantages (lower wages, etc.) would be dissipated by the higher cost of protected inputs. An additional problem for the furniture industry is that protection results in less style selection of inputs as well as higher input prices. Thus Canadian upholstered furniture often fails to offer either competitive quality or range of fabric covers. As one manufacturer said, "I can beat my U.S. counterpart on price all the way up to the cover, then I really am forced to step aside."

[43]10 percent is the U.S. MFN rate for all items except chairs and metal furniture, which have a 17 percent rate.

[44]Another possibility would be for Canadian firms to sell in Canada at the high current Canadian prices, and achieve scale by selling in the United States at the domestic U.S. price (and hence absorb the U.S. tariff). It is not clear that this would be economical, even in competition with Illinois; and it will be evident in the next section that meeting North Carolina competition would be even more difficult. An added important factor is that Canadian firms would become vulnerable to U.S. anti-dumping regulations. Hence the greater their success in invading the U.S. market, the more likely would be retaliation. For an extended discussion of the economics of double pricing, see Wonnacott and Wonnacott, *Free Trade*, chaps. XIII and XV.

3. Prospects under North American Free Trade

If Canadian and U.S. tariffs on all manufactured goods were to be abolished, many of the higher costs of production in Canada would be eliminated. We now turn to the even more critical question: "Would the Canadian industry be eliminated?"

To answer this, it is necessary to consider explicitly whether free trade would allow Canadian cost reductions to competitive U.S. levels. Higher Canadian input costs due to protection (D_m and C_d) would automatically and immediately disappear. Nor could higher Canadian costs due to the restricted market (U) continue. It is evident from Figure 1 that a Canadian industry burdened by higher costs of this kind simply could not compete with low-priced imports entering duty-free from the United States. The continued existence of the Canadian industry, therefore, would require the elimination of inefficiency by scaling up to levels appropriate to the North American market.[1]

One barrier to past Canadian rationalization (i.e., the U.S. tariff) would be removed; thus duty-free access to the U.S. market would provide an incentive for Canadian rationalization. But this is not the *only* necessary incentive. In addition, Canada must be a low-cost location for furniture production; otherwise the Canadian industry will exercise its other option, i.e., close down.

An examination of the estimates below the base line in Figure 1 indicates that, given industry rationalization, Ontario manufacturers could indeed compete with those in the U.S. East North Central area. The relevant information is reproduced in the upper left-hand corner of Figure 2. Canadian free trade cost advantages W and T_m are again measured below a U.S. price/cost baseline. The Canadian cost disadvantages that would continue under free trade (C_t and C_i) are appropriately deducted in column 2, leaving the potential net free trade advantage for a fully rationalized Canadian industry (A).[2]

---

[1]Although Canadian producers would initially enjoy a wage advantage, it is not clear that this would persist in the long run. This issue is analyzed later.
[2]Recall that such an industry need no longer incur higher costs D_m, C_d, and U.

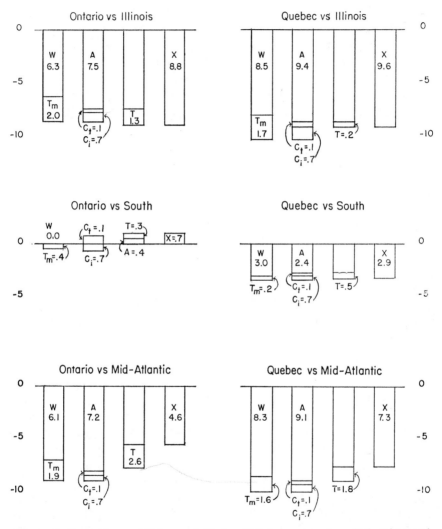

Figure 2. Comparison of Prices and Costs, 1962 (percentage by which prices and costs in Canadian region exceed those in U.S. region)

There is one other cost estimate required in evaluating the Canadian competitive position—i.e., the cost involved in shipping final products to North American markets. Since furniture markets are in population and income centres, they are concentrated in the United States. It does not follow, however, that Canadian producers are at a disadvantage. For example, in shipping furniture to the largest market (New York City),

Toronto firms enjoy an advantage (T) over Chicago firms equivalent to an estimated 1.3 percent of total costs.[3] In column 3, this is added to other cost advantages (A); in combination they provide furniture-makers in Toronto with an 8.8 percent cost advantage (X) over Chicago firms in delivering furniture into the New York market. (Clearly, the Toronto advantage would be substantially less in delivering furniture to, say, St. Louis; in this case the Chicago producer would enjoy a transport-cost advantage.)

Six comparisons are shown in Figure 2, each representing the competitive position of a Canadian location (Toronto or Montreal) vis-à-vis a U.S. location (High Point, New York, or Chicago).[4] In terms of potential free trade costs, either Toronto or Montreal compares favourably with U.S. locations in the north. But the picture is quite different in comparisons with the U.S. South; Ontario costs would be at least as high as in North Carolina, and Quebec costs would be only slightly lower. A key issue is clearly the U.S. region with which Canadian producers must compete; and this depends on product line.

It is now appropriate to consider the different impacts of free trade on various product groupings. It will be evident from the discussion below that prospects vary widely among the four sectors into which we have divided the industry. Nor does variation end there. Even *within* any of these sectors (e.g., case-goods), some subsectors would fare better than others. Indeed, because of differences in management energy and outlook, one might expect a differential effect of free trade even at the firm level; that is, the impact may vary widely among firms engaged in precisely the same furniture-making activity. This is not an argument against the average cost figures presented in this study or against the broad conclusions inferred from them; these have been necessary to give an over-all picture of the competitive strength of the industry. It is simply a warning that these figures cannot be uncritically applied to all activities nor to all Canadian furniture firms. Our only observation is that these estimates are, to our knowledge, unbiased; that is, one may expect a roughly equal distribution of firms in a weaker competitive position *and* in a stronger position than our averages imply. Canadian specialization will be concentrated in the latter group. With this

[3]The differential was calculated in the same way as shown in chap. 2, n. 17. The market centre was taken as New York City, and the distances from that city to the points of production were calculated; in each case the difference between each of the Canadian and American centres was found. This was then multiplied by the cost of shipping furniture per dollar mile times the total output of furniture. The resulting product was in turn divided by the total output of furniture shipped in Canada and expressed as a fraction.

[4]Note that in the bottom two comparisons, T is negative—i.e., either Canadian location faces a transport-cost disadvantage vis-à-vis the U.S. Mid-Atlantic region in delivering final output to New York.

caveat in mind, it is now appropriate to consider how free trade might affect the four major sectors of the furniture industry.

1. *Local cabinet shops*

Regardless of the exact nature of the trade agreement, the portion of the industry devoted to local or custom work will be relatively unaffected.[5] These small cabinet shops typically employ fourteen persons or less and manufacture furniture to order. They number slightly more than one-half of all the establishments listed in the annual DBS surveys and employ 8 to 10 percent of the total labour force in the industry. Regardless of how much tariffs rise or fall, or how extensive the penetration of imports, these firms are likely to continue their present operations; they will be about as immune to lower priced imports in the future as they have been to lower priced domestic factory furniture in the past.[6]

2. *Upholstery, mattresses, and bedding*

The sector of the industry with the best free trade growth prospects may well be the bedding and upholstery business. High weight/value ratios make distant shipment of these products unprofitable; hence the industry is market-oriented. As a consequence, Canadian locations would compete against northern U.S. locations, but not against locations in the U.S. South. If Canadian firms were able to develop their own designs or to manufacture American designs under licence, they should be able to survive; they might even expand through sales in urban markets along the border. It is evident from the Canadian/U.S. North comparisons in Figure 2 that lower wages would allow an efficient Canadian manufacturer near the border to produce and distribute his product across the line in the United States at a lower cost than that of his U.S. counterpart.[7] Moreover, since this is the most labour-intensive segment of the industry, its wage advantage would be even greater than the average estimates for the industry shown in Figure 2. Hence, there seems to be an incentive for the reorganization and scaling up of Canadian facilities to exploit these border markets.

It would be only in the very highest-priced lines, where exclusive designs

---

[5]Except in a city such as Windsor, which is part of the same metropolitan area as Detroit.

[6]Any reduction in their sales is more likely to come from the increased variety of available imports, rather than from their lower prices.

[7]Provided there is free trade in all manufactured goods. If free trade is limited to furniture, higher input costs (D_m) would erode this Canadian advantage.

and fabrics are essential, that Canadian firms might be unable to compete. Here production costs are of second-order importance, and a marginal advantage for Canada of this kind might not provide sufficient incentive to overcome major design problems. In any case, it is not clear that continental markets would be able to support more than the several firms of this type already existing in the United States. Rather it is in the lower-priced lines of upholstered furniture and bedding that the Canadian industry will have the greatest chance for survival, and perhaps even expansion.

3. Case goods

This is the most vulnerable Canadian sector because it *does* have to face southern competition. Relatively low weight/value ratios make case-goods profitable to ship longer distances. This, along with substantial economies of scale, has resulted in spatial concentration of the U.S. industry in the low-wage South. Under free trade, southern case-goods producers would be able to sell in Canadian markets on roughly the same terms that they now sell in the U.S. North. Could Canadian producers meet this competition?

A. INCENTIVE FOR REORGANIZATION
From Figure 2, it is evident that Canadian producers—especially in Ontario—would have little incentive for rationalizing their production. Their costs would not be substantially lower than in the U.S. South because, unlike most Canadian industries, they would enjoy no wage advantage. It is quite true that any efficient Canadian firms now geared up to hit U.S. markets with distinctive designs and quality workmanship should be in a reasonably competitive position because of rough potential equality with southern costs. But Canadian firms embedded in the inefficiencies of the traditional Canadian market would need to change rapidly or face deep trouble. Furthermore, it is not clear that there would be a great incentive for them to embark on a program of change. From Figure 2, it is evident that they could hope for little cost advantage, even after they completed a rationalization program; and during the interim overhaul period, they would face substantial once-and-for-all adjustment costs and problems.

B. PROBLEMS OF ADJUSTMENT
(a) *Rising wage rates.* Our analysis of comparative costs is based on the assumption that Canadian wage rates remain in their present position relative to U.S. rates. But across-the-board free trade is likely to change

relative wages. The general equilibrium effects of free trade have been analyzed elsewhere;[8] if expected general equilibrium pressures materialize, the Canadian dollar would appreciate towards parity with the U.S. dollar,[9] and/or the Canadian wage level would shift up towards the U.S. level. The problem is not that furniture wages in Canada would rise towards U.S. levels (they are already at par with the U.S. South); rather, the difficulty is that a possible appreciation of wages in other areas of Canadian manufacturing may tend to attract the labour force out of furniture. Given the present equality of costs in Canada and the U.S. South, it is not clear that Canadian case-goods manufacturers could retain their labour force by matching upward shifts in wages in other Canadian sectors. The major consolation is that shifts within the U.S. wage structure are likely to occur at the same time. Thus, wages in the U.S. South are likely to continue to close on the U.S. average; and in particular furniture wages in North Carolina may come under upward pressure with increased concentration of the industry there.

(b) *Problems of industry structure, finance, marketing, and design.* The average Canadian firm with sales in the $1–$3 million range would face other major difficulties. Typically it operates in a building some fifty years of age, producing a limited line of well-built pieces selling in the middle- to upper-price range. It is family-owned and suffers from undercapitalization and lack of trained engineering skills. It has a sales force working on commission and no established line of access into the U.S. market. Such a firm, lacking originality of design, with extended delivery dates, and with limited ability to extend finance to dealers, would be exceedingly vulnerable to competition from the giant U.S. firms. Unfortunately, it is these firms, often located in small towns where they are the most important employer, that do the bulk of the business and employ a major portion of the labour force in the industry.

Structural detail on the industry is shown in Table VIII. The major portion of business (92 percent) is done by incorporated companies. Moreover, Canadian ownership dominates the industry: privately owned Canadian firms account for almost 70 percent of total sales, while U.S. subsidiaries account for only about 10 percent.

Note from Table IX that U.S. subsidiaries are spread throughout the industry, while U.S.-licensed firms are mainly concentrated in bedding. The most plausible explanation is that brand identification is greater in bedding than in any other sector of the furniture industry; thus the major advantage

---

[8]Wonnacott and Wonnacott, *Free Trade*, chap. xi.
[9]Because our wage comparisons have been in terms of domestic dollars, this parity assumption has already been built into our comparative cost analysis.

TABLE VIII

STRUCTURAL CHARACTERISTICS OF THE CANADIAN FURNITURE INDUSTRY

Type of ownership	Establishments	Value of shipments	Percentage of total value shipped
		($000)	
Individual	1,007	23,450	5.1
Partnership	196	12,870	2.8
Incorporated companies:	837	425,880	92.1
U.S. subsidiaries	18	47,500*	10.2
U.S. licensed	16	22,000*	4.8
Canadian public companies	19	41,000	8.9
Canadian private companies	784	315,380	68.2

Sources: DBS, *Miscellaneous Furniture Industries*, 1963, *Office Furniture Industry*, 1963, *Household Furniture Industry*, 1963, and Department of Industry work sheet.
  *Estimates.

TABLE IX

BREAKDOWN OF FURNITURE-MAKING ACTIVITIES
IN EACH OWNERSHIP CLASSIFICATION
(percentages)

	Bedding	Metal office	Uphol-stered	Comm. cabinets	Wooden household	Miscel-laneous
U.S. subsidiaries	24.8	22.8	21.3	16.8	11.7	2.6
U.S. licensed	95.0		5.0			
Canadian public companies		37.9	2.6	23.2	28.9	7.5

Sources: DBS, *Miscellaneous Furniture Industries*, 1963, *Office Furniture Industry*, 1963, *Household Furniture Industry*, 1963, and Department of Industry work sheet.

of association with a U.S. firm is acquiring its well-known brand name. To do this, a Canadian firm requires only a licensing agreement.

While the cost equality in Figure 2 suggests little incentive for firms of this kind to reorganize, it also implies that Canadian firms which are already at, or near, U.S. efficiency levels should be in a competitive position. In addition to matching production costs, there will be other tests of survival: quality design and the ability to market aggressively in the United States as Canadian sales are lost to imports. These two problems are interrelated and may require imaginative solutions. For example, a Canadian firm may seek a custom contract with a large U.S. department store (or chain) to produce a quality line to its design specifications. Such a contract might cover the interim period of adjustment of the firm and provide it with a breathing spell in which to plan a broader attack on U.S.

markets by independent sale of its own designs. Canadian firms correctly recognize that, even if they can compete in terms of price in Canadian markets with U.S. imports, they may still lose sales as consumers exercise choice over a greater variety of (imported) designs. Hence, even if they can effectively compete in the North American market, they will tend to lose sales in Canada. But it is important to recognize that this argument cuts both ways. A Canadian firm need carve only a very small segment out of the vast U.S. market to more than compensate for its loss of Canadian sales; and the more attractive and unique its design, the more will its segment of the market be insulated from price competition. In such a taste item as furniture, quality design and craftsmanship may provide the "protection" in the North American market in the future that tariffs have provided in the Canadian market in the past. Developing tasteful and unique designs is no simple matter. For example, the "Swedish modern" designs characteristic of Scandinavian furniture were not developed over-night, but only after a prolonged process of trial and error extending over a period of ten to thirty years.

In any circumstances, the disciplines of a broader, more competitive market yield substantial benefits, both for consumers facing more attractive prices and for labour and management receiving higher rewards for efficiency. Competition, however, involves a cost as well, albeit temporary: the inefficient must find work elsewhere. Tariff elimination would provide the sudden equivalent to many years of competitive change. Because Canadian firms now operate well below optimum scale, survival would require expansion; those unwilling to seize the new opportunities for expanding sales in the United States are almost certain not to survive.

It is extremely difficult to predict resulting patterns. The authors' tentative view is that a large number of privately incorporated Canadian case-goods firms would cease to exist in their present form; many would be merged with more efficient, expanding Canadian firms or U.S. firms; and the present trend of the elimination of obsolete Canadian furniture firms would be greatly accelerated. This would be offset, at least in part, by the expansion of the more efficient Canadian firms. It is not possible to estimate the combined effects of these cross forces on Canadian furniture employment. However, the complete elimination of case-goods production in Canada seems vastly too pessimistic a prediction; on the other hand, continued Canadian employment at present levels in case goods[10] seems an overly optimistic view.

[10]With increased efficiency and productivity, this implies an increase in Canadian production, both in absolute terms and relative to production in the United States. A more modest target for the industry, therefore, would be to maintain its share of North American production.

4. Special products

It is likely that there would be an equally severe adjustment problem in metal furniture. The market for dinette suites is characterized not so much by price competition as by originality of fabrics and design and increasingly complex production techniques. This sector of the industry would attach less importance to low Canadian wages, but more importance to high pre-vailing Canadian capital costs.[11] An advantage accruing to Canadian pro-ducers of inexpensive items is that they may be partially protected by distance, since the value/weight ratio of these finished products is low. Hence, assembly plants may continue in the major urban markets of Toronto, Montreal, and Vancouver. In inexpensive lines, these Canadian cities may have wages sufficiently below those of the U.S. North to allow them to assemble products for distribution to nearby American markets.

5. Summary of the sectoral impact of free trade

The Canadian furniture industry would face special problems not faced by many other Canadian industries.

The most mobile segment of the U.S. industry (case-goods) that might otherwise find low Canadian wages an attraction has already gone (or is in the process of going) to the equally low-wage U.S. South. Moreover, the sunk capital of an established industry in Canada would provide little insurance that the industry would continue here, since it is at present ill-adapted to the new set of circumstances. Since most firms have limited themselves to the small Canadian market, they are unprepared both for meeting import competition and for seizing market opportunities in the United States. On the other hand, there is no reason why Canadian firms that are prepared to reorganize and expose themselves to the cut and thrust of international competition cannot expand on the basis of increased U.S. sales. Adjustment of the industry would be easier if the initial free trade period is one of rapid over-all economic growth.

Continued existence of custom work in Canada and (to a lesser degree) of upholstery and bedding is to be expected because of the localized or semi-localized nature of the product. On the same grounds there are good prospects for the assembly of relatively inexpensive lines of metal furniture in Canada.

---

[11]This is especially true of stamped metal furniture. Similar difficulties would be involved in the production of institutional items (e.g., hospital beds) which are also capital-intensive.

4. Implications of a North Atlantic Free Trade Area

If North American free trade were extended to include Europe and Japan, case goods would be the only furniture items substantially affected. Even in such a broader free trade area, the survival of the Canadian industry would remain contingent on its ability to face competition with U.S. producers in North American markets. Therefore, Canada's prospects under North Atlantic free trade must be projected from the best available estimate of the outcome of Canadian competition with the United States. Specifically, we must consider the two extreme limits (defined in chap. 3, section 3) within which North American adjustment is almost certain to fall: the far too pessimistic view that Canadians will be totally unable to compete with U.S. case-goods manufacturers and the Canadian industry will disappear; and the (probably) overoptimistic assumption that the Canadian case-goods industry could succeed in retaining its present share of North American employment. The implications of these two extremes will now be examined in turn.

1. *An extreme case: The demise of the Canadian case-goods industry and the pattern of increased imports*

Canadian producers unable to meet U.S. competition in Canada can hardly be expected to compete in third markets. With the decline of Canadian case-goods production, North Atlantic trade patterns would be determined by competition between European and U.S. producers. In these circumstances, the only major question for Canada becomes the pattern of case-goods imports. These would increase for two reasons: first, to displace domestic Canadian production and, second, to satisfy increased demand in Canada induced by lower prices and greater style selection. In this (admittedly unrealistic) set of limiting circumstances, case-goods imports would increase by many times their present level.

Where would these imports originate? U.S. producers would be likely to capture the lion's share of new Canadian imports for several reasons: geographic proximity, low transport costs, and style preferences in Canada induced by U.S. advertising. However, U.S. producers are unlikely to corner this market. For one thing, European competitors would enjoy a substantial wage advantage; European success in Canadian markets seems most likely in handmade lines, which allow maximum exploitation of this advantage. (The European transport-cost disadvantage would also be less critical in these expensive lines.) In such expensive items, style becomes a critical factor. The European ability to exploit (and induce) taste changes in North America is likely to be the key issue—especially because rising U.S. and Canadian incomes will allow indulgence in wide swings in taste. This argument, of course, cuts both ways: style and taste variations in Europe may also be exploited by U.S. producers.

Given the pessimistic assumptions of this section, the effects of free trade can be sketched out. For reasons of both price and style, U.S./European trade (in both directions) would increase with free trade. Both U.S. and European producers would increase sales in Canada, displacing Canadian production; but it seems likely that U.S. manufacturers would capture the larger portion of these markets.

2. *The other extreme: Suppose a rationalized Canadian case-goods industry retains its present share of North American employment*

In this more complicated case, three effects must be considered. The first two follow from the elimination of U.S. and Canadian tariffs only, regardless of whether or not Europe cooperates; the third is the additional effect of tariff removal between Europe and North America.

A. THE EFFECTS OF CANADIAN/U.S. TARIFF REMOVAL ON
   CANADIAN/U.S. TRADE

Reciprocal tariff reductions by the two countries would result in a large, balanced[1] increase in Canadian exports to, and imports from, the United States. The rationalization of North American production implies a concurrent rationalization in consumption. To the degree that Canadian furniture-consumption patterns come anywhere near approximating those of the United States, a many-fold increase in Canadian imports from the United States would result; this follows strictly from the relative size of Canadian and U.S.[2] markets and production.

[1]This follows (approximately) from Canadian retention of present share of North American employment.
[2]U.S. furniture production now represents over 90 percent of North American consumption and would, under the circumstances here considered, continue to dominate to this degree. If Canadian consumption patterns approach those in the United States, U.S. production would satisfy over 90 percent of Canadian (as well as U.S.) con-

B. THE EFFECTS OF CANADIAN/U.S. TARIFF REMOVAL ON TRADE
   WITH THIRD COUNTRIES

Successful rationalization implies substantial Canadian cost reductions. Hence Canadian producers would be able to compete more effectively with third-country producers in third-country markets and *also* in Canada. This suggests an increase in Canadian exports to third countries and a reduction in Canadian imports from these areas.

It is extremely difficult to predict the size of these increased trade flows. The only benchmark of any kind available is present U.S. performance vis-à-vis third countries. Canadian cost reduction to U.S. levels not only implies the ability to compete on equal terms with U.S. producers in North America; it should also imply the ability to match U.S. competition in third markets.[3] Thus, in competing in third countries, Canadian producers would face the same advantages and disadvantages U.S. producers now face.

Multilateral trading patterns are shown in Table X. It is not surprising that U.S. trade with third countries greatly exceeds Canadian trade with third countries, given the relative size of Canada and the United States. This table is more useful in pointing up the stronger competitive position in third markets of the present (lower-cost) U.S. industry: U.S. exports to third countries are roughly 65 percent of imports, but the equivalent export/import fraction for Canada is just over 25 percent. To the extent that reduced free trade costs would allow Canadian producers to emulate U.S. performance vis-à-vis third countries, increased Canadian exports to third countries and decreased Canadian imports from third countries should tend to increase the Canadian export/import fraction towards the U.S. level. Canadian trade would be unlikely to reach this level, since, at best, U.S. performance is only a long-run benchmark guide. But even if this trend did run its full course, the resulting changes in Canadian trade flows would not compare in magnitude with the potential changes considered in section A above.

---

sumption. This implies that Canadian imports from the United States would grow from their present level of less than 10 percent to over 90 percent of Canadian consumption. (Imports would grow not only from this structural change, but also because of normal market growth and the growth in Canadian sales induced by lower prices. A similar growth in exports implies that Canadian producers would be selling about 90 percent of their output in the United States.)

No one would predict this sort of change. Even under free trade, and even considering only the most mobile product (case goods), consumption patterns in the two countries would be unlikely to conform to this degree. Instead, a producer in either country would likely capture a larger proportion of domestic than of foreign markets. But even conceding this, the rationalization of consumption is likely to increase Canadian imports by many times their current levels, and (smaller present) Canadian exports by an even greater multiple.

[3] A difficulty arises in cases where Canadian and U.S. exporters do not face similar tariffs by third countries. This issue is dealt with below in n. 5.

C. EFFECTS OF TARIFF ELIMINATION BETWEEN NORTH AMERICA AND EUROPE

Since the effects of tariff elimination between Canada and the United States have been traced out in A and B, it is now appropriate to turn to the further effects of free trade between North America and Europe. M. E. Kreinin's estimates indicate that trade flows between the United States and Europe would increase in both directions by about 50 percent as a result of free trade.[4] Similar effects on Canadian trade flows with third countries are likely.[5] Though sizable, these effects would not compare with the changes considered in A.

[4]In his not yet published manuscript, "Trade Arrangements in the Atlantic Community—Effects on the United States," he estimates 1960 trade flows, as they would have been affected by free trade, as follows:

U.S. TRADE IN FURNITURE ($ MILLION)

	1960 U.S. imports	Hypothetical increase in U.S. imports from tariff reduction	1960 U.S. exports	Hypothetical increase in U.S. exports from tariff reduction
U.S. trade with:				
AFTA (Atlantic Free Trade Area)*	18.9	10.0	20.0	9.0
AFTA (ex. EEC)	13.4	7.1	19.1	8.8

*Includes the EEC, EFTA, Canada, and Japan.

A comparison of the figures in the two rows indicates that it makes some difference whether or not the EEC participates. With EEC participation, the slight present U.S. surplus of exports over imports would be reduced by free trade. On the other hand, without EEC participation the conclusion is reversed: the present U.S. surplus would be increased somewhat. In either case, however, the mix of production in the United States and Europe remains basically unaltered, with furniture trade increased in the order of 50 percent.

[5]A difficulty arises because of the different third-country tariffs now faced by Canada and the United States; e.g., Canadian participation in the Commonwealth preference system. Thus the trends examined in B should be modified to the extent that Canada and the United States would face different tariffs by these third countries. But for precisely the same reason, the estimates in (3) would require modification because the tariffs being removed against Canada and the United States would differ. But these modifications to B and C cancel out; so no conceptual problem is involved if they are ignored in both instances.

If difficulty with this argument remains, the reader may view the move to Atlantic free trade as involving two distinct stages. First, the formation of a Canada-U.S. customs union with a common external tariff set at the present U.S. level. Its effects are analyzed in A and B. Thus B becomes an estimate of the effects on Canadian third-country trade of Canadian cost reductions *and* a shift onto the U.S. tariff position vis-à-vis third countries (including Canadian exit from Commonwealth preference). The second stage is the formation of a North Atlantic free trade area by the elimination of tariffs between the North Atlantic customs union and Europe. This is estimated in section C; in this final stage Canada and the United States would enjoy equivalent tariff reductions by third countries.

TABLE X

MULTILATERAL TRADE FLOWS IN FURNITURE, 1961
(mil. $ U.S.)

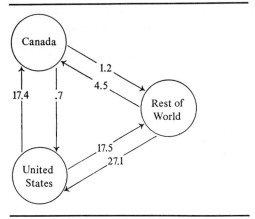

Source: U.N. *Commodity Trade Statistics, 1961.*

3. *Summary of the prospects of the case-goods industry in a North Atlantic free trade area*

It has simply not been feasible to quantify each of the effects discussed above; instead, only the likely direction and rough magnitude of changes have been defined. A fairly clear picture does, however, emerge. The key for the case-goods industry is its ability to compete with U.S. producers in North American markets. At the pessimistic extreme, if it fails completely (as in 1), then there is no prospect that it can survive by capturing third markets.[6] At this extreme, domestic consumption defines the deficit in case-goods trade, and the multiple increase in imports would be drawn largely from the United States.

At the optimistic extreme, if the industry shows sufficient competitive strength to retain its present share of North American employment (as in 2) the picture becomes more complicated; prospects can be defined only by considering the combined effects of 2A, B, and C above. The effect of B is to increase exports but decrease imports. The effect of either A or C is to increase

[6]Even Commonwealth preference would no longer afford Canadian producers any protection, since this system could hardly survive under North Atlantic free trade. (In any event, the only significant Canadian furniture exports to the Commonwealth now are to Bermuda and Trinidad, and these combined in 1961 scarcely exceeded half a million dollars.)

both exports and imports by roughly equal amounts. In sum, these imply a multiple increase in both exports and imports, with the present export-import deficit in furniture slightly reduced in absolute terms but greatly reduced in relative terms. The other question is, "With whom will Canada engage in all this new trade?" A implies a multiple increase in trade in both directions with the United States, while B and C imply increased exports to Europe.[7] Since A would dominate B and C by a wide margin, this new Canadian trade will be heavily concentrated with the United States.

[7]The effect on Canadian imports from Europe is not clear, since the influence of B and C operate in opposite directions.

5. Free Trade Benefits and Costs

1. *Effects on the Canadian consumer*

A. LOWER PRICE ON PRESENT CANADIAN PURCHASES

The major benefit of free trade would be that the Canadian consumer would pay less for all purchased furniture which is now domestically produced. (He would also pay less for imported furniture; but this would be offset by the equal burden he would bear as a taxpayer, since the import duty on furniture would no longer be collected by the Canadian government.[1]) The factory price of domestic furniture production in 1962 in Canada was $363 million; deducting exports of $3 million leaves a balance of $360 million. This domestic product would have cost Canadians an estimated 15.3 percent less[2] under free trade—or a saving of about $55 million.

B. BENEFITS ON INCREASED PURCHASES

While the above represents the benefit involved on present purchases, it must be recognized that purchases would be increased at this lower price. The benefits involved on these additional purchases[3] depend on the response of consumers to lower prices. Our statistical estimate of the price elasticity of Canadian furniture demand was substantially less than unity, which intuitively seems on the low side.[4] However, even this figure yields an estimated $2–$3 million of free trade benefits to consumers on additional

---

[1]For a clarification of this and other issues in this section, see Harry Johnson, "The Cost of Protection and the Scientific Tariff," *Journal of Political Economy*, Aug. 1960.

[2]I.e., the present Canadian price is 18 percent above the world (i.e., U.S.) price (see above, section 1A); or the world price is 15.3 percent below the present Canadian price.

[3]This is the consumer surplus triangle in Johnson, "The Cost of Protection and the Scientific Tariff."

[4]From a time series regression of (price-deflated) furniture sales on price and (price-deflated) GNP. Because this is a relatively insignificant free trade benefit, no attempt was made to improve on our single-equation, least-squares estimate by taking account of identification difficulties, etc.

furniture purchases. And if demand elasticity were to be as high as two, estimated benefits would exceed $8 million.

C. WIDER RANGE OF CHOICE

There would be an additional benefit for consumers, who would face a much wider choice. It is impossible to estimate the value the consumer would place on increased variety; but it is almost certain to fall within the range of 0–$67 million.[5] This is clearly a consideration of major importance; restricted choice *may* be more costly to Canadians than higher price.[6]

In total, therefore, the per annum benefits of free trade to the Canadian consumer are valued on a 1962 base at $57–$125 million.[7]

[5]This maximum figure is derived by estimating the cost to the consumer of exercising his option of purchasing U.S. imports instead of Canadian furniture. Because of the tariff alone, these imports would cost 25 percent more than the U.S. price. But that is not all. Additional handling and distribution charges are imposed on imported items; or the consumer who takes the trouble of shopping in the United States incurs substantial cost and inconvenience. (There also may be a problem of paying sales taxes in both countries.) The maximum figures in the third column of Table I indicate that selected Canadian items can be priced almost 40 percent above U.S. equivalents without inducing Canadians to exercise their option of purchasing in the United States. This suggests that the frictions involved provide Canadian producers with an additional 15 percent of price insulation above and beyond the 25 percent provided by the tariff.

If this U.S. price plus 40 percent is assumed to be the price at which Canadians would opt to purchase in the U.S. market, then the Canadian consumer is worse off by this same 40 percent because of protection. Of this, 18 percent reflects higher Canadian price and has already been estimated as a cash equivalent of about $55 million. The remaining 22 percent, or roughly $67 million, is our maximum estimate of the cost of restricted Canadian choice.

This is regarded as a maximum bound, since many Canadians undoubtedly place a lower valuation on variety than this estimate implies. (Note that the argument above is based on the assumption that all Canadians would behave like those who place a high premium on variety—i.e., those who would switch purchases to the United States if the Canadian price were to reach the U.S. price plus 40 percent.) However, in another sense this estimate may understate; there may be a group of Canadians for whom the cost and inconvenience of shopping in the United States exceeds 15 percent. Such individuals may accordingly place a higher valuation on variety than the 22 percent figure we have used.

[6]A very limited sample of couples who have lived in both the United States and Canada were asked, "Which do you find to be a greater disadvantage in purchasing in Canada: higher price or more restricted variety?" Husbands generally pointed to price; and wives, variety. Which set of preferences is more appropriate? Once purchased, furniture apparently provides more satisfaction to women than to men. Moreover, manufacturers typically aim their advertising at women because they feel that wives make the final selection. However, this must be regarded as a restricted exercise of choice, since it is generally within a budget restraint set by the husband. This line of enquiry clearly leads to no firm estimates; but it does support our conclusion that restricted choice may be as costly to Canadians as higher price.

[7]For two reasons, even this figure represents an underestimate. No account has been

2. *Income and employment effects*

Effects on income recipients in the industry depend on Canadian employment displaced by imports and on labour mobility into new occupations. Since available information is inadequate on both counts, our cost estimates will be even more tentative than our benefit figures. As in similar perplexing circumstances, we shall try at least to bracket the answer by arguing from two extreme sets of assumptions.

A. THE OPTIMISTIC CASE, WITH MINIMUM RESOURCE-TRANSFER COSTS
A completely cost-free adjustment requires that *only one* of the following two assumptions hold: either (*a*) the industry successfully rationalizes to retain its present share of North American employment or (*b*) any employment shifts into other sectors involve benefits at least equal to transfer costs.

(*a*) *If the industry does not contract.* This first possibility has already been discussed in chap. 3, section 4 above. Continued Canadian furniture employment does not imply that the industry would be frozen in its present pattern. Indeed, substantial structural and geographic shifts would almost certainly occur. In this circumstance, a costless adjustment would require that losses from sunk costs[8] and the inconvenience and cost of labour relocation be covered by the increased income benefits. The new employment of the labour force will be with surviving Canadian firms, which *ipso facto* are the most efficient. They would also be expanding. For both reasons, one might expect this shift in employment to be at a higher wage rate.

---

taken of the increase in consumer surplus that would result from increased purchases due to a greater range of choice. Even more important, no account has been taken of a whole set of benefits that might accrue to the consumer if distribution and retail margins in Canada were to be affected by free trade. In this analysis, these margins are assumed to remain constant at their present *absolute* value. But in a world of falling prices, this is the assumption that *percentage* markups rise. If percentage markups do not rise in this way, then the consumer will receive an additional benefit. And this seems almost ensured—at least in border areas—by the access of Canadians to highly competitive retail outlets in the United States, such as Detroit. To evaluate this would take us too far afield, into an analysis as extended and complicated as the one here undertaken on furniture manufacturing. Suffice to note that the estimate of the free trade benefits to the consumer is almost certainly understated in this study.

[8]In the furniture industry, sunk costs are not what one would expect. By and large they would not involve furniture factories, which in many cases were fully depreciated many years ago. Instead, the major losses would fall on the host community, which frequently looks to the furniture industry as the major, if not the only, source of employment. With any departure of the furniture industry, there might be both private sunk costs (housing) and public costs (schools, etc.). But this would depend on the ability of the community to attract new employment.

Moreover, since it is a per annum benefit, a small wage increase would offset an apparently large, once-and-for-all set of adjustment costs.

(b) *If resources are sufficiently mobile.* Even if furniture employment in Canada were to contract, a costless adjustment might still occur if labour[9] were sufficiently mobile into other industries. Costs and benefits similar to those in the previous case still apply, although with minor modification.

A psychic cost may be involved for furniture workers who have to take up new tasks.[10] On the other hand, their new wages would be higher on two counts: first, because average wages in other industries exceed those in furniture[11] and, second, because Canadian wages would be rising across the board with free trade.[12] (Recall that it is this pull on labour by other industries that would make it difficult for the furniture industry to retain its labour force.) One condition for a costless transfer in this instance is, therefore, that these new wages be high enough to offset any psychic income loss in new employment, and once-and-for-all sunk costs and transfer costs.[13]

With a costless adjustment process for any of these reasons, the net benefit of free trade would be the consumer windfall of $75–$125 million.

B. THE PESSIMISTIC CASE, WITH MAXIMUM RESOURCE-TRANSFER COSTS

The most expensive conceivable cost would be incurred if resources now in furniture were to be left permanently unemployed. This outcome would require that *both* of two extreme conditions occur: that the entire portion of the industry subjected to import competition fails; *and* that resources are permanently unemployable in other sectors. Clearly, either is so unlikely that the (necessary) combination of the two may be rejected out of hand. Nevertheless, this cost will be computed as a benchmark for evaluating potential unemployment costs of a less severe nature.

The localized output of about 30 percent of the industry (e.g., custom work) leaves only 70 percent of the industry vulnerable to import compe-

---

[9]Labour is used in this discussion as a proxy for the more general term "resources."

[10]This cost can, of course, be negative—i.e., workers may find they enjoy the new tasks more than the old.

[11]This transfer into more productive occupations is one of the major benefits of free trade, and one that is often overlooked. In 1962, average hourly earnings of production workers in manufacturing exceeded those in furniture by 34 cents per hour. Workers now in furniture might have increased their income by as much as $16 million per annum by transferring into a mix of alternative industries paying average wages.

[12]See Wonnacott and Wonnacott, *Free Trade*, chap. XI.

[13]For this case to hold, we require only that labour be *sufficiently* mobile to satisfy this condition of cost-benefit equality. Labour would still be employed in various sectors at differing wage rates. Hence this is far less restrictive than an assumption of "perfect" mobility.

tition. On a 1962 base, maximum lost wages are estimated at 70 percent of a total payroll of $121 million, or about $85 million—a figure which is bracketed by the estimated range of $57–$125 million of consumer benefits. Hence, the cost-benefit balance can be restated as follows: free-trade consumer benefits of $57–$125 million will exceed payroll losses unless most[14] of the present Canadian labour force engaged in import-competing furniture-making becomes permanently unemployed, with no prospect of ever again becoming employable.

Permanent payroll losses, of course, are an inadequate indicator of possible costs[15]; even so, it is difficult to see how continued protection of this industry can be justified in the light of these estimates. There seems to be no way of reasonably arguing that permanent unemployment of even, say, a quarter of the labour force would follow as a result of free trade. This would require arguing a whole set of propositions; regardless of the likelihood of any of these alone, in combination they become highly implausible. These include (1) a pessimistic view of industry prospects under free trade; (2) permanent inability of displaced labour to get alternative employment at any wage rate—a proposition which is directly contradicted by every historical precedent; and (3) a paralysis of government policy, involving the payment of staggering sums in unemployment insurance but no effective monetary or fiscal response, relocation, or retraining assistance. And anyone bold enough to argue such a case must then recognize that even though this implies that costs equal benefits initially, they cannot continue

[14]I.e., 67–100 percent.
[15]For example, equity earnings and government corporate tax receipts would be reduced in a declining industry. (These have been estimated at roughly $11 million in 1962.) Furniture-supplying industries might or might not contract their operations, depending on elasticities of domestic and foreign demand from other sources; if they were forced to contract (or reduce their prices to foreign purchasers), a cost might be involved. Finally, unemployment has familiar multiplier effects, as reduced purchases by the unemployed result in reduced sales of consumer goods, and so on. These multiplier effects could be very large if they were to apply to all lost furniture payroll. But they do not; since the unemployed would receive unemployment insurance and tax reductions, these multiplier effects would apply only to a fraction of their income loss. Even this might be offset by compensating monetary and fiscal policy.
It is not clear by how much payroll losses of the permanently unemployed might understate total costs of a declining industry. However, it is the authors' view that total costs are unlikely to exceed permanent payroll losses by more than 50–100 percent.
Except for factories that are closed down, no sunk costs are involved; the unemployed labour force would continue to use its present housing, schools, etc. Its income (unemployment insurance) is an income transfer, rather than a cost. It is assumed in this argument that workers receive the same psychic satisfaction from leisure as from building furniture. In other words, the only reason they would be less happy when unemployed would be because their income would be reduced to the unemployment insurance level.

to do so. For costs must decrease over time as the permanently unemployed "retire" from the labour force; but benefits will increase over time with the increase in Canadian consumption of furniture.

There is, of course, the non-economic argument that there is a social benefit involved in maintaining a large Canadian furniture industry—i.e., that there is some inherent advantage in having present furniture-makers continue in their present tasks, rather than turning their hands to the production of aluminum or automobiles. Since this is a value judgment rather than a conclusion following a logical chain of reasoning, it can be neither proven nor disproven.[16]

[16]Two other economic arguments deserve comment. The infant-industry argument can scarcely be used to support continued protection of an industry so heavily marked by age. Another conceivable justification for protection is that management, like labour, is unable to turn its hand to other activities and that furniture-supplying industries would be unable to find either alternative domestic or export markets. In other words, if one takes the view that the Canadian economy is frozen into a rigid structural pattern, then any attempt to induce a more efficient allocation of economic activity is doomed to failure. Given this view, any change (such as tariff reduction or automation) is likely to involve a net cost. While this argument cannot be contradicted logically, it may be rejected on empirical grounds; the economy is just not that rigid.

6. Policy Options

In the preceding sections, the effects on the furniture industry of across-the-board free trade have been examined. In this section, a number of alternative policy options are considered; each will be compared with free trade (i.e., unrestricted, across-the-board tariff elimination), on the one hand, and present protection, on the other.

1. *A negotiated reduction of present MFN rates by one-quarter to one-third*

A. CONSUMPTION EFFECTS

With a one-quarter to one-third reduction in the present 25 percent Canadian tariff, the price of imports would fall by 6 to 8 percent. Substantial gains would go to the consumer because his present import purchases would cost less. However, this does not represent a "social gain," since it would just be offset by an equivalent loss in duty revenue to the government.[1] The net gains to the consumer/taxpayer, therefore, would come from the purchases he now directs at domestically produced furniture. If price reductions are forced upon domestic producers by lower-cost imports, the Canadian consumer benefits as a consequence. Even if Canadian producers do not lower their prices, the Canadian consumer still stands to gain; additional U.S. imports will result, and the Canadian consumer will select from a greater variety of imported items, all more attractively priced than in the past.

B. PRODUCTION EFFECTS

A reduction in the 25 percent Canadian tariff to about 17–19 percent would seriously threaten the Canadian industry in its own domestic market, since the price of landed imports would be reduced to the present level of domestically produced items.[2] If Canadian producers maintained present

[1]This "loss" is involved even though total government tariff receipts may not fall. Duty receipts from additional imports induced by the tariff reduction may offset the duty reduction on present imports.
[2]Recall that Canadian price was estimated in chap. 2, sect. 2, as about 18 percent above the U.S. price. Any error in this estimate becomes critical in evaluating the

prices, they would lose whatever small price advantage they now enjoy and hence would lose a portion of their markets to imports. Alternatively, Canadian producers attempting to maintain their competitive edge by matching this price reduction would find their profits reduced. The prospect for domestic producers is therefore bleak, unless they could use the U.S. tariff reduction to exploit new export markets.

There is little prospect that the U.S. tariff cut would allow the Canadian industry to capture sizable markets in the United States. At best, a fully rationalized, high-volume Canadian industry could produce at costs only roughly equal to those prevailing in the United States, but Canadian producers would still face a competitive disadvantage in the form of a 6 to 8 percent U.S. duty.[3] There is therefore little prospect that the industry could make up for its domestic losses in increased exports. And without wider markets, volume efficiencies could not be achieved.

C. EVALUATION

As far as the furniture industry is concerned, it is difficult to make much of an economic case for the option of MFN tariff reductions. It is true that the over-all effect could be an improvement on the present (protection) situation, but this is not a clear case and would depend on how consumer benefits might trade off against production problems. It is clear, however, that this MFN option is inferior to free trade. This is true from the point of view of the consumer, who would get less price reduction and variety from the more modest MFN cuts. It is also true from the point of view of the producer, who would face increased import competition without compensating advantages of improved access to the U.S. market.

There are two general observations that apply in any comparison of complete free trade and partial MFN tariff reductions. There may be political advantages in working towards free trade via reciprocal MFN reductions. Politicians may view a gradual program as easier to sell than a once-and-for-all dismantling of tariffs.[4] On the other hand, it is unlikely that such a process is the most efficient route to free trade. Even if one could assume that tariffs could be completely eliminated by a set of such bargaining rounds (and this is an extremely optimistic view), Canadian

---

effects of a one-quarter to one-third MFN tariff cut: if Canadian price is less (more) than our estimate, then Canadian producers will be in a stronger (weaker) position to meet import competition as a consequence.
[3]I.e., the present 10 percent rate less the one-quarter to one-third cut.
[4]It is generally assumed that Canadian industry would prefer gradual tariff reductions. However, the view of industry leaders is by no means unanimous—for the reasons cited below.

industry would become involved in a whole series of reorganizations. Thus, even if a situation of optimal efficiency is eventually reached, the path leading to it would involve needless cost. Above all, any industry rationalizing its operations by shifting from a domestic to an international base requires stable expectations of future export markets. Yet a series of MFN reductions would involve a large element of uncertainty about the eventual outcome—as well as the outcome of each particular bargaining round. And this uncertainty alone might prevent industry rationalization.

These considerations are important for any industry, but they are critical for furniture. Even if the industry were to be viable in Canada after complete tariff elimination, it may not survive the first step (i.e., the one-quarter to one-third tariff reduction) in a staged process. Furniture seems to be a marginal industry in any case; and its situation would be likely to get worse in any staging process before it got better. It must be remembered that the existence of many industries in their present locations depends heavily on inertia. If inertia is at all important in furniture-making, the contraction of this marginal industry at any point in a staging process might be irreversible.

2. Single-industry free trade

Unrestricted free trade for a single industry would allow anyone and everyone to move the product across the border duty-free; the precedent is farm implements. This is not to be confused with the limited free trade scheme in autos (discussed in the next section), which involves a number of restrictions designed to guarantee continued Canadian employment.

Unrestricted free trade in furniture would have similar effects to negotiated MFN tariff reductions. The major difference would be one of degree; the single-industry scheme would have a far greater impact on both consumers and producers.

A. CONSUMPTION EFFECTS

Consumers would enjoy maximum benefits. The free entry of imports would drive furniture prices down to the U.S. level; at the same time the consumer would enjoy the full benefits of variety provided by free access to U.S. lines.

B. PRODUCTION EFFECTS

With present techniques and volume, Canadian manufacturers would be unable to meet competition from imports; the elimination of the 25 percent

Canadian duty would leave Canadian producers at an approximate 18 percent price disadvantage vis-à-vis imports, rather than the 7 percent advantage they now enjoy.

The one hope of the industry would be to increase volume (by selling in the United States) and thus decrease costs. The most favourably situated firms might succeed; however, our aggregate figures for the industry do not indicate that rationalization of production in Canada would be profitable for the average firm in Canada. Figure 2 suggests that Canadian producers could maintain costs roughly competitive with those in North Carolina in an all-industry free trade area; but in a single-industry scheme Canadian furniture-makers would be at a substantial competitive disadvantage because of their higher cost of protected inputs. (On average, Canadian furniture costs could be almost 8 percent higher for this reason alone.)[5] This is critical in upholstered goods, since an important protected input is textiles.

The outlook for Canadian producers in such a scheme is not promising. They would face the full force of foreign competition in domestic markets. However, there would be little offsetting advantage provided by duty-free access into U.S. markets; Canadian costs would remain higher because of the protection left on other industries.

C. EVALUATION

Any comparison of such a scheme with present protection is difficult. On the one hand, Canadian consumers would enjoy maximum benefits from price reductions and increased variety. On the other hand, this scheme would involve maximum pressure on Canadian producers, and it is unlikely that most of the industry would survive. It is not clear how consumption advantages and production disadvantages would trade off. Any firm conclusion would require a cost/benefit calculation similar to that undertaken in chapter 5. And conclusions would be more difficult to reach. In this case, it would no longer be clear that benefits exceed costs by a wide margin; hence, a number of difficult issues would require clarification— e.g., how permanently displaced labour might remain unemployed and how quickly present suppliers of furniture inputs might develop alternative markets in other industries and countries.

Hence it cannot be concluded that such a scheme is superior or inferior

5Canadian producers could receive a drawback on import duty for export sales. This would not reduce their input costs to the U.S. level, however, since only a portion of their inputs is imported and subject to duty remission. The large portion of their inputs is purchased from domestic producers who charge a higher price because of the protection they receive. Moreover, the industry has not taken full advantage of the drawback scheme in the past.

to present protection. However, this scheme can be rejected in comparison with across-the-board free trade. The consumer would enjoy similar benefits in either case. However, producers would be worse off in a single-industry scheme because of higher input costs; accordingly, they would face greater pressure from import competition and less prospect of compensating export sales.

D. SOME DIFFICULT ISSUES RECONSIDERED

It should be noted that there are two difficult issues that arise in an analysis of this kind. First, it is necessary to argue from the present exchange rate and from present relative wage rates—even though it is recognized that these may change with tariff reductions. Thus, for example, if an MFN tariff reduction gives rise to a general shift in Canadian wages relative to those in the United States, Canadian furniture production would become more or less attractive than this impact analysis suggests. (Indeed, as long as general equilibrium shifts of this kind are allowed to take place, they ensure that Canadian labour will be fully employed—at least in the long run.)

When wages are considered variable, conclusions for a single-industry scheme are also complicated. For example, the Canadian industry might survive the severe pressure of foreign competition by suspending wage increases, thus allowing its wages to lag further below those in the United States. The conclusions above, however, remain unaffected. This scheme is less attractive than across-the-board free trade because it would involve a continuing cost—in this case the depressed Canadian wage necessary to compensate for high input costs.

The second issue that arises is the normal presumption that labour and other factors of production are worse off as their industry contracts. Superficially, this seems highly plausible. But it does not necessarily follow in a long-run analysis of a low-income industry. Unskilled labour (and indeed management with skills not specific to furniture-making) may be better off if unemployment induces them to find more rewarding jobs elsewhere. The issue is more complex for other factors of production. Owners of a contracting industry become involved in once-and-for-all sunk-capital losses; on the other hand, the capital they do manage to extract may be invested in another industry yielding a higher return.[6] Labour and management with skills specific to the contracting industry may also become involved in sunk-capital losses,[7] along with higher income in new employment. The

---

[6]This may be important in furniture-making. There is evidence that a number of owners have kept their capital in this industry despite a depressed return.
[7]In this case, sunk capital is investment in training.

conclusion is that the long-run production effects of a contracting industry need not necessarily be unfavourable.

3. Restricted single-industry free trade

It has been concluded that complete across-the-board free trade is preferable to either of the partial schemes examined above. But if for political reasons this cannot be undertaken, some modified single-industry scheme may be considered. If there is an additional restraint that free trade can only be introduced if the existence of the industry is assured, then a limited scheme like the Automotive Agreement with its balance of payments or production constraints would become the active option. The essential difference between a limited auto-type scheme and an unrestricted single-industry plan is that the latter directs gains to the consumer, while the former initially directs gains to the producer.[8]

Provided domestic prices in Canada are reduced sufficiently to offset the duty loss to the taxpayer (as has been the case in the, admittedly tardy, auto precedent), a restricted single-industry scheme would leave the consumer no worse off than under present protection. Any net increase in production efficiency[9] would represent a windfall gain, which would initially go to the producer; this might eventually be distributed to the consumer (via further price cuts) or to labour (in higher wages) or as increased profits to owners. Hence, so long as it induces rationalization of the industry, such a scheme may be judged preferable to protection. However, problems would remain.

A. THE EQUITY ISSUE

Assurances of minimal necessary price reductions to the consumer[10] would have to be incorporated in such a scheme. Otherwise, the consumer/taxpayer might not be left equally well off, and this scheme would be complicated by equity issues arising from the redistribution of duty revenue from the taxpayer to the importer.

B. ADMINISTRATIVE PROBLEMS

Complications would arise if Canadian furniture producers were to become the sole agents for the import of U.S. furniture. For example, what would happen to present furniture importers? (Administrative problems have

[8]Eventually these gains may go to the labour force or the consumer.
[9]I.e., cost saving due to rationalization less changeover costs.
[10]I.e., sufficient to cover the reduction in government duty revenue. A simpler alternative would be the imposition by the government of a compensating sales tax; this could be covered by the producer from his duty savings without raising prices.

been minimized in the auto industry because that industry is characterized by parent-subsidiary ties.) Any marketing of a U.S. firm's output in Canada through a Canadian firm would raise anti-trust problems. Furthermore, marketing economies might induce the takeover of Canadian firms by U.S. companies. There would be other administrative problems as well; but these are not pursued, since they would be secondary to fundamental economic difficulties to which we now turn.

C. RATIONALIZATION OF CANADIAN INDUSTRY IN DOUBT

It is by no means certain that any windfall efficiency gains would come from such a scheme, since it is not clear that it would be profitable for the Canadian industry to increase volume by exploiting the duty-free U.S. market.

The option for a Canadian firm under such a scheme would be to specialize for export, while importing (duty-free) items of equal value in the lines it would be dropping from Canadian production. Its profit would come from the sale of U.S. imports in Canada and could run up to the 25 percent protection that would still remain as a price seal on the Canadian market.[11] However, there would be loss incurred on its export sales, since high-cost Canadian units would be sold in the United States at low prevailing prices there. This loss would initially be about 18 percent,[12] but with increased Canadian specialization might be reduced to about 8 or 9 percent.[13]

Thus manufacturers would incur losses on exports in order to make even greater profits on imports. From the social point of view, two windfalls would be involved for Canada, one of production and one of exchange. The production windfall is any increase in efficiency that results from more specialized production in Canada. The exchange windfall is the consumption gain involved in exchanging Canadian-built furniture[14] for U.S.-built furniture.[15] This suggests that, from either the social or the private point of view, this scheme is preferable to the present situation of protection.

There are a number of reasons why this favourable conclusion would

[11]And perhaps even higher; the inconvenience consumers would face in shopping in the United States might allow a price up to 40 percent above the U.S. level (see n. 5, chap. 5).
[12]I.e., Canadian furniture would be sold in the United States at a price about 18 percent below the price at which it is now sold in Canada (see Figure 1).
[13]I.e., the higher cost in Canada that would remain after rationalization. This is made up almost entirely of higher input costs that would remain in a single-industry scheme (D_m in Figure 1).
[14]Which the Canadian market now values, marginally, at 18 percent above the U.S. price.
[15]Which Canadians marginally value at 25–40 percent above the U.S. price (see n. 5, chap. 5).

need to be modified. If the consumer/taxpayer is to be reimbursed for his loss of duty revenue, furniture prices on *all* Canadian sales would have to be reduced by 1 or 2 percent.[16] A price reduction on a product involving so many complex, differentiated items would be extremely difficult to measure, let alone enforce. This price reduction would reduce the incentive facing a Canadian furniture-maker; his incentive would be further reduced by whatever costs he might face in marketing imports in Canada and in marketing his own lines in the United States.[17] It is therefore not clear that Canadian firms would rationalize to engage in export-import trade under an auto-type scheme.

D. THE CHOICE OF INDUSTRY

Regardless of whether or not rationalization occurs and windfall gains result, the authors do not recommend a restricted single-industry scheme for furniture. It is less desirable to introduce limited free trade in this industry than in almost any other—for a number of reasons.

(*a*) One rationale for such a scheme is that it provides protection and subsidy to ensure that an industry will survive during the period in which it is reorganizing; once efficiently set up, it can then weather real free trade. But if the government wishes to use subsidy measures to ensure the survival of an industry, it surely should select a high-income, rather than a low-income, industry. So long as the Americans are prepared to cooperate in such asymmetrical agreements, high-wage industries such as the auto industry should be chosen.[18]

(*b*) Not only is this a low-wage industry in Canada; it is also one of the few industries in which U.S. wages are about at the Canadian level, largely because Canadian furniture-makers in Ontario and Quebec are competing with a U.S. industry in North Carolina. Hence, in the event of eventual complete free trade, this industry is unlikely to be in as strong a competitive position as many other Canadian industries that do enjoy a wage advantage.

(*c*) This industry is very sensitive to higher-priced protected inputs. While this would not affect the industry in the event of across-the-board free trade, it does jeopardize any single-industry scheme. Accordingly, incen-

[16]The Canadian government would lose its present 25 percent duty on imports, which comprise about 6 percent of domestic consumption—a loss equivalent to 1.5 percent of total domestic sales (i.e., $.25 \times .06$).
[17]The Canadian producer may find it difficult to market his product in the United States. Adequate sales staff, inventory maintenance, and advertising support would take time to develop. Furthermore, it might take time to adjust to the different technique of furniture wholesaling in the United States.
[18]The industry selected should be one capable of paying high wages (and other incomes) with unrestricted trade; logically, this need not be an industry which pays high wages under protection, although the two are likely to be the same.

tives might be insufficient to induce Canadian rationalization; and even if it were to occur, it would not spread back into major supplying industries (e.g., textiles). In the auto case, most important component suppliers could be incorporated into the scheme, and those that could not (e.g., steel) were selling at reasonably competitive prices in any case. In the furniture industry, some supply components could undoubtedly be included; but one of the most critical suppliers—textiles—is an industry in its own right and, indeed, an industry many times the size of furniture-making. It is difficult to see how it could be included without transforming the plan into a two-industry scheme.

4. *Comparison of options*

Of all the schemes discussed in this study, economic considerations indicate that unrestricted free trade in all industries should be preferred. Not only would efficiency gains be introduced in many industries rather than just in the furniture industry. In addition, reduced input prices would allow the furniture industry to compete more successfully.

A negotiated step-by-step move to free trade by all industries (e.g., a series of GATT bargaining rounds) would be less attractive, since the first such multilateral tariff reduction would be more effective in increasing import competition than in opening export markets.

If for political reasons it is feasible to introduce free trade in only one industry at a time, then the options become either an unrestricted single-industry plan (such as farm implements) or a restricted single-industry scheme (such as autos). However, if there is a further restriction that such a scheme must "prove successful" in terms of maintaining factor employment in that industry (rather than increasing real income of factors now in the industry), then there remains little choice. An auto-type scheme is indicated, since this is the only option that would ensure continued existence of a furniture industry.

But if economic choice is so restricted that only auto-type schemes may be undertaken, then furniture seems to be one of the last industries to qualify. Instead, the authorities should seek out industries in which (i) incomes are high in both countries, (ii) Canadian producers enjoy a substantial wage advantage, and (iii) Canadian input protection is relatively unimportant and/or inputs can easily be included in the scheme. Finally, industries selected should face a clear-cut inducement to rationalize, with strong competitive strength indicated if and when a final step to real free trade is undertaken. Substantial administrative difficulties might remain for industries selected on these grounds; but they are unlikely to be more severe than the administrative problems involved for the furniture industry.

7. The Path of Adjustment

1. *Problems and objectives*

Timing and adjustment assistance would be important determinants of the final success of any trade-liberalization program. In this section these issues are considered, and a proposal is set out for staging tariff reductions to unrestricted free trade.[1]

While the consumer wishes as rapid tariff reductions as possible, the issue is not as clear for the producer. Although some producers may favour rapid tariff reductions (e.g., to reduce input costs and open U.S. markets), some may not. Many may prefer delays to provide time for at least partial depreciation of any Canadian machinery and equipment that has been installed in the past to service Canadian markets but is inefficient under free trade. From the point of view of the firm, sunk-capital losses would be reduced, and firms would be in a stronger position to raise funds necessary for rationalization.

Hence there may be a conflict of interest between consumers and some producers. The speed of tariff removal may involve an implicit value judgment by the authorities on the strength of each case. But even if an extended staging process is chosen, it must not be so drawn out over time that it removes the incentive to reorganize. In this case, equipment inefficient by North American market standards might be reinstalled in Canada even after the staging process to free trade has begun.

Any proposed scheme should meet two primary objectives. First, it should encourage the most efficient to expand. Second, it should facilitate the re-employment of resources released by declining, inefficient firms. And the distinction between the efficient and the inefficient should be left to the market.

---

[1] It is assumed that tariffs on all manufactured goods are removed; however, the implications for the furniture industry only are considered.

2. *A possible scheme*

The present 25 percent Canadian tariff might be eliminated by a five-stage reduction of 5 percent per year.[2] This period would allow firms time to rationalize their output and marketing to the wider continental market. Furthermore, five years in the half-life of machinery in the industry;[3] while there is no timing sequence that would completely eliminate capital losses, this seems to be a reasonable guideline for limiting them.

Coincident with the first reduction in the tariff, an excise tax would be imposed on all furniture sold in Canada. This tax could be as much as the 5 percent reduction in the tariff and still leave the consumer as well off. On retail sales of $620 million,[4] the government would collect about $31 million in revenue. About $1 million would represent compensation for the loss in duty revenue because of the lower import tariff. The remainder could be used for relocation and retraining of any displaced labour and/or as an interim subsidy for firms in the industry. For example, tax exemption might be allowed on the base profits of firms in operation before the scheme was initiated. These base profits would be equal to their average annual profits earned in the five-year period prior to the initiation of this scheme; any additional profit would be taxed at the normal corporate rate. Such a policy would clearly encourage the efficient, but not the inefficient: no profit, no tax relief. This relief would be provided either to firms remaining in furniture-making or to those which exit. In the latter case, this tax credit would represent a major asset to bring to a new manufacturing activity. This tax relief could be further restricted to apply only if a certain percentage of value added is maintained in the present site of furniture-manufacturing. Such a policy is not strongly recommended in this study; however, if a high premium is placed on maintaining present small furniture towns, such a proviso could easily be incorporated.

This would not be a costly subsidy, since it would probably involve less than $5 million of tax remission.[5] A net addition of over $25 million in government revenue would remain. This could be used to subsidize increased output of furniture firms, a measure which would encourage expanding firms; these firms are more likely than not to be the relatively efficient.[6] Alternatively, this sum could be used to subsidize job retraining

[2]The U.S. tariff would also be eliminated at this rate, or faster if the Americans are willing.
[3]As allowed by the U.S. Internal Revenue Service.
[4]Estimated for 1965 from figures supplied by the Department of Industry.
[5]The 443 profit-earning firms filing a federal tax return in 1963 paid $2.8 million in corporate tax.
[6]But this is not guaranteed. Note that even corporate tax remission would not abso-

and relocation of the labour force; if used exclusively in this way, this subsidy would be equal to almost one-quarter of the recent industry payroll.[7] Which of these two additional subsidies is chosen would depend on a value judgment: the former is appropriate if a high premium is placed on maintaining the present Canadian industry structure and, in particular, a furniture industry; the second is appropriate if the objective is high-income employment of the labour force.

Such a scheme would initially direct all benefits to furniture firms and factors, rather than to the consumer. In subsequent years, as tariffs are further reduced, increased production subsidies would be possible, financed by an excise tax that could be as high as 10 percent in the second year, 15 percent in the third, and so on. Thus, the government's ability to subsidize would increase as the pressure of price competition from imports on the industry builds up. To what extent this should be entirely expended on subsidies to producers rather than to consumers would be an arbitrary judgment. But regardless of how justified production subsidies may be as an interim measure to ease reorganization of the industry, little case can be made for continuing them beyond the short term. Therefore, in the long run both the import tariff and the excise tax should be completely removed, with the consumer enjoying maximum benefits of free trade.

---

lutely guarantee a subsidy to the most efficient; for example, a very efficient firm may have had depressed profits in the base period prior to the scheme because of a costly reorganization for export. And there would be other problems; for example, in a diversified firm, how is total profit in the base period to be allocated between furniture-making and other activities?

[7]The industry payroll in 1962 was $121 million.

Appendices

Appendix A: Classification of furniture

Furniture is not a homogeneous good. The furniture industry is composed of separate subsectors with some common features, but more often differing greatly in inputs, outputs, and production techniques. There are three ways to subdivide the industry.

It can be divided by major input or component. Thus we would have the wooden-furniture portion ($126,232), metal furniture ($75,651), upholstered products ($71,323), and bedding ($38,051). The principal advantage of this classification is that it facilitates analysis of manufacturing techniques, costs, inputs, etc.

An alternative DBS classification scheme divides the industry by end use. This yields: household furniture ($219,996), office furniture ($37,764), and miscellaneous (including institutional furniture, bedding, and upholstered items) ($100,823). The advantage of this scheme is that it facilitates analysis of marketing problems and income, price, and demand relationships. But it makes analysis of component costs more difficult.

The third form of classification is the *de facto* ordering used in the industry. This classification is by component and end use as shown in Table AI. This scheme permits easy analysis of cost and input relationships as well as of marketing problems. Unfortunately, the data that are available are classified by the DBS end-use method. Problems of comparability of data frequently forced us to use higher levels of aggregation than was our original intent. It will be noted from the text that we generally used the industry's classification scheme, as shown in Table AI.

TABLE AI

Type of Furniture	Shipped in 1962
	($000)
Wooden houshold furniture (referred to as "case goods" by the industry); e.g., bedroom and dining-room furniture, end tables, and other occasional pieces	81,662
Wooden institutional furniture; e.g., school desks, church pews, etc.	32,786
Wooden office furniture; e.g., desks, filing cabinets, tables	11,784
Metal household furniture (referred to as "chrome ware" by the industry); e.g., dinette suites, metal frame chairs	30,138
Metal institutional furniture; e.g., hospital beds and tables, metal frame desks and chairs	21,813
Metal office furniture; e.g., desks, files, tables	21,070
Upholstered furniture; e.g., furniture more often than not used in the household. Some is used in institutions and business (such as hotels), but the bulk is in the form of sofas, chairs, and ottomans and is sold to households	71,323
Bedding; e.g., mattresses, pillows, and box springs	38,051
Total	308,627

Appendix B

TABLE B1

COMPARATIVE WAGES BY JOB CLASSIFICATION IN THE WOODEN-FURNITURE INDUSTRY
UNITED STATES AND CANADA, 1962
(in domestic dollars)

Job	U.S. region			Canadian region	
	Middle Atlantic	East North Central	South Atlantic	Quebec	Ontario
Assemblers, case goods	2.12	1.87	1.34	1.55	1.69
Cutoff saw operators	1.89	1.82	1.39	1.30	1.38
Gluers, rough stock	1.76	1.71	1.29	1.28	1.37
Maintenance men	1.50	1.54	1.21	1.03	1.25
Packers, furniture	1.73	1.64	1.27	1.13	1.30
Ripsaw operators	1.85	1.78	1.36	1.29	1.51
Rubbers, furniture	2.04	1.74	1.27	1.25	1.49
Sanders, furniture	1.79	1.73	1.37	1.27	1.40
Tenoner operators	1.98	1.99	1.53	1.42	1.58

Sources: U.S. data as of July, 1962: "Earnings in Wood Household Furniture, July 1962," *Monthly Labor Review,* July 1963, pp. 814–16.
Canadian Data: "Wooden Furniture," *Wage Rates, Salaries and Hours of Labour, 1962,* Report no. 45, Economic and Research Branch, Department of Labour, Ottawa, p. 113.

Comparisons and classifications may not be exact in all cases. The U.S. source lists twelve classifications, while the Canadian data have twenty-seven separate headings. But the evidence remains clear: Ontario wages are slightly higher, and Quebec wages slightly lower, than wages in the southeastern region of the United States.

RELATED PUBLICATIONS BY THE
PRIVATE PLANNING ASSOCIATION OF CANADA

CANADIAN TRADE COMMITTEE PUBLICATIONS

THE WORLD ECONOMY

The World Economy at the Crossroads: A Survey of Current Problems of Money, Trade and Economic Development, by Harry G. Johnson, 1965.

The International Monetary System: Conflict and Reform, by Robert A. Mundell, 1965.

International Commodity Agreements, by William E. Haviland, 1963.

CANADA'S TRADE RELATIONSHIPS

Canada's International Trade: An Analysis of Recent Trends and Patterns, by Bruce Wilkinson, 1968.

Canada's Trade with the Communist Countries of Eastern Europe, by Ian M. Drummond, 1966.

Canada's Role in Britain's Trade, by Edward M. Cape, 1965.

The Common Agricultural Policy of the E.E.C. and its Implications for Canada's Exports, by Sol Sinclair, 1964.

Canada's Interest in the Trade Problems of Less Developed Countries, by Grant L. Reuber, 1964.

CANADA'S COMMERCIAL POLICY AND COMPETITIVE POSITION

Prices, Productivity, and Canada's Competitive Position, by N. H. Lithwick, 1967.

Industrial Structure in Canada's International Competitive Position: A Study of the Factors Affecting Economies of Scale and Specialization in Canadian Manufacturing, by H. Edward English, 1964.

Canada's Approach to Trade Negotiations, by L. D. Wilgress, 1963.

CANADIAN-AMERICAN COMMITTEE PUBLICATIONS

CANADA-U.S. ECONOMIC RELATIONS

Constructive Alternatives to Proposals for U.S. Import Quotas (a Statement by the Committee), 1968.

U.S.-Canadian Free Trade: The Potential Impact on the Canadian Economy, by Paul Wonnacott and Ronald J. Wonnacott, 1968.

The Role of International Unionism in Canada, by John H. G. Crispo, 1967.

A New Trade Strategy for Canada and the United States (a Statement by the Committee), 1966.

Capital Flows between Canada and the United States, by Irving Brecher, 1965.

A Possible Plan for a Canada-U.S. Free Trade Area (a Staff Report), 1965.

Invisible Trade Barriers between Canada and the United States, by Francis Masson and H. Edward English, 1963.

Non-Merchandise Transactions between Canada and the United States, by John W. Popkin, 1963.

Policies and Practices of United States Subsidiaries in Canada, by John Lindeman and Donald Armstrong, 1961.